Jonathan Raban

Hunting Mister Heartbreak

Jonathan Raban is also the author of *Soft City, Arabia, Foreign Land, Coasting, For Love and Money, Old Glory,* and *Bad Land.* He won the W.H. Heinemann Award for Literature in 1982 and the Thomas Cook Award in 1981 and 1991. He also edited *The Oxford Book of the Sea.* He lives in Seattle.

241 LOUCHE
P. 245 OBJECTED - COVERED BY A HARDENED
SOLUTION

Hunting
Mister Heartbreak

A Discovery of America

Jonathan Raban

Vintage Departures
Vintage Books
A Division of Random House, Inc.
New York

FIRST VINTAGE DEPARTURES EDITION, NOVEMBER 1998

Some parts of this book appeared, in different form, in *Granta*.

Library of Congress Cataloging-in-Publication Data
Raban, Jonathan.
Hunting Mister Heartbreak : a discovery of America / Jonathan Raban.
p.   cm.
Previously published: New York, NY : Edward Burlingame Books, c1991.
ISBN 0-375-70101-X
1. United States—Description and travel.
2. United States—Social life and customs—1971–3. Raban, Jonathan—
Homes and haunts—United States. 4. British—Travel—United States.
5. Atlantic Ocean—Description and travel. I.Title.
[E169.04.R32 1998]
973.928—dc21   98-26450
CIP

ISBN-13: 978-0-375-70101-6

Author photograph © Marion Ettlinger

www.randomhouse.com

Printed in the United States of America
10   9   8   7   6   5   4   3

Mr. Heartbreak, the New Man,
come to farm a crazy land . . .

—John Berryman, *Dream Songs*

What, then, is the American, this new man? . . . *He* is an American, who, leaving behind him all his ancient prejudices and manners, receives new ones from the new mode of life he has embraced, the new government he obeys, and the new rank he holds. He becomes an American by being received in the broad lap of our great *Alma Mater.*

—J. Hector St. John de Crèvecoeur,
Letters from an American Farmer

Contents

ONE
The Atlantic Passage
1

TWO
The Biggest Department Store in the World
44

THREE
Free Spirit
105

FOUR
In Our Valley
125

FIVE
The Friendly Sky
219

SIX
Gold Mountain
239

SEVEN
Land of Cockaigne
317

Hunting Mister Heartbreak

ONE

The Atlantic Passage

THERE IS A SENTENCE that has stirred the imagination of Europe as powerfully as any call to arms. I've seen it written a hundred times, and have always felt a pang of envy for its lucky author. It is so jaunty, so unreasonably larger than life. It promises to deliver the unexpected—some fantastic reversal of fortune, some miraculous transfiguration in the character of the writer. It deserves a paragraph to itself, and should be printed in ceremonious italics.

Having arrived in Liverpool, I took ship for the New World.

Behind the sentence crowd the emigrants themselves—a crew of people dingy enough to take a little of the shine out of the words. They stand in line: the long-out-of-work, the illiterate, the chronically drunk, the hapless optimists, the draft-dodgers, the bankrupt adventurers. Some, like the Jews escaping the Pale of the Czars, are dignified by the involuntary heroism that attaches itself to any persecuted people; but most of the single men and families on the dock are not—were not—refugees. If they were on the run, they were more likely to be fleeing tallymen and creditors than cruel kings and despots. Very few of them could seriously claim to earn the sentimental welcome which would meet them on the far side of the ocean as their ship passed the Statue of Liberty on its way into the dock at Ellis Island. Few of them would be able to read (or understand) the words of Emma Lazarus's poem on Liberty's plinth, that grandiloquent advance-advertising of America as the sanctuary of freedom and democracy. To most of the immigrants America was simply a tantalizing rumor of easy money—of jobs, clothes, food.

In *Letters from an American Farmer* (1782), J. Hector St. John de Crèvecoeur (Mr. Heartbreak, in John Berryman's happy literal translation) wrote:

> What attachment can a poor European emigrant have for a country where he had nothing? The knowledge of the language, the love of a few kindred as poor as himself, were the only cords that tied him; his country is now that which gives him his land, bread, protection and consequence; *Ubi panis ibi patria* is the motto of all emigrants.

What turned the Atlantic passage into *the* great European adventure was not so much the character of America as the character of the ocean. It was simply a space too big for you to be able to imagine your way across it. It was as deep as the highest mountain you'd ever seen. It was a place of terrible winds and weather, with waves as big as crashing churches. That gigantic desolation of angry water was a source of terrible stories of shipwreck, sickness and death. The moment you stepped on to the gangplank, you committed yourself—not to America, but to a strange and frightening sea ritual, which would ineluctably transform you from the person you had been on the dock into the person you would eventually become when, and if, you reached the far shore. *Over there,* after the ocean had done its job, you'd have a different identity, and very probably a different name. You would not be *you,* at least not as you had known yourself to be up to this extraordinary moment.

A Yiddish memoirist—who in New York became "George Price"—wrote a booklet called *Yidn in Amerika,* in which he warned his fellow emigrants that the Atlantic crossing was "a kind of hell that cleanses a man of his sins before coming to the land of Columbus." The journey to Ellis Island from Rotterdam, Bremerhaven, Genoa, Le Havre, Glasgow, Liverpool, was a grim and protracted *rite de passage.* Before the invention of the steam turbine (which shortened the trip to nine days, in fair weather), it lasted for two weeks. For thirty-four dollars, you were treated to a symbolic death, in a stinking wooden coffin, with the promise of an uncertain and hazardous resurrection.

Before it was anything else, America was the voyage itself. Few of the emigrants (and very few of those who traveled in steerage) could think sensibly beyond their coming trial-by-water. Many of them, from landlocked villages and towns in central Europe, had never even seen the sea before this day. The United States was a sketchy, if glittering, fiction, its unreality sustained by the ungraspable breadth of the ocean.

It was a country they had read about in pamphlets and in letters home that sounded more like fables than descriptions of any recognizable reality. In America, the houses were as high as the sky. Everyone had enough to eat. Everyone had an alarm clock to wake them in the mornings. You could buy "several kinds of food, ready to eat, without cooking, from little tin cans that had printing on them." The poor people dressed in exactly the same finery as the rich . . . Who could seriously believe tall tales like these?

Yet they'd seen evidence of miracles. Returning emigrants, in American hats and American coats, brought souvenirs home—razors, penholders, music boxes. These tangible authentications of the tale were like the gold that Hansel and Gretel brought back to their father from the gingerbread house. To reach the land from which these treasures came, you had to trespass on forbidden territory. In German fairytales, the forbidden territory was the Forest, a realm of solitude and danger, with its evil woodcutters, wolves and bears. In nineteenth-century European history, it was the Ocean, the fierce North Atlantic with its fogs and sudden storms.

For most emigrants, it was sufficient transformation to become an *alrightnik*—to eat, dress and talk like an American. But an impressive minority of the steerage passengers achieved success on a scale that would have been unimaginable to their old, forsaken selves. It was as if the voyage had robbed them of all their European sense of deference and proportion. In Isaac Bashevis Singer's story "The American Son" a pair of elderly peasants living in Poland are frightened half out of their wits one morning by the arrival of a gorgeous cuckoo, a "nobleman," their son. Emigrants turned themselves into lords of the New York garment industry, millionaire realtors, Hollywood magnates. Their children became senators and congressmen, Pentagon strategists, CIA officers, secretaries of state. In the twentieth century, America's foreign policy has been haunted by the ancestral memories and nightmares of the transatlantic emigrants, just as its domestic political rhetoric has been colored by their sense of the magical melodrama involved in becoming—and remaining—an American.

For many years now, the modern emigrant has been more likely to fly the Pacific in the cramped vinyl pod of a 747, cross the Rio Grande, or sneak ashore among the mangroves on a Florida key, than to make the journey to New York by ship. Yet the long Atlantic crossing is still the one on which America feeds in its sleep. Again and again it turns to the Atlantic for its sustaining memories, and to those sepia images of ragged troops of Europeans disembarking at Ellis Island. So I took ship at Liverpool.

The Old World was in bad shape. It was coming down around my ears as I drove north out of the city through the Victorian docks that line the Mersey. At least they had been docks. Now they were smoking heaps of brickdust. I drove through an orange fog of dust. Dust caked the windshield of the car. Even from behind closed windows, one could taste the dust, its moldy sweetness, like stale cooked liver. Ball-swinging cranes stood idle in the muggy afternoon heat. Raised over the dustheaps were the yellow Portakabins of the demolition contractors, on tall stilts of scaffolding.

"The last of England," I said.

My wife said nothing. She'd imagined a more romantic maritime setting to say goodbye in, and I could see it too . . . worn paving stones, old iron bollards, trapdoor warehouses with cantilevered blocks and tackles. The swinging balls had demolished everything, including our goodbyes.

Every so often there was a gap between the ruins and the improbable glimpse of a ship. I saw the listless flags of Japan, Liberia and Greece, but no British ensign. Most of the British mercantile fleet had been either scrapped or "reflagged"—registered in Liberia, or the Isle of Man, or some other country where taxes were low and shipping regulations easygoing. In the last ten years the "red duster" had turned into a nostalgic rarity, and there was none on view among the dustheaps, where a duster of any color would have been welcome.

In the middle of the wasteland, the demolition men had left behind a sailors' pub whose scrolled Edwardian stuccowork lent an ironic touch of moldering finery to this devastated place. I parked the car on a patch of cinders and we crossed the dual carriageway to the pub. Inside, the flavor of brickdust was seasoned with the eye-watering tang of Old Holborn cigarette tobacco. We sat side by side on a wooden bench holding glasses of Spanish brandy.

"Cheers," my wife said cheerlessly.

After ten silent minutes of pretending an exaggerated interest in the sluggish movement of the colored balls around the pool table, I said, "I suppose we'd better find my ship." The Old Holborn in the air seemed to have got the better of my wife's eyes.

The ship was easy to find. At what had once been Seaforth it towered over the dustheaps, in wedding-cake tiers, topped by a spinney of radar scanners. Its name, *Atlantic Conveyor,* was clear from half a mile away, and it was flying a Red Ensign the size of an embroidered wall-hanging. Between us and it lay a shantytown of steel containers with mobile gantries and forklift trucks plying in the streets, a mile or so of twenty-foot-high chainlink fencing and a Portakabin guardhouse in which a bored attendant was staring at the *Sun.*

My wife and I embraced wanly. I lugged my bags from the trunk of the car to the guardhouse, and watched the car lumber and sway over the potholes in the tarmac and disappear into the orange fog of the Waterloo Road. It was not the dockside farewell that either of us had planned. Proper farewells need a suitable architecture on which to stage them. Kissing was not an activity that was catered for by the bald amenities of the Seaforth Container Terminal.

At first sight the ship was bigger than the dock in which it floated, a whale sprawled in a hip-bath. For although the North

Atlantic seaway was almost completely closed to passengers in the 1960s, it is still one of the most important freight routes in the world, and giant container ships like the *Atlantic Conveyor* maintain a continuous trucking service between the ports of Europe and those on the eastern seaboard of Canada and the United States.

Nine hundred-and-something feet long, fifty-six-thousand tons gross, the *Conveyor* was a custom-built marine pantechnicon. It had a toppling Hilton hotel mounted at its back end, with a long city block of slotted containers stretching out ahead of it. For the last ten days it had gone tramping round the small seas of Europe, picking up cargo from Le Havre, Antwerp, Rotterdam, Bremen and Gothenburg, and it was now gorged with exports. The car decks, on the waterline and below, were a luxury traffic jam of unplated Jaguars, Porsches and Mercedes. The containers were packed with many thousands of tons of bizarre odds and ends: Swedish matches, French brandy, frozen seal meat, Dutch tulip bulbs, paint, perfume, laughing gas, helium. Two containers were bound for Macy's on Herald Square in Manhattan: one, loaded at Le Havre, was billed on the manifest as "French wearing apparel"; the other, which had come on at Liverpool, was billed as "English bric-à-brac." A Robinson Crusoe, salvaging stores from the wreckage of a container ship, could drive round his island in an XJS, clad in Dior, reeking of Joy, blind drunk on Courvoisier and armed with enough high explosive to blow an unsightly mountain to smithereens. No wonder that so much chainlink fencing and so many rolls of barbed wire were needed to keep the locals out; every container ship that was locked into this ruined Liverpool suburb was a treasure chest of expensive toys and frills. By this measure, Europe itself had turned into a giant gift shop supplying America with high-fashion trinkets. I wondered what the afternoon drinkers in the pub, with their whippet-like bones and wretched teeth, thought of the trade; did they ever picture the Long Island mansions and Palm Beach ranches in whose garages those cars would soon be stabled, and did they ever try to guess at the real distance between Seaforth and the world the ships were servicing?

The accommodation for the crew of the *Atlantic Conveyor*

matched the grandeur of its cargo. I was traveling as a guest of the owners, Cunard Ellerman, and was assigned the cabin of Officer B, on the tenth floor of the wedding cake. Officer B lived well. His cabin was a roomy studio apartment furnished with bookcases, a refrigerator, a king-size bed, a comfortable sofa, a long desk of varnished pine, a cabinet for drinks and glasses, a coffee table and his own lavatory and shower. Just down the hall, Officer B could swim in the heated pool, put in a sweaty half hour on the squash court, work out in the gym and open his pores in the sauna, before showing up in the Officers' Bar and Lounge, where the bonded Scotch was twenty cents a measure, and where a new film was shown on the video at eight-fifteen each night.

I spread myself in Officer B's fine quarters, and loaded his bookshelves with the accounts of the nineteenth-century visitors and emigrants whose company I meant to keep during the voyage. I'd brought Irving Howe's *World of Our Fathers* and Moses Rischin's *The Promised City*, for their descriptions of Jewish peasants in steerage; Henry Roth's *Call It Sleep*, for the arrival in New York Harbor; Robert Louis Stevenson's *The Amateur Emigrant*; Charles Dickens's *American Notes for General Circulation*. Officer B's cabin compared well with the stuffy dormitory-cum-canteen in which Stevenson made his crossing, or Dickens's "stateroom" on the steam-packet *Britannia*, which turned out to be an "utterly impracticable, thoroughly hopeless, and profoundly preposterous box . . . no bigger than one of those hackney cabriolets which have the door behind, and shoot their fares out, like sacks of coals, upon the pavement." Lounging in Officer B's swivel chair and looking out over the smoking dustheaps through Officer B's picture window, wondering whether to pick up Officer B's telephone and ask the purser if he could bring me a bottle of Famous Grouse, I felt a tide of resentful envy coming my way from the voyagers on the bookshelf. Ian Jamieson, the purser, said that he'd be around with the whiskey in five minutes. I got Stevenson down from the shelf.

> . . . the second cabin is a modified oasis in the very heart of the steerages. Through the thin partition you can hear the steerage passengers being sick, the rattle of tin dishes as they sit at meals,

the varied accents in which they converse, the crying of their children terrified by this new experience, or the clean flat smack of the parental hand in chastisement . . .

Come to think of it, I had some complaints of my own on this score. The air conditioning was annoyingly loud. It sounded as if a large dog was stationed overhead and was growling through the vent at me. Turning the milled screw, marked Lo and Hi, red and blue, resulted in no change in either the noise or the temperature. I rolled up a dirty shirt and tried stuffing the vent with it. The growling dog backed off into the distance for a while, then the shirt took wing, flapped across the cabin and made an ungraceful landing on the sofa; the dog returned, sounding, if anything, bolder and growlier than before.

When the purser showed with the Famous Grouse, together with an electric kettle, a jar of coffee, a carton of milk and a pair of rather pretty cups and saucers, I decided to put a stoic face on the hardships inflicted by the air conditioning. Sailing, he said, had been delayed till tomorrow noon. There would be drinks in the Officers' Bar at half past five, followed by dinner, then a film on the video . . . The emigrants booed and whistled from behind their covers.

The next morning a steady drizzle softened the hard edges of the demolition work and turned the surrounding landscape to the even color and texture of gray porridge. There was a humming, banging, swaggering cheerfulness aboard the ship as people woke to the imminent prospect of Liverpool bobbing soddenly in our wake. At breakfast, there was already talk of Halifax, Nova Scotia, the first stop. I had imagined Halifax to be a fishy nowhere, and was set upon for my prejudices by the captain, the chief engineer, the first officer and the purser, working in chorus, as if they'd been commissioned by the Halifax Chamber of Commerce to sing an advertising jingle on the town's behalf. The bars! The discos! The amiability and comeliness of the people! The safety of the streets, where never a police horn sounded! The excellence of the restaurants! The Split Crow! The Palace! The Red Fox! The Misty Moon!

"It's the little town that has everything," said Captain Erin Jackson.

"Lobster lunches . . ." said Ian Jamieson.

"Ladies—for those who have need of ladies," said the chief engineer, David Meek, whose wife, Helen, and daughter, Wee Helen, were traveling with him on this trip.

"It's the social center of Nova Scotia," said First Officer John Brocklehurst.

"Everyone likes Halifax," said Captain Jackson.

I nodded politely and kept my disbelief to myself. I suspected that this paradise was a peculiarly Liverpudlian fantasy. If your ship's home port was Liverpool, or, rather, an empty un-urb of that depressed and beaten-about city, then anywhere on the far side of the ocean would take on the glow of a Samarkand, especially if you happened to be sitting in Liverpool, eating your breakfast by electric light, a day late in sailing, watching the rain fall on a range of low hills of brickdust and cinders.

When the ship at last began to move, it did so with the ponderous delicacy of an elephant sidestepping the tea things in a drawing room. I was on the bridge, a hundred feet above sea level and ceremoniously remote from the operations that were going on down in the bows and the stern and on the dock. The silence was churchy. A hushed voice over the radio announced that the stern line was off; another came in to say that the bow was now clear. We were so many stories up that the only way to tell that the main engine was running was to put one's palm on the bridge-console and feel the metal surface tremble with an even beat, like the skin of a breathing creature. The Sunday-suited pilot stood by the captain's elbow as the enormous ship eased itself, inch by steady inch, away from the wharf. To reach the open estuary, it had to move forward, turn on its axis in a space shorter than its own length, then feed itself into a long double lock that was half as wide as the ship's beam. It was a camel-through-the-eye-of-a-needle job, and I stood holding a rail, waiting for the million-pound crunch.

No one raised his voice. Wives and children were inquired

after, the weather was grumbled over, Liverpool's draw at Anfield on Saturday was derided, while the *Atlantic Conveyor* squeezed itself in, spun itself round and shrank itself into the lock.

"How much clearance do we have on either side?"

"Oh—a good eighteen inches."

While the lock filled to bring the ship level with the open water outside, we enjoyed a view of a ragged alp of rusty junk. The first officer said, "Liverpool's chief export. Scrap."

"Who's the lucky recipient?"

"The Japs. It all comes back to Liverpool eventually, as Toyotas and Hondas."

We slid gingerly forward, feeling for the cross-tide at the entrance with our bows, made a slow turn to starboard, and began threading our way north through the sand and mud banks of the Crosby Channel. The water was camouflage brown, flecked with the spittle of small, triangular breakers raised by the stiff southwesterly wind. From up on the bridge, the waves looked like ripples; though a fishing boat, a hundred yards or so away from the *Conveyor,* was jouncing about in them as if they were a serious running sea.

The captain and the pilot were conducting their professional business in a continuous gentle murmur around the wheel. Gossip and navigational instruction were laid on each other like the strands of a two-ply rope. "Old Rowntree—port ten—bought a bungalow up there recently—steady as she goes—cost him an arm and a leg, by the sound of it—starboard five—seventy thousand someone, I think it was Jack Elstree, told me—three four zero—two bathrooms, three bedrooms—steady as she goes—he's got a champion view, of course, south-facing—three three five—you heard his daughter got married in August?—steady on three three five—yes, Heswall man . . ."

The coast of Lancashire faded into a dim smear in the rain. The breakers, bigger now, were beginning to drool, with a sandy-yellow foam as thick as cotton candy. I'd never been on a ship as big as the *Conveyor,* and found it hard to adjust to its silence, its absence of palpable motion. It was as if we were at anchor while the Mersey estuary and Liverpool Bay were being slowly dragged away from under our hull. I was used to seeing the sea at close quarters, to treating each wave with respectful deference, but from the patrician height of the *Conveyor*'s bridge I saw the Irish Sea (which I knew to be a bully easily roused) humbly licking our boots.

We passed a coaster of about a thousand tons which was dipping its bows into the swell like a long spoon. Every time she came up, a cascade of ice-green water poured from her scuppers. The crew in her wheelhouse must have been like so many dice being shaken about in a cup.

"Only a little fellow ... We could tuck him into a spare corner of Three Deck," said one of the second officers.

The *Conveyor* lorded it over the small fry of struggling trawlers and tinpot freighters. We were the biggest ship in the sea, we were America-bound. There was a splendid arrogance about the way we drove our cargo of colored containers far ahead of us into the murk while the mountains of Snowdonia, dramatically and perversely sunlit, closed with us, fine on our port bow.

The pilot was dropped in the lee off Anglesey, where he was borne away in a tumbling orange walnut shell. With a very faint churning sound, somewhere deep down in her lower intestinal arrangements, the ship moved to Full Ahead. Seventeen and a half knots. Six days to the Elysium of Halifax.

Captain Jackson came over to where I was standing. "Well, what do you think of the ship so far?" He was a squarely built, deliberative Welshman, who counted out his words like coins and whose voice had a dry, North Walian creak to it.

I said, "It feels like going to sea in a block of flats, it's so motionless. Does she never roll?"

"Oh, yes. She rolls."

He checked the glowing bronze screen of one of the several radar sets on the bridge, targeted a white blip on the six-mile ring, glanced up at the digital readout of our speed, and studied the anemometer, which showed forty-five knots of apparent wind on our port bow. The *Conveyor* was moving at full speed, perfectly upright, through a near-gale.

"It takes a lot to make her move, but when she moves, she moves."

In the winter of 1986, Captain Jackson said, the *Conveyor,* bound, as now, for Halifax, ran into a violent storm three hundred miles east of Newfoundland. The tops of the waves were higher than the level of the bridge. The needle of the anemometer was glued solid to eighty-five knots, its highest reading. The actual speed of the west wind was one hundred knots, perhaps more.

"She was making forty-degree rolls."

"You mean rolling twenty degrees each way?"

"No. Forty degrees to port. Forty degrees to starboard."

I couldn't see it. In my view, if you cant a floating block of flats over at forty degrees, it falls into the sea with an enormous splash, and doesn't come up again. Somehow the *Conveyor* had managed to retain her footing and return to the vertical, despite her shallow draft and the towering, topheavy weight of her superstructure.

For two days the crew had fought to keep her facing up into the wind and sea. As she hit the face of each new wave, her bows had "fallen off," and the ship had done her best to slew sideways. The screw kept on coming out of the water and at one stage the engine failed. For a time, while the engineers worked to get the main engine back on line (with errant tractors threatening to fall in on their heads), Captain Jackson had kept the ship's head up to the wind with the bow-thrusters—ancillary propellers in the front of the ship, normally used only for maneuvering in harbor.

"And if she had been caught broadside?"

"God only knows what would have happened." He checked his instruments again, and made a slow, dry, Welsh inventory of that voyage. "We had a lot of cargo damage. One man was injured. He still has the scar. The accommodation was in a terrible state. After thirty hours up here, I went down to my cabin; it was un-recog . . . niz-able."

Leaning forward, hands planted on the console, his meaty fingers spread wide, he was reading the sea. He searched the horizon from end to end, and nodded. "Yes. She rolls. When we get round the corner of Ireland and meet the swell . . . she'll roll a bit then."

*   *   *

Only a few years before, a cargo ship the size of the *Conveyor* would have been a large and multilingual floating village, with Cape Verdian deckhands and Chinese laundrymen; now it was a tiny hamlet of ten officers and eleven crew-members. On the French and Swedish sister ships of the *Conveyor* everyone ate and drank together; but we were British, and both officers and men had chosen to recreate, on board, the ritually stratified and segregated life of a Cerne Abbas or a Chipping Campden in miniature.

The crew bar, a deck below the officers' quarters, was a cheery pub, with a dartboard, a jukebox and posters on the bulkheads. Upstairs, on the gin-and-tonic level, we signed our chits in a setting of consciously refined gentility. Framed color portraits of the Queen and the Duke of Edinburgh regarded us with a somewhat chilly marital gaze. We perched on sofas of imitation leather. An embroidered sampler showed the *Conveyor* floating on a stitched blue sea above the words of John Masefield's "Sea Fever." A letter from Prince Andrew to Captain Jackson thanked the captain and crew for their felicitations for the prince's forthcoming wedding. Guppies and angelfish swam decorously through the greenery of a tropical aquarium.

For dinner, you changed into uniform—at least into a white uniform shirt worn with epaulets and a tie. You had to help yourself from the galley, but sat down to a table laid with rolled linen napkins in silver rings, and seating was by rank, with the first officer, the chief engineer and the purser at the captain's table by the window, while the junior officers had a table to themselves.

Most of the officers and many of the crewmen had been aboard the *Conveyor* since her launching in 1985. Some, including the purser, the first officer, and the assistant cook, had been on the original *Atlantic Conveyor* when she was sunk by an Argentinian Exocet missile twenty miles north of Teal Inlet during the Falklands War in 1982, with the loss of her captain, Ian North, and several of her crew. So the community of the ship was tight and memorious. The *Conveyor*, though she might appear to the outsider to have the character of a new glass-and-steel office block, was a creature of fixed habits and customs.

In the ballroom-sized officers' dining room, the two small knots of diners had all known each other for so long, and had sat down with each other to eat so often, that conversation had been reduced to a sort of gruff Morse. If you were in on the code, a single word could do the job of an entire story.

"Meatloaf," said Donald, one of the second officers.

The second engineer, the electrical officer and Donald's colleague, Vince, chuckled clubbishly, as at the end of some elaborate tale of malarkey, while the radio officer touched his mouth with his napkin and went self-deprecatingly pink. It was a tough world for a stranger to horn in on; my own stories sounded impossibly long-winded by comparison, and I was cautious of using words like gorgonzola or Telex, in case they enshrined stories either so hackneyed or so blue that I'd condemn myself to social ostracism even before we left the Irish Sea.

Dinner over, we withdrew formally to the bar for coffee and stickies. Stickies were liqueurs—tots of Tia Maria, Cointreau and Drambuie—and these ladylike, sugary concoctions signaled an abrupt change in the tenor of the talk. We were in the drawing room now, and could gossip cozily about life ashore—about wives, children, girlfriends, mortgages, cars, house improvements. Helen, the chief's wife, and Wee Helen, his daughter, a schoolgirl of sixteen, were now the focal center of our circle—the official representatives of the families we'd left at home. We talked curtains, in-laws, C.S.E. exams and summer holidays, while the sea began to heap outside the window and the wind made lonely fluting sounds down the ship's empty corridors. Craning my head round and peering through the glass, I saw lights on the Irish coast and recognized them as old acquaintances. There was Wicklow, to the northwest, making its triple wink every fifteen seconds—and, up ahead of us, the Arklow Lanby buoy, flashing twice every twelve seconds. Before, I'd always fought anxiously to identify them as they disappeared behind the tops of waves, and had been worried sick about getting too close to the line of offshore sand banks that they marked. Up here, nursing a sticky and chatting to Wee Helen about her set passages in *Hamlet,* I saw them as pretty twinkles in the night.

I climbed up to the darkened bridge. The sea was looking more like a real sea now. The wind had started to cry in the rigging and in the tall stalks of the radar antennae. The anemometer showed fifty-five knots, dead on the nose—or about forty knots of true wind, a full gale. Far ahead of us—so far ahead that they looked as if they belonged to another ship—there were sudden, explosive gouts of flashpowder white as our bows hit the building swell. Yet the ship continued to plow uprightly ahead, with no more than the occasional bump and rattle that one might expect from a well-bred tram.

I made myself a mug of coffee in the chartroom at the back of the bridge. A fax machine was stuttering out a silver weather map of the Atlantic. On another day, in another vessel, this brittle, smudgy document would have reduced me to panic and a desperate run for a safe harbor. I'd never seen so many isobars so closely packed. The map showed half a dozen different weather systems, each one like a giant whorled thumbprint; cyclone hurrying on the heels of cyclone, in too many directions and speeds to follow. Our gale was taking place in one of the few areas of the map that looked relatively isobar-free.

Captain Jackson came in, scanned the map, and said, "Yes, looks as if we might be in for a bit of a blow in a day or two . . . This hurricane here . . ."—he pointed somewhere down in the region of Bermuda—"Helene, seems to be changing direction now. See, she was going along this track, westwards; now she's started to head north. We'll be keeping an eye on her over the next few days." He spoke of the hurricane as indulgently as a teacher might have spoken of a mildly naughty child in the classroom. I didn't at all like the look of Helene; she was not so much a thumbprint as a dense black stain, with her isobars coiled as tightly as the loops of a watch-spring.

"Very probably she'll peter out long before she gets to us. She'll just be another low, like the one we're in."

I thought, forty degrees to port, forty degrees to starboard, wave tops higher than the bridge, engine failure, caught broadside . . . and saw the quick, dit-dit flash of Tuskar Rock ahead of us. Rosslare, a few miles short of it, was a good deepwater port, and County Wexford is a genial and beautiful place to find one-self stormbound. Captain Jackson, though, had abandoned the alarming weather map for the bridge, where his attention appeared to be wholly engaged with the question of the unloading schedule in Halifax.

By six the next morning, the *Conveyor* was beginning, in the captain's word for it, to "move." I lay in Officer B's comfortable double bed, figuring out the ship's peculiar style of motion. First, there was the sound of a bomb going off far up front—nearly a fifth of a mile away—as she rammed an advancing sea; then the impact came shunting, trainlike, through the frames . . . *whump, whump, whump, whump* . . . until it disappeared with a valedictory wallop under the stern counter, by which time a new shock wave was already shunting its jerky way down the ship's length. It was not remotely like being rocked on the bosom of the ocean deep.

After some intimate slapstick with socks and trousers, I drew the curtains on a morning of brilliant early sunshine and a sea of low, ribbed hills, loosely crocheted with foam. The North Atlantic was in sparkling form, looking every bit as angry, cold and blue as the books had cracked it up to be. I jammed a woolly hat low over my ears and tackled the passageway leading to the afterdeck with a drunkard's concentration on the difficult motor skill of planting one's feet squarely and in good order. Outside, I was knocked sideways by the stinging, salty wind, and took shelter in the lee of a fire-box, where I wedged myself tight, just in time to see Ireland fall astern.

The Fastnet Rock was lying on our starboard quarter like a large blackened molar. Some miles behind it, Cape Clear and its attendant headlands showed as jagged atolls of moss green and granite purple. High over the Fastnet, the wind was whirling the gulls away like so many tumbling smuts in a chimney. It was a view so obvious, so piercingly vivid, so laden, that it sent a shiver down my spine to see it—and, by seeing it, to see the quiet crowds at the stern rails, watching and waiting until these last few crumbs of Europe were swallowed by the sea.

*   *   *

My ghostly fellow travelers were *emigrants;* they were not, or at least they were not yet, *immigrants.* At ten degrees west, America was still an empty hypothesis; it was the land, the family, the village or city they were leaving that must have occupied their thoughts at this stage of the voyage. They were making their exit—a phrase which, in *Roget's Thesaurus,* leads straight on to "resign, depart this life, die."

Too little has been made of this resignation and deathliness. Most American historians have preferred to stress the glorious resurrection that awaited the immigrants on the far side of the ocean, just as they've preferred to stress the vitality of spirit that the emigrants brought with them to the New World. I find it odd that Stevenson's *The Amateur Emigrant* (which is by far the most graphic and searching first-hand account of nineteenth-century emigration) is so rarely referred to in general histories of the United States. It may be because what Stevenson has to say about the matter is unpalatable to the point of being un-American. His emigrants are not the hardy and red-blooded ancestors of whom politicians like to boast when on the stump at Ellis Island. They are pathetic creatures, much too listless and moody to be seriously stirred by the American Dream.

One says that he is going to America because he's heard that "you get pies and puddings" there; and his horizon is noticeably more extended, and more optimistically set, than that of most of his companions in steerage. In Stevenson's words:

> Those around me were for the most part quiet, orderly, obedient citizens, family men broken by adversity, elderly youths who had failed to place themselves in life, and people who had seen better days. Mildness was the prevailing character; mild mirth and mild endurance.

And again:

> We were a company of the rejected; the drunken, the incompetent, the weak, the prodigal, all who had been unable to prevail

against circumstances in the one land, were now fleeing pitifully
to another; and though one or two might still succeed, all had
already failed. We were a shipful of failures, the broken men of
England . . .

And again:

As far as I saw, drink, idleness and incompetency were the three
great causes of emigration, and for all of them, and drink first
and foremost, this trick of getting transported overseas appears
to me the silliest means of cure . . .

As the ship at last drew clear of the known world, few of the
passengers at the stern rail can have harbored many tangible
hopes of the unknown one. They had amounted to nothing much
in Europe. Some had already been bankrupted by America, like
those Swedish farmworkers whose small fields of acid and stony
soil had been made valueless by the colossal success of the Midwestern grain belt. It's hard to imagine that the garment district
of New York could have meant much to the Jewish tailor from
some muddy *shtetl* in Poland, trusting himself to his luck and his
already-settled *landsmen*. Many of the passengers must have
been carrying precious addresses whose place-names gave away
the fundamental unreality of America. Could anyone really live
in a town called Fertile? Eureka? Promise City? Eden? Harmony?
Eldorado? Cosmos? Hopeville? Arcadia? Was Defiance, Iowa, a
farming community, or was it just your friend's idea of a rather-
too-hearty joke? The map of the United States was dotted all over
with fantasies and fictions. These ludicrous names belonged to
the landscape of allegory, not real life. They inspired skepticism.

So you stood and watched the ship's wake trailing back in the
direction of your own failure, which was your only established
reality, while the ship's head was pointed at an enormous blue
emptiness. Maybe you checked that doubtful address again, to
give the world beyond the blue a touch of reassuring substance.

Paradise? Kansas?

Better, perhaps, to go on gazing at the wake, unspooling from the stern like the thread of gum on which the abseiling spider hangs, on its pioneer descent into the unknown.

At lunch that day, both Helen and Wee Helen were white-faced and queasy. Wee Helen was staring into her plate of oxtail soup as if she'd just noticed a hatch of mosquito larvae wriggling about in it. The captain was trying to introduce a more cheerful note.

"It looks as if we'll have a lovely day tomorrow—there's a nice ridge of high pressure coming up. We'll have lost this wind by the evening, and after that we should have a flat calm for a day at least. Lots of sunshine. You'll be able to take those folding loungers out onto the afterdeck and put in some sunbathing time . . ."

Water slopped in the jug. A spoon slid across the table under its own steam. Wee Helen headed for her cabin, making swimming motions as she floundered up the slope of the dining room floor.

"It's not the rolling I mind," Helen said. "It's this pitching I can't stand. Anyway, like I always say on every voyage, this is *definitely* the last time."

"Is that a threat or a promise?" said her husband, tucking, with unkind gusto, into his plate of bangers and mash.

"What about the other Helen?" I asked the captain.

"Oh—Helene, you mean? They demoted her this morning. They've got her down to a tropical storm now. I don't think she's going to be any serious problem." But there was a note in his voice which suggested that he might be putting a comforting gloss on the facts for Mrs. Meek's benefit. After lunch I sneaked a look at the latest printout from the fax machine.

TROPICAL STORM "HELENE" 37.5N 47.0W EXPECTED 47.5N 37.0W BY 30/0600 GMT. THEN BECOMING EXTRA-TROPICAL BUT REMAINING A VERY INTENSE STORM, EXPECTED 58N 26W, 950 BY 0100 GMT, 63N 19W UNCHANGED BY 0200 GMT, 67N 07W 960 BY 03/0000 GMT. BRACKNELL W'FAX.

At 950 millibars, the atmospheric pressure of Helene's heart was very low indeed—a hungry vacuum trying to fill itself by sucking in the surrounding air and making it spin, counterclockwise, like a plug-hole draining water from a bath. This whirling mass of unstable air, with winds of 75 to 90 knots at its center, was moving northeast up the Atlantic at about 25 miles an hour. The *Conveyor*, on her Great Circle course to Nova Scotia, was heading west-by-north on what looked to me like a probable collision-course with angry Helene, whose temper, according to the forecast, was declining from hysterical to just plain furious. Before hurricanes achieved sexual equality (Helene had been preceded, a fortnight before, by Gilbert, who had wrecked a few of the West Indies and torn a broad swath through northern Mexico), they used to be called "whirlygirls." The more closely I looked at the chart, spreading the points of a pair of dividers between where we were, at 51.30N 11.07W, and where Helene was going, at 58N 26W, the more suspicious I became that we had a firm date with a whirlygirl. I also noticed that the title of the main North Atlantic chart, FROM THE AZORES TO FLEMISH CAP, had been amended, in the shaky pencil hand of some past officer-of-the-watch, to read FROM HERE TO ETERNITY.

Still, there was the captain's ridge of high pressure to look forward to. It bulged fatly out over the Porcupine Abyssal Plain, while our rendezvous with Helene looked set to take place somewhere around the Faraday Fracture Zone. The names of these bits of ocean were so much more solid, more likely, than the names of America—and the names were reminders that the Atlantic was a *place* with a geography just as particular as that of a continent. The sea floor was shelving steeply away from under our keel—1,500 meters . . . 2,000 . . . 2,500 . . . 3,000 . . . Since midmorning, the sea's character had altered, from being superficial to being seriously profound.

Meanwhile, the inked track of the barograph was climbing as fast as the sea floor was falling. It had risen fifteen millibars in eight hours and was passing the 1010 mark. Crossing the Atlantic from east to west, you meet far more weather than if you go from west to east. For, as the ship streams westward, it races through the advancing weather systems with their eastward drift. Going the other way, you can, apparently, ride a single bubble of weather from New York to Europe; if you time it right and leave the American coast in the southern quadrant of a vigorous depression, you can carry the same tailwind with you for the duration of the voyage. So, on the westward passage, the barograph needle tends to sweep up and down, leaving a pattern of exaggerated loops, where on the eastward route it can remain motionless for days on end.

Out in front, the containers stretched ahead in railway-line perspective, almost to vanishing point. The rectangles of ocher, green, rust red, gray and blue looked like a third-rate Mondrian as they shoveled their way through the breaking swell. I needed a pair of binoculars to see what was happening to the front of the ship. I got the stubby foremast in focus and watched it twisting stiffly from side to side as the whole structure of the *Conveyor* groaned and flexed, trying to fit itself to the uncomfortable sea.

The wind was blowing from west-northwest at Gale Force 8 and gusting to Severe Gale 9. Vince, the officer-of-the-watch, put the swell at thirty feet, though from the bridge it looked less.

"That's the danger of a ship this size. Up here, you're so far removed from the elements, you get blasé. If you were down on Three Deck now, that sea would look bloody terrifying. High as houses . . . and in this sort of weather you have to know exactly what you're asking the ship to do. Otherwise you'll overstretch her."

I didn't care for the sound of "overstretch." Studied through binoculars, the torque looked painful. There was a distinct bow in the line of containers, while the bridge and the foremast were rolling in opposite directions.

"That's good. It shows she's got some give in her."

Down in the cabin, it was hard to concentrate on reading. Dickens was drowned out by the drumroll noise of the swells as they came jolting through the hull. *Rivets*, I thought, and instantly heard them popping like buttons all over the ship. *Metal fatigue*, I thought, and lost myself in a maze of empty-headed speculations about molecules growing fatally sleepy under stress. At dinner, I felt aggrieved when someone, at last acknowledging that we were eventually going to meet up with Helene, or at least tangle with her skirts, talked of "this blow that's coming up." To live in a world where Force-8-gusting-9 didn't even count as "a blow" struck me as dangerously unnatural.

After the ritual dispensation of stickies, a group of officers sat down round the table in the bar to play *Colditz,* shaking dice and drawing cards to break their way out of a prison camp; *as well they might,* I thought. Wee Helen was sufficiently recovered to join them. I looked in two hours later and they were still at it, with Wee Helen trapped, in fiction as in fact, in the Officers' Quarters, while Dave, the radio officer, was making a break for the Perimeter Wire, as the ship slammed and shuddered her way through the dark.

By dawn the sea was swollen and hillocky, but smooth. Slopping lazily about over the Porcupine Abyssal Plain, it looked as thick as treacle. Out on deck, the air was slack and dead. Up on the bridge, the main steering compass was showing a new course. We were now heading southwest on 210°, aimed not for Halifax but for the Bahamas.

The original plan had been to scoot north over the top of Helene and be safely west of her by the time she reached our latitude. But the latest fax printouts showed that she'd been picking up speed overnight, and the winds at her center had been accelerating too. So the captain was now trying to dodge her by running down her eastern flank and ducking south of her.

For the time being, though, we had the barograph needle perched high on 1027 millibars, a rising sun in a cloudless sky; an ocean-cruising day in perfect keeping with our new Bahamian heading. At 10 A.M., the two Helens were gently grilling on sun-loungers on the afterdeck, while the revolving spoke of light on the radar screen combed through a forty-mile radius of ocean and found not a blip or a speck to interest it.

We were shrinking. We seemed to be a lot shorter and a lot closer to the water than before. With nothing to measure itself against now except the open Atlantic, the ship, so enormous in Liverpool, so lordly in the Irish Sea, was dwindling into a dot, a cell of dry little British jokes, fine little British caste distinctions and surprisingly formal British manners. I had once spent three weeks aboard a coaster whose crew had behaved like a rollicking gang as they nipped and tucked between the ports of Cornwall, France, the Netherlands, Northumberland and Lincolnshire. On the *Conveyor*, things were very different, and it was as if the bigness of the sea itself had subdued us, made us more polite and respectful of the terms of the social code that goes with sailing under a Red Ensign. We talked in lowered voices. We spent hours just staring at water, watching it change color as it bulged and contracted, bulged and contracted, or went sifting lacily past the side of the hull. We didn't seem to be going any*where;* we were merely *going,* intransitively, like the movement of a clock.

"At times like this," said the officer-of-the-watch, "the captain's job is to be like a fire extinguisher in a box, with a sign on the front saying 'Break Glass Only in Emergency.'"

We'd reached the stage where not only was it impossible properly to imagine the land we were headed for, it was impossible properly to remember the land we'd left. There was simply too much sea around to think of anything else but sea. It sopped up every other thought in one's head. It must have been at this stage that the emigrants began to shed their *emi* prefix, and turned into pure migrants, as oblivious as birds to anything except the engrossing mechanics of their passage.

"Anything happening?" asked Vince, relieving Donald of his watch.

"Nothing. Nothing at all."

"The pressure's starting to drop," Vince said; and it was—the barograph needle was sliding from 1026 down to 1025.

"When will we meet Helene, do you think?"

"Not for hours yet. Not till well into tomorrow morning, and then she should be a good three hundred miles or so off."

At lunch, both Helens had turned to a bright shrimp pink in the sun.

"This weather will do us very nicely, thank you, Captain. You'll be arranging for it to stay like this?"

"I'm sorry to say that I can't make that guarantee, Mrs. Meek. I'm afraid it's going to be a bit . . . on the blowy side tomorrow."

"As bad as yesterday?"

"Yes," said Captain Jackson. "Much like yesterday. Perhaps a little worse, even. But not much. No, not much."

The barograph needle was trudging downhill and, as the pressure-gradient steepened, the wind began to blow. First it was a summery breeze out of the south, which sprinkled the water with dancing highlights and cleared the afterdeck of the lingering smell of Ambre Solaire. It took an hour or two to build into a wind with any serious weight in it; a further hour to pile the sea into lumpy, blocklike waves with collapsing crests of foam. The sky turned overcast and I sat by the window in Officer B's cabin watching the Atlantic make its final preparations for the storm to come.

I was surprised to see so many birds so far away from land; and armed with the captain's bird book I set to naming them. The little black-and-white ones that skated and pattered in our wake were storm petrels; the bulky brown high-fliers were skuas; the gull-like birds, riding the wind at cabin level and matching themselves, canvas by canvas, against the speed of the ship, were fulmars. But the really fanciable birds, the aeronautical aces, were the Manx shearwaters. They hugged the waves on wings as stiff as those of model airplanes, gliding, banking, swiveling, diving, as they followed the continuously changing contour of the water at a distance so close that you couldn't tell where the face of the wave ended and the wingtip of the bird began. They seemed to be courting death by drowning, and as the waves grew steeper and whiter, the exploits of the shearwaters grew more audaciously cavalier. Tilted in perfect parallel with the toppling front of a breaker, the shearwater was wedded in a daredevil union with the ocean. I was thrilled by these birds, with their air of having been constructed out of balsa wood, tissue paper and dope; they made the sullen North Atlantic look fun.

Late in the afternoon we "spoke" two ships. The first was a Russian weather-surveillance vessel, usually on permanent station in midocean. It was running to Greenland for shelter. The second was a Greek freighter, only a little smaller than the *Conveyor*. Her captain wanted to know if we had a Weatherfax machine on board. The latest silver map, a worms' nest of isobars, was described to him in flat, matter-of-fact terms. For ten minutes, the Greek ship kept on its westerly course, then made a wide U-turn and steamed back in the general direction of Europe.

There was now a bilious tinge to the rim of sky ahead of us, a streaky, greenery-yallery look, as if Helene had been lightly currying it in turmeric, saffron and coriander.

"That's a classic storm sunset," Donald said, as if it was exactly what he'd been hoping for. The *Conveyor* stood on course. She was just beginning to shunt again. I felt a pang of envy for the retreating Russians and the lily-livered Greeks, and wondered whether we weren't all being a shade too British about Helene.

At midnight, the barograph was drawing a fair outline of a tufty precipice. It had fallen nearly three millibars in the last hour, and was skidding down toward the 990s. The wind yodeled round the bridge. I tried putting my shoulder to the door on the lee side which gave access to the bridge deck, but it felt as if a burly club bouncer was leaning hard on the far side. From the inch or two of space that I managed to gain against the bouncer, there came a blast of unseasonably hot air—vagrant African air that had traveled a long way from home.

Hurricanes, or tropical cyclones, are hatched in the Cape Verde Basin, ten degrees or more north of the Equator, off the coasts of Senegal, Guinea, Sierra Leone. They feed on moisture from the sea, charging themselves with water that has been warmed over the tropical summer. As this water vapor condenses in the air it releases energy in the form of heat, and the infant hurricane begins to spin. Moving like a top across the surface of the Atlantic, it crosses the Fifteen Twenty Fracture Zone and the Barracuda Ridge, gaining speed and confidence as it goes. By the time it hits the Puerto Rican Trench, it is a mature storm with a name of its own (given to it by NOAA, the happy acronym of the National Oceanic and Atmospheric Administration of the United States). Here, it either keeps on going west into the Caribbean or, like Helene, swerves north and east up the middle of the ocean, where the coldness of the sea usually reduces it to a tame Atlantic Depression.

Helene had more stamina than most of her kind. She was now

past the fortieth parallel, but the Weatherfax machine was still reporting winds of seventy-five knots at her center (a hurricane-force wind starts at sixty-four knots). We were more than three hundred miles away from her now, but inching closer, our speed reduced by half. The *Conveyor*'s anemometer was showing fifty to fifty-five knots of true wind, as the ship bullied her tonnage through the sea.

Trying to sleep, I was unpleasantly teased by the image of the *Conveyor* as a giant Italian breadstick. She was so long, so slender, so brittle—why couldn't the waves simply snap her between their fingers? Then she turned into a shunting train. For some reason best known to himself, the driver was ramming the buffers, again and again and again. Then she became my own boat, a cork on a billow, and the slow recollection of her actual tonnage, her huge and ponderous stability at sea, worked on me like a shot of Valium. I woke only when I found myself sliding, half in, half out of the bed.

It was still dark. The ship was leaning over to starboard, pinned there by the steady brunt of the wind. A cautious uphill walk to Officer B's picture window turned out to be an unrewarding exercise. It was impossible to see out for the gluey rime of wet salt which had accumulated on the pane overnight.

Up on the bridge, I found that someone had broken the captain out of his glass box, for he was standing by the wheel in slippers, pajamas and dressing gown.

"Morning." He treated me to a polite nod. "Bit of a windy morning we've got today." Slow-smiling, slow-moving, swaddled in paisley, Captain Jackson had the knack of conjuring around himself a broad ambit of suburban calm and snugness. Far from piloting his ship through the remains of a hurricane on the North Atlantic, he might have been pottering among the geraniums in his greenhouse on the morning of the local flower show.

"Didn't you sleep well?"

"Fine," I said, doing my best to match his tone. "I just wanted to see what was going on up here."

"There's nothing much to see. We're down to five knots at present. The wind's come up to about sixty. It's looking as if we won't make Halifax until first thing Tuesday morning now."

I had quite forgotten about Halifax.

". . . which is rather a nuisance, I'm afraid," the captain said, as the *Conveyor*'s stern crunched on a big one, making the whole bridge-and-accommodation section of the ship boom like a struck gong.

". . . because that's going to put us three days, possibly four, late in Baltimore. I'm afraid I'll have to Telex Liverpool—"

The howl somewhere behind and below us was the ship's screw, taking a brief airing out of the water.

I tried to divert the captain from his preoccupation with dates and schedules and interest him in the drama of the storm. I told him of Dickens's passage in January 1842, when the *Britannia* steamship had met weather so bad that Thackeray had suspected Dickens of making it up for literary effect. On his own Atlantic crossing, Thackeray had put his doubts to the captain of his ship and been told that the *Britannia* had indeed been lucky to have survived one of the most famously awful storms on record. I showed Dickens's magnificent description of being tumbled about in a small ship on a wild sea to Captain Jackson:

> The water-jug is plunging and leaping like a lively dolphin; all the smaller articles are afloat, except my shoes, which are stranded on a carpet-bag, high and dry, like a couple of coalbarges. Suddenly I see them spring into the air, and behold the looking-glass, which is nailed to the wall, sticking fast upon the ceiling. At the same time the door entirely disappears, and a new one is opened in the floor. Then I begin to comprehend that the state-room is standing on its head.
>
> Before it is possible to make any arrangements at all compatible with this novel state of things, the ship rights. Before one can say "Thank Heaven!" she wrongs again . . .

"Yes," Captain Jackson said. "It's good. It's . . . vivid. But when he says *wrongs,* that's not a nautical term he's using there. *Righting herself,* yes; *wronging herself*—no, I don't think you'll find that term has ever been used at sea. It gives away the fact that he wasn't really a seaman, doesn't it?"

With this unanswerable piece of scholarship, the captain went back to glooming over the damage inflicted by Helene on his precious timetable.

There was no sunrise; only a slow erosion of the darkness into a thin gray twilight—and what the twilight showed was not sea so much as a shifting mass of piled and driven snow. The *Conveyor* was plowing into snowdrifts, her forward containers now buried in a tumble of white, now taking off from the top of the drift like a ski-jumper launching himself into the empty air. Though this wintry appearance was contradicted by the way that the whole ship felt sweaty with Helene's body heat. The bank of low cloud overhead was an illusion too. Every so often one could spot ragged clouts of blue sky showing through it; the cloud ceiling was just salt spray, pouring past the ship at seventy miles an hour.

"The trouble *is,* you see, there's only one container berth where we dock in Halifax, and there's a Maersk Line ship due in there Monday. . . . That's what worries me."

The *Conveyor* seesawed clumsily over a hulking wave which was trailing spume like the smoke of an old steam train.

"How high are the waves now?"

"Oh, forty, forty-five feet. It's *nothing* like December eighty-six. They were up to the level of the bridge deck then; the swell was *twice* the size of this. No, I don't think there's too much malice left in this sea now. It hasn't had the time to *really* get up—"

We rammed another giant snowdrift, the ship went through its standard repertoire of creaks, bangs, shudders, jolts and groans, a ton or so of seawater came sluicing down over the bridge windows, and the captain said, "There's a book I've been trying to lay my hands on . . . a book that our agent in New York asked me to find for him . . ."

In the chartroom, the barograph was bottoming out at 994. Helene's center, about two hundred fifty miles off, was supposed to be 950, so we were on the rim of a deep cone of pressure. Five miles to a millibar is a very steep gradient in a weather system. On the faxed map of the Atlantic, it looked as if we'd sailed into a black hole in the ocean, with the isobars packed so tightly together that you couldn't see the gaps between them. I scanned the deck log, to see if the captain was holding out on me, but the only entry in the Comments column was "Pitching easily," which seemed a characteristically Jacksonian description of our thundering ride over this warm, alpine sea.

All day, and for most of the next night, the wind stayed up at storm force, but it was veering. It slowly hauled itself round from south to southwest and then to west, as Helene went north ahead of us; and these shifts confused the sea. The waves began to pile up on top of each other's shoulders. They crashed into each other and exploded into pyramids of froth. By noon, the ship was forced to heave to. With her engine slowed and her bows pointed up to the weather, she lay in the sea like an enormous log, making no progress over the ground at all.

There were few takers for lunch. The ship's kitchen sounded like a poorly conducted steel band. An incoming tide of gravy washed over the edge of the plate and made a black pool on the tablecloth. I asked the chief engineer how his wife and daughter were.

"They've both got their sheets pulled over their heads and they've turned their faces to the wall."

In the tropical aquarium, the fish were having a bad time. Most of their habitat had been uprooted from its floor of colored gravel and now floated on the surface of the water, which was slopping about and spilling over onto the floor. The big striped angelfish was beating on the glass with its fins, its mouth framing round *O*s of panic as it tried to recover its lost equilibrium.

Lying hove to is a state of mind. You mark time in a world that tilts and slides a lot but is going nowhere. You can't remember when it wasn't like this and you can see no particular reason why there should ever be an end to it. The tangled shaggy ocean strikes you as the ultimate emblem of meaningless activity. For as far as you can see, it goes on heaping itself up and pulling itself to bits. There is something profoundly numbing in the monotonous grandeur of the thing. Staring at it makes you feel as empty-headed as the angelfish.

As the wind shifted, the *Conveyor*'s bows followed it round through sixty degrees until we were aimed once more at Halifax, and the ship moved cautiously forward, as if on hands and knees. When we finally parted company with Helene, a knot of off-duty officers were sitting in the darkened lounge watching *Morons from Outer Space* on the video while we stumbled about in search of Newfoundland.

The next day, the wind was down to a Force 7 out of the northwest—an easy breeze, by the *Conveyor*'s disdainful standards—and the two Helens were back at the captain's table.

"But when do we see *life*, Captain?"

"Not long to go now, Mrs. Meek. Not long now."

Everyone was impatient for land. Halifax itself was still nearly eight hundred miles off, but we'd picked up the scent of North America and it was suddenly real enough to plan on. These plans were evidently part of an old and exhaustively rehearsed ritual. They were the treat you allowed yourself on crossing the forty degree longitude line. So the Meek family settled, in lascivious detail, on dinner at the Halifax Sheraton, while the first officer, the purser and I fixed on drinks at the Split Crow, followed by lunch at Oregano. The captain was booked in for a formal lunch at the Yacht Club; the radio officer was bound for a disco called the Palace. Only two more days of sea to go! After our brush with Helene, this substantial remnant of ocean presented itself as little more than a ferryboat ride.

It must have been at just this point of the voyage that the migrants, lately emigrants, found themselves slipping into their new characters as immigrants—comers-to, not goers-away-from. From here on in, you could begin to sketch your new life to yourself, to fill the obscure vacancy of "America" with solid objects. Somewhere west of Flemish Cap in the North Atlantic Basin, Paradise, Kansas, acquired a barn, a fence, a herd of cows with shitty tails, a log house, a spread table.

There was no horizon. The lightless water and the lightless sky formed an evenly laid wash of flannel gray. The wind had died during the night and the sea poured smoothly past the ship, as inert and heavy as sludge. This deathly calm was broken by the madhouse life of the birds, who lay in the water in rafts, several hundred to each raft, where they jostled, chattered, gobbled, barked and squealed. As the *Conveyor* pushed through, the birds budged resentfully out of our way in a last-second scramble of wings. Birds stood on the containers, leaking guano. Birds mobbed the ship's wake.

Vince, the officer of the watch, had his head jammed into the rubber hood of the radar. Looking out into the gray, I saw why he was so unsociably preoccupied: faintly printed on what I had taken to be sky was the outline of a big trawler. Searching left and right, I saw another, and another—a pack of pale shadows fishing in the clouds. A shadow on the starboard bow began to darken like a photograph in a tray of developer. It materialized into a black-funneled factory ship, its plates patched and stained with rust. There were men in woolly hats out on deck. One waved as we slid past, and had it not been for the gibbering of the birds, we were close enough to conduct a shouted conversation.

"Russians," Vince said from inside his radar, targeting blips of light.

Sometime in the small hours, we had crossed on to the Grand Banks, an enormous apron of sandy flats that fans out south and east from the coasts of Newfoundland and Nova Scotia. Here the cold water of the southgoing Labrador Current collides with the warm water of the Gulf Stream as it bends east toward Europe. This sudden mixing of hot and cold produces the chilly steam in which the area is almost continuously enshrouded. It also produces the kind of busy, circulating, aerated water in which krill and zooplankton breed; and the food chain that starts with krill and zooplankton ends with cod, whales and man.

John Cabot lit upon the Grand Banks in 1497, on the return voyage from his search for the North West Passage to Cathay. On the Banks, his men (aboard the tiny ship the *Mathew*) found cod shoaling so densely that they only had to lower baskets over the side to bring them up groaning with fish.

It was a miraculous draft of fishes—an image that fitted nicely with the theological rhetoric in which so much of the European colonization of America was conducted. The New World was Canaan, the land across the water that God promised to the Israelites. Man's duty was to "plant a Christian habitation and regiment" there, to "redeem the people of the Newfoundland and those parts from out of the captivity of that spiritual Pharaoh, the devil." So Cabot's baskets of fish, with their clear echo of the disciples casting their nets on the other side, were seen as happy confirming portents that the conquest of America was an evangelical mission.

The view from the *Conveyor*'s bridge was of a watery world so dank and sun-starved that it was hard to imagine anyone being thrilled by it. Yet in the sixteenth century the fish of the Grand Banks inspired as much excitement as the gold, spices and tobacco of the southern discoveries. In Hakluyt's *Voyages* the Banks earn as much space as Florida and the West Indies. They were the place where fishermen's tall stories came true: ". . . as great an abundance of cods as in any place can be found. In little more than an hour we caught with 4 hookes 250 of them." ". . . a great Turbut which was an elle long and a yard broad . . ." "140 lobsters in one small draw-net . . ." The fishermen had never seen so many salmon, so many herrings, so many whales. Ashore, they found raspberries and strawberries, "as common as grass"; "roses as common as brambles"; wild peas, game, timber for ship repairs, the raw materials for making tar and rope. The local "savages" gave them little trouble; Sir Humphrey Gilbert's expedition to Newfoundland in 1583 placated the Indians by mounting musical entertainments for them whenever the fleet put ashore—with Morris dancing, a maypole, hobby horses, hautboys, trumpets, cornets, drums and fifes.

Although Cabot, sailing under letters patent from Henry VII, had claimed "the Newfound land" for the English Crown, the British were latecomers to the Grand Banks fishery. In 1578— nearly thirty years before the settlement of Virginia and more than forty before the arrival of the colonists in Massachusetts— an adventurer called Anthony Parkhurst wrote a letter to Hakluyt in which he reported that he'd counted about 380 fishing vessels working the Banks during the previous summer. There had been 50 English boats; the rest were Spanish, French and Portuguese.

In 1583, Edward Hayes, a ship's captain on the Gilbert expedition, called the Grand Banks "the most famous fishing in the world."

It is a hard fact to grasp. Europe was not fished out. There were huge stocks of cod in the North Sea and the eastern Atlantic. Although the Church (in England, the Crown) had stimulated the fishing industry by turning Friday into a pan-European fish-eating day, the demand can't have been so great as to force a crossing of the Atlantic in order to meet it. Yet the fishermen came. Their "rutters" or "sea cards" were not charts so much as diagrammatic instructions of the sort one might scribble on the back of an envelope. They had no reliable way of fixing their longitude, and could get only a rough-and-ready idea of their latitude by aiming a backstaff at the Pole Star. They had wonky compasses. Their boats were very small—forty to fifty feet long seems to have been an average size. The one-way voyage to the Grand Banks took at least three weeks with untypically favorable winds and weather; the Gilbert expedition took seven weeks to get from Plymouth to Cape Race, Newfoundland.

These fishermen (who have effectively been written out of the standard history, which usually begins with John Smith and the Jamestown colony) were the first modern Europeans to make themselves at home in America. They fished the Grand Banks from April to July every year, traded with the Indians, laid up stocks of gear and provisions in the natural harbors of Newfoundland, Cape Breton Island and Nova Scotia. In an ad hoc, part-time way, they farmed the land. Anthony Parkhurst wrote to Hakluyt: "I have in sundry places sowen Wheate, Barlie, Rie, Oates, Beanes, Pease and seedes of herbes, kernels, Plumstones, nuts, all which have prospered as in England."

The Russians, working along the extreme easterly fringe of the Banks, were the last survivors of the international floating city of boats which used to fish over Whale Bank, Green Bank, St. Pierre Bank, Misaine, Banquereau, Canso and the rest. Everyone on the *Conveyor* could remember the time when the last few hundred miles to Halifax were an intricate slalom course, as the ship twisted and dodged through the fishing fleet, more often than not in thick fog. When Canada increased its fishing limit to two hundred miles in the 1970s, the Grand Banks emptied of boats. An hour after we'd sighted the Russians the radar was drawing a blank again, and we were alone with the squabbling birds, the colors of our containers looking vulgar and strident against the sober gray.

Then the containers, or most of the containers, disappeared. One moment we were pushing a long street of them up over the horizon, the next we were perched high over a vestigial stump of half a dozen or so. Looking over the side of the bridge, one could just see down as far as the water, which showed as tarnished silverfoil.

"Somewhere on board this ship," Vince said, "there's got to be a jinx." He lit a cigarette, and the long roll of smoke he blew inside the wheelhouse was cousin to the rolls of fog outside. "We're getting a bit too much of bloody everything, this trip."

I heard a ship sound, two or three miles off; a long, muffled burp. Worried that Vince hadn't noticed this disturbingly close neighbor, I said, "There's a ship out there . . ."

"Yeah. Us."

I listened again. The horn was dead ahead, but sounded spookily far away.

"Women on board is always bad, of course," Vince said. "Rabbit's bad. Vicars are bad. I never heard anything about authors before."

"Authors are bad."

"I suppose it must all be meat and drink to you—hurricanes, fog, engine trouble . . . Chapter Three: 'Fog on the Grand Banks' . . . pity we're past the iceberg season, I expect you could do with a few icebergs."

"I was really hoping for a shipwreck. Second Officer in Heroic Mercy Dash . . . that sort of thing."

"Yeah," Vince grunted from the radar hood. "The *Titanic* went down not far from here—just south of the Grand Banks."

The fog lifted in midafternoon and let a few feeble rays of sunshine through. The sea was brown and dusty looking, more inclined to take its color from its own shallow bottom than from the distant sky. Later, after the stickies, after the Harrison Ford movie on the video, after the game of *Colditz,* I went out onto the afterdeck to clear my head and was startled by the ship's wake. For a mile at least, it stretched behind us in writhing, braided flames of phosphorescence, as brilliant as liquid steel in a smelter. The sea was swarming with microscopic life, with meganyctiphanes, dinoflagellates, noctiluca doing their dazzling thing. Slightly drunk, I clung to the rail, watching as the ship's screw went on stirring up this rich, protozoic, Grand Banks soup.

Radar has taken the edge off the traditional excitement of landfall. Long before the coast of Nova Scotia showed up in life, it was there on the screen, as a broad ribbon of gold. When it finally emerged through the drizzle—uniformly flat, mossy, starved of landmarks, unpeopled—it was like Lancashire without the funfairs and boarding houses. The immigrants crowding at the starboard rail must have felt cheated to have crossed 2,500 miles of ocean only to arrive in a climate and a landscape of such unpromising familiarity.

The moment the pilot came aboard, three miles off Halifax, he brought with him a breezy, genial draft of North American air. As he marched the ship down the line of buoys, he talked of his own affairs as if they were a matter of general public interest. Yes, he said, in answer to no one's question, he'd just spent *his* weekend hauling his boat out of the water. Thirty-foot cutter. Built her himself. Took three years over it. This last summer, he'd sailed her down to Maine. Great trip. Reckoned he was going to redesign the rig to improve her performance to windward . . .

"Oh, yes?" Captain Jackson said. He and I had been this way before. He regarded yachtsmen with deep Welsh skepticism.

So much less guarded and jokey than the *Conveyor*'s British code of manners, the pilot's easy frankness belonged to another, less crowded, less self-conscious continent than ours. Black-bearded, lazy-voiced, dressed for the weather in a great plaid lumber jacket, the pilot roused my envy for his here-I-am, this-is-what-I-have, take-me-or-leave-me style.

While the pilot talked, the ship began to swell. Suddenly she was towering over the narrow inlet, over the suspension bridge ahead of us, over the midget shipping in the channel. Moving on cautious tiptoe at five knots, she rounded an island a quarter of her size and shaved past the Canadian navy in its dockyards.

Her sternquarters came into line with a miniature American city of lighted cloudscrapers, packed in tight crystalline formation like spars of quartz, while her bows were already exploring a hillside of pastel clapboard bungalows with open yards. Halifax was a stage designer's preliminary model of the real thing; it was New York, Chicago, Seattle, on a toy scale of one to one hundred, with an intricately pretty waterfront, a business district, towers, domes and residential suburbs, all gathered in an ambit that you could embrace with the sweep of an arm. We parked at the container terminal on the edge of a wide wood-fringed lagoon, a hundred yards or so beyond the end of this Lilliputian metropolis.

It was 10 A.M. on October 4th, and we were back on the calendar after a week of living in the shifting bubble of Ship's Time. The Canadian leaf season was in full swing, with the trees round the water colored henna, strawberry and ocher like a punk's hairdo. There was a wet bonfire smell on the wind, and the suburban surf of traffic on a nearby highway.

As the first Jaguars began to roll off the car decks, there was a half-term holiday air upstairs. The officers, unrecognizably clad in jeans, sweaters and snappy windbreakers, were queuing at the purser's office for dollars. Someone had collared the local newspaper and was reeling off the list of the week's attractions. Who was for Nelson Blick at the Palace, or Heart Surgery at the Carlton? Did anyone want to share a taxi?

It was easy to see why the crew loved Halifax. It was a compact and gentle town where the visiting sailor was a serious factor in the economy. The bars (or "beverage rooms") were full of men off ships. The cab drivers knew the names of all the ships in harbor, and where their moorings were. You could get blind drunk in Halifax, and someone would pour you out on your home gangplank without robbing you.

Half Scottish and half Irish, the town was in perfect balance between the Presbyterian rectitude of its architecture, whose granite, slate and dark red brick looked as if they'd been imported from Dundee or Galashiels, and the Catholic talent for having a good time that showed itself as soon as you broached this upright and stony facade.

I joined the sailors' round. There were tallboys of thin and gassy beer at the Split Crow; a stripper with a bad cold at the Lighthouse, where hulking men in gimme caps and fur-lined parkas grinned shyly while the naked girl stopped her act in order to blow her nose with a borrowed Kleenex; antique songs at the piano ("I Can't Give You Anything But Love, Baby," "Whatever Will Be Will Be," "Red Sails in the Sunset," "The Mountains of Mourne") in O'Carroll's Lounge. One could have taken one's maiden aunt even to the stripshow, where the frayed floral curtains at the windows, the little heap of used tissues on the stage, the auntly awkwardness of the watching men and the amateur, skinny unsexiness of the girl herself turned the event into a harmless, Haligonian oddity. It was Presbyterian striptease.

". . . through those streets broad and narrow, crying 'Cockles and Mussels, alive, alive-oh,' " wailed the pianist in O'Carroll's Lounge to an audience of office workers, who took up the chorus with big, confident, Canadian voices. In my shore-going tie, I was overdressed for the town. Everyone else appeared to have just come in from an afternoon's duck shooting. They dressed, not to stand out but to blend in, in muddy browns, greens, beiges and plaids, as if the height of Haligonian fashion was perfect camouflage. There was an above-average incidence of beards, a below-average incidence of jewelry. That cardinal provincial sin, of "getting above yourself," was not a Nova Scotian weakness; the people of Halifax had carried unshowiness to such a point of fine moral principle that I felt my striped Italian tie was standing out among them as an act of insufferable urban arrogance.

Where they were rich, and showily rich, was in body space. Everyone carried at least three hundred cubic feet of the stuff round with them on the streets. Life on a sidewalk in Halifax was a lonely business, with people swerving aside to give you a wide berth, as if you had a contagious social disease. Even in the enclosed shopping mall of Scotia Square, the Haligonians made a point of announcing that they lived in a luxuriously underpopulated country where bodily privacy and the right to one's own air were treasured. Once, I accidentally brushed against a woman pushing a supermarket cart; from the expression on her face, I feared that an arrest for criminal assault was imminent.

I'd gone to Scotia Square to renew my failing supply of socks, and was trudging up and down the aisles of the Woolco department store. The goods on sale were all depressingly useful, with the significant and sole exception of the flimsy nylon fancies in the Intimate Apparel section: snow boots; racks of green and khaki parkas; hairy plaid shirts; legwarmers; rubber overshoes; knitting wool in Haligonian earth colors; large agricultural implements for digging shelters and hacking away scrub. An early settler out of Hakluyt's *Voyages* would have felt perfectly at home in the Halifax branch of Woolco's.

The crew were right. In thirty-six hours of knocking about the town, I never heard a police siren. Taking a ride back to the ship at midnight, I mentioned this conspicuous silence to the cab driver, who was mildly indignant.

"We got a whole lot of police in Halifax," he said. "You see their cars all the time."

"What's the big crime round here?"

"Traffic violations," he said, without a flicker of identifiable irony.

Under way again, the *Conveyor* steamed southwest. Next stop, New York. Down in steerage, the immigrants were bursting with excitement and anxiety. On Robert Louis Stevenson's ship in 1879:

As we drew near to New York I was at first amused, and then somewhat staggered, by the cautious and the grisly tales that went the round. You would have thought we were to land upon a cannibal island. You must speak to no one in the streets, as they would not leave you until you were rooked and beaten. You must enter an hotel with military precautions; for the least you had to apprehend was to awake next morning without money, or baggage, or necessary raiment, a lone forked radish in a bed; and if the worst befell, you would instantly and mysteriously disappear from the ranks of mankind.

Little had changed by 1988. As Nova Scotia slid past in the dark, the talk on the bridge was of muggings, murders, crack, heroin, of bug-eyed addicts with shaky fingers on the triggers of their Saturday Night Specials, of the subway as a tunnel of hate in which passengers were casually butchered, on a daily basis, and by the dozen and the hundred. In the telling of these stories there was a persistent note of reverence and wonder, as if New York's otherness, its majestic status among world cities, could only be adequately honored by bloodcurdling tales of the unnatural. Aboard Stevenson's ship, people prepared themselves for their imminent rebirth in America by scaring each other with terrible rumors, and for them the stories were a way of facing up to the momentous fact of their own exile. The strange cannibal islanders of Manhattan rang true to the mushrooming sense of unreality in the immigrants themselves, and to their fear of finding themselves helplessly vulnerable in their new world. *You would instantly and mysteriously disappear from the ranks of mankind...* That was everyone's reasonable dread, of vanishing without trace—and had America not already been well supplied with homicidal felons, the immigrants would certainly have invented them.

By morning, we were off the jaws of the Bay of Fundy, with the coast of Maine a hundred miles away to starboard. A high-pressure ridge gave us a blue sky in which a few clouds floated like splashes of beaten whites-of-egg, a light easterly wind, and a prettily tousled sea. A big school of dolphins was larking just ahead of the ship; the Helens had taken to their sun-loungers. It was Vince's watch, and I stood with him on the bridge as we overtook a coaster with a red hull and a dazzlingly white superstructure.

"How far away is it?" Vince said.

"A mile . . . a mile and a half?"

"Look on the radar."

But there was nothing there. The sea was empty, except for a speck of light on the sixteen-mile ring, lying on roughly the same bearing as the coaster.

"That's high-pressure refraction."

We weren't seeing the ship; we were seeing the ship's image, telescoped across the curve of ocean in a brilliant optical illusion.

As we approached St. George's Bank, the Atlantic took on a domestic, inshore air, though we were still far out of sight of land. A fleet of small trawlers cruised over the shallows; passing freighters were recognized as old acquaintances.

"He's the gypsum ship, on his way up to Halifax from the West Indies . . ."

The first real sign of the United States was a close-packed archipelago of buoys marking lobster pots or fish traps. Around the British Isles, the standard equipment consists of a bundle of old plastic detergent bottles or a lump of tar-encrusted polystyrene, together with a length of garden cane topped by a torn rag. These buoys were smart, high-tech contrivances, freshly enameled in scarlet, with aluminum masts and tetrahedral radar reflectors. Each buoy was flying the personal pennant of its owner, racing-yacht style. They bobbed past on the beam and danced in our wake—new, snazzy, *American* symbols.

When night fell, we caught the wink of the Nantucket light. *Almost there.* But we had lost our ridge of high pressure, and the weather was blowing up hard behind the ship, with a building swell and banks of low cloud gathering in the eastern sky. By midnight the wind was moaning round the bridge and the *Conveyor* was beginning to corkscrew in the following sea.

The telephone on Officer B's bedside table rang at 4 A.M. It was Captain Jackson, calling to say that we'd passed the Ambrose lightship and that the New York pilot had just come aboard. I fought my way back into my clothes and went up to the bridge. It was the middle of a wild night, with a forty-knot wind caterwauling in the ship's rigging, rain sheeting down in diagonal bolts and a confused sea pluming whitely ahead of the containers. The lights of Long Beach and Rockaway on the Long Island shore showed through the rain as a faint, wobbly smear. The pilot had brought with him the early editions of the papers. The *Post*'s headline was TWO COPS SLAIN!

The city was hiding behind the low hills of Brooklyn and the thick weather—a distant glow of ruddy smoke, like a forest fire in another county. It took an age to reach the Verrazano Bridge and enter the Narrows, from where New York was suddenly on top of us. Manhattan was a dozen glittering sticks of light, through which livid storm clouds were rolling, lit from below, sooty orange in color, as they swirled past the middle and upper stories of the buildings. The choppy sea in the harbor was like a lake of troubled mercury, and the water glared so fiercely that it was almost impossible to find the tiny red and green sparks of the buoys marking the deepwater channel. Then one's eye adjusted and the city's famous icons began to emerge from the general dazzle of things. *There* was Brooklyn Bridge, a sweeping curve of white lights to the north; *there,* on her rock, was Liberty, weirdly floodlit in leprechaun green. Manhattan's freakish height and narrowness, rising in front of the low dark industrial sprawl of the Jersey shore, defied gravity, proportion, nature. It was brazen in its disdain for the ordinary limits of human enterprise. I watched the storm and the city battling it out, high in the sky. For a few moments, the sailing clouds exposed a large, low moon. It was drifting over the boroughs like a huge corroded gilt medallion. Given the air of high melodrama in the surrounding landscape, I would have been only mildly surprised to see the moon come crashing out of heaven and set the whole of Queens on fire.

If the moon had crashed, the event would not have much interested the crew of the *Conveyor,* who were otherwise engaged, getting ropes out to tugs and talking into radios. With his back firmly turned on the brilliant scene to starboard, Captain Jackson was saying, "You see, you have to keep an eye on the set of the tide in the Kill Van Kull; it's very narrow there, and there are some nasty shallow patches . . ."

I tried to think about the set of the tide in the Kill Van Kull, but it was no match against the scowling splendor of the illuminated city in the storm, the racing clouds, the hideous light in which Liberty was bathed, the exaggerated sense of occasion that this moment must always have inspired. The immigrants, crowding against each other's backs, shoving and straining, must have felt that all the reports and letters home had understated the awful truth about New York. The real thing was even taller and more intimidating than the tallest story. So you looked out, numbed by the gigantism of the city, asking the immigrant's single overriding question: is there really a place *there*, for *me?*

With tugs attached to the bows and stern, the *Conveyor* rounded the corner of Staten Island and nosed her way slowly into the tricky canal of the Kill Van Kull. The darkness was turning to gray now, and Manhattan began to dissolve into the clouds astern of us, as if it had just been one of those vividly awful things you see on a disturbed night. We docked, in the dead light of dawn, at a container terminal that looked like nowhere at all.

After breakfast, the ship's New York agent volunteered to drive me to Newark Airport, from where I could catch a bus to the city, and we drove through a landscape that only a guard dog could have looked at with any pleasure or anticipation. There were several miles of wire mesh, concrete, sheds, containers, dumps. The place, if it could properly be called a place, was a storage and service area for New York. Everything the city didn't want, or didn't want yet, or was just about to run out of, landed up here, where it lay about in mounds and piles and crates and tins. It was a glutton's backyard, on an epic scale. As evidence of Manhattan's insatiable appetites, it was impressive. Here came the fleets of ships, trucks and cargo planes that were needed to keep the city fed and entertained. To these heaps of packaged consumables, the *Conveyor* was now adding its minuscule contribution.

The airport was quiet, the bus stop deserted. I waited with my bags, feeling marooned and short of sleep. I missed the easy community of the ship and the imminence of New York felt oppressive.

"Hey! You want the bus? I sell the ticket—" The man was light on his feet, his walk close to a dance step. He looked as if he was wearing a fatter man's clothes, and his black pant-legs flapped thinly round his knees. I suspected that he was working some kind of minor scam, but the ticket looked official.

"Where you from?"

I explained my eccentric way of getting from London to Newark Airport, and he shook my hand up and down, beaming ferociously.

"I am . . . Sam Zokar." He said it importantly, as if it ought to ring a bell. It didn't. "From Liberia."

He'd been in America for three months. He was staying in Newark. He was alive with the springy hopefulness of the greenhorn. "This," he said, waving his wad of bus tickets, "is, for me, just *tempo-*rary."

He laid his plans out for me. Everyone was going places today, so Sam Zokar was going to get into the travel business. There were a few things to sort out, but pretty soon he was going to have his own agency. Right here in Newark.

"Start small, right? But then you got to *expand.* Move out to Manhattan . . . maybe a chain . . ."

In seconds, Zokar Travel grew from a single room over a derelict grocery in downtown Newark to a corporate giant with branches scattered over the subcontinent.

"Don't have no business card right yet, but if you have a piece of paper on you . . . ?" He wrote out his name in careful block capitals, with a Newark phone number. "Just ask for Sam. They'll know. Soon, I get Telex. Next time you need a plane flight, call that number—maybe then I'm in business already."

When the bus arrived, he loaded my bags into the hold, and as it was about to move off he stuck his head through the door and shouted, "Hey, John! Give me that call, right? You never know!"

I watched him dancing back into the shelter of the airport terminal. He was on air, fired up with the sense of his own boundlessness. Like the other immigrants whose ghostly company I'd been keeping, he had discovered the world's capital of *maybe* and *you never know.*

TWO

The Biggest Department Store
in the World

First of all—the land itself. A land flowing with milk and
honey. People with money left and right. Beggars use two
hands. They rake it in. And there's so much business there, it
makes you dizzy. You do whatever you please. Want a factory—it's a factory. Want to open a store—fine. Want to push
a pushcart, that's permitted too. Or you can become a pedlar,
even work in a shop! It's a free country. You can be bloated
with hunger, die in the street—and no one will bother you; no
one will say a word.

> —Sholom Aleichem, "On America"

Alice's apartment was a cell in a concrete honeycomb on East
Eighteenth Street between Gramercy Park and Union Square.
I had never met Alice; I knew someone who knew her and had
arranged to sublet her apartment, sight unseen, for two months
while she was working abroad. This deal was a technical breach
of the regulations of the building, so I had been told to present
myself to the doormen and the super as Alice's cousin, or at least
her intimate friend. So far as the handicaps of sex and voice
allowed, I had to be as nearly Alice herself as I could manage.

I let myself into a neat but rather gloomy cabin, barely half the
size of Officer B's—the fully furnished life of someone small,
slender and dainty in their movements. Alice must once have
trained in ballet and gymnastics in order to negotiate the doll's
house routes and spaces of her apartment without breaking

something every time she yawned. Everything was little: little table, little chairs, little couch, little bureau, a very little upright piano with its lid open and a piece of Schumann's on the stand. Only the bed was big, it reigned over the rest of the room from its alcove, where it was surrounded by books, angle lamps, card index files, and apparently served a dual function as Alice's head office. A patchwork mammal was crouched on top of the pillows. It probably had a name like Merriwether or Smudge.

With blundering caution I sniffed and snooped, trying to get the measure of this rented new life. I studied the grainy framed photographs on the walls, each one inscribed "For Alice with Love" by its photographer; a winter landscape, a woman in bed (could this be Alice herself?), a timber barn somewhere in the Far West. Alice had a serious library of modern poetry, photographic books, some stuff on Egyptology and the ancient world. No history, no politics, no obvious bestsellers. There was something fierce and exclusive in her taste for Robert Lowell, Alfred Stieglitz and the pharaohs, as if her apartment was too small to admit entry to the eccentric strangers who manage to worm their way onto most people's bookshelves.

Her kitchen—a narrow tiled slot, like a shower stall—revealed a preference for herbal teas and decaffeinated coffee as well as a reassuring weakness for vodka and white wine. The bathroom cabinet gave nothing much away: she was prone to headaches and occasional trouble with her sinuses. I liked the smell of her shampoo.

There was a useful find on the bureau—along with a stack of snapshots, a brittle clipping from a local newspaper in Mississippi, *circa* 1954. It showed a family of small children restraining an exploding huddle of Labrador pups, under the headline COON-HUNTERS OF TOMORROW? The caption identified the child in the middle as Alice. So Smudge—or Merriwether—had survived from a rural childhood in the deepest South into a north-facing single life in New York City. The clipping, with its cozy-cute headline, was rich in tantalizing suggestions. It conjured a great white Greco-Roman Baptist church, a segregated school where Alice would have been the clever one in the second row back, a landscape of flat cotton fields and stands of cypress and bog-oak.

There was a dusty, back-country road . . . Alice swinging her school bag . . . the lazy, grown-up talk of dogs and guns . . . It was all further away from New York than New York could possibly imagine—a lonely distance for anyone to travel on their own.

I ousted Smudge, or Merriwether, from the bed and tried out what it might feel like to be Alice. The last things she'd been reading were Joseph Brodsky's essays, an advanced French grammar (she still did her homework, evidently) and the October issue of *Vanity Fair.* I switched on the TV. She'd been tuned to the Cable News Network.

"Preserve your heritage of freedoms—join the National Rifle Association," then the picture changed to shots of Michael Dukakis and George Bush on the presidential stump. Alice would be rooting for Dukakis, but rooting reluctantly, I guessed. She'd wince at the too-new suede jacket and too-stiff checkered leisure shirt in which he was now cajoling an audience of Iowa farmers. He kept on blinking, as if at the glare of footlights; a big-city actor trying, unsuccessfully, to pass himself off as a down-home country boy. Bush, by contrast, also somewhere out in the sticks, looked as if he'd just strolled off the golf course; his clothes were clearly his own, and he seemed worryingly at home with the people he was talking to.

Half attending to the garble of the candidates at my back, I lay propped on one elbow looking out through the window at Alice's view. The rain had stopped, and on the roof of the building across the street a potbellied man was pegging out his laundry on a line. A rowan tree, rooted far down in someone's yard, was still in full leaf, its fernlike greenery straggling up through a jungle-gym of pipes and fire escapes. High above the street, a squirrel was making an intrepid passage from house to house: down a drainpipe, up a tree branch, along a fire escape, up another drainpipe . . . an urban aerialist, sprinting and jumping through the neighborhood, as footsure as a purse-snatcher.

The view was dominated by a single building: a distended Florentine *palazzo,* clad in bright red brick, encrusted with ornament, which grew, story by fantasticated story, to a huge water tank masquerading as a campanile. This good-humored, elderly monster loomed protectively over Alice's small quarter of New

York, with its nineteenth-century houses, its bar, its rowan tree, its rim of foliage showing over the tops of the roofs from Gramercy Park. Beyond the loony *palazzo,* the gray cliffs of midtown Manhattan began—a mountaineer's territory of ribbed outcrops and fissured slabs. No wonder that Alice had come to roost here on the seventh floor of East Eighteenth; it was a gentle village in the foothills, a place that anyone might choose to set off from in order to climb the dangerous peaks of the city.

Yet even in this relatively quiet corner, one could feel New York trembling under one's feet. The building shook with the wet sea-surge of the traffic as it bulleted away from the stoplight on East Eighteenth and Third Avenue. In place of birdsong there was the continuous angry warble of ambulances, patrol cars, firetrucks. It was the sound of heart attacks and heartbreak, of car crashes, hold-ups, fire-raisings, hit-and-run, flight and pursuit, sudden death; the sound of a city in a round-the-clock state of emergency.

The squirrel attained the guttering of Pete's Tavern. The man opposite, his mouth full of clothespins, was taking a last anxious look at the sky before disappearing down the hatch on his roof. If you were going to learn to live here, you'd have to go deaf to the sound of New York and set up house in the silent bubble of your own preoccupations. Therefore never send to know for whom the siren wails; it does not wail for thee.

Alice must have schooled herself to abide by this breezy motto. For me the New York air was full of robbery and murder; for her, it would all be inaudible white noise. She would be placidly sitting at her piano practicing scales and waiting for the kettle to come to a boil for her cup of camomile tea, snug in her cell, with uniformed guards standing watch down in the lobby. I resolved to try and learn to be like Alice.

Her name, and the shoebox scale on which she lived, made her belong to Lewis Carroll and the Tenniel illustrations to *Through the Looking Glass.* Her shoulder-length hair was fastened back with a snood; she wore a pinafore and striped knee socks. More importantly, she had the other Alice's sturdy bourgeois sense of normality. Alice was the touchstone of what was right and proper, a pillar of common sense in a world turned inside out.

Keeping one's footing in New York would need just the Alicelike gumption required by life on the chessboard at Looking-Glass House.

In the promised city at last, the immigrants found themselves in a cacophonic bazaar. So many *things!* The streets were awash with commodities undreamed of by the poor of Europe—new foods, smart clothes, mechanical novelties, luxuries made cheap by American techniques of mass production. Your own berth in New York might be no more than a patch of floor in a dumbbell tenement on the Lower East Side, where the roaches marched in platoons and every lungful of air was freighted with the bacillae of typhoid, dysentery and tuberculosis; yet no building was so squalid that its tenants were entirely excluded from the bounty of American life. In the midst of rack-rent poverty, in conditions as bad as anything they'd suffered in the old country, the immigrants were surrounded by symbols of extravagant wealth. There were ice cream parlors, candy stores, beefsteaks, fat cigars. In New York ordinary people, wage earners, dined out in restaurants; they had Victrola machines on which they played "jass" music; and by the standards of Europe they were dressed like royalty.

Two pictures. The first is a photograph, taken in 1900, of immigrants at Ellis Island. In the peasant costumes of central Europe, in clogs, shawls, long skirts, aprons, ragged coats and baggy trousers, they form an impossibly heterodox group. Nothing fits, and nobody fits. The only thing the people have in common is the expression of stunned vacancy on the faces of everyone except the very young. The second picture, taken at the same date, is of a Sunday crowd in Union Square. In this photograph, men are in snap-brim hats, sharp suits, striped shirts and fancy ties, women in fresh shirtwaist dresses. To be transformed from a character in the first picture to a character in the second—a magical metamorphosis—took perhaps a month. It was often done (as Abraham Cahan, Louis Adamic and other immigrant memoirists have recorded) within twenty-four hours.

The immigrant ships supplied the raw material out of which

the New York garment industry manufactured off-the-peg Americans. The clothes were machine-made on Singer treadles. The operatives were themselves mostly immigrants, working for desperately low wages, in the sweatshops of the garment district. The combination of the sewing machine and a limitless supply of cheap labor made stylish American clothes available to almost everyone.

You had a new name, assigned to you at Ellis Island by an immigration officer who was too busy to bother with the unpronounceable *z*s and *x*s of your old one. (*Gold*, because the streets of New York were supposed to be paved with it, was a favorite standby.) You had new clothes. You might be able to speak only a word or two of English, and live in a filthy den somewhere off Delancey, but you could still promenade as a suave, fashion-conscious New Yorker.

In 1904 Henry James spent an appalled couple of hours at Ellis Island, watching the officials admit "the inconceivable alien" to his native country. "It is a drama that goes on, without a pause, day by day and year by year, this visible act of ingurgitation on the part of our body politic and social, and constituting really an appeal to amazement beyond that of any sword-swallowing or fire-swallowing of the circus." James was consumed by the sense of his own "dispossession"; it made him ache for "the luxury of some such close and sweet and *whole* national consciousness as that of the Switzer and the Scot." Theodore Roosevelt voiced the same feeling, in less anguished grammar, when he said that immigration was threatening to turn America into a "polyglot boarding house."

The garment industry at least made the boarders look like residents, and the movies taught them what clothes to choose if they wanted to pass as regular American swells. There is rather too sanguine a flourish in Daniel Boorstin's paean to the industry, when he claims that it produced "a democracy of clothing," and more unkind truth in Michael Harrington's observation that it made the American poor into an invisible class. But it was huge (in 1914 a survey claimed to have counted 572,514 garment workers in New York City alone); it put the stamp of America on the new arrivals (as well as supplying many of them with their first jobs); and the costumes it had to offer were fantastically various.

So far, the experience of the immigrants had been a long shedding. On the way from Europe, they'd lost their names, families, occupations, uniforms, languages. The Ellis Island photographs show people who look as if they've forgotten that they've ever been anyone in particular at all. In New York, like so many children with a dressing-up box, they were faced with the choice of who they wanted to start being.

Identity in Europe wasn't a matter of individual fancy. Even if you had the money for the materials, you couldn't dress as an aristocrat simply because you liked the look of the local nobleman's style. If you were Jewish, you couldn't even pass yourself off as a gentile without incurring punishment under the law. Every European was the product of a complicated equation involving the factors of lineage, property, education, speech and religion. The terms were subtle and they could be juggled; even the most rigid class system has some play in it, some room for people to move up and down within the structure. But once your personal formula had been worked out by the ruling mathematicians, the result was precise and not open to negotiation. A over B times X over Y divided by Z equaled a calico shirt, a leather jerkin and a pair of clogs.

For anyone brought up in such a system, arrival in New York must have induced a dizzy sense of social weightlessness. Here identity was not fixed by society's invisible secret police. The equation had been simplified down to a single factor—dollars. There were a thousand different ways of being an American and (within the limits set by the amount of money you could raise for the game) you were invited to experiment with them, to fantasize, to play with strange and colorful self-images. Billboards (themselves an exotic feature of New York life) offered a free education. You learned the American language from them at the same time as you absorbed pictures of the savvy American that you might yourself become. In the five-cent nickelodeon, you sat in the dark dreaming your way into the clothes, and then the skin, of the screen lover, the gangster, the millionaire, the tender heroine—everyone his, or her, own Douglas Fairbanks or Mary Pickford.

The windows of the department stores were theaters. They showed American lives as yet unlived in, with vacant possession. When your nose was pressed hard against the glass, it was almost yours, this other life that lay in wait for you with its silverware and brocade. So you were a presser in a shirtwaist factory on Division Street, making $12.50 a week—so what? The owner of the factory was your *landsman,* very nearly a cousin; he had the start on you by just a few years, and already he lived in a brownstone uptown on Eighty-fourth. Success in this city was tangible and proximate; it was all around you, and even the poorest people could smell it in the wind. The distance between slum and mansion was less than a mile; hard work . . . a lucky break . . . and you could roam through Bloomingdale's and Macy's, buying up the life you wanted to lead. This Horatio Alger version of the American career was full of blithe and guileless unrealism; many, many more immigrants died in their tenements than commanded grand funerals on the Upper East Side. Yet the sheer compactness of Manhattan (where Alger himself, a Unitarian minister, had lived in a newsboys' hostel, obsessed with the idea of his own social failure), the nearness of the rich to the poor, the relative cheapness of American fashions and luxury goods, made stories like *Ragged Dick* and *Tattered Tom* seem more likely to come true in New York than in any other city in the world. The temper of New York itself was at least as unrealistic as anything that the Reverend Alger could dream up in his hostel.

The department store was the great treasury of New World culture. It was a splendid edifice—a many-storied exhibition hall, part opera house, part classical temple. It aimed, or at least pretended, to house a whole civilization within the space of a city block. Ranged in order, section by section and floor by floor, according to a system of classification as ingenious and arcane as that of the Brothers Roget in their *Thesaurus,* were the prestigious materials and objects of American society, its domestic arts and sciences; its inventions, foods, costumes, furnishings and accoutrements. Long before Chicago mounted the World's Columbian Exposition in 1893, the department stores had been running their own Columbian expositions, and they transformed the act of going shopping into something more like an educative tour of a museum of contemporary life. In pillared halls littered with statuary on plinths, you were taught the social values of the age—whatever was new, worthy and of good report.

Rowland H. Macy opened his store on Sixth Avenue, just below Fourteenth Street, in 1858. He had failed four times over in the dry-goods business in Massachusetts and California; in New York, twenty years before the Alger books came out, he was the prototype of the Alger hero. His line was that he bought for cash, sold for cash, and undercut all his competitors; in fact he bought on credit which was constantly running out on him. But he was perfectly placed, on the edge of the growing garment district and on the brink of the great wave of immigration. As he branched out from selling dry goods and notions into jewelry, silver, clocks, Paris fashions, furniture and food, the store ate up the neighboring shops and quarried its way down Sixth Avenue and back along Fourteenth Street. Macy died in 1877, and the Straus family—rich Jewish immigrants from Germany—began to move into the store, first leasing space in which to sell their own lines in dinnerware, then, in 1896, buying out the last of Macy's heirs.

In 1900 the Strauses bought an enormous site, between Broadway and Seventh Avenue on Thirty-fourth Street, and commissioned the architects who'd designed the new Flatiron Building (a masterpiece of New York unrealism, with its hatchet-blade face and twenty-two ribbed stories) to draw up the plans for what they were now calling the World's Largest Store. The thing was a monster. The ten floors, laid end to end, added up to a strip a mile long and more than 150 yards wide. It mixed uplifting "classicism" with high technology. At the entrances, grinning satyrs waving horns of plenty supported the name of R. H. Macy; perched on a frieze above the street, a mixed bunch of goddesses sported sheaves of corn, panpipes and unidentifiable pieces of kitchen equipment. Inside, there were more divinities in togas, marble pillars, mountainous electric chandeliers. The place had the general atmosphere of a palace belonging to one of the bibulous, later Caesars, of the kind who ate babies and brought about the downfall of the Empire. It was, at the same time, a boastful monument to twentieth-century know-how. Every latest gizmo had been incorporated into the building: banks of high-speed elevators, tricked out in teak like staterooms on ships; the first stepped escalators; a system of overhead rails on which the merchandise traveled cable-car style; several miles of pneumatic tubes in which messages were sucked, or blown, from floor to floor in a few seconds.

In *The Art of Memory* Frances Yates described the memory theater of the sixteenth-century Venetian Giulio Camillo. It was on seven levels with seven gangways, and each of the seven segments of the theater was assigned to one of the seven planets, the seven angels and the seven stages of mystical ascent from the corporeal to the Infinite.

> The student of it is to be as it were a spectator before whom are placed the seven measures of the world *in spettacolo,* or in a theatre. And since in ancient theatres the most distinguished persons sat in the lowest seats, so in this Theatre the greatest and most important things will be in the lowest place . . .

In Milan at the end of his life, Camillo dictated the plan of the theater, which was meant to embody the secret of knowledge, to a fellow Hermetic philosopher, Girolamo Muzio. The dictation took seven mornings. If you were in on the cabalistic symbols used by Camillo, you could move about the theater as if inside the mind itself. Everything the mind had ever conceived was there, on one level or gangway or another, and in the theater you could take in the working of the universe at a glance.

There was a teasing likeness between the new Macy's and the Renaissance memory theater. New York's great retail theater was not so much a store as *the* store of American life—a three-dimensional encyclopedia, in commercial and vernacular form. The Straus brothers' taste in pillars and sculpted deities further strengthened the resemblance. Macy's was a show, the customer was treated as a spectator. Riding up through the levels, propelled by the newest electrical engines, you passed through every rank and category of material object. If you could hold Macy's in your head, with all its distinctions and discriminations, you would be close to possessing the key to the workings of America at large.

A small Korean woman was wrestling a large microwave oven through the swing doors on Broadway and Thirty-fifth. I made a show of trying to help, but she muttered furiously at me, cuddled her precious oven to her breast and broke into a run for the subway. Feeling foolish, I fed myself into the avid Saturday crowd as it streamed into the store.

I'd been to Macy's once before, in 1972, when I went foraging in the basement for a change of clothes. On a hot June afternoon the store had been blessedly cool and cavernous. The motherly assistant had made an old-fashioned fuss over my British accent and the clothes themselves had been, by European standards, amazingly cheap. Made of some kind of acrylic stuff, they were smart, bright, all-American. I bought a striped summer jacket in synthetic seersucker, a pair of washable trousers with creases built in and guaranteed to last forever, two button-down shirts with white collars and blue fronts. The bill for everything came to less than $70—which, at an exchange rate of $2.40 to the pound, seemed like a steal. Out on the street in my new American camouflage, I melted into the city, a regular guy at last.

Something had happened. Macy's in 1988 smelled of serious money. The air trapped in the swing door reeked of new leather and Rive Gauche. Inside, a man in white tie and tails was rattling off popular classics on a concert grand. Above the glassy aisles and mahogany-paneled boutiques there was a heraldic blazonry of expensive trade names—Louis Vuitton, Calvin Klein, Givenchy, Dior, Ralph Lauren. It was platinum-card country; a twinkling gallery, as big as a battlefield, of gold, silk, scent and lizardskin. When I'd last been here, there had been a slogan painted over the entrance: IT'S SMART TO BE THRIFTY. Sometime between the age of Richard Nixon and the last days of Ronald Reagan, that homely touch of American puritanism had been whitewashed over. Only frumps were thrifty now.

The crowd ran sluggishly through the long, marble-pillared corridors of jewelry, handbags and cosmetics. It eddied round the women in high heels, fishnet tights, frou-frou skirts and top-hats who were squirting scent samples at everyone, male and female, who came within their range. For a few moments, I was gridlocked with someone's reluctant husband, a tubby man wearing a bomber jacket and a leatherette helmet with earflaps who gave off a powerful odor of sweat and attar of roses. He was hauled away, whining, to the escalators by a twin-engined Brillo pad in a fox-fur stole, while the current of the crowd bore me along into Men's Furnishings.

These "furnishings" were disappointingly dull in themselves—plain cotton shirts and ties that in England would be the badge of having once belonged to an obscure county regiment or minor public school. It was the way they were displayed that was extraordinary. Each counter had been converted into a grotto of evocative junk. Between the shirts and ties were piles of antique fishing rods, golf clubs, snowshoes, hatboxes, tarnished silver cups, gumboots, antlers, broken leather suitcases with labels from hotels in Split, Prague, Venice, Florence; gold-banded walking sticks; a pair of crossed oars; a horn phonograph; a battered schoolroom globe; shotgun cartridges; bits of splayed cane furniture left over from the Raj; old family snapshots in ornate silver frames.

So this was what had been in the container billed as "Bric-à-brac" on the *Conveyor*'s cargo manifest. There was a new life waiting in America for all the rubbish in the attics of genteel England. Macy's must have ransacked half the Old Rectories and Mulberry Lodges in Cheshire in order to assemble this hoard of moth-eaten Edwardiana. The rubbish apparently served some alchemical purpose: after a day or two spent in the company of a croquet mallet, a hunting flask, a box of trout flies and a pair of old stirrups, an ordinary white shirt would, I supposed, begin to stiffen with exclusiveness and nobility as it absorbed the molecules of stables, servants, log-fires, field and stream. Certainly the shirt could only justify its ninety-dollar price tag if you were prepared to pay at least fifty dollars for the labor of the alchemist and not be too pernickety about the standard of shirtmaking.

The crowd poured onto the escalators. When Macy's opened in 1902, these escalators with their woodblock steps had been the latest thing; now they were of a piece with the antique luggage and the wind-up Victrola, valued the more highly for being old than being new. They rumbled up through timber-paneled shafts. We piled, hip to haunch, onto this creaky Jacob's ladder, talking in Spanish, Haitian French, Brooklyn, Russian. There was a noisy elation in the crowd, as if the act of going shopping was working like an inhalation of Benzedrine.

We climbed through a cloud bank of bras and negligées; a meadow of dresses went by. Suppose you'd just arrived from Guyana or Bucharest—here would be your vision of American plenty, the brimming cornucopia of the fruits of capitalism. Here goods queued up in line for people, not vice versa. Here you were treated as an object of elaborate cajolery and seduction.

Nothing was too much for you. At every turn of the moving staircase, Macy's had laid on a new surprise for your passing entertainment. You'd like to see the inside of an exclusive club for Victorian gentlemen? We've built one. A pioneer log cabin? Here it is. After the log cabin, a high-tech pleasuredrome of mirrors and white steel. After the pleasuredrome, a deconstructionist fantasy made of scaffolding, with banks of video screens all showing the same picture, of beautiful people modeling leisurewear. The whole store was wired for sound, and each architectural extravagance had its own musical signature. Duke Ellington . . . Telemann . . . Miles Davis . . . Strauss . . .

Macy's was scared stiff of our boredom. This was a world constructed for creatures with infantile attention spans, for whom every moment had to be crammed with novelties and sensations. To be so babied and beguiled, all for the sake of selling skirts and jackets, sheets and towels! It was gross, even by the relatively indulgent standards of London. Many of the people on the escalators were fresh from that other world of clothing coupons and short rations; had I been one of them, I'd have been swept by a wave of blank helplessness in the face of all this aggressive American fun.

To get by in Macy's, a sturdy sense of selfhood was required. Everything in the store whispered *For you! Just for you!*—and you needed to love yourself a very great deal to live up to this continual pampering, for there was an insidious coda to the message, whispering *Are you sure that* you *belong here?*

At each floor, we had to leave the escalator and walk round to the far side of the shaft; and on the way we were ingeniously tormented with mirrors, each one placed so that it appeared to be an innocuous part of the display. I kept on barging into a figure who darkly resembled Henry James's inconceivable alien. I first spotted him in the Victorian men's club: a lank and shabby character in scuffed shoes and concertina trousers whose hair (or what little was left of it) badly needed pruning. He could have done with a new set of teeth. Had I seen him in the subway station, shaking a polystyrene cup under my nose, I'd have given him a couple of quarters and walked on fast, but in Macy's there was no escaping him. He jumped out at me from behind a rack of padlocked fur coats, and was waiting for me at the bookstore. Wherever he was, he looked equally out of place and I grew increasingly ashamed of him.

Shame was a central part of the deal in this show. The luxurious artifice had been designed to soften you up; first, by making you feel good about yourself, then by slugging you below the belt with a surprise punch and making you feel rotten about yourself. It worked, too. By the time I was halfway up the store, I had an American haircut and a new pair of shiny oxblood Italian loafers. It was a pity that, though Macy's sold almost everything, they didn't seem to have a boutique where you could buy new teeth.

By the ninth floor the crowd had thinned to a trickle and the air was sepulchrally cool. Here on the summit of the store, in Furniture & Carpets, was where the serious money got blown. The place exuded solemnity and elevation. The salesmen, seated in padded chairs behind bland vice-presidential desks, looked like the top guys in their world, as remote as kings from the girls who peddled cosmetics down on the ground floor. The music here was a discreet baroque tinkle on a harpsichord, the smell was of oiled potpourri.

A salesman, talking confidentially into a telephone, had spotted me and was sizing me up as a prospect. His disdainful, pouchy-lidded eyes were hoisted above a pair of halfmoon specs. In a second, the eyes slumped and the man returned to his conversation. I was not Furniture & Carpets material. *No way.* The harpsichord continuo was a muted babbling, like water flowing over stones; the salesman was beating time to it on his desk with the fleshy middle finger of his left hand.

The furniture was arranged over an acre or so of fully dressed theatrical sets—whole lives for sale. The owners of these lives had just stepped out of their rooms, leaving open books beside their beds, half-drunk glasses of champagne, plates of painted plaster food on dining tables laid for eight. Macy's had rigged things so that the customer was made to feel like a burglar. On the ninth floor, people walked on tiptoe and talked in whispers as they padded round the enviable existences of these ghostly creatures.

The ghosts, I was interested to notice, were bibliophiles. There were no broken-spined paperbacks in their lives, only books bound in calf and morocco with tooled gilt lettering and marbled endpapers. I flipped back to the title page of a book left by a ghost's fourposter: *The General Assembly of the Presbyterian Church: Reports of the Boards, 1919.* It was stacked on top of *Archives of Ophthalmology, 1945,* which in turn was stacked on a commentary—in Icelandic—on the Sagas. This scholarly Calvinist eye doctor (I saw him as a grizzled, hatchet-faced New Englander with a small-town practice somewhere in Maine) had an endearing weakness: he kept a bottle of Moët & Chandon handy, to swig at as he read in bed.

Next door was a drawing room roughly twice the size of Alice's entire apartment; soft-lit by sconces on the walls, this place belonged to a ghost who'd been toying with *Outline of Economics* by Richard T. Ely and *A Book of Famous Explorers* in the Marco Polo Library edition—a bond-broker with ambitious notions of foreign travel, perhaps. To stress the height of his ceiling, he kept a full-size palm tree in a half barrel. His coffee table, long as a stretch limo, was made of tweedy brown marble with a silver frame and smoked-glass top. The table served as a plinth for a three-foot-high ceramic Chinese dragon with a price tag of $2,400. A lacquered screen, gold on black, stood by an unglazed urn with Japanese characters painted on it. The screen cost another $2,400. Above a fine carved timber fireplace there hung a big still life of fruits and flowers, done in the general style of Fantin-Latour, but apparently painted by numbers, and a shade on the expensive side, I thought, at $3,500. The L-shaped oatmeal sofa, which would have seated a conference of arbitrageurs in decent comfort, had a single occupant, an old acquaintance of mine. The pyknic type in his World War I airman's cap with earflaps was trying on the bond-broker's life for size. Ignoring the supercilious gaze of a pearl-gray-suited salesman in the middle distance, he was using his own well-upholstered can to test the suspension of the broker's sofa. There was an expression of deep oblivion on his face as he joggled powerfully up and down, earflaps flapping, bomber jacket unzipped to the waist; a creature of pure unembarrassed ego.

Each haunted room played a variation on a theme first stated down on the ground floor among the shirts and ties. I'd never seen so much hill-station cane and wicker furniture, so many grandfather clocks, such heavy chintz. Walls were hung with antlers, horse pictures and sporting prints. There were assorted views of Oxford colleges and of the Thames ($125). For $225, you could carry off a print of a nineteenth-century soldier in the uniform of the Yorkshire Hussars or the South Salopian Regiment. For $995, you could claim an ancestor, painted by "Burton" in oils that looked as if they'd been kippered in woodsmoke.

This Burton was the *genius loci* of the Furniture floor. His work was everywhere, and after half an hour of coming face to face with Burtons in unlikely places, I found his style growing as familiar to me as that of a genuine old master. He'd been deeply influenced by John Singleton Copley, the eighteenth-century Boston portraitist. Like Copley, Burton was in thrall to an aristocratic ideal and had a knack of turning all his sitters into thin-lipped and Roman-nosed gentlemen of the Lord Chesterfield type. Their dark hair curled over the collars of their black coats, and one of the hallmarks of a true Burton was the care he lavished on the spray of lace at his gentlemen's necks. His backgrounds consisted of murky hints of broad acres and country estates.

At first I couldn't place just what it was that gave Burton's work its odd twist of originality. His pictures had *something*—a something that wouldn't immediately yield to stylistic analysis. Then, on my eighth or ninth Burton, I got it; it was to do with the olive sallowness of the sitters' skin and the not-quite-Boston cast of their eyes. This ancestor, like all the others, was the great-great-great-great-great-grandfather who could trace a line of direct descent back to that Puerto Rican pilgrim settler who came over on the *Mayflower.*

I took the escalator. Ancestors at a thousand bucks apiece, along with mementos of the hunting field and the shooting party, were not what I had in mind when I set out for America. I wanted to see what a new life might look like, not be shown a makeshift reconstruction of the life of one of my own widowed Wiltshire great-aunts, *circa* 1952. I remembered *their* rooms with a pang of claustrophobia—the smell of mothballs and bruised apples; the shelves of unread, unreadable books; the portraits of family worthies, as bad in their way as anything by Burton; the shabby keepsakes of lost empire, like the sheathed krises and elephant's-foot wastepaper baskets.

These gruff-voiced aunts lived in a world that was stiff with self-conscious gentility. Whenever we went to their houses, it was *Don't touch* and *Don't play.* They served grim teas, on trays of Benares brass, and talked about the dead. Lightly mustached, dressed in old tweeds and clumping brogues, they used to fill me with dread at being touched—and, worse, kissed—by them. They hated the twentieth century, its noisy cities, its rude young people, the way it took no notice of the aunts' violent opinions.

Now, by a stroke of irony that would have astonished them as much as it astonished me, the aunts were the cynosure of New York fashion. On sale on the top floor of Macy's were *their* hidebound devotion to the conventional, *their* reverence for lineage, which only just stopped short this side of necrophilia, *their* obsession with the insignia of social rank, *their* taste for all things stolid, rural and out-of-date.

At the Club Room, the escalator crowd wound slowly past an armorial display of crossed polo sticks. I wondered what on earth other people must be making of the world that Macy's was trying to conjure for us. In their Nike trainers, dreadlocks, tracksuit tops, surely they found all this emptily fantastic. Clearly the store knew what it was doing, for on every floor I could see the inexhaustible green flow of moving money. It was pouring into the tills at a rate (as I discovered later) of around $175,000 an hour, or $50 a second. Fed by this stream, Macy's could easily have afforded to transform itself into a perfect replica of far Araby, the court of Louis XIV, or any other historical dream world that caught its fancy; but at this late stage of the twentieth century, the cash and the *cachet* were in genteel, undemocratic dowdiness.

It was good to be back on the street, to escape this puzzling multistory fiction and return to the low realism of Broadway at dusk, with a hard nip in the air and a frank scowl of aggression on everyone's face as people shoved and jostled each other round the choked entrance to the subway. Two men were out of the race. One was blind and black; he stood his ground in the swarm, holding a tin mug and wearing a sandwich-board that said *I AM Blind / PleASE HELP me / thank you & / GOD BLESS YOU.* The other sat on a camp-stool, warbling on a birdwhistle, the self-appointed nightingale of Herald Square. He held the whistle to his lips with his left hand; the sleeve of his duffel jacket was fastened with a safety pin where his right elbow should have been. There was an expression of pure benignity on his face as he trilled and fluted at the angry crowd. His eyes were wide, their pale blue exactly matching the color of the faded denim cap that he'd pulled down over his Harpo Marx tangle of white hair. After the elaborate cunning of Macy's approach to the retail trade, his sales pitch was refreshingly direct. On a sheet of torn cardboard he had written in ballpoint *BIRD WHISTLE / ALL COLORS / $1.00 EACH WHISTLE.* I know a good bribe for four-year-olds when I see one, and bought five whistles, in red, yellow, green, white and blue. As I picked them out of the box at the man's feet, he smiled—a big, untidy, open smile that looked as if he really meant it.

"For to make the whistle, must first to put the water in the hole!" He shook his own whistle under my nose to show me.

"Where are you from? What country?"

"Me?" He seemed surprised and pleased that anyone should ask him such a question. "I come from Kiev. Kiev. In *Ukraine.*"

"How long in America?—how many years?"

"I come in . . . nineteen—eight-oh. I have eight years in New York."

"What was your job in the Ukraine? What did you do before you came here?"

He grinned, sighed, blinked. "Excuse me. Not understanding. Too bad English." His eyes, candid and friendly, remained on me as he piped a long, robin-like territorial demarcation call. It was a disappointment—I badly wanted to know why he seemed so happy. To escape from the Soviet Union, only to find yourself hawking plastic toys on a cold Manhattan street corner, would take an extraordinarily sunny disposition if you weren't to feel ground down by your fate. But the birdwhistle man didn't seem ground down at all. Nor did he seem mad or particularly slow-witted; just not much of a linguist. Down in the tiled warren of the subway station, I kept on hearing this blithe Ukrainian spirit sprinkling his plastic woodnotes on the New York air, and wondered how often, and how bitterly, he wished himself back to Kiev.

Still, he had a trade of sorts; by comparison with the beggars who took shelter in the subway stations, he was an *alrightnik.* Every station had its resident population of forlorn supplicants, and every journey across the city entailed a descent into a Third World of helpless distress.

The smartest beggars restored the literal meaning of the word "panhandler": they wielded long-handled saucepans with inward sloping sides to protect the alms within. When shaken, these pans made much the best noise: the mournful slather of quarters and dimes on Teflon was a sound in the same key as one's heartstrings. After the saucepan came the aluminum tankard, the tin plate, the greasy cap, the Styrofoam cup, the cracked and dirt-lined open palm. In as many yards, there were a dozen men and women—a desperate chamber orchestra of rattles, chinks and plunks.

Competition meant advertising. Some of the beggars rolled up their sleeves and trouser legs to expose weeping patches of violet scar tissue, growths, amputations, open sores. Others used techniques learned from radio and television. One well-dressed Third Avenue beggar was expert at delivering his slogan, which went, "I'm poor, I've had no breakfast/lunch/supper, and I want to work." He stood facing the drift of the crowd, and reeled off his words like an actor playing with variant meanings in a passage from *Hamlet.* He had a throwaway, cocktail party version: Oh, by the way, d'you know that "I'm poor, I've had no supper, and I want to work?" He shifted to truculence: "*I*'m poor! *I*'ve had no supper! And *I* want to work!" His voice took on a tearful, beseeching note: "I'm *poor* . . . I've had no *supper* . . . and I want to *work* . . . " He was a saucepan man.

Whenever I paused on the street, or hesitated over which subway line to take, someone new materialized beside me, and always the voice was discreet and confidential. I was a mailbox for muttered stories about lost wives, lost children, lost bus fares, lost jobs, hunger and thirst. Fifty cents or a dollar—never more—was what people asked for. With a bagel, a burger, a cup of coffee, a subway token, they said, their problem would be solved.

Always, I noticed, I was addressed as "sir." In the Great Depression, it had been "Buddy, can you spare a dime?"; fifty years on, we were buddies no longer. *They* were the outcast; *I* was the tenant of an apartment with uniformed doormen in the lobby— and there was no calling on my sense of fraternity to answer their need. I was sorry about the passing of that *buddy;* its disappearance registered something newly cruel in New York life.

The beggars slept much of the day away on benches on the subway platforms. The lighting was fierce, the noise of the trains was an incessant slamming and screeching. With their filthy topcoats pulled all the way up over their heads, the beggars looked like victims of a fatal accident; you knew they were alive only because they sometimes moaned and cried out in their sleep.

By night, they scavenged. Returning home late after dinner, I would meet them on the cross-streets around East Eighteenth, where small knots of them went tipping over trashcans in search of a bit of half-eaten pizza, or the lees of someone's can of Coors. They flopped and stumbled, far too feeble to be figures of menace, even on the darkest street—and at this hour none of them spoke to me; they knew that well-fed middle-class men take to their heels when strangers talk to them after dusk in Manhattan.

The current term for these misfortunates was "street people," an expression that had taken over from bag ladies, winos and bums. The Street People were seen as a tribe, like the Beaker Folk or the Bone People, and this fairly reflected the fact that there were so many more of them now than there had been a few years before. In New York one saw *a people;* a poor nation living on the leftovers of a rich one. They were anthropologically distinct, with their skin eruptions, their wasted figures, poor hair and bony faces. They looked like the Indians in an old Western.

The term was too easy by half. It casually lumped together the criminal and the innocent, the dangerous and the safe. It included long-term mental patients discharged from hospitals under what was called, in a sublime euphemism, the "de-institutionalization program," along with crack addicts, thieves, alcoholics, hobos, the temporarily jobless, the alimony defaulters, rent-hike victims and everyone else who'd fallen short of the appallingly high standards that Manhattan set for staying properly housed and fed.

You were meant to be scared by the Street People, to take one look at this defeated crew and see—Crack! Mugging! Homicide! Pathological vice! This simplified things wonderfully for the apartment dwellers, for at a single verbal stroke it canceled a great chunk of the city from our vision.

Within hours of my arrival, I was pumped full of propaganda. Don't loiter—always walk purposefully and signal that you have an imminent destination. Keep to the outer edge of the sidewalk. Avoid doorways. Never make "eye contact." If asked the time, or for directions, don't reply. Don't go north of Ninety-sixth, south of Canal or west of Ninth Avenue. Stick to the "white" subways, like the Lexington Avenue line, and never use the subway system after dark. Treat every outing on the New York streets as a low-flying raid over enemy territory.

This advice had the ring of that given to Alice by the Red Queen:

Now, *here,* you see, it takes all the running *you* can do, to keep in the same place. If you want to get somewhere else, you must

run at least twice as fast as that . . . Speak in French when you
can't think of the English for a thing—turn out your toes as you
walk—and remember who you are!

Alicelike, I tried to follow it as politely as I could, with curious
results.

I straightened my shoulders, focused on an imaginary point in
the far distance, and marched, swinging my arms like a marathon walker. Almost immediately, I started to acquire Manhattan
tunnel vision. The Street People moved from the center to the
periphery of the frame; within a minute or two they became
virtually invisible—bits of stationary furniture, on a level with
the fire hydrants and the trashcans. Left, left, left, right, left
. . . The stoplight flashed "Walk!" and I strode at a steady six miles
per hour on the flank of the sidewalk; it flashed "Don't Walk!" and
I halted, drawing my stomach in and throwing my chest out in
the best parody I could manage of a guardsman on duty in a
sentry box. There were no Street People now; just the marching
backs of men in city suits. The entire physical fabric of New York
had turned into a sheer trajectory, a bullet path (with one right-
angled ricochet) between subway exit and apartment block.

It was a tiring exercise. My fixed stare kept on slipping, to
include faces, shop windows, restaurant menus. On East Twenty-
second at Broadway I found a vacant fire hydrant and settled on
it, as into an armchair, like the Street People did, to watch the
crowd file past. Everyone moved with the same stiff clockwork
action; everyone wore the same boiled look on their faces. As they
approached my fire hydrant, they accelerated slightly from the
waist down, locked their eyes into the horizontal position, and
swept by, giving me an exaggeratedly wide berth. I tried making
eye contact, and managed to catch a few pairs of pupils offguard;
they swerved away in their sockets, as quick as fish.

It was interesting to feel oneself being willed into nonexist-
ence by total strangers. I'd never felt the force of such frank
contempt—and all because I was sitting on a fire hydrant. Every
one of these guys wanted to see me wiped out. I was a virus, a bad
smell, a dirty smear that needed cleaning up. After only a minute
or two of this, I began to warm with reciprocal feeling; had I
stayed on my hydrant for an hour, I'd have been aching to get my

fist round a tire iron or the butt of a .38, just to let a zombie know that I was human too.

There were the Street People and there were the Air People. Air People levitated like fakirs. Large portions of their day were spent waiting for, and traveling in, the elevators that were as fundamental to the middle-class culture of New York as gondolas had been to Venice in the Renaissance. It was the big distinction—to be able to press a button and take wing to your apartment. It didn't matter that you lived on the sixth, the sixteenth or sixtieth floor; access to the elevator was proof that your life had the buoyancy that was needed to stay afloat in a city where the ground was seen as the realm of failure and menace.

In blocks like Alice's, where doormen kept up a twenty-four-hour guard against the Street People, the elevator was like the village green. The moment that people were safely inside the cage, they started talking to strangers with cozy expansiveness. As we rattled up through the floors, it was "Hi!" and "Bye!" and "Where'd you *get* that?—I just love it" and "Don't you hate this weather?" ... little trills and squawks of sociability that registered everyone's relief at having escaped the dreadful flintiness of the subway and the street.

Returning to Alice's apartment—to the camomile tea, the sheet music on the piano, the patchwork creature on the bed—I unlocked my own temporary castle in the air; a soap-bubble life, as far out of touch with the city below as if I'd pressed a rogue button on the elevator and been whisked from East Eighteenth Street to a sedate small town in Mississippi or a gnome's den in Zurich, Switzerland. Like the *tableaux vivants* on the top floor of Macy's, Alice's room was a fully furnished fantasy; not so much an actual living space as a fond idea of how you might live, if only you didn't live in Manhattan. Its shoebox tidiness, its over-careful taste, its museumlike display of little-girl things from Alice's childhood, were set against the encroaching city—its wild disorder, its vulgarity, its tough grown-upness. When Alice came home to New York, she was in flight from New York. I saw her closing the curtains against the street, putting a Bach cantata on the stereo system, and drifting up and away, a balloonist floating high over the lawless wreckage of the city.

Everyone I knew lived like this. Their New York consisted of a series of high-altitude interiors, each one guarded, triple-locked, electronically surveilled. They kept in touch by flying from one interior to the next, like sociable gulls swooping from cliff to cliff. For them, the old New York of streets, squares, neighborhoods, was rapidly turning into a vague and distant memory. It was the place where TV thrillers were filmed. It was where the Street People lived.

Diane, my friend of twenty years, had turned into an Air Person since I'd last seen her. Once, she'd been down on ground-level, in a small terraced house in Greenwich Village; now she had a twenty-ninth-floor rental in a new fortified apartment building on Thirtieth Street.

Paying a call on her nowadays was hardly less difficult than stopping by at Buckingham Palace to have a quiet word with the Queen. The vast marble lobby of the building was patrolled by men in braided caps and so much gold frogging on their jackets that they looked like officers in the service of some fierce South American dictatorship. Unsuccessful applicants for interviews sat about on upholstered benches, disconsolately waiting for their accreditation to come through. If you managed to be escorted to an elevator by a member of the Tontons Macoutes, you felt marked out as a conspicuous social success.

"It's what people boast about now," Diane said. "Everywhere you hear women talking about how many 'men' they've got. We've all got men now. Have you got men?"

Her apartment was a rectangle of sunlight, adrift in the thin air of High Manhattan. Long windows framed a heady view of brick pinnacles and pale sierras. Only the faint purr of the air conditioning disturbed the alpine silence. Diane's white drawing room was lightly furnished, as if she'd had to throw out all the ballast from her life in order to ascend this far. There were some framed photographs of her family on the walls, two small paintings, both by friends, a typewriter on a table, a single spray of flowers.

"It's sort of nowhere, really. That's what I like about New York—it's *nowhere.* Nowhere, with a view."

So it was. She'd found an airy vacancy.

"Look—you can see the East River—"

It took some finding. A very short section of it was sandwiched high up between the walls of two office buildings. A distant barge slid from behind a smoked-glass window and was immediately swallowed by an insurance company.

"I like to watch the ships when I'm working. Sometimes, at night, you hear their foghorns."

Extraordinary. All I ever heard in New York was the barbarous wailing of police sirens; in Diane's soap bubble, the sound of the city was of solitary ships at sea, riding downtide in the early-morning mist. Perhaps it did matter what storey you were on, after all. The higher up you were, the more free you were to live in a world of your own imaginative making. By the thirtieth floor, you could probably tear loose from reality altogether. By comparison with Diane's apartment, Alice's seemed flatly realistic, dragged down by the gravitational field of the street and its people.

Here you had to stand with your nose pressed against the double-glazing to see the street at all. Far below—a world away—was turmoil. Down around the knees and ankles of Diane's tall block, nineteenth-century tenements were being torn down by cranes and bulldozers in a low cloud of red dust. Stores were boarded up. Cabs were stalled at a light in an unbroken line of dirty yellow. With a really powerful telescope, you might pick out the sprawled beggars, the crack dealers with telephone bleepers in the back pockets of their jeans, the addict sweating off his high in the doorway of the derelict warehouse; but on the twenty-ninth floor you had no more reason to pay attention to these things than you would have to go rubbernecking down the sewage system of the city.

In her apprenticeship as an Air Person, Diane had learned how to stay aloft for days on end. Every morning her Romanian maid would arrive with bloodcurdling news from ground-level. A secretary came to type in the afternoons. At sunset, friends presented themselves to the guards and showed up—ears popping from their ascent—for drinks.

Her days were punctuated by the arrival of "men." "Men" brought cartons of groceries, ordered by telephone, to the door; "men" came with sticks of her French cigarettes, crates of wine and Stolichnaya vodka, fresh flowers, books, magazines and newspapers. I doubted if she knew where any of these commodities came from. Far down in the uninhabitable city there were stores that were just telephone numbers to the Air People; there things were counted, parceled, charged and posted up, via guards and elevators, like so many messages to another world.

Diane used her TV set as if it were a video intercom, to inspect what was happening in the street outside her front door. Four blocks to the west, a building collapsed, trapping a woman under a filing cabinet for thirteen hours. It was on television. One block south, a man was found shot dead in his laundry truck. It was, said a police spokesman on television, "a very professional job." Every day our neighborhood yielded a drug raid, a hold-up, a rape, a killing; it was constantly on television.

For Diane, places like Brooklyn and the Bronx were as remote as Beirut and Teheran. *Nobody* went there. The subway system was an ugly rumor—she had not set foot in it for years. She did quite often go walking alone in the knot of streets around East Thirtieth, as a seriously entrenched Air Person would not have dared to do; and sometimes what she saw on television led her to take the elevator down to the street, where she would prowl through her own neighborhood to the site of a disaster or the scene of a crime, like a war correspondent braving the battlefield for the sake of a story.

I sometimes joined her on evenings when she was dining out uptown—evenings that had the flavor of a tense commando operation. At eight o'clock, the lobby of her building was full of Air People waiting for their transport. A guard would secure a cab, and we'd fly up through New York to the West Sixties or the East Eighties. I thought the cabs far grimmer and more alarming than the subways. Their suspension had usually been long wrecked by the potholes on the Avenues; the bulletproof Plexiglas screen between us and the driver had knife scratches on it and had turned milky and opaque with age; the blood-colored seat covers were ripped and holed. The driver was nearly always in a state of uncontained fury, and inclined to treat his cab as a weapon, an Exocet missile in the War of New York. Swaying and shuddering over the terrible roads, while the driver burbled obscenities at everyone who came within his sight, was an experience calculated to make Air People fervently wish themselves back in their safe eyries.

On my first night-raid with Diane, the driver was forced to stop at the light on Lexington. The heating in the cab was savage, and I'd wound my window down and was gazing out of it with the unfocused curiosity of a man who's quite forgotten the cardinal rules of Manhattan street life. Obedient to the gaze, a long, skinny figure came limping out of a pool of shadow. He wore a greasy embroidered *yarmulke* on his head. "Sir . . . " Phrases I'd heard twenty times before during that day came dribbling listlessly out of his mouth. *Ain't had nothing to eat . . . no place to sleep . . . Sir, will you give me fifty cents?*

I fished out my wallet, searched for a one, but could find only a ten. A hand, with broken lampblack fingernails but delicate musician's fingers, seized it. The man stared at the note. He might as easily have been seventeen or thirty-five. "Ya gotta be kidding! Oh, God! Ya *got* to be kidding!"

Diane, embarrassed by this display, stared dead ahead, practicing her tunnel vision. The light was stuck solid on red.

The man held up the ten-dollar bill to the streetlamp, shouted *Oi veh!* and crushed the bill into a pocket. Then he began to dance—a crazy, limping, jittery dance—and as he danced he moaned words in what I took to be Yiddish. He went on dancing until the light turned green, when he stumbled back into the shadow where he lived.

As we pulled away, I saw the driver's eyes fixed on me in his rear-view mirror. They were not friendly. He said, "Stoopid motherfucker—get that fuckin' window *up!*"

It was a white-knuckle ride. Diane sat bolt upright, wordless, clinging to the strap, while the cab flew through the dismal Thirties. At this level, at this hour, all of New York looked ugly, angular, fire-blackened, defaced—bad dream country. The sidewalks were empty now of everyone except the Street People. This was the time when things began to happen that you'd see tomorrow on breakfast television, and read about, in tombstone headlines, in the *Post* and *Daily News.* Father stabs three-year-old son, believing him to be Satan. Kin held in two bludgeonings. Woman slain as stray shot rips into hall. Mistaken identity—convicted murderer on run.

Few of these journeys lasted more than ten or eleven minutes, they were just long enough to let you catch a glimpse of the world you feared. Then, suddenly, there was another guard, dressed in a new exotic livery, putting you through Customs & Immigration in another lobby.

An elevator, identical to the one we had just left, spirited us upward with a long, low, mechanical whispering in its guts. At the appointed altitude, we stepped out into a mock-Tudor hall, where a Filipino servant was taking coats; and beyond, a splendid drawing room whose high ceiling was lavishly encrusted with mock-Georgian cornices. The guests who'd arrived before us were sitting on a brass-and-leather club fender, round a blazing log-fire in an open hearth decorated with *trompe l'oeil* plastic wood-ash. The carved timber mantelpiece was packed, end to end, with embossed invitation cards to charity dinners and memorial services.

There were several touches of Macy's ninth floor: a wall of books in claret leather bindings; a vast Japanese screen; a still life, French, of a spatchcocked hare with assorted fruits and flowers, which was three times the size of the one in Macy's. My first impression was that we had somehow stumbled on a house party assembled in the library of a castle, probably Scottish, in, perhaps, the middle of the 1920s.

I couldn't concentrate on the conversation, which was about German pedantry in the new edition of Joyce's *Ulysses;* a topic that I would have quickly warmed to in the ordinary way of things. Perched on the edge of the club fender, watching the gas flames leap from the make-believe logs, I was thinking of woman slain, father stabs, kin held, of the man in the *yarmulke* and of the word *motherfucker,* which was ringing unpleasantly in my head. *Up here,* you could barely credit the existence of *down there;* just as *down there* you couldn't conceive of the armored extravagance of *up here.*

This New York, the city of the Air People, was straining to break free of that other, accursed city of the same name. One day, perhaps, you'd feel a tremor under your feet and hear a sudden cracking and tearing as the fibers of steel and concrete gave way . . . At present the two cities were held together, one on top of the other, by the slender umbilical of the elevator, and by the Air People's dependence on the traffic that came up it—the *Times* and *Wall Street Journal,* beefsteak and zucchini, laundered shirts, Château Léoville-Barton, maids, flowers, guests, invitations.

Cry your heart out, man in the *yarmulke!* Up here, we're sailing through the sky where the air is keen and the view is of a flawless sweep of luminous indigo blue. You're way below the cloud ceiling. You're not even a dot to us, *buddy.*

"What was the name of that Dublin physician?"

"Did you read Susan's piece in the last issue?"

Fogheaded, unused to the altitude, I took my place at table.

Everyone was dreaming. The word came at one from every direction. On the subway platform at the Twenty-second Street station, one bench was permanently occupied by a head-covered sleeper who, as day followed day, I began to suspect was really dead. He (or she, or it) lay below a poster for the New York Lottery. It said, ALL YOU NEED IS A DOLLAR AND A DREAM. Whenever I switched on Alice's TV, I found politicians talking about their dreams. The Republican candidate for the presidency kept on reiterating his dream of a kinder, gentler America. The Democrat was reported by his advertising staff to have "lived the dream," because he was the son of an immigrant. Every congressperson and senator seemed under a weird compulsion to summon the ghost of Martin Luther King by slipping in the phrase "I have a dream" before going on to spell out their ghostwritten positions on Star Wars, or Medicare, or the federal deficit.

"In *our* country," said Alice rather sternly, "I'm afraid that we wouldn't much like it if politicians talked about their dreams as they do here. People would tend to think that they were a bit soft in the head. Where I come from, dreamers are impractical folk who have difficulty tying their own shoelaces. Still," she added politely, "I suppose that in America everything is as different as possible, and dreams are *far* more real to Americans than they are to us."

They were, too. *Dream* was the codeword for that ache for transcendence, for moving up and moving on, which had been sanctioned by the republic as a democratic right. As the grave voice-over in a TV ad for an investment company put it, "Because Americans want to *succeed,* not just survive. . . ." Success here didn't merely mean moving from position *A* to a more comfortable berth at *B;* it was, rather, a quality endemic to your personality and your national character—a peculiarly American state of being, in which you were continuously aspiring, striving, becoming. To dream was to keep faith with the idea that there was always a new frontier, a story at least one floor above that on which you were now living. It was an authenticating mark of the true-hearted American.

So—after more than a century of staying loyal to the slogan *It's Smart to Be Thrifty*—for the last fifteen years Macy's had been making a fuss of living the dream, by "trading up" and "going upscale." The store which used to serve the hard-pressed, bargain-hunting working class of New York had embraced the social ambitions of the Air People; and the change in Macy's reflected a profound—and unhappy—change in the life of the city itself.

I sat in the office of the Herald Square store manager, and listened to him tell a corporate rags-to-riches story. "Before Finkelstein—" he said; in Macy's, 1974 was zero-year. *Before Finkelstein* and *After Finkelstein.*

"We were dowdy . . . old . . . declining. There was no excitement in the place. We had this dowager reputation. We were floundering—changing presidents every year, all the bad signs. We'd drifted into being a lower-end-type business."

Then came Finkelstein, the new president of the New York division. In the manager's story, Finkelstein bore a more-than-glancing resemblance to another president that I could think of. He too had ridden in from the West, from Macy's California, and he was credited with having made Macy's people feel proud once again to belong to Macy's.

It was Finkelstein who erased the sign saying that it was smart to be thrifty. "Before Finkelstein, Macy's was just a store for moderates."

"Moderates?"

"Moderates. Moderate income, moderate spenders. The 'less affluent.'"

I liked the sinisterly Orwellian flavor of the word.

"Now we look to hit the upper echelon."

Finkelstein had begun to "lose the moderates" by emptying the bargain basement for which Macy's had been famous. In its place he had installed the Cellar, an arcade of glassed-in boutiques where you could buy "French" bread, handmade chocolates, espresso machines, fondue sets, chafing dishes, canteens of silver cutlery and "gourmet" hampers. *Before Finkelstein,* the ground floor had been occupied by counters of candy, drugs and notions; *After,* it was given over to scent, scarves and handbags, along with concert pianists and girls in tights and tophats. On the upper floors, he weeded out the jeans and cheap acrylics and brought in the big rag trade names—the Calvin Kleins, Giorgio Armanis, Ralph Laurens.

Macy's went on selling a lot of inexpensive, functional things that couldn't be found in grander places like Bloomingdale's or Bergdorf Goodman; but they were increasingly relegated to the further reaches of the building, on floors a long ride away by escalator.

"Dealing with the moderate customer, it's not a problem where to place your merchandise. The moderate, she'll go out there and *find* it."

Finkelstein, who had himself grown up in the New York suburb of New Rochelle, where his father was an egg-and-butter merchant, had the measure of the city. It was an astute decision to take Macy's "upscale," even though the store stood in what was now one of the seediest quarters of midtown Manhattan, on the rat run between Times Square and Penn Station; an area of welfare hotels, beggary, purse-snatching, addiction. Macy's main rival for the moderate trade was Gimbel's, a spit away on the south side of Thirty-fourth Street; and Gimbel's continued to stick with the moderates. For ten years, its business steadily crumbled. By the beginning of Reagan's second term, Gimbel's was holding desperate one-day sale after one-day sale in a last-ditch effort to regain its customers. Finally it went bust.

There was no percentage in moderates any more. No self-regarding moderate wanted to be treated *as* a moderate; and Finkelstein set about lapping his customers in the illusion, at least, of aristocratic luxury.

The stages of this exercise in social mountaineering could be tracked in the changing language of the store's advertising. In 1933, for instance, a mail-order catalog set out the Macy philosophy in the penny-plain terms that marked out Macy's from all the other New York department stores:

> We sell only for cash. Resulting economies including efficiency and volume save, we estimate, six per cent. We endeavor to have the prices of our merchandise reflect this saving, subject to limitations over which we have no control . . .

In the early 1970s, just before Finkelstein, the underlying tone was still the same, even if the phrasing was a great deal snappier:

> CAST YOUR THRIFTY EYE OVER BARGAINS YOU'LL FIND HARD TO BELIEVE! *(Christmas catalog, 1970)*

> Captain Rowland H. Macy believed in bargains 113 years ago when he started Macy's. We still do!
> *(Christmas catalog, 1971)*

It took the advertising department a little while to catch up with Finkelstein's style of doing things. In their 1977 catalog for the Cellar—once the bargain basement—they hit on a language of expensive golden words:

> Come on down to where the four corners of the world meet in a bustling melange of shops. A Marketplace with wares to tempt

the palate, titillate the senses. From succulent delicacies to old
world confections. A quaint Apothecary . . .

So it went on—with little dabs of French, self-conscious archa-
isms, bursts of indulgent alliteration. Yet this was restrained by
comparison with the catalog of 1988. *Think Status* . . . it said:

> Wrap her in tapestry . . . Mark Cross leathergoods collection,
> patterned for success, to carry her through her busy day . . .
> Princess Gardner solar calculator clutch. Karung lizard em-
> bossed leather . . . Baccarat, the crystal of kings, once reserv-
> ed for royalty. Hare sculpture, especially for animal lovers,
> $69.00 . . . Lace and silk charmeuse gown . . . Judith Leiber's
> jeweled goldtone monkey. A work of art that just happens to be
> a handbag . . .

This last—and most peculiar-looking—object cost $1,980. Even
the most pedestrian goods were painted over with words designed to associate them with royalty, antiquity, exotic zoology,
art. What would have been a "line" was now a "collection," and
the vocabulary of the art museum was borrowed by the copywrit-
ers to give the merchandise the glow of "timeless" (a favorite
word) value. Brand names were now artists' signatures, and everything possible was done to suggest that the personal hand of
the designer had "crafted" each individual commodity in the line.
In an unwitting echo of Karl Marx, whose theory of value-as-
labor had now been generally discredited, the advertising men of
Macy's invited you to buy, not a dress or a handbag, but "a work."

In this thriftless language, the New York garment industry
was slyly recast as something like the Gobelin family factory—a
great *atelier* of visionary artist-craftsmen. Here, in a dusty upper
room with leaded windows, you'd find Ralph Lauren patiently
stitching his "Polo" logo onto the left breast of a shirt . . . *for you,
just for you.* It was all as far away from Daniel Boorstin's idea of
a "democracy of clothing" as it was possible to imagine.

In one sense at least, the language answered to reality. Its
immoderacy corresponded to something that had happened in
the surrounding city—a squeezing out of the wage-earning mid-

dle class, the moderates for whom Macy's had traditionally been *their* store. Unable to afford "men" to protect them, they had been frightened away by the crime figures, while at the same time rent hikes had made Manhattan increasingly untenantable by everyone except the immoderately rich and the immoderately poor. When Finkelstein went courting the "upper echelon," he was following a clear demographic trend. The moderates were on their way out. The real middle class in New York now consisted of that uniformed army whose job it was to save the rich from the unwelcome attentions of the poor.

One Sunday, I sat in Alice's apartment doing sums. There was barely room in the place to accommodate both me and the 103 separate sections of the Sunday *New York Times*. This low-ceilinged, one-person box in a "safe" but unsmart block cost $1,350 a month, or $16,000 a year. My New York friends all told me that this was a snip; asked to guess my rent, everyone named a figure closer to $2,000 a month.

In the *Times* I searched for a job that would keep me in the unluxury to which I was trying to get accustomed. I knocked fifteen years off my age, gave myself a Harvard degree in literature and several years' experience in advertising, publishing and magazines. I was a thirtyish single, a yuppie type; the kind of guy to whom *New York* magazine might speak with special intimacy.

There were yards of job advertisements, and they sounded like good jobs, too. I could be an editor, a reporter, a media representative, a librarian—all sorts of things. The only snag was that none of them would pay enough to let me stay on in Alice's apartment. It would be easy for me to earn $25,000 to $30,000 a year; if I had luck, strong references and shone at the interview, I might just manage to pull in $40,000; but that would still be $10,000 short of the $50,000 minimum that I calculated was necessary to support life in a small studio in Manhattan.

So I'd have to move—out to Jersey or the boroughs. I'd ride in and out each day on the subway, or take the bus to the vandalized shambles of the Port Authority Terminal. Despite my B.A. from

Harvard and my straight-from-the-laundry Brooks Brothers shirt, I was, I realized with a sinking of the spirits, a moderate.

Isabel was one of the Air People. Her weekends lasted till Tuesday, when she took the train down to Grand Central from her farmhouse in upper New York State. Her husband was an investment broker on Wall Street; he had a complicated ancestry, an Albanian surname, and spoke American with a still-distinct French accent. He kept a stable of horses and rode regularly to hounds. I pictured him tally-hoing across the Berkshires in a pink coat, hot in pursuit of—maybe a real fox, maybe only a scented bundle of rags. Isabel disliked horses. She painted: delicate watercolors of plants and flowers on vellum.

The couple had an apartment on Park Avenue, in the Eighties, and from the picture window of the dining room you could look clean over Madison and Fifth avenues to the open greenery of Central Park. By this window, Isabel set up her painting things. Installed here, she could altogether forget that she was in New York. While Paul spent his day bawling into a telephone down on Wall Street (or whatever it was he did there—Isabel was vague about this), she moistened the tip of her brush between her lips and quietly vacated herself from the "ghastliness" of Manhattan. When she looked up from her work, she saw blue sky and a green field with sandstone boulders in it. She could as easily have been in the farmhouse, two hundred miles away.

One Wednesday morning, she was beginning to color in the purple, pincushion bloom of *Dipsacus fullonum,* the common teasel. The fine crosshatching of brush strokes was taking on body nicely. She was working against time; the real teasel, which she'd brought down with her from the farm, was already dying in its jam jar. She looked out for a moment toward the park—and found the park gone.

She must be out of her mind! As her brain received the message transmitted by her eyes, it registered, ERROR—RESET. She tried resetting; ERROR came up again.

Where Central Park should have been was now a gray, ribbed *thing* of concrete, with men in hard hats working on it. A man with a wheelbarrow of cement slop was staring at her. He was twenty yards away. She couldn't *believe* it. She was in the wrong apartment, on the wrong floor . . . If she could just calm down, her vision would clear, the man would go away, Central Park would come back . . . But it didn't.

She was shaking badly when she rang her husband at his office on his private line. The first time, she misdialed because she didn't dare to remove her eyes from the thing in the window. The second time, she got through.

He had shifted something over $2 million since breakfast time. He had just lit the first of the five cigarettes that he allowed himself during the day. He wasn't pleased to hear his wife's voice over the phone. He stirred the paper cup of coffee on his desk with a plastic spatula, and kept on saying, "Ya! . . . ya! . . . ya!" He held the receiver a few inches away from his ear; when Isabel's voice rose with indignation, it hit a pitch that he found unendurable. Finally he said, "Okay, honey, okay. I'll fix it later when I get back home," and, blowing a long plume of smoke ahead of him, slotted the phone back into its cradle.

After that, Isabel *hated* teasels.

The new Macy's owed a lot to Ralph Lauren. Its theatrical assemblages of English bric-à-brac and antique sporting goods were edited versions of what was on show at the Lauren store, once the Rhinelander Mansion, on Madison Avenue. In 1985, Lauren had spent $30 million converting this building into a delirious baronial fantasy, where customers were treated as if they had not so much entered a shop as strayed into the private home of the 14th Earl of Ardnamurchan. Dodging side-tables with vases of cut flowers, you had to sign a leatherbound visitors' book under the supervision of a butler doubling as an FBI heavy. There were ancestors and antlers everywhere; stuffed foxes, stuffed pheasants, stuffed fish, butterflies in cases, shotguns, riding tackle. The prices of goods on sale were inscribed on discreet handwritten notices, in sepia copperplate.

For a long time, Lauren had fought shy of selling his lines at Macy's. He didn't want his precious *objets* to be seen in a discount store for moderates, and Finkelstein had spent many months persuading Lauren that his dreams of social elevation were perfectly in sync with those of Macy's. Now the turnover of Ralph Lauren gear in Macy's stores across the United States was climbing past the $250-million-a-year mark.

Lauren was a local kid from the North Bronx, where his father, a Russian immigrant named Frank Lifshitz, was a house painter. He went to DeWitt Clinton High School, dropped out of CCNY and worked for a few months as an apprentice salesman at Brooks Brothers, where he fell into a lifelong infatuation with Old Money. Ralph Lifshitz became Ralph Lauren. A photograph of him when he was twenty-two shows a young man deeply smitten by the glamour of Groton and St. Mark's, of summers on the Cape, the Princeton-Yale football game, the old family house on Beacon Hill.

Since then, Lauren had become the arbiter of urban American taste in the age of Reagan. As a Bloomingdale's ad in the *New York Times* reverently phrased it, "Ralph Lauren. In our time, no American designer more perfectly embodies the way we live, the traditions we value, the style we share." By 1988, Ralph Lauren had won for himself an extraordinary iconic status. His name was now a magical signifier. It was like *Kennedy* or *Scott Fitzgerald* or *Rockefeller*. It stood for very much more than itself. Lauren himself boasted, "I don't do a shoulder—I do a world."

The world of Ralph Lauren was a version of pastoral. With besotted unrealism, Lauren idolized the countryside, the past, and a class system that America had never experienced at first hand. Like an Arcadian poet of the seventeenth century idealizing the lives of shepherds and shepherdesses (those poor Corydons and Phyllises), Lauren found his sublime in an imaginary society of Ladies and Gentlemen. Pastoral was traditionally a form in which aristocrats doted sentimentally on the working class; in Lauren's new American pastoral, the boy from the Bronx and DeWitt Clinton found happiness, simplicity and innocence, the great pastoral virtues, in the lives of the English upper class in the heyday of Empire and the Raj.

In Macy's, Bloomingdale's and the Lauren store at 867 Madison, I spent whole days trying to piece together the separate bits of Ralph Lauren's world. It was a strange place, not unlike Look-ing-Glass House in its bending of the familiar into the profoundly foreign.

There was no agriculture in Ralph Lauren country; no tenant farmers, no peasantry. Industry was restricted to game conserva-tion, domestic service and taxidermy. Some ancient system of enclosures had turned the country into a gigantic stretch of park-land. Like Yellowstone, it was conceived on an American scale, but its vegetation and wildlife were, broadly, Kentish, with the odd Yorkshire grouse moor and Scottish deer forest thrown in for good measure, along with polo pitches from Jaipur.

It was a landscape constructed for the exclusive pursuit of sport, mostly of a bloody kind. It rang to the sound of the hunts-man's horn; there was always the faint smell of spent cartridges in its otherwise crisp air. Purling brooks delivered fat brown trout to the fisherman's fly. Pheasants and partridges dickered up from their coverts on boxy wings. The climate was odd; even in high summer (and it was always high summer in Ralph Lauren country), the white slopes of the hills were decorated with skiing figures. On the rivers, there was a continuous plash of oars as insect-like eights competed for trophies. The sea coast was stud-ded with the kind of yacht clubs that blackball ninety-nine per-cent of their membership applications. Every paddock held its horse, and there was a pedigree dog by every open fireside.

Girls played lacrosse; boys were instructed in the art of gently squeezing the triggers of their Purdeys. The architecture was of weathered brick and white clapboard. Strict regulations ensured that no building in Ralph Lauren country exceeded four stories. There were, somewhat surprisingly, no churches.

The essential symbolism of this pastoral vision was not drawn directly from England but from PBS. Television—from "Master-piece Theatre," and its repertory of British serials with introduc-tions by Alistair Cooke. Lauren had built his world out of the set designs for *Upstairs, Downstairs, Brideshead Revisited* and *The Jewel in the Crown.* The whole thing was the work of a devout television fan. The difference between Lauren and the original filmmakers was that, while there had been much fudging of his-tory in the television serials, Lauren had succeeded in eradicating the last trace of historical reality from his version. He had turned it into a distinctively American fiction as pure as a tale of Cockaigne.

If you tried to judge Lauren's world by what it proclaimed itself *for,* it was an insubstantial cobweb—such silly stuff that no one in their right mind could seriously fall for it. Its real power lay in what was now being called the hidden agenda. It was what it was *against* that made it work.

It was in revolt against the city—an urban style that was sick to death of urban life. Its glorification of the cottage and country house, the wide open space, the hunting field, the horse and the yacht had far more to do with modern Manhattan and the Bronx than it ever did with England, Old or New.

It vaunted craft over industrial mass production. In fact Ralph Lauren's goods were factory-produced on a mass scale that would have staggered any garment district sweatshop boss in the 1920s. Yet the Lauren signature, the Polo emblem, the fake hand-stitching, together with the envelope of arts-and-crafty images in which the clothes were marketed, were designed to assure the customer that, by buying Ralph Lauren, she was returning to the world of her great-grandmother, where the personal tailor stood by with scissors and tape measure. People called him "Ralph," as if he was Abe or Ziggy from just down the block.

It rejected the present day. In the world of Ralph Lauren, the past was always better, richer, kinder, gentler—an idea that would have bewildered Lauren's father, as indeed it would have bewildered most of his generation of New Yorkers, for whom the past had meant poverty, hunger, repression. That the son of an immigrant should seize on the Europe from which his family had escaped as the fountainhead of prosperity and elegance was a sour and curious irony. Yet the idea evidently struck a deep chord in America at large.

It recoiled from the melting pot. Ralph Lauren's America was aggressively Anglo-Saxon. Nothing in it derived from Mediterranean Europe, let alone from Afro- or Hispanic America. It was the Lowell-Cabot axis of the Commonwealth of Massachusetts, pitched squarely against the teeming masses of blacks, browns, yellows and off-whites. When you kitted yourself out with Ralph

Lauren in the paneled Club Room at Macy's, you aligned yourself with the *Mayflower* screwballs versus the Rest.

Like so much in New York now, it was in flight from New York—from the dense streets, the mix of peoples, the electric up-to-dateness of the place. It was marketed as a "conservative" vision—as a return to "the classic," to "things that endure," to a "style beyond time." In fact no one could go back to Ralph Lauren country, since it had never existed, on any continent in any time. It was a brand-new American invention, as vividly of its own moment as the Reebok and the Space War machine. It struck me, a European, as a strange means of escape.

If you had dreams of flying, there were other ways of making them come true. On some of the cross-streets around East 18th, it was impossible to walk on the pavement without feeling the constant scrunch of powdered glass under one's soles. Here teen-agers with swivel-eyes monopolized the pay phones, making deals; they carried pagers, and were bleeped to their assignations. On their bikes, they could run rings round the squad cars which occasionally showed up on their territory.

Every so often, a ragged banner would go up, strung between the third floors of buildings on opposite sides of the street. The banner read, POLICE ARE WATCHING THIS CRACK BLOCK—CLEAN-ING CRACK OUT OF THE CITY. This neither reassured nor frightened anyone. The dealers moved a couple of blocks up the avenue until the cops took the banner down.

The volume of trade was enormous. It was conducted on much the same level of openness as the sale of pretzels and knishes from sidewalk carts. The city, with its police force already stretched beyond reason, was in no position to clean crack out.

The one big victory in the drug war had been the isolation of tobacco smokers into a leprous minority. This pleased everyone, including me. But I was an addict: every three or four days I hit the streets to cruise for a bearable brand of imported pipe tobacco. I could have scored a vial of crack many times over before I found a pusher of my drug. As the corner cigar stores went broke, so the crack dealers multiplied—a mobile guerrilla army of skinny kids in windbreakers, their success no less spectacular, or characteristic of its time, than that of Ralph Lauren.

A vial of crack cost five dollars. That was enough to make a single smoke, which would take you way off the streets for just long enough to make you feel bad about coming back again. As soon as the drug hit your system, the experience came in a rush. You were on air. You could feel the blood fizzing in your arteries. For five minutes, you were invincible. It cost just a dollar a minute to be King of Manhattan.

Crack was (so people said) instantly addictive: not because the bloodstream became chemically hooked on the stuff, as mine was on tobacco, but because you couldn't bear the way life looked when you came down. You'd been out of the ugliness, the dirt, the noise—that *shit*!—and now it was redoubled. You had the shakes, and a fierce thirst. After smoking crack, you craved liquid almost as keenly as you would soon crave crack again.

In the late-night grocery on Third, I'd be waiting at the checkout, then be shouldered out of the line by a jittery child clutching a liter-bottle of Pepsi. He was *down*—back on the street with a vengeance after his brief taste of the sky. He looked like someone whose elevator had gone into free-fall and slammed them into the basement from thirty stories up.

What this country needs is a good five-cent cigar . . . But what it had got was a good five-dollar fix. People were killing each other for crack. It was constantly being named now as the primary cause of street crime. The primary cause of crack use was not so easily named—though if you sat quietly on a fire hydrant a few blocks away from where I lived, you could begin to feel the cause in your own bones.

Edward Finkelstein converted Macy's into a nickelodeon. The customers were now spectators of an unrolling fantasy about the goings-on of an imaginary *haute bourgeoisie*. The gap between the real lives of the people who crowded onto the escalators and the ghostly leisure class who haunted the Club Room and the ninth floor was enormous; but, because that leisure class was so explicitly imaginary, the gap could be bridged by a three-inch credit card. With your $150 purchase, you were not even pretending to buy yourself into the English landed gentry; you were buying a ticket to move in the society of Ralph Lauren's wholly fictitious Arcadians. This gave a new twist to the loose talk of living the dream.

At the same time, Finkelstein engineered a great structural change in the store that was just as important, and every bit as typical of its age as the craze for Ralph Lauren. He "took Macy's private." Since 1924, Macy's had been a public company; through 1985 and 1986, Finkelstein got together a consortium of three hundred fifty members of his senior management and, despite furious opposition from the last surviving members of the Straus family, forced a "leveraged buyout," or, as everyone now called it, an LBO.

In its acronymic form, the leveraged buyout had a peculiar hold on New York dinner tables. People took stands on LBOs, as if they were declaring their position on capital punishment or the drug problem. Your opinion of the LBO, in general and on principle, was the big test as to whether you were a liberal or a conservative. I heard the term again and again. I knew that Macy's had undergone one of these fashionable operations. I no more understood it than I understood the intricacies of heart bypass surgery. Every time it cropped up, I saw a long spade digging into thick wet clay and levering out a solid rectangular chunk of the economic action. How that leverage was applied I had no idea.

It was meant to sound mysterious, for the leveraged buyout was basically a financial conjuring trick, a sleight of hand in which the success of the operator depended on his skill as an illusionist. It was the miracle of the loaves and fishes in reverse. It turned a lot of credit into an even greater quantity of debt, and then, if the illusionist had timed things right, it made a gigantic profit out of the debt.

It was a dazzlingly simple device for turning people on salaries into overnight millionaires. When I got the hang of it, I felt backward for not having invented it myself. It was pure mousetrap.

You are the employee of a big public company, with its empire of real estate, stock and industrial plant; the more of a behemoth it is, the better. If you put all the company's assets in hock, you can raise the money to buy out the stockholders. The company itself is now deep in the red, and what used to be profit is now required to pay the interest on the loan you secured against the company's assets. You now do nothing for a while, except let the company go on trading in the normal way.

There are one or two *if*s at this stage. You may not be able to keep up the interest payments, in which case the company will go spectacularly bankrupt—as Revco had recently done. In a growing national economy, though, your volume of business should soon outstrip the fixed level of payments on your mortgage. In any case, the company was probably undervalued when you bought it, as most public companies are. You go on sitting tight.

Now the trap springs shut. After five or six years, you sell the company back to the public again, at a price which reflects the true value of its assets and its growth over the period it has spent in pawn. You are now very, very rich, and you will never be anyone's employee again.

So Finkelstein and his consortium bought Macy's. The store, with its outposts strung across the United States from Florida to California, cost $3.7 billion. At the time, Finkelstein was on a salary of more than $780,000 a year, and was no doubt able to put away a few of those dollars in a personal savings account; but $3.7 billion is a figure unimaginable in practical terms—even to a man earning $780,000 a year.

The amount of cash that Finkelstein and the rest of the 350 Macy's executives had to raise on their own sureties was just $17.5 million. The rest—all $3.683 billion of it—was up to Macy's; to the stores, shopping malls, warehouses and stock that Finkelstein had previously been managing on the shareholders' behalf.

The executives came in on the deal at three levels. The top managers chipped in for $200,000 apiece; senior vice-presidents were allowed to invest $70,000; unadorned vice-presidents were limited to $17,000, or little more than the price of a couple of stiff drinks. For this last group, the promise (and it was a promise based on realistic forecasts of Macy's performance) was that when the company went public again, in five to seven years, their

$17,000 would be transformed into around $1,500,000. In an LBO that works, a return of a hundredfold is reckoned as a good average for the course.

The thing had to be irresistible: who says no to such fantastic personal enrichment—when all you have to do is to continue doing your job? It offered a ride in a magic elevator, straight from the ground floor to the thirtieth in a single swoop.

This was very wonderful for the executives concerned. For Macy's as a company the rewards were a little dubious. Its solid profits had been turned into a black hole of debt. It was now spending $600 million a year on interest payments. Various outlying bits of the Macy empire had been sold off to lighten the deficit. But Finkelstein talked of "the unleashing of a new entrepreneurial spirit" in the company; executives were now working in concert, instead of trying to push each other off the promotional ladder; several who had threatened to leave Macy's before the LBO were now staying, their eyes firmly fixed on those putative millions.

The rise of the LBO under the Reagan administration was the despair of liberal economists. To people like J. K. Galbraith and Benjamin Friedman, the LBO was a symbol of the way in which America was paying for its determination to live in a fantasy world of extravagant richesse by going into overdraft. Under Reagan, the United States had become a debtor nation; as under Finkelstein, Macy's had become a debtor store. The federal deficit, the great unaddressed issue of the presidential campaign, now stood at $155.1 billion; Macy's deficit alone was $3.7 billion—and all over the country, heads of corporations were putting their company assets in escrow, in the hope of raking in the jackpot in a few years' time. Meanwhile, Nancy Reagan disported herself at her husband's second inauguration in outfits that had cost—and not cost *her*—$46,000; in Macy's Club Room, people were cajoled into seeing themselves as members of a new class of idle rich; high above Manhattan, the Air People floated, safe in their armored apartments, far out of reach of the facts of life in the street below.

Some people saw in this a return to the 1890s and the rise of the robber barons like Jim Fisk and Jay Gould. Galbraith saw the Great Crash coming again. He wrote of the LBOs:

> We are now required to act—or not act—in accordance with the belief that uninhibited financial operations, however disastrous for economic performance, however verging on insanity, must be left strictly alone . . . There is the same massive substitution today (as in the years leading up to the Crash) of debt for equity; it is one of the inbuilt destructive features of capitalism.

When eventually I met Edward Finkelstein, I taxed him with Galbraith's line of argument. Finkelstein winced slightly as I pronounced the name. "He's just viscerally a socialist," he said. "Hates capitalism. Doesn't understand it. He'd like to see every business in this country owned by the government."

Every day I went to Macy's, I saw the birdwhistle man crouched on his stool, warbling to the crowd; and every day he stopped to return my nod with a big uncomplicated grin. Curious about the life of this visceral Ukrainian capitalist, I asked friends if they knew anyone who spoke Ukrainian—and one day I was able to introduce the birdwhistle man to a bilingual publisher's editor. He seemed thrilled to meet a *landsman* on the alien ground of Herald Square, he shook out his overcoat, put away his whistle and settled to monologuing happily in a language that meant no more to me than the sound of breaking glass.

Later, I heard what he'd said. His father was Polish, a cobbler. He'd grown up in Kiev. He'd learned to make shoes too, but it was a hard life, with never enough to eat. He had married, but his wife had died, leaving him with their daughter. Then—he had no explanation for this—the Russians had sent him to a camp, a *gulag*, in Saratov, a thousand miles from Kiev, on the Volga. He was eight years in the camp. Many people died when he was there. Every day someone new was dead. Things were very bad. On his release, in 1979, he had applied to go to America, taking his daughter with him. That was very difficult. So many questions! So many forms! So many offices to go to! It had taken him a year to get permission. At last, he and his daughter had come to America by train, and then by airplane—a big adventure for her, and for him too.

Yes, he was happy in America. He and his daughter had an apartment, in Brooklyn (I had thought he probably slept in a padlocked night shelter); and his daughter had a good job, in a bakery close by. He didn't want for anything. He didn't go out in the evenings—it was enough to be in the apartment with his daughter.

As for the birdwhistle business, that was slow, but it suited him. The whistles themselves he bought up in the Bronx, for twenty-five cents each. He had friends—from the Ukraine—in the Bronx. They sold him the whistles. He had chosen his pitch outside Macy's because it was the best, the busiest, intersection in the whole of New York. So many people! He sold thirty to thirty-five whistles a day; on a good day he could make twenty-five dollars, sometimes thirty dollars, clear profit.

God willing, he survived. He was fine. He had his daughter and his business here. He had friends. He liked New York; it was so very different from Kiev. No! He would not think of going back. Never! He would not go back for a million years—not until communism dies.

His last words were "Tell the Englishman—no one helped me!" It was said as the proudest boast that an immigrant could make; a defiant gesture of Emersonian self-reliance. The birdwhistle man was all right; he was doing okay in the promised land.

Within a few weeks I found that I had instinctively constructed a *neighborhood.* The word itself was old-fashioned, warm and reassuring. It summoned echoes of the whitewashed Puritan township, built around its meeting house, of borrowing twists of salt and pats of butter from the family next door. In New York, the reality was more like the enchanted circle cast around oneself by a primitive tribesman to ward off evil spirits. Here, you had to will a *neighborhood* into being in order to dare to go out on the nearest street.

So I laid down my own magical grid of lines, enclosing an arbitrary space that was nine blocks long and two blocks wide. It held everything necessary for survival—a Polish bistro, a Korean supermarket, a laundry, a cigar store that sold the *Nation* and *New Republic* as well as imported pipe tobacco, a good florist, two bars, a proper butcher, a diner. I could address the doormen on my block by name, and I had two beggars to whom I regularly gave alms.

At two in the morning, dropped from a shared cab on Seventh Avenue, I would march, sidewalk-craftily, along Eighteenth Street until I gained the eastern side of Broadway, which was where neighborhood began. Here my shoulders would unhunch, my pace slow, and I'd start nodding at strangers.

The curious thing about New York was that your neighborhood was always "safe"; it was only the places where your friends lived that were dangerous. Everyone I knew lived in a dangerous quarter, while my rectangle of streets was miraculously exempt from all the terrible generalizations that people made about Manhattan.

At dinner high over East Eighty-fourth Street (a grim battleground, to my unneighborly eye), I was sitting next to a woman who was bringing up two small children down on the Bowery, near Canal Street. I wondered what desperate straits had brought her to this fate, and how on earth she could afford the Air Person's uniform in which she was clad.

"Isn't that scary? Don't you endlessly worry for the children?"

"Oh, no, it's a nice neighborhood. People are very friendly, round our block. Where are you living?"

I tried not to look too annoyingly complacent as I said, "On East Eighteenth. Just off Third."

"Is that *safe?*" she said.

I had an appointment with Linda Lee of Macy's by Appointment. Ms. Lee was a counselor who specialized in social anxiety. If you were new to New York and were unsure of how to look the part in your job, or if a gold-encrusted invitation card to a charity dinner came winging your way out of the blue, you could go to

Ms. Lee for advice, and she'd prescribe clothes that would make the timid feel authoritative and the plain beautiful.

In a society as mobile, as imitative and as attentive to the outward and visible signs of inward wealth and status as that of modern New York, Ms. Lee offered a service that was at least as useful as psychiatry. She was in herself a wonderful advertisement for her profession. She had the kind of clear tanned skin that put one in mind of ski slopes and gymkhanas. Her dark hair had the luxurious and shining body that conditioners promise in advertisements but never, in real life, seem to deliver. Suited in black, with a pale gold chain around her neck, she was formidably beautiful without being in the least intimidating in her beauty. You'd *trust* this woman, and confide to her things that you wouldn't tell anyone younger—or older—or richer—or poorer. She was just right. I took her for thirty, and was astonished when she let fall that she had graduated from college two years before I had done so myself.

"I have a problem," I said.

"You've come to the right place," said Ms. Lee.

"I've just won the New York Lottery."

"That's no problem."

"But I'm forty, I'm a woman, I work in a deli in the Bronx. You know the slogan—'All You Need Is a Dollar and a Dream'? My dream is to own a co-op on Central Park West. It doesn't just take money to get into those places. You have to convince a whole committee that you're their kind of person. They put you through hell—"

"So you want a total makeover, right?"

"Is that what it's called? D'you get many total makeovers?"

"Not many. Some. So—you want to be an aristocrat."

"Roughly speaking."

"Okay. We're talking English Heritage here—the classic that endures. The country look ... Harris tweed, glen plaid ... " She measured me up for my new identity. "I'd put you in trousers— suede or leather, beige or brown. And a white silk shirt ... silk because it says, 'Look, I can go *riding* in this, and not care if it gets muddied up.' Then a cashmere tweed hacking jacket by Ralph Lauren, and a Hermès scarf—though I hate to say it, because we don't *do* Hermès at Macy's. Leather gloves . . . I'll have to *accessorize* you right: give you a little discreet gold jewelry; a brooch, a chain, a gold-and-stainless-steel watch. That's it."

"And I'll be able to walk out of the store and carry it off? I'll be a real Old Money equestrienne?"

"You'll get your co-op. Though, of course"—she eyed me—"it'd help if you were naturally blond and tall and happened to have that long, leggy stride—"

Outside Alice's apartment, the rowan tree was shedding its leaves on the wet street. Inside, the candidates were slugging it out on the TV screen. Both men had now spent so long repeating themselves in front of cameras that they seemed to have moved into a merely pictorial dimension, like cut-out heroes from the backs of cereal boxes. They belonged to that simplified moral realm of Skeletor, He-Man and Castle Greyskull.

Dukakis was the lean and hungry one. He came on like the ghost of yesterday's America, bringing to the election something altogether too conscience-stricken, too immigrant, too moderate for the bullish party mood of 1988. He badly needed Linda Lee to get his wardrobe right. His chronic blinking was perhaps meant as an earnest of his sincerity, but on TV it made him look like the uncomfortable outsider, caught in the act of gatecrashing a function hosted by his worst enemy. He seemed paralyzed. Again and again his supporters urged him to speak openly on the big issues—on the budget deficit, Central America, defense expenditure, the homeless and the poor—but Dukakis only fudged and blinked. Somehow or other, in the face of nearly all the available facts, the incumbent president had managed to persuade a lot of people that under his administration the American Dream had been restored—and evidently Dukakis did not dare to disturb the nation's slumbers for fear of turning into the messenger who gets shot for bringing the bad news.

Bush was Club Room in person, a Ralph Lauren Arcadian. Before the election, he'd been written off as "a wimp," but now the very qualities that had made him appear feeble were reinterpreted as dignified marks of his patrician status. His manner, bred at Phillips Academy in Andover and Yale University, was leatherbound, ancestral. In World War II and on the oil fields of Texas, he had proved himself as a self-reliant American. He went in for manly recreations, taking good care to invite the TV crews along when he sank himself up to his midriff in the Florida surf and lashed the water with his fishing rod. (In *Who's Who,* Bush listed his hobbies as "tennis, jogging, boating, fishing," beside which Dukakis's taste for "walking" and "gardening" looked suspiciously tame and introspective.)

The genius of George Bush, or his handlers, lay in his, or their, ability to identify the cause of patriotism with the policy of *laissez-faire.* He was photographed walking down avenues of rippling American flags, at military installations, or at the joystick of an antique bomber plane. Yet hand in hand with these images of Bush as a bold, loyal, intrepid American went Bush's reiterated promise, that he would do nothing whatsoever to upset the status quo.

Much the most famous phrase of the election was his proclamation "Read my lips: No . . . new . . . taxes!" That was truly intrepid, and no serious economic analyst that I read seemed to believe that Bush could really deliver. Reagan had cut America's taxes in 1981 with the Economic Recovery Bill (the "Kemp-Roth Amendment"), on the grounds that lower taxes would mean greater personal spending, which would, in its turn, lead to higher tax revenues. This was the theory. Only a year earlier, Bush had jeered at Reagan's approach as "voodoo economics." The federal debt (as opposed to the annual federal deficit) had risen from $914 billion in 1981 to an accumulated total, in 1988, of $2.6 trillion . . . a figure that deserves to be written out in noughts, as $2,600,000,000,000, or something over $12,000 for every man, woman and child in the United States.

Yet now the dream had been restored, no one must be woken from it. I watched Michael Dukakis timidly touching the occasional sleeper's shoulder with his fingertip before moving quickly on. I found his awkwardness sympathetic. I'd have given him my vote. But in an America sold on the leveraged vision of Ralph Lauren, it was hard to see how he could possibly be elected president. George Bush looked as if he'd sail into office by default.

Among the Air People—at least among the liberal Air People whom I knew—things seemed so foregone that only a spectacular scandal could save the day and let the Democrat in. A suitable rumor began to make its way around the dinner tables. It drifted across the Avenues; in a couple of days, it shot from Greenwich Village to the Nineties and back again, changing substance as it went. I heard it in several forms. The woman named was X, then Y. She was Irish. She was British. She was American, but had been married to a Brit. She was a newscaster—no, she was a political aide . . . There were two impressive aspects to this rumor. One was its sheer velocity, as it sped round the dense circuitry of New York, making the city seem a community as enclosed as a boarding school. The other was the way it was seized on and spread by serious people who would ordinarily have held themselves to be above such tattle. It was a measure of their candidate's hopeless position that they now clung to this tale as a desperate last chance.

One afternoon, share prices on Wall Street dived—the brokers had heard that the *Washington Post* was going to publish the rumor next morning. But that was just rumor too. There was nothing in the paper; the Dow-Jones climbed back and my Democratic friends abruptly lost the air of high good fortune that had settled on them for the past few days.

I had never watched so much TV. In the security control cubicle at Macy's, I sat with a store detective watching people shopping on a bank of sixty separate screens. Some pictures were in color, some in black and white. The cleverest of the hidden cameras could be controlled from inside the cubicle: if you found an interesting character browsing in Lingerie, you could zoom in on their face and track them across the floor. It was all a good deal more absorbing than the over-rehearsed opera of the hustings, as we spied on people who had no idea that they were being watched.

Under surveillance, everyone looked criminal or eccentric. Here was a man tenderly fondling a pair of socks; there was a woman furiously cuffing a blouse with her bunched fist before returning it to the rack. People scratched, picked their noses, practiced superstitious walks. Behind a rack of coats, a woman changed her baby's diaper. Everybody seemed strangely oblivious to the presence of everybody else. Pursuing his or her own private route through the store, driven by some inscrutably private desire, each customer showed up on the screen as a naked ego, adrift in an over-abundant sea of things. There were no smiles, no polite masks. The reigning expression was one of resentful anxiety. It was hard to believe that these people were engaged in this grimly solitary occupation for their own pleasure; it looked rather as if they were undergoing some kind of ritual punishment.

Every so often a message was broadcast over the security intercom system. "A ten-ninety-three sleeping by the Salad Grill." I asked the detective what she was looking for.

"Anyone who takes something off a rack without looking at the size first; thieves aren't interested in sizes. Often there'll be two of them working together—you look for the lookout guy. But mostly you can tell by the way they're underdressed for the merchandise. Like, the second floor is for moderates, mainly; but if you see a moderate in Calvin Klein, or the Little Shops, you *follow* that guy."

So we went on a moderate hunt, searching the pleasuredrome for people who were too fat, too short, too unfashionable to earn their place there. We tracked men with dreadlocks, men in jeans and sneakers, dumpy women in rollers—anyone whose aspect was sufficiently proletarian to stigmatize them as unworthy of the department in which they were, for the most part, innocently window-shopping.

"See those guys on seventeen?"

The couple on screen seventeen were moderates in their early twenties, both dressed in cheap plastic zip-up windbreakers. The man was wearing dark glasses. He tugged at his zipper, and his windbreaker turned into a yawning mouth. He was feeding the mouth with women's blouses. The movement was fast and skillful; it was over in a few seconds.

". . . he has shades, a down jacket, very puffy, a ten-ninety. She's kind of ninety-threeish, I can't see her too good. Both of them scored, and they're exiting as of now . . ." The detective was talking into her hotline, her voice up half an octave with the rising adrenaline of the chase. "Now! Now! You got him? Great. What about her? Shit. No, I told you, she was mostly out of shot. Kind of ninety-threeish, puffy jacket like the guy . . ."

"What's a ten-ninety?" I asked.

"Black male," she said. She was black herself. "It's a pity they're going to lose that girl. I never got to see her face. They must have exited separate. Guy on the floor says only the guy came out."

"It's satisfying work," I said.

"Yeah—I like to make a hit." She was studying the screens again. She brought the face of a male moderate in Women's Shoes into close-up and investigated it. It looked vacant of any discernible intent. "You get a lot of picks in Shoes. I'm keeping my eye on him."

Another woman detective joined us in the cubicle.

"You doing any good?"

"I just got one. Shoulda been two, but the girl got away. They were scoring blouses in Liz Claiborne."

"It's crazy down there now," the woman said. "There's some guy down on his knees in there, crying—real old guy, like fifty. Anyway, he's shouting, and weeping; a minute or two ago, he was *praying* to them. Like in a goddam church."

"That right?"

"Right down there on his knees." She lit a cigarette, her eyes drifting professionally from screen to screen. *"Crying."*

In this steep and unkind city, downward mobility took extreme forms. You could get rich quick, and you could get poor just as quick as you got rich. One week you'd be soaring over Manhattan in a tuxedo, martini in hand; the next, you could find yourself on Riker's Island, locked up in the company of the Street People. New York fed greedily on these Icarian stories. Failure here was meant to happen in the same exotic dimension as success.

There were plenty of stories to fuel the myth. Ivan Boesky, the great corporate raider, was serving time in a Florida jail. Stanley Friedman, the ex-president of the Bronx, was also in jail. Donald Manes of Queens had killed himself just before he was indicted for corruption. Financiers, congressmen, city officials were regularly to be seen handcuffed to police officers, being hauled off to the cells. In the newspapers, these stories were called "tragedies," but the way in which they were presented was jubilant. They were New York's own version of the Roman holiday.

At that moment, New York was feasting happily on the story of Bess Myerson, lately Mayor Koch's commissioner for cultural affairs. Ms. Myerson, a famous partygoer, a friend-of-everyone-who-mattered, stood accused of abusing her public office and bribing a city judge. The judge, Hortense Gabel, was also on trial. According to the DA, Bess Myerson had given Judge Gabel's unemployable daughter, Sukhreet, a well-paid job as her assistant, in return for a large favor. Judge Gabel's side of the deal, or so the prosecution said, had been to slash the alimony payments made by Myerson's lover (who was himself currently in jail) to his ex-wife.

The star of the show was the chief prosecution witness, Sukhreet Gabel. Each morning she turned up on the steps leading up to the court and gave a regal audience to the TV crews. She was not an Air Person. In early middle age, she retained a disconcerting quantity of puppy fat. She went in for little-girlish party dresses, with red bows and lacy frills; and the descriptions of Sukhreet Gabel's wardrobe frequently went on for longer than the accounts of the day's proceedings inside the courtroom. Out on the steps, in the hard glare of the November sunshine, she shopped her mother and her ex-employer in a mincing voice, like a bright but narcissistic child doing a class recitation. She was impressively equipped with the latest brands of psychological and sociological jargon, and she communicated a mixture of intelligence and self-pitying fey scattiness. The court case had at last brought her the fame and importance that, one suspected, she had always believed herself to deserve, but which had always, up to this moment, somehow evaded her. She was half heroine, half comic turn, and the cameras lapped her up.

Her air of thwarted great expectations touched a New York

nerve. It was almost too good to be true that such a one as Bess Myerson, who had lived so long, so conspicuously, in the unassailable stratosphere of city life, should be brought down by this galumphing child-woman. Her lost jobs, her fatness, her unfailingly bad taste in clothes were of the street and the subway. They made one think of shared walk-up apartments out in Jersey City, of welfare payments and fast-food dinners. To see Sukhreet, as everyone now called her, flying so high and Bess dragged down so low was to see the whole system of the city turned temporarily upside down. Like the medieval festival of the boy-bishops, it simultaneously asserted the abiding power of the system and mocked it, outrageously, just for the day.

At the end of the trial, the charges were thrown out by the jury. But Sukhreet had had her stardom, as Bess Myerson had suffered her public humiliation. We'd been treated to a fine spectacle, we'd watched an Air Person tumbling head over heels from a high window, and seen someone from the street grotesquely elevated to the Manhattan heights.

For New York was a piecrust. If you put your foot in the wrong place, you could go straight through it. There was a patch I knew, on the corner of Lexington and Fifty-third, where the actual crust of the city felt thinner than anywhere else: waiting to cross the street, I'd feel the sidewalk drumming and shivering under my feet as the traffic tore past at ground-level and the trains rocketed through the cellarage. Here it seemed that at any second the city might suddenly collapse in on itself, the tall blocks splitting open, the great ones falling, the whole enormous, delicate structure of shafts, pipes, tunnels and chutes bursting apart like a rotten cantaloupe.

Visiting Edward Finkelstein was like tracking down the Minotaur at the heart of the labyrinth. It was hard to reach him, since he spent so much time in the sky, jetting between New York, Florida, Texas, California, keeping the Macy empire under continuous surveillance. In a city where everyone was known as Bob, or Kay, or Bill, or Susan, Finkelstein had kept his surname; only senior vice-presidents referred to him as plain Ed. One junior VP spoke of him as The Ultimate, tipping her chin fractionally heavenward as she said it.

He lived in a mahogany-paneled office on the thirteenth floor, whose double-glazed picture window afforded a fine view of the ruins of Gimbel's, just down the street. He was a man of immediate and visible substance: heavy-bellied, heavy-jowled, with eyes that lay half in hiding behind soft pouches of flesh. His own clothes made no concessions to the social fantasies on sale a few floors below. At this height, he was beyond the need of fantasy. There was no English Heritage for Mr. Finkelstein: he was content to be plain American Corporation, in slacks, tan jacket, blue shirt and a tie that didn't hint at membership of anything except, perhaps, the Lear Jet Club.

Behind him, a gallery of framed photographs of his family advertised an immaculate American life of smiling people with wonderful teeth doing healthy things in the open air. In front of him, a rectangular ginger jar of boiled sweets confessed the only vice that Mr. Finkelstein wanted to admit to strangers.

But his face was complicated. It was like the facade of a mansion, with windows on many floors. Only one window would be open at a time, but whenever he spoke, or looked at me, it was always a different window. I saw a staff of housemaids busily rattling these windows up and down in their frames as Mr. Finkelstein gave them their orders—Blue bedroom! Library! Red bedroom! Lounge!

"I'm basically just a meat-and-potatoes person," he said, making you understand clearly that he wasn't any such thing.

He talked of how he'd engineered the LBO. In the early spring of 1985, there had been rumors on Wall Street, there were "mergers in the air," and the price of Macy's stock began to jump, then sink, then jump again. "There were people out there . . . nipping, taking shots at us. I don't know who they were." One of his upstairs windows slammed shut.

He spun out a military metaphor. He was "the strategist" of the LBO; his second-in-command, Mark Handler, was "the tactician"; the sales force and the buyers were "the people down in the trenches." Macy's was an army under one flag, with fifteen-thousand-dollar-a-year sales clerks falling in line under their general.

Wasn't it taking an enormous risk, I said, to hock the corporation's assets, just on the basis of a few unsubstantiated rumors?

Mr. Finkelstein treated me to a slow, tolerant smile. "Look," he said, and rested his left elbow on the table, with his forearm sloping up at an angle of about fifteen degrees. "You fix your debt at this. Now . . ." He lay his right forearm above his left. It was pointing at a steep diagonal toward the ceiling. "Your business is *this*. Where's the risk? The danger point in LBOs is always early. The first year is the most dangerous time; after that . . ." He nodded at the widening gap between his two forearms.

"That's assuming that your business is bound to get bigger and better as the years go by."

A window briefly opened, and closed again.

Mr. Finkelstein explained to me the benefits of LBO—a great shower of blessings. After an initial stage of "plumbing problems," the whole "culture and character of the business" had changed as the enterpreneurial spirit was let off the leash. The lumbering structure of the organization had been simplified. There were now three major divisions, each with "cohesive trading areas." Management had learned how to pull together for the sake of the company. Much dead wood had been cut down. Even in the trenches, there was a new spirit abroad, as more and more staff were given the incentive of selling on commission. The new Macy's was lean, efficient, go-getting, where the old Macy's had been tainted with "narcissism."

Yet why, I asked, did it take an LBO to accomplish all this? Couldn't Finkelstein have made these admirable changes when Macy's was a public company and he a chairman answerable to his shareholders?

No, said Mr. Finkelstein. "It doesn't work—not in a company where management doesn't own a good hunk of the business."

Now he was looking for "geographic balance," for profitable outposts across the length and breadth of middle-class America. "I like to select real estate in areas where there are sophisticated fashion customers. I like the area to grow, I like it to be medium to high income, I like it to be conscious of fashion . . ."

"Aren't you in danger of being altogether too sophisticated for your own good?"

"If you've walked this store for fourteen, fifteen years, yes, you'll see a general trading-up, but it's still a family store. You don't need a passport to get into Macy's."

"But isn't there a ceiling to this trading-up? Some point where you start losing customers because they simply can't afford Louis Vuitton luggage and clothes by Ralph Lauren?"

"If there's one thing I've learned in this business, it's that as people prosper, so they'll buy up to the level of their prosperity."

That was the great hypothesis. In Edward Finkelstein's vision of America, as in Ronald Reagan's, people just got richer. It was a natural law. As the grass grows, so Americans prosper. Every year, they have more money to spend, greater social ambitions, more extravagant tastes. And Mr. Finkelstein had customers to prove it. Fifteen years ago, the store on Herald Square had had a turnover of $165 million a year; now it was up to $450 million. Who would deny the reality of such patent prosperity? Only killjoy Harvard economists, redundant executives from the Rustbelt and the weirdo denizens of the night shelters. Not me—or, at least, not to Mr. Finkelstein, who was by now telling the last housemaid to close the last window.

People in New York evidently kept their children locked in closets or hidden in secret attics. For weeks, I'd been moving in what seemed to be a childless city. The six or seven children whom I'd met—and issued with birdwhistles—had themselves been as rare as golden orioles.

Now, on Thanksgiving Day, the children were out of the closet. As I walked across Central Park at breakfast time, it seemed as if a whole generation had mysteriously sprouted overnight. There were children in strollers, children perched on fathers' shoulders, babes in arms, children on tricycles, in gangs, in orderly crocodiles, every infant muffled to the ears against the icy brilliance of the morning. For once, the harsh and rascally air of New York had a wholesome smell of candy, milk and cookies.

There was a religiose flavor to the language in which the Macy's Thanksgiving Day Parade was spoken of within the store. It was Macy's way of Reaching Out and of Serving the Community. It was also the store's most famous advertisement: broadcast live on national television, the parade announced the beginning of the Christmas shopping season. The parade was a spectacular endorsement of Macy's special claim to be "a family store." It underpinned the wording of the jingles that were broadcast several times a day on local radio and television: "Macy's! Macy's! We're a part of your life!" and its variant, "Macy's! Macy's! Now more than ever, you're a part of my life!"

In every apartment overlooking the parade route, there was a party. I was bound for a tenth-floor co-op on Central Park West—an alpine roost with balconied windows overlooking a view of rocks and trees and shaggy grass. It was packed to the seams with pale and scholarly-looking Air Children holding glasses of orange juice like cocktails and shooting the breeze about the respective merits of their nursery schools.

They broke cover to a cry of "Garfield!" as the first battalion of the parade, with its gas-filled balloons, floats and marching bands, came heading our way. A creature, famous to them but not to me, swayed above the treetops in giant, inflated effigy, then loomed at our window, its whiskers on a level with the balcony. Far down below, a team of a dozen or more burly winch-men was needed to keep the thing tethered to the ground. They hauled and pumped on their ropes, and when a flutter of wind came through the park, a man was lifted clean off the tarmac as the balloon tried to reach for the sky. There was rapture on the balcony. "Big Bird!" "Superman!" "Woodstock!" "Snoopy!"

The Radio City Rockettes went past—a band of girl hussars from Pennsylvania—a troop of clowns—a tumble of acrobats. Here came the Statue of Liberty in painted polystyrene . . . and there were the Pilgrim Fathers in stovepipe hats. The Minute Men of Lexington had brought their muskets; and a three-masted ship, all guns firing, blasting the crowds with paper streamers, turned out, a shade surprisingly, to be the *Mayflower.* Most of the floats had a throne, on which sat a real, live New York eminence. The children beside me named these people. A TV weatherman was being cheered down the length of Central Park West as if he were personally responsible for the dazzling sunshine.

"He pitches for the Mets."

I pointed out the woman in furs who was riding on the front of the Statue of Liberty. I held out a distant hope that she might be Bess Myerson. "Who's that?"

"Oh that's . . . just some celebrity."

"Is Mayor Koch anywhere?"

"Major *Koch?*—if he came, they'd *throw* things at him," said a cynical seven-year-old.

The religiose language had more point than I had given it credit for. The Thanksgiving Day Parade was the secular, American descendant of the European Catholic Easter procession in which all the icons and saints' bones are removed from the churches and carried ceremonially around the town. The baseball hero, the gaseous, rubbery Mickey Mouse, the *Mayflower* pilgrims were the totems and treasured relics of a culture, as the New Orleans jazz and Sousa marches were its solemn music. Here was America going by.

Had a serious-minded Martian been standing at the window, he would have learned a good deal by studying the parade's idyllic version of American history. He'd see at a glance that this was a revolutionary nation, in which the gun was an entirely happy symbol of selfhood and independence. He'd notice that refugees and rebels had a special standing in the culture. Black people here contributed much of the entertaining local color, but for some reason they got to be in charge only of the smallest and least interesting balloons. The imaginative life of children was honored to a degree unknown on Mars—which was, perhaps, why matters of fact and matters of fiction were so confusingly jumbled up here, with Santa Claus and George Washington and Superman and Abraham Lincoln all stirred into the same pot.

He would be struck by the extraordinarily mythopoeic character of life in this strange country. People made myths and lived by them with an ease and fertility that would have been the envy of any tribe of Pacific islanders. Sometimes they were big myths that took possession of the whole society, sometimes little ones, casually manufactured, then trusted absolutely.

A little myth was floating past the balcony—a blimp decorated with the burgundy-colored, five-pointed star that was the Macy's trademark. The store liked to use it in its name, instead of an apostrophe, *MACY*☆*S;* and in the parade these star balloons were employed as punctuation marks between the floats. The symbol went back a long way. I'd seen it in photographs of the store's horse-drawn delivery vans, taken in the 1870s, and had tried to find out what its origin was.

The vice-president in charge of advertising had said, "When Captain Macy was a young man in the Navy, he had a star tattooed on his arm, just above his wrist—and when he opened his store, he incorporated the star for good luck."

Doris Carey, who looked after the archives, had said, "That star comes from the time when Captain Macy was shipwrecked. He was in a lifeboat . . . and his, like, *sexton*, you know, was broke? He was ever such a long way out from land, and the only thing he had to steer by was that star. It took him I don't know how many weeks, but that star brought him all the way home safe to Massachusetts, with every one of his men. And that's why he always wanted his star painted up on everything to do with the Macy's store. It was his way of giving thanks for his salvation."

There was just a trace of fact to support this happy invention. Rowland H. Macy did go to sea. He was fifteen when he enlisted as a deckhand on a New Bedford whaler, and one long voyage proved enough for him. After that he took a job as a clerk in the dry-goods business. He was never a captain, and never shipwrecked. But the story was a classic useful fiction. It established Macy as a solitary American hero, in the line of Leatherstocking, Captain Ahab, Huck Finn—a self-reliant adventurer of the outdoors; and, by extension, it turned the management of a store into a heroic enterprise. The sale of dry goods and notions was, after all, something you could set alongside the conquering of the frontier of the pursuit of the white whale.

As with "Captain" Macy, so with the astounding conflation of the parade, which was strung out over more than a mile of Manhattan, with Garfield and Woodstock sailing between the buildings south of Central Park. The mythical America represented by the floats—that marvelous, heroic, sentimental land—was an object of faith. It challenged you to make the believer's leap over the rude facts at your feet. The great success of Reagan's presidency, it seemed to me, was that he had somehow managed to assure a large number of people that they were actually living in the America of Macy's Thanksgiving Day Parade.

THREE

Free Spirit

"How fur ye goin?"
"I dunno . . . Pretty far."
—John Dos Passos, *Manhattan Transfer*

The dirty porcelain of the Holland Tunnel opened out into a six-lane highway that climbed the bluffs of Hoboken and Jersey City, but the traffic was locked hull-to-hull for as far ahead as one could see. Killing time, I monkeyed with the side-mirror on my rental car, slewing the landscape around in the glass until I got the view I wanted, of grilles and windshields scowling at the sun. In the background, behind the cars and trucks, was an enormous graveyard. The mirror reflected hundreds of bleached obelisks and fuzzily lettered headstones.

So many dead! Turning my head to inspect this unmapped necropolis, I saw that the white tombs were only the tall buildings of Manhattan on the far side of the Hudson River. Liberty was down there on her island, surprisingly close by; a damaged angel, streaked with gull droppings, standing guard over a vandalized and neglected family vault.

As the cars inched, growling, up the slope, New York slid down and out of the mirror. Sick of the city, its tense days and sleepless nights, I was glad to see it go. I lacked the buoyancy it took to be an Air Person. I wanted to feel the ground under my feet, to find some green and pleasant place where life felt more like life and less like a guerrilla war. I wanted to go down to the Deep South.

I liked the ring of the name, with its suggestion of a profundity unavailable elsewhere in the country. A diver, tumbling from the high board of Manhattan, might reasonably hope to touch bottom somewhere down, deep down, in the South; or so I hoped.

Sleeping alone in Alice's broad bed, listening to the sirens of the ambulances taking the casualties of New York life to Bellevue, I had kept on remembering, or half remembering, a sentence first read twenty-five years ago but never properly parsed till now. It was Allen Tate's, and was the call to arms of the Southern Agrarian movement in the early 1930s. *Only a return to the provinces, to the small self-contained centers of life, will lay the all-destroying abstraction America to rest.* Now I'd felt the destructive power of the abstraction on my own pulse and was pining for a province, for a small self-contained center of life. If such a thing still existed in the United States, I wagered that my best chance of finding it lay in the Deep South, in some uncelebrated nook of Georgia, Alabama or Tennessee.

As the traffic began to peel off into the unlovely Jersey suburbs, I kept on, heading for Interstate 78, Pennsylvania and the Mason-Dixon line. It took less than half an hour for the great tentacled city to lose its grip on the land, and for the freeway to turn into a concrete duct running bullet-straight through what appeared, at least, to be open forest. Outcrops of shale and dripping rock shouldered the road. Although we were on the cusp of March and April, the trees were still bare and cobweb gray from winter.

I pressed the search button on the radio and let it browse through the shelves of audial junk: an ad for a new kind of submarine sandwich, a snatch of Schubert, Marlee on the line from Elizabeth, someone plugging a factory outlet, an old Mamas and Papas number, a bushy-tailed chipmunk chorus singing "Macy's! Macy's! We're a part of your life!"

Not anymore, I thought with the stony-hearted elation of the traveler moving on. I waited for the Schubert to come round again on the airwaves and locked the radio to the classical station. It was Dietrich Fischer-Dieskau singing "Die Forelle," and I sang along, though not in German.

"Ta *room* ti-dee-dee-*dah,* dah! Ta room ti, di-di-di-di-*dah!*"

With a thousand miles and more to go, I settled into my position in the mercurial society of the freeway. Here, as not in Europe, people wore their cars rather than drove them. They were costumes, *habiliments.* From my teens, I had noticed with pleasure that no American thriller was so fast-moving that it could not afford to take time out to tell you that the hero was now dressed in "a dark blue seven-passenger sedan, a Packard of the latest model." Cars expressed the essence of character. You instantly knew what kind of girl it was who stepped out of her '62 candy-apple red Mustang white-top convertible, just as you doubted the honesty of the man who flat-mashed the throttle of his silver T-Bird. Even I could grasp that; but there were grave subtleties, inaccessible to the foreign reader, in this encoded world of Caddies, Chevies, Plymouths, Pontiacs, Buicks. What did possession of an Olds mean? More to the point, as I-78 came up with exits to North Branch and Wilmington, what did *I* mean? I was the guy in the '89 white Dodge Spirit. That clearly signified something, but what? Was it like wearing a gold ring in the lobe of one's left ear? Like sporting an Elks pin? Dreadlocks? A hairpiece? I didn't know.

Hoping that I was behaving in character, I floored the gas pedal. The needle bounced across the top of the arc to seventy-five, dickered about for a moment as the guts rumbled in the automatic shift, then came sweeping cleanly down through the eighties and into the nineties. I couldn't see any state troopers in the rear-view, and the left lane was wide open. The car was drumming like a boat in its own airstream, and I sailed at a hundred past a ragged little fleet of city-battered Volkswagens and Datsuns; left a big truck standing, its chromium gothic bullnose a receding twinkle in the mirror; tangled, briefly, with a metallic gray Buick Park Avenue (date not known); then eased off on the gas, thinking that I was chancing my luck to try living in such thoroughbred American prose for more than a sentence or two at a time.

Sunk low in the seat, arms out stiff, feathering the wheel of this surprisingly nimble Spirit, I shucked off the skin of Alice, her tidiness and scruples, her doll's-house way of doing things. For my new life as a misdemeanant, a burner of rubber on the open road, I needed another name—a fast, sawn-off American name. Trav would do. Or Ty, or Lew. Trav, hauling ass down the interstate, wouldn't *reach* places; he'd *hit* them. If the traffic cops didn't interfere with my itinerary, I thought I might hit Roanoke, Virginia, before nightfall; then, toying with words like *hit* and *hauling ass,* I realized that no Trav or Lew would be caught dead listening to Schubert on the car stereo, and so I put the radio on search again and found a heavy metal band that went straight to a tender patch inside my cranium, but was the sort of thing that I imagined Trav might like. After a couple of minutes of organized brain damage, I switched the radio off and resolved to stop this playacting.

At only 180 miles long, I-78 was hardly an interstate at all; it was a feeder road, an overextended ramp, for a really big *I,* 81(40), which absorbed it just short of Harrisburg, Pennsylvania. I-81 began up in Canada, on the north bank of the St. Lawrence near the neck of Lake Ontario. It dropped due south to Scranton, Pennsylvania, then coasted along the eastern edge of the Appalachian range down as far as Knoxville, Tennessee, where it changed its number to 40 and ran west, through Tennessee, Arkansas, Oklahoma, Texas, New Mexico and Arizona to an unplace in California eighty miles northeast of Los Angeles. It was an epic road, a three-thousand-mile trans-American ribbon that tied up the subcontinent in a single wide loop. If such roads had ever been conceived in Europe, there might be one from London to Tehran, or from the French Riviera to the outer reaches of Novaya Zemlya.

I poured the Spirit into the southgoing stream. A stately, plump Winnebago with Michigan plates was doing a sedate fifty-five in the center lane, while the left lane had been commandeered by a West Virginia pickup which was idling through the landscape at fifty, and refused to give over when I flashed my lights behind it. Coming alongside West Virginia, I watched him sink a can of Michelob, crumple it in his fist and flip it out onto the median strip. By the expression on his face when he glanced back at me, I gathered that a white Dodge Spirit was not a car that inspired much respect where he came from.

For miles, I saw nothing but plates: Ohio surging past Florida

. . . South Carolina sinking back behind Maine . . . Kentucky slipping past New York on the inside. . . . The states of America had all been shaken up in solution on the freeway, and there could be no image more expressive of the chronic restlessness and mobility of the nation than this race of the plates, with their jostling crests and mottos—the Puritan stovepipe hat of Massachusetts, Florida's pistol-shaped map, The Empire State, Land of Lincoln, First in Freedom, Live Free or Die, Famous Potatoes, Land of 10,000 Lakes, The Last Frontier.

Many of the cars were towing U-Haul trailers—potted, aluminum versions of the covered wagon—in which were stowed the drivers' worldly goods. Each time I passed U-Haulers, I tried to guess what had happened to them. The moth-eaten blond man in the rattletrap tan Chevy had been given the boot by his pregnant girlfriend. The elderly couple in the Mazda, closely followed by the biggest U-Haul that I'd seen, were under doctor's orders. The old man had worked all his life at Bethlehem Steel. He had a circulation problem. "You want to see another winter out? You'd better head for the Sunbelt." The wife had relatives in Houston. They were going to look around for a while, maybe rent first, then buy later. The single woman, thirtyish, whey-faced behind her tinted glasses, with a medium-sized U-Haul, was heading for a new job, in Atlanta. She looked to me like a Macy's buyer. She drove a brand-new Corsica sedan.

U-Haul's slogan promised that it made Moving an Adventure, and there was adventure in all this motion—a great deal of "chance . . . hap . . . luck . . . speculation," as the dictionary defines the word. If you live with a road like I-81 on your doorstep, I thought, how different it must be to the world I knew. Europeans cannot move more than a few—at most a very few hundred— miles without traveling out of their own language; but Americans can, as it were, go from London to Tehran, from Marseilles to Novaya Zemlya, and still be perfectly at home, with Johnny Carson on the TV and the Burger King drive-in two blocks down the street. No wonder that people hitch U-Haul wagons to their cars and go. If the winters get too cold for old bones . . . if the farm's foreclosed . . . the factory shut down . . . the divorce papers are served . . . call U-Haul and take to the road. In America, there is always someplace else where you might yet find heart's-ease, whether it's the condo in Florida or forty bucks an hour on the rig in Alaska.

Breezing south in my wicked Spirit, my eye was tuned to watching other vehicles on the road, while the landscape spooled by far too fast for me to follow the story. It came to me in totemic fragments, observed only after they were already miles behind. That bridge back there *was* the Mason-Dixon line; and it took the slick new tarmac and trim white picket fences of Maryland to make me realize that Pennsylvania had, on the whole, been like an unkempt family back yard with bald turf, a vegetable plot and the children's tricycles left out to rust in the rain. Only the sudden deterioration in the road surface as I hit West Virginia made me see Maryland, in retrospect, as a rich man's garden, with sprinklers playing on mown and rollered lawns, a pony in a paddock, rhododendrons, a bronze Pan on a stone plinth.

In West Virginia, the freeway began to twist and steepen, enclosed by darkening forest, and, unlike most of the residents of that disreputable statelet, I went legal. Down to sixty, peering anxiously into the twilight, I felt abruptly tired and thirsty. I slowed before each forthcoming exit to scan the board reading LODGINGS NEXT RIGHT by the beam of my headlights. Mac's Motel. Sunset Motel. Econo-Lodge. Howard Johnson's. Dean's Motel. Rack-rent Motel . . . Their scabby advertising boards were strung up in the trees, and the best recommendation they could make for themselves was that they were EZ-OFF EZ-ON, as if the true aficionado of the freeway could only sleep comfortably with the breaking surf of overnight traffic in his ears.

I knew those places. They were all one. Sometimes, emptying the pockets of your trousers to take them to the cleaner's, you come across a credit card slip crumpled into a spiky ball. You carefully unfold it. It reads, bewilderingly, "Peek's Motel, Wardensburg." You do not know where Wardensburg is. You cannot remember ever having been there. It goes on: "Lodgings, one night, $18 + tax . . . " So you presume that you must have been alone, at least. You search in the eaves of your memory and dig out a slowly developing image.

There was . . . a cigarette burn in a too-thin coverlet . . . a cracked shower curtain gone parchment yellow . . . a carpet, of sorts, with a quilted brown pile . . . an ice machine and a Coke machine in a windy open hallway . . . a room infected with the smell of slovenly solitude. You didn't sleep; you lay, oscillating continuously between quick, violent dreams and unhappy wakefulness. Yes, that was Peek's.

I didn't want to stay at Peek's—or Dean's—or Mac's—or Sunset—and so I kept on driving. Another fifty miles went past, another state line. I was in Virginia proper now. LODGINGS NEXT RIGHT . . . WAYSIDE INN. Nothing about EZ-OFF EZ-ON. I took the turning.

It was well out of earshot of the freeway. It was a real hotel. Roadshocked, I lumbered into the bar.

"And what can I do for you this evening, sir?"

I stared at the girl. She had a voice out of *Gone with the Wind.* I set to wondering stupidly if it was her own voice or if she was putting it on.

"Sir? Do you want a drink?"

"Sorry. A vodka martini, very dry, straight up with a twist. Please."

This was not to do with any great desire for a vodka martini (I would actually have preferred Scotch); it was a small salute to a dead man. For I had once lunched with John D. MacDonald, the creator of Travis McGee—the Trav whom I had spent some time earlier in the day trying to be. MacDonald himself had been surprisingly gentle and homely, with clumsy hands, not at all like his intrepid, know-it-all hero. There had been just one flash of McGee in MacDonald, when we were ordering our drinks before the meal. Without looking up from the menu, he'd growled, "Vodka martini, very dry, straight up with a twist." It was a fine line. I couldn't match MacDonald's delivery of it, but it was nice to say it, and to think of him, and Travis McGee, in this timbered bar somewhere in northern Virginia.

Sipping at John D.'s martini, I followed I-81 through the pages of the Rand McNally atlas, trying to work out exactly where I was.

"This is Winchester?" I said.

"Here? No, you're in *Middletown,*" said the bartender. She sounded mildly scandalized.

I found it—a dot on the map, near nowhere special.

"Where are you heading for?"

"I'm not sure yet. Alabama, maybe."

"Alabama? I drove through there once. There was a lot of crazy rednecks down there. Ran me right off the road, one time."

"They did?"

"Sure did. The whole state was full of them. Real crazy guys." She polished a glass, biting on her lower lip as she did so. "You say Alabama? No. That wasn't Ala*bama*. That was Louisi*ana*. Must've been. I never was in Alabama."

Early next morning, I pulled the curtains in my room and looked out over rolling hills, woods, a field full of cattle, a white grain silo. Shaving, I wondered if Middletown was the small self-contained center of life that I was looking for. My breakfast egg came served with hominy grits, and the waitress who brought it dawdled over her vowels, making even the word "egg" itself sound rich and strange. The way she said it, it came out as *aieyaiegg,* floating on the air, swooping and dipping like a balsa-wood toy glider. But this was the shallow, the superficial South; I needed to go down deeper, much deeper, than Middletown, Va.

It was Sunday, and the interstate was almost empty. Were the truckers and the U-Haulers at church? Or were they still trying to shake themselves back into life after a lousy night at some EZ-OFF, red-eye, EZ-ON motel? The Spirit whistled past a couple of pickups with local plates and settled down on a comfortable broad reach through the middle of Virginia. The trees that had been skeletal and gray the day before were coming into leaf this morning, buds into blossom, bare earth into green pasture. The harder I stepped on the gas, the faster I could make things grow. I made the first magnolia burst suddenly into flower, woke the first snake from hibernation, turned the first orchard petal-white. At the rate I was going, it would be fall by Tuesday morning.

The landscape itself had fallen into a fixed pattern. On the right, the Appalachian Mountains formed an endless, lumpy blue-green bolster. On the left, little cities came and went between tracts of farmland and miles of thick deciduous forest. Above the greenest, most virgin-territory stretches of the forest were raised, on gleaming stalks and gantries, dwarfing the Appalachians, the heraldic devices of the freeway chains—the great looping mustard-squirt *M* for McDonald's, the double-cross of Exxon, the five-pointed Texaco star. STUCKEY's! WENDY's! HARDEE's! There was something at once innocent and anachronistic in this triumphant blazonry over the tops of the wild woods, as if we were still living in that frontier world where technology was on the right side in the battle against nature; the world of Stephen Crane's "The Blue Hotel," where the inhabitants of a hamlet in the prairie boast exultantly about the coming of the railroad, the "line of 'lictric street-cars," the factory and the new hotel. I began to warm to these gaudy signs in the sky: they had a saving naïveté that just, or almost, compensated for the ugly holes they made in these forests of sycamore and beech.

By lunchtime I was nearly two hundred fifty miles farther down the road, when I saw a promising exit labeled RURAL RETREAT. The town was a mile and a half off the freeway up a bumpy farm lane. It was small all right—a grid of half a dozen brick streets that petered out into fields after a few yards, bisected by a grassy railway line. It was self-contained; at least to the extent that City Hall, the post office and the barber's shop all appeared to have combined forces within one small two-story house on Main. Its shingled white church was attached to a surprisingly populous cemetery: in Rural Retreat the dead looked as if they outnumbered the living by about twenty-five to one. It had no bar that I could see—not a fatal disadvantage, but a setback for me. The Country Diner, smack in the middle of the township by the railroad, served no drinks more stimulating than milk shakes. The large family at the table next to mine were talking about the sermon that morning; and most of the town seemed to have assembled here for their Sunday lunch. Was this, I wondered, as I forked down mouthfuls of chicken that tasted of stale dishcloth, the kind of place that Allen Tate had in mind?

From the moment I walked in, I felt there was a vague air of expectancy in the room. Maybe someone was about to spring a birthday surprise, like a topless kiss-o-gram, helicoptered over from Winston-Salem in North Carolina. People kept on going quiet and sneaking glances at the window. Then, at 1:57, it happened. The freight train came through. The moment the rails began to telegraph the pounding wheels a mile or more up the line, people rose from their half-eaten meals and crowded round the long window. For four and a half minutes, Rural Retreat shook with excitement. The shuddering boxcars blew a pall of white dust around the town. My own plate took on a life of its own, trying to shimmy across the Formica tabletop in response to the almighty train. Suddenly, it was all over. There was a faint, lingering whimper in the rails. A dog barked up by the church. The people in the diner returned to their tables, and a sad, postcoital silence reigned over the remnants of chicken, mashed potatoes and corn bread.

I was pining for a province, but there were provinces and provinces. By the end of lunch, I knew that I was not pining for Rural Retreat.

Each time I stopped, to fuel the Spirit or grab a mug of boiled coffee to keep my reaction time on edge, I noticed people's vowels getting twistier, their sentences more drawled and long-drawn-out, their formal civilities growing more numerous and elaborate. Fresh from New York, I had forgotten the America where *please* and *thank you* and *'preciate it* were the habitual punctuation marks in almost every sentence. At one gas station, a woman, as curious about my accent as I was about hers, asked me what I was doing. I told her. "Why! I am *so* glad to make your acquaintance," she said.

The phonetic characteristics of Southern speech—its varying tinctures of Jacobean English, Irish, Scots, French and African-American, with every state and county having its own way of making up the prescription—have an obvious historical explanation. What struck me, hearing people talk to me, a stranger with New York plates, was the way those lengthened vowels and conscious courtlinesses seemed to be used as defensive weapons. The slightest of exchanges were charged, I thought, with a tacit subtext. It was as if everyone was saying: *They may do things fast and rude up where you come from; but down here, we do different. And if it takes a whole hour for me to get to the end of this sentence*

*that I'm saying now, it won't do you no harm to just set there still
and listen.*

In 1861, the South had seen itself as fighting a holy war on
behalf of a godfearing, ordered, rural society against the wanton,
godless, urban, industrial forces of the North. It had been, from
the South's point of view at least, as much a war of the Country
against the City as a war about the issue of slavery. The humiliation inflicted on the South by Reconstruction had only strengthened the Southerners' wounded pride in their—essentially
rural—culture, shabby and makeshift as that culture was. Tate's
Agrarians were reviving, for the umpteenth time in Southern
history, the assertion made by an anonymous Alabamian, quoted
in James M. McPherson's *Battle Cry of Freedom,* who wrote in
1858:

> That the North does our trading and manufacturing mostly is
> true, and we are willing to grant that they should. Ours is an
> agricultural people, and God grant that we may continue so. It
> is the freest, happiest, most independent, and with us, the most
> powerful condition on earth.

Thirty years after Tate and his friends took their stand, the South
was turning into the industrial Sunbelt; by the 1980s, it was
hardly less urban—and certainly more successfully urban—than
the North with its Rustbelt. Yet the South's hard feelings toward
the North, its sense of itself as a society rooted in the countryside,
its resentful provinciality, were far too deeply ingrained to be
easily overturned by a couple of decades of building work and
industrial investment. The old attitudes clung on, in Southern
speech, Southern religion, and in the fetishistic cultivation of
"Southern manners." Even the man working at the Exxon station
on I-81 was somehow able to see himself in his mind's eye in a
rocker, on a porch, overlooking his greensward and fending off,
by force of arms if necessary, the incursions of the fast-talking,
atheistical city slickers from up North.

He turned my credit card over in his hands as if Visa was a
new name to him, glanced across at the Spirit and registered its
alien plates, took a cumbrous while to fill in the form and stamp

it on his machine, passed it back across the counter, said, "Now, if you wouldn't mind just giving me your autograph, right there, I'd appreciate it." He was putting me down, in that sweet, polite, Southernly way that registered a century and a half of bad blood.

The road climbed steadily for several miles, with the car flagging a little on the bends; Virginia leaked into Tennessee; and on the long downhill run the Appalachians had shifted, from the right-hand side of the highway across to the left. The South was deepening fast now. There was more wildness and more decrepitude, fewer townships, even thicker forest, scattered farms looking lonely and uncared for. A creosoted barn, its timbers splayed and tottering, was like a wounded hippopotamus going down on its knees in an empty field. A brick chimney with an open hearth stood by itself in a clearing. The family farmhouse that had once surrounded it had burned down or rotted to bits long ago.

Knoxville, a pasta-tangle of white concrete expressways, was a sudden burst of the New South, but it was here and gone in less than fifteen minutes. Weaving through the end-of-the-weekend traffic, tunneling through underpasses and skyriding up overpasses, I kept the balls of my toes hard on the floor as the Spirit rocketed through the city and back into the woods.

I took the exit for I-75 S, for Chattanooga, Atlanta and, ultimately, Tampa, Florida, leaving what had now turned into Route 40 to make its own Ulyssean way to California. I disliked I-75 on sight. It was flat, straight, crowded with trucks powering down from the big cities of Ohio and Indiana to Atlanta and Mobile. After less than an hour on this thundering racetrack, I was sleepwalking through the driving. The cowardly Spirit shrank into the inside lane. Sag-bellied old Buicks, more rust than metal, were romping past it now. The speedometer needle was shivering in the middle fifties. I wanted a drink. *Vodka martini, very dry, straight up with a twist.*

A Holiday Inn came up, high on a bluff beside the highway. There are times when even a Holiday Inn can shine with the promise of a lighted harbor seen across a dark and lumpy sea. I took a right, hoisted my bags out of the car and stood in line at the reception desk. The woman ahead of me had some kind of executive deal worked out with the hotel chain, and was asking where she could take delivery of her complimentary cocktail.

"We can't serve you a cocktail here, ma'am. This is a dry county."

There are times when even the best-lit harbor can turn out to be so uncomfortable that you wish you were at sea again.

Interrupting, I said, "Where's the next wet county, going south?"

"Chattanooga. Thirty miles on down the highway."

I hoisted my bags back aboard the Spirit and sleep-drove to Chattanooga where, deep in the downtown business section, I found an old, modestly restored traveling salesmen's hotel with a brassbound bar as long as a cricket pitch. Up in my room, repaired by two martinis, I switched on the TV to find out what had been happening in the world. The picture came up strangely pink, and for a moment I couldn't figure out what was going on. It appeared to be some kind of instructional medical program set in an operating theater. Then I got it. It was a close-up shot of a woman's lips working their way slowly up and down a man's penis. Superimposed on this image was the flashing word, in neon-red, PAY! PAY! PAY! PAY! The screen then went blank. I tried another channel. On this one, two girls were carefully unsheathing a man from his underpants. PAY! PAY! PAY!—blank. And so it went. I could find nothing on television except vaginas, penises, mouths and busy fingers, all photographed from angles so ingenious that they looked like creatures in a sci-fi movie. I considered telephoning down to the desk to ask the exceptionally pretty college student who was working there if this television was capable of receiving CNN or CBS, or whether it was exclusively reserved for watching sex at a price; but I feared that the question would strike her as so silly that it would only be answered by a peal of giggles.

In McMinn County, you couldn't get a drink; in Chattanooga you could get a drink and hard-porn videos, but you couldn't watch the news. Being in Tennessee meant making some tough choices. That such extreme rural puritanism should go cheek by jowl with such extreme urban license seemed to me to have a distinct, distinctly Southern, logic. If you came from a society where the City had traditionally been regarded as the temple of ungodliness, it made good sense to turn your own cities into ghettos containing every vice you could think of, thereby preserving the pious order of the Country while simultaneously confirming all your worst fears about the evils of the City. Then, when the restaurant and motel owners in your district began to lobby for the legalization of liquor, you could say—and rightly— *Look what happened in Chattanooga.*

At nine next morning, the black porter who helped me with my bags was all friendliness. He checked out the Spirit and quizzed me on its performance.

"And now you're going to drive all the way back to the Big Apple?"

"No, I'm going south, into Alabama." I'd spent some time over dinner with the Rand McNally, and had found a route that would take me down along the course of the Tennessee River on a minor road.

The expression on the porter's face changed sharply, and for the worse. "Oh, man, you going down to the *country.*" He pronounced the word as one might say *penal farm,* and I saw Walker Evans pictures in his eyes. His interest was gone, but he said, colorlessly, "Where'bouts in Alabama?"

"You ever heard of a place called Guntersville?" It looked promising, a river town, pop. 6,491, deep in the apparent sticks.

The porter shook his head. "I thought you was going to the Big Apple."

It was raining hard, and the surface of the interstate felt treacherously slick under the tires. I let the big trucks wash past me in their cauls of spray, with the Spirit like a dinghy caught up in a fleet of warships, and was glad when my turn-off came up, marked to Scottsboro and Huntsville. Because of the switch from Eastern Standard to Central Time, I drove into Alabama twenty minutes before I had set off from Chattanooga.

The time-lag felt a good deal longer than an hour. There were potholes in the road, tarpaper shacks, ancient trailers propped up on piles of bricks. Round here, people traded in worms, with signs for "Nite Crawlers," variously spelled, posted in front yards. *Crorlers. Crawliers. Crorls.* Like the conjugation of an irregular verb. A closed café had a sign hanging askew in its window advertising catfish dinners. The Tennessee River itself, the source of all this economic activity, was tantalizingly hidden behind a mile-thick belt of forest. Then a rip-rap causeway carried the road across a broad slough of open water, where an open boat held two figures in storm gear hunched sullenly over their poles.

Scottsboro. I couldn't immediately identify the bell that the name was trying to ring in my head. It carried the same bleak echo as *Selma,* but the image was older and mistier than that. A night train . . . a lynch mob . . . some black teenagers . . . *the Scottsboro Boys.* I drove through the town. It was small, strag-gling, shabby, rainswept; nothing to stop for, nothing to nudge that moment in the 1930s into sharper focus.

Out of Scottsboro, I picked up a country music station broad-casting from Guntersville. The voice of the announcer was more elaborately squiggly-voweled than any Southern voice I'd ever heard. He rolled them, stretched them, swallowed them and gar-gled with them, turning the simplest sentence into a linguistic conjuring display. He must have said "jayuiest layissayien tu hays laiayd-iayesd noyiumbah" four times at least before I cottoned on.

The landscape grew steadily more watery; seen through a streaming windshield, the dripping pines, the puddled road, the quickening creeks and sloughs amalgamated into a world like that of a weedy, algae-infested aquarium. At any moment, one might have had to brake hard to avoid colliding with a large fish.

The news from Guntersville came in small dollops between long stretches of banjo plucking and songs about mothers, gran-pappies and lost sweethearts. The biggest thing in town was the auditions for the upcoming production of *The Sound of Music.* There was to be a public hearing that evening about someone's proposal to build a lounge (so Guntersville had lounges, at least). A girl's body had been found in the lake. A "twister" had been sighted somewhere in western Alabama, and there was a tornado watch in Marshall County. I thought that I had better keep quiet about Hurricane Helene when I hit town, or my reputation as a jinx would get me run out on a rail before I could even stop for lunch there.

The wind was certainly freshening, though it was still well

short of being a full gale. It roused the water round the causeways into short, steep, houndstooth waves and rimed the shore with a margin of frothy yellow scud. If and when the tornado watch turned into an alert, the announcer said, you should go down to your basement, taking blankets, pillows, plenty of soft drinks and your radio. This frightening news was followed by an advertising jingle in which a girls' choir sang, *con spirito,* "Loudermilk's Pest Control is the very best pest control you ever did have," or words to that effect, words that were now exactly one thousand miles away from Madison Avenue, according to the clock.

The Spirit emerged from the woods into a wide flooded valley. The Tennessee River, dammed fifty years before by the Tennessee Valley Authority, still looked as if it hadn't gotten used to the idea that it was more lake than river. There were no banks, no hard edges between the land and the water, which lapped at the grass and round the boles of trees along an arbitrary contour. The breaking waves on the leeward ground were like a tide stealing through the fields.

On the far side of the river lay a range of low forested mountains, looking as spongily green as tumps of sphagnum moss. Two separate bridges took the highway over a strait of water nearly half a mile wide. Southbound traffic was led on to an elderly iron contraption of crocheted spars and girders, where the Spirit's tires went flap-slapping over the dodgy surface of studded plates. On the crest of the bridge I came face to face with a soaring turkey vulture. Its great Hershey Bar–colored wings were braced in a shallow vee. It slid and teetered on the wet wind like a beginner on a skateboard, so close to the car that I could see the wrinkles in the skin of its bald head, its legs tucked up under the tail like a retractable undercarriage, the expression of dim malignancy in its small button eyes.

It was only at the last moment that the dense green ahead opened up and yielded Guntersville, its new white City Hall and police department standing proud of the turn-of-the-century brick stores that lined the wide main street. I parked the Spirit outside God's Kritturs, which looked and smelled like a pet shop deep in my childhood; next door, the barber, strop in hand, paused to watch me go by. I passed a very possible-looking small restaurant with (good sign) today's menu chalked up on a blackboard inside the window. A department store had gone on a triumphal march down a long stretch of this side of the street, gobbling up one-story businesses as it went. Shop after shop, emblazoned in various periods and styles of signwriting, had been taken over by someone called Hammer, evidently the Rowland H. Macy of these parts.

I liked the look of Hammer's sprawling little empire, its jovial, throwaway air. On the sidewalk outside stood a line of bright, blood-red lawn mowers, seedboxes of garden plants, a Coke machine. Inside, under fierce striplights, were displayed heaps of clothes, piled up, in a higgledy-piggledy way, on trestle tables. Handwritten notices said TROUSERS $3.98, T-SHIRTS $1.29, DRESS SHOES $9.98, DOCKSIDERS $4.98, CASH ONLY and DO NOT SPIT ON STAIRS—THANK YOU. Hammer's looked like a place where some serious shopping might be done. Eat your heart out, Ralph Lauren.

Beyond the Coke machine was a newspaper dispenser. For a quarter I got the latest issue of the Guntersville *Advertiser-Gleam.* I crossed the street to the Rexall drugstore, where there was a lunch counter and soda fountain, and settled down to read the paper over coffee.

On the front page, a local murder trial competed for headline space with *In 29 Years He Has Built 5 Additions to His Home* and *Express Lube to Offer Service While You Wait.* Doot Norrell, Milford Painter and the Rev. Lincoln Drain had died, while the goings-on of the living were recorded in a breathless gossip column:

Chester and Caroline Sparks have sold their place on Wyeth Drive and bought another over on Spring Creek . . . Holly Walley is out and walking the levee again following surgery several weeks ago . . . Bonnie Segui had the program at D.A.R. with Katherine Richter and Lindy Hard as hostesses. Lindy reported a dozen bluebirds already building in boxes along her trail and is looking for many more to nest on her place . . . Valda Pizitz was over from Huntsville this week with her father Bentley Huggins and Katherine Duncan . . . Two busloads of Jolly Seniors went to Georgia and Calloway Gardens . . .

The minutes of the county commission were dominated by an attempt by the sheriff's department to raise five thousand dollars to buy a "drug dog."

Deputy Paul Evans, who would handle the dog, said they are hoping to buy a dog from a place in Indiana that trains them to sniff out marijuana, heroin, etc.

The commissioners were apparently reluctant to fork out, even though six hundred fifty dollars had already been raised by private subscription.

Sheriff Big John Colbert: "We're not asking you to fund all of the dog."
Commissioner Howard Rowe: "I'd like to help you, but our budget's mighty close."

I was deep in the *For Rent* ads when I was joined at the counter by the pharmacist, who'd heard my outlandish accent and wanted to give my voice a routine check-up.

"So what do you think of our paper?" he said. *His* voice was careful, soft, whispery; his face serious and mild.

"Well . . . it's a lot different from the *New York Times*. I like its personalness. I like reading all the names of people . . . I like the obituaries . . ."

"Oh, yes—the *Gleam*'ll tell you exactly what a person died of . . . heart attack, cancer, high blood sugar, liver failure, stroke, it all goes in the *Gleam.*"

The wind was beginning to racket round the town, and people from Hammer's were taking in the stuff that was on display on the sidewalk.

"What about this tornado watch? Is it serious?"

"No, we don't get bothered too much by tornados in Guntersville. We got real good protection from the mountains here. Any twisters that's going, they'll slide right by over the top of you. And it seems they have some kind of aversion to water, I don't know why. You get a twister heading right for the lake, the moment he smells water, he'll swerve right off down south, like he's got a mind of his own. They're strange things, twisters; I don't think that no one understands them rightly . . ."

Thinking of blankets and pillows and soft drinks, I was still anxious to know if the drugstore had a basement.

"Like when a twister hits a trailer home? You know about that? It'll explode from the inside. The walls'll bulge, and it'll blow out like a balloon. Bang!—and the whole trailer, it'll be just a whirl of dust? What they say is that it's something to do with a differential in the pressure between the outside and the inside, but I don't know . . ."

I was impressed by how such a meek-seeming man could harbor such a feeling of fraternal tenderness for tornados. I saw him quietly mixing his medicines while dreaming of sublime catastrophes.

"Sometimes I think they're *meant,*" he said. "Oh, a tornado can bring good as well as bad, you know. I remember . . ." He named a town in southern Alabama that I'd never heard of. "It was all real old homes from way back. They got the people out before the twister hit, and when it came through, it blew that town apart. It didn't leave but *nothing* standing. Houses and stores, they were torn right out of the ground, they were flying over the fields. When that twister was through, it was just *bare.* You go back there now, you'd never know the place; it's so smart, with new homes, new stores, new churches—why, it's paradise to what it was before. And that was down to a twister."

He looked wistfully out to the old brick of Guntersville. I imagined Hammer's and the pet shop spinning in the sky, to be replaced by spanking new buildings of cinderblock and white concrete, and was glad that Guntersville was shielded from twisters by the mountains and the river.

The pharmacist eased himself up from his stool. "You know what they say about Guntersville? It's not the *end* of the world, but you can see it pretty good from here."

The line was a little too well honed to be a Guntersville original; I suspected it of being a chestnut from the cracker barrel that had seen useful service in small towns across the length and breadth of the United States. It was also delivered with a slight upward inflection that turned it into a question—a trick question. *You want to find our town quaintly amusing? We know how to play along with that.*

I said, "I wonder if there's any chance of my renting a furnished house or apartment here? A trailer would do."

The pharmacist sat back on his stool. "You want to *live* in Guntersville?" It was pronounced *Gunnersvull;* a pronunciation I had better learn.

"Just for a while. A month or two."

The light in the street outside had turned a bilious sea green. What I took at first to be a long roll of thunder resolved into a big "semi" going on down south. I watched it swim heavily past the drugstore window with a smug sense of arrival, of having broken free of that alienated, unstable society of the road. Guntersville smelled right. It felt like a place one might touch bottom in. I didn't want to peer curiously out at the town from the perspective of a motel room; I wanted to learn to live here, in a house of my own, with a back yard, neighbors, a Welcome doormat, the litter and unwashed dishes of home.

"I don't think you're going to have too much of a problem. I can ask around for you . . . and you can talk to the real-estate guys like Ed Neely, and Tom Mosley, and Ray Brannum—we got a whole bunch of realtors in this town.

"You know? I think you're going to like it here. I *do* so hope you do."

FOUR

In Our Valley

A great Plan, a moral and indeed a religious purpose, deep and fundamental, is democracy's answer to both our own homespun would-be dictators and foreign anti-democracy alike. In the unified development of resources there is such a Great Plan: the Unity of Nature and Mankind. Under such a Plan in our valley we move forward. True, it is but a step at a time. But we assume responsibility not simply for the little advance we make each day, but for that vast and all-pervasive end and purpose of our labors, the material well-being of all men and the opportunity for them to build for themselves spiritual strength.

—David E. Lilienthal, *T.V.A.: Democracy on the March*

There was a cardinal in the dogwood tree, just six feet away from where I was sitting in my porch swing. The bird was blinded to me by the screens of the veranda. I didn't move a muscle. Against the flurry of white petals, the cardinal's crimson feathers were like a holy wounding, a splash of fresh blood on a laundered sheet. Its head swiveled to exhibit its horned crest, combed and oiled to a fine point. A skirl of wind rattled the map of Guntersville on my knee, the chains of the swing creaked in their ringbolts, and the cardinal shot out of the blossom in a flaming streak of red.

Things happened fast in this town, a lot faster than they happened in Manhattan. I'd crossed the bridge to Guntersville a little after ten in the morning; by four in the afternoon, I had assembled the materials of a complete new life. I was a resident of Polecat Hollow, with a two-bedroom cinderblock cabin in the woods at the edge of the water. My telephone was connected. I had a box number at the post office; I had engaged a once-a-week maid, stuffed the Frigidaire with a sackful of groceries, ordered a typewriter so that I could be a useful and productive citizen.

That freedom to move—the hallmark of being an American—entailed a corresponding freedom to settle. My demand for instant membership of the community was met without a glimmer of surprise. Footslogging round the realtors, I picked up the low-down on the local bars and restaurants, accumulated a deck of business cards with people's home numbers scribbled at the top ("Just call *any* time"), was invited to a party, and was introduced to the elaborate network of cousinship in which a few related families appeared to have the town's affairs sewn up. Posted from uncle to wife's brother-in-law, to father, to nephew, to wife's mother and on to wife's mother's sister-in-law, I felt I'd strayed back into some great tribal house on the Arabian Gulf. The Lusks, Neelys, Alreds, Smiths and Willises had coagulated into something like the Al-Thanis or the Al-Makhtoums. Walking past the hilly, well-tended graveyard on O'Brig Avenue, I noticed that the names on the tombstones of a hundred years ago still worked as a reasonably efficient business directory for Guntersville in 1989, and that even the longest dead were still honored with tributes of cut flowers.

It had taken half a dozen meetings, a few telephone calls and a windy promenade around the town to find my cabin in the woods. At $250 a month, it was reckoned to be discouragingly expensive by Marshall County standards; I decided not to let on what I'd paid for living in Alice's shoebox on East Eighteenth.

The Hedgepeth place was a summer house; it was gloomy, cold and smelled of damp and desertion. A souvenir teacloth showing a map of Puerto Rico was the main ornament to the living room, while the ceiling of the main bedroom had been tiled with squares of tarnished mirror glass. When I lay on the bed I was appalled to find myself staring at the body of a bald man, his image broken up Hockney-snapshot-fashion into a grid of angled planes. Who on earth could bear to wake to the sight of their own nakedness so splayed and deranged? Guntersville people, apparently. Maybe this Narcissean ceiling was all the rage in Alabama; and it was with some anxiety that I tried switching on the TV set—but there were no flesh-pink operations, just Oprah Winfrey, *Knot's Landing, Newsday, Bugs Bunny* and *Hawaii Five-O*.

It took me a while to notice the ants. Unpacking my shaving kit in the bathroom, I thought I saw the brown shag carpet ripple like a corn field in a wind. Looking closer, I saw a colony of ants the size of wasps out on some kind of jungle exercise in the woolly undergrowth. When I flushed the cistern, a hundred or so ant-marines tumbled into the toilet bowl from their positions under the rim.

I drove the Spirit back into town, a mile away, and consulted my new friend William, the pharmacist.

"They black ants? Or are they a kind of reddy-brown?"

"Black—I think."

"I *hope* it's black ants you got out there. If they're a *brown* ant, it could be you got *fire ants* on your place. Then you got problems." He was searching round among his poisons. "Friend of mine, he had fire ants once . . . he just went out into his back yard one morning . . . end of the day, his daughter came home, found him laying there *dayud?* Fire ants. Yes—he was killed by the fire ants," he said with the same soft twinkle that he'd used to speak of tornadoes. "That was a misfortunate man."

As he spoke, my ants started changing color rapidly from black to brown.

"But if they're inside your house, they'll most likely be black ants. I hope so, anyway; I wouldn't like to think of you with fire ants in your house. How big you say they are?"

I found it hard to control the trembling of my forefinger and thumb.

William nodded and smiled; he looked significantly pleased by what I'd shown him.

"Oh, yes, we do get them real big around here—"

Before I left the drugstore with two bottles of sweet antbane, he asked me if I knew about brown recluse spiders. They were worse than fire ants, far worse. There was probably a brown recluse somewhere out at my place; most people had them, without knowing. They were inconspicuously small—no bigger than William's thumbnail. They didn't spin giveaway webs. They just hid, and waited to get you. If you left a pair of boots in a closet, a brown recluse might well take up residence in a toe. If there was some rotten wood in your porch, or up in the rafters . . . The brown recluse was the duke of the dark corners of Alabama. William knew a lot of people who'd died, or been permanently paralyzed, after being bitten by a brown recluse.

"Why, the Reverend Billy Graham—*he* was bitten by a brown recluse. He got treatment, but that's why he still walks so stiff. That was a brown recluse spider."

Back at the cabin, I moved as cautiously as if I was burgling it, examining each patch of carpet before I dared to plant a foot there. But there was no question: my ants were coal black, not deadly, just a nuisance to be gotten rid of. Following the instructions on the bottle, I booby-trapped the house with half-inch rectangles of white card, then shook out on each card a couple of drops of the poisonous clear syrup. Within a quarter of an hour, the ants were assembled round the cards like so many guests at an all-male black-tie dinner. I watched over them with an odd hostly feeling of benevolence. Poisoners, I remembered, tend to have milk-and-water manners—like Dr. Crippen, described by the sea captain who was responsible for his arrest as "the acme of politeness."

As they rose from their banquet to return to headquarters, the ants blundered away from the table, limped, staggered, fell to their knees. Their legs kept on waving feebly long after their thoraxes had hit the deck. Quietly cheered by the slaughter, I poured myself a finger of Scotch and went out to sit in my swing on the porch and admire the scenery.

Beyond the dogwood tree, a rickety flight of steps led down to my own pier and boathouse on this narrow neck of lake. The water, luminously brown after the rain, was pockmarked with the circles of rising fish, and the far shore, a hundred yards or so away, was colonized by a string of ample, single-story wood-frame houses, each on its acre of green woodland, each with its private dock and electrical boat-hoist. My ant-ridden cabin was by far the poorest house in sight. The standard bungalow in this cozy waterside suburb boasted white Doric pillars in molded fiberglass, floodlights on the lawn, a barbecue pit big enough to roast a whole bullock and a satellite dish big enough to detect signs of life on distant planets. Beyond the houses, a slow freight train was stalking through the trees. The intervening water magnified the sound of its whistle—that long, low oboe-chord of the American railroad, a sound perfectly contrived to strike a note at once imperious and deeply wounded.

Whiskey in hand, I walked down to my boathouse. As my foot touched the pier, it triggered off a series of bellyflop splashes, making me spill my drink. A fallen beech tree, its bark stripped bare, lay out along the water, and turtles were tumbling in from their perches on its trunk. They came in all sizes, from babies the size of silver dollars to grown-ups as big as soup tureens. They crashed into the lake like a row of falling bricks. I was glad they were shy: a snapping turtle could amputate whole hands of fingers with a bite, or take a clean halfmoon of flesh from your calf, if you were caught at close quarters with it.

My forehead snagged a cobweb, slung between the boathouse and the corrugated iron canopy over the pier. As I flinched away, my glass followed the turtles into the lake.

It was how Europeans had always seen American nature—as shockingly bigger, more colorful, more deadly, more exotic, than anything they'd seen at home. When the urban European thought of the countryside, he imagined a version of pastoral that was akin to—if a good deal less exaggerated than—that on offer in Ralph Lauren's Rhinelander Mansion on Madison Avenue. The "country" was an artifact—hedged, ditched, planted, well patrolled. The dangerous wildlife—the bears and the wolves—had been exterminated; the few remaining "wild" animals, like foxes, hares, boars, were permitted to exist only because they provided sport for man. The European landscape was a mixture of park, farm and garden; the nearest we came to wilderness was the keepered grouse moor and the occasional picturesque crag. We were astonished by America, its irrepressible profusion and "savagery."

Crèvecoeur's *Letters from an American Farmer* set a tone that has survived for more than two hundred years. America was a place where, if you went on a quiet country stroll, you might come across:

> . . . something resembling a cage, suspended to the limbs of a tree, all the branches of which appeared covered with large birds of prey, fluttering about and anxiously endeavouring to perch on the cage. Actuated by an involuntary motion of my hands more than by any design of my mind, I fired at them; they all flew to a short distance, with a most hideous noise, when, horrid to think and painful to repeat, I perceived a Negro, suspended in the cage and left there to expire! I shudder when I recollect that the birds had already picked out his eyes; his cheek-bones were bare; his arms had been attacked in several places; and his body seemed covered with a multitude of wounds. From the edges of the hollow sockets and from the lacerations with which he was disfigured, the blood slowly dropped and tinged the ground beneath. No sooner were the birds flown than swarms of insects covered the whole body of this unfortunate wretch, eager to feed on his mangled flesh and to drink his blood. I found myself suddenly arrested by the power of affright and terror; my nerves were convulsed; I trembled; I stood motionless, involuntarily contemplating the fate of this Negro in all its dismal latitude.

This was Mr. Heartbreak's quintessential American scene, and the image of the sightless Negro in the cage, found while botanizing in "a pleasant wood," hangs over the whole of his book like a great question mark. How could this come to happen? Did exposure to the awful wildness of American nature bring out an answering echo of brute savagery in human nature?

Crèvecoeur was fascinated by the brilliancy of the hummingbird and by its rapacious temper:

> . . . from what motives I know not, it will tear and lacerate flowers into a hundred pieces, for, strange to tell, they are the most irascible of the feathered tribe. Where do passions find

room in so diminutive a body? They often fight with the fury of
lions until one of the combatants falls a sacrifice and dies.

Writing about American snakes, he described how the spirit of
the copperhead possessed the body of its human victim:

> I have heard only of one person who was stung by a copperhead
> in this country. The poor wretch instantly swelled in a most
> dreadful manner; a multitude of spots of different hues alter-
> nately appeared and vanished on different parts of his body; his
> eyes were filled with madness and rage; he cast them on all
> present with the most vindictive looks; he thrust out his tongue
> as the snakes do; he hissed through his teeth with inconceivable
> strength and became an object of terror to all bystanders.

In all these passages there is an undercurrent of suggestion that
Americans have been somehow snakebitten by their natural surroundings—that something venomous and predatory has entered
the American character. If you live in such proximity to the alligator, the snake, the vulture and the hummingbird, you will find
that to crucify a Negro in a cage soon comes quite naturally.

For all its seeming factuality, *Letters from an American
Farmer* was a work of fiction. Crèvecoeur made his America up
as he went along; the book works by symbolic logic, and the truth
it tells is a symbolic truth. However much he stretched the facts
of his country walks and fantasized his natural history, he was
true to a European perception of the United States that has barely
altered since his death.

Two centuries after Crèvecoeur, a notably cool British historian, Hugh Brogan, described the battles over civil rights in the
South in the 1960s, in the Longman *History of the United States
of America.* He wrote:

> The savagery lurking in American life was welling to the sur-
> face . . .

I have tried that phrase out, substituting other words for "American"—and it doesn't work. *The savagery lurking in German life?*
That would betray the writer's Germanophobia. *The savagery*

lurking in English life would have too florid a ring to it. Yet Brogan, whose understanding and affection for America is matched by no other contemporary European historian's, can allow the phrase to pop out as if it were an accomplished fact. Oh, yes, that lurking kind of *American* savagery . . . it is as unexceptionable—as platitudinous—as associating America with the hamburger and Coca-Cola.

Sitting in the swing I could see a vulture quartering the sky, the snapping turtles on the dead tree, a very large poisoned ant like a collapsing Degas dancer. I had been warned that water moccasins swam near my dock. I was landlord to a number of invisible brown recluses, and probably fire ants as well. I had heard a serpentine slithering in the fallen leaves beyond the bedroom window, and could reckon on meeting the odd rattlesnake, copperhead and diamondback. Polecat Hollow was mildly infested with poison oak and poison ivy. Black widow spiders were common. One of the realtors had said that both black bears and cougars were occasionally spotted in the suburbs of Guntersville. There was more savagery lurking in my plot—in the water, up the trees, under the dead leaves, in the woodwork, behind the shower curtain—than there was in the whole of Europe put together; and if the Crèvecoeur hypothesis held good, I had lit on the cradle of American savagery, in the state that harbored more venomous creatures than any other in the Union.

It was a relief to see the lights coming on all round the lake and hear the neighborly susurration of tires on distant gravel. There was the smell of barbecue charcoal in the air, evening voices in the trees, the *tink* of ice cubes in a cocktail glass, someone calling "Hon? Hey, hon?" I swept the bathroom carpet with a straw broom, blackening the dustpan with ant corpses. Then, too tired to make the journey back to town and seek out strangers for company, I tried to pretend that I really lived here, grilling a sirloin steak, watching *Larry King Live* on television, doing my best to push to the back of my mind the image of the coiled snake and the deadly spider no bigger than the pharmacist's thumbnail. A discussion of the minimum wage went suddenly out of focus and out of earshot, drowned by the sound of something, or some-body, moving in the leaves outside—but it was only a stray breeze eddying from the lake. Across the water, a dog set up an angry yodel, and was answered by a bass growl on my side; in a mo-ment, every German shepherd, Doberman and Rottweiler in the neighborhood had joined the dog-telegraph. It occurred to me that I must be the only resident of Polecat Hollow who didn't have a dog to warn them of intruders.

I woke at 2 A.M., to the telephone ringing. There was slow breathing on the line, then the caller hung up. Twenty minutes later, the phone rang again. This time there was a voice. "Will you quit shittin' me?"

"Look," I said, "I'm not—" but he'd gone.

At 3 A.M. he was back. "I know you're there, Bri. What you scared of? Afraid of talking, Bri?"

I shouted into the phone that I wasn't Bri, that I was English, that I'd just moved in; but all I got in reply was the dial tone.

My persecutor left me alone until just before eight, when he, or rather his just-audible breath, was back on the line. I filled the silence with indignant gabble; he cut me short with a click, then the one-note tune of the empty telephone.

I called the real-estate agents, the telephone company and the police department. I was told that the cabin wasn't on a party line—that it had been vacant for several months—that no one called Bri or Brian or Bryant was known to the owners of the place. The woman in the police department said that they'd be happy to help, but only when the voice had made some specific threat, "like if he says he's going to kill you."

Who the hell was Bri? And what was I doing in his life? If he was usually available for conversation at two and three in the A.M., Bri kept foxy hours. I had found a half-finished plate of tortilla chips on the breakfast bar: were they his? Had he been squatting here secretly for weeks, and moved out only when he saw me moving in? What had he done to provoke the spook, and why should the spook be so unsurprised to hear Bri putting on a phony British accent and pretending to be someone else?

Sleep-starved and jumpy, I raced ahead on Bri's biography. He'd ratted on a drug deal—maybe run off with the stash. The cabin in Polecat Hollow had afforded him a quiet asylum until I'd shown up; and now his friend, having tracked him down to a phone number, would soon be round to finish off whatever business was still outstanding . . . Did this taciturn friend actually know what Bri looked like? If the friendship was based on the trade in crack, coke or heroin, friends had very often never met their friends.

Quit shittin' me, Bri.

I stood by the gas cooker, glumly watching for signs of life in the glass belvedere on the domed top of the percolator. A trickle of water popped into view and disappeared. Where was Bri now? I saw him Huck Finning it out in the woods, lying low, waiting to see what my next move would be.

The phone rang again. *"Bri?"* This time it was a woman, and this time she heard me out. "Must've got a wrong number," she said; but then she called again.

"Who *is* this?"

"What number are you dialing?"

"Five eight two, three two seven three," she said, stretching the vowels out like so many lengths of knicker elastic.

"That's *my* number. That's not Bri's. I've never heard of Bri—"

"That's the number Bri goes under. Five eight two . . . aw, shit," and she hung up on me.

It was one thing to play at being Alice; quite another to be taken for Bri. I was seriously scared of being Bri. I knew Bri, or at least Bri's kind. He'd be twenty-three, maybe twenty-four, with skinny whippet bones, thin fair hair spread over his low forehead like stalks of moldy hay, no lips, chips of dull flint for eyes, cheekbones like ax-blades. Bri was the kind of person who gets killed in back alleys outside bars.

This was absurd. I was winding myself up with old Travis McGee stories. I sat out on the porch with a mug of coffee and studied the dogwood blossom, the ruffled water, the Spirit parked sedately in the driveway. I identified the white flashes on the wings of a passing mockingbird. I was sitting in the middle of a life so sunlit, so comfortably suburban, that nothing could be badly wrong in it.

The phone was mewling in its cradle again. I let it go on

crying. I thought, all I need is a German shepherd to keep watch at night, a dog with a basso-profundo voice to scare my spook back into the woods and out of my dreams.

The man in God's Kritturs was tending a bank of illuminated aquariums. "You want to . . . borrow . . . a dog. For a . . . month." He straightened up and turned round to face me.

"Well, I thought more like—rent."

"Rent-a-Dawg."

"I've got a spook caller, in the small hours—"

He smiled patiently. In the pet shop business, you get to meet all kinds of crazy people. " 'Fraid I just can't help you there," he said. "But if a Siamese fighting fish was any good to you . . ."

William the pharmacist suggested the dog pound at the Animal Hospital on Henry Street, where I raised only a faint zephyr of amusement ("Gentleman here wants a tempo-rary, re-turnable dog") and was shown to the cells at the back of the building. The dogs were short of ears, eyes, fur and teeth. They had the resigned manners of long-term detainees. Some slept, whiffling asthmatically; some raised a single bored eye as I peered at them through the wire. One growled, but it was a countertenor, not a bass, and I could see Bri's friend skying it contemptuously—a brindled football, sailing over the lake, hitting top C as it went. It wouldn't do.

A technician came over to say, "You looking to borrow a dog? I got a dog you can borrow if you want." She occupied every available inch of an outsize T-shirt that asked *Have You Hugged Your Horse Today?* "She's a black lab, she's *trained.* She's old, but she still barks real good at strangers in the night."

"And she won't mind?"

"Gypsy? No, she'll just mooch all the love out of you she can. She's a big love-dog."

"Won't you miss her?"

"I got more dogs out at my place'n I can keep a count of. You want to borrow my dog, you're most welcome."

So at noon I followed Janet Potocki out to her place "on the mountain," a ten-mile drive that led from highway to crooked lane to dirt road to rutted track. The isolated farms still looked like bold and novel intrusions on the forest, even though their white shingles were flaked and scabby and some were drifting from decrepitude into ruin. Bony cattle stood up to their knees in the swollen creeks. Old men in dungarees stopped in their work to check out what a Spirit with New York plates was doing hereabouts, and farm dogs shifted grudgingly from their sleeping quarters in the middle of the road to let our cars go by.

The Potocki place was a trailer on several acres of its own green hilltop. Mountains were cheap in Alabama. Here even someone working for something close to the minimum wage of $3.35 an hour could be the landed proprietor of a handsome estate. Away from the town and the main highway, this kind of mixed woodland and rough pasture went for around $400 an acre. I'd seen tracts of it, in thirty- and forty-acre lots, advertised in the classified section of the *Gleam*. For $60 down and $60 a month, you could buy a fine parcel of American wilderness on which to improvise an ad hoc, self-reliant life. A secondhand trailer home could be had for less than $3,000. The man who sold birdwhistles in Manhattan might have set up as a country squire in Marshall County, Alabama.

As we pulled up, a horse shoved its head into the open window of my car. I nervously patted the bridge of its nose, feeling incompetently urban and out of touch with these rural courtesies. A troupe of dogs clowned and tumbled round Ms. Potocki, breaking off every few seconds to yell at me to go home where I came from.

"Gypsy? Gypsy!" Then, to me, "There's your dog—"

She was by far the staidest of the troupe, plump and matronly, with big teats and a grizzled face. She waddled as she walked toward me, a little stiff with rheumatism in her hindquarters. The skin of her forehead was wrinkled in a puzzled frown. Her tail swayed uncertainly from side to side. She had shy caramel eyes. The words "black lab" had conveyed to me something altogether more fierce and coyote-like than this faded old biddy, who was deferentially sniffing at my shoes.

I could see Gypsy cowering under the bed if the spook ever phoned again, let alone showed up in person. "She can bark?"

"If I wasn't here with you, Gypsy'd see you right off the property. That's a trained dog. You just give her a bit of love and see she gets fed right, she'll be real good protection for you."

With Gypsy following behind, tail at half mast, we went into the trailer. It was hot, cramped, overpoweringly doggy. A spaniel with a litter of week-old pups lay in a basket at the foot of the narrow bed. The floor was carpeted with newspapers on which the dog troupe had strewn bits of food. For the dogs' entertainment, *As the World Turns* was playing on the TV. The horse pressed its long head against the trailer window and neighed to be let in.

Looking out over the valley to the vaporous blue of the next range of hills, I said, "You've got a wonderful view. It's great out here."

"Well, it suits me."

Certainly her life in the trailer on the hillside looked as chosen, as wanted, as Thoreau's in his log cabin in the woods. By suburban standards it was bare and makeshift; it did smell strongly of dog farts, but there was no hint of quiet desperation in it. If I imagined someone like Janet Potocki in England, I saw her as thwarted and unhappy. There, it would be painfully hard to be in your mid-twenties, too large for society, too poor and constrained to make an independent break. But here she was free, working happily, part-time, in the animal hospital, comfortably supporting herself, her acres, her family of animals out on the mountain. I doubted if anyone thought of her as cracked or eccentric to live like this. The mountains were made for nonconformists, and there was still a soft spot in American culture for the idea of going it alone on your own private frontier.

"My parents didn't like me living out here by myself; not at first. They got used to it. I told them I was a whole lot safer up here with the dogs than they are down in the city."

Gypsy had fallen instantly asleep on Janet Potocki's bed, looking more like a stranded dugong than a dog—my blind date. It was too late to stand her up now, with Ms. Potocki fetching her collar and lead, her tin feeding bowl, her rations of Canine Maintenance—brown vegetable pellets that looked like the artificial soil in which people keep rubber plants in pots. At the sound of the dry rattle of food in the paper sack, the dog opened an eye and crooned. A trickle of frothy saliva leaked onto the bedspread.

"She may like to eat some candy on the drive." Doing my best to hide my feelings, I pocketed half a dozen bright red miniature bones. "She *loves* candy, don't you, honey?"

The dog raised herself carefully, in sections, clambered off the bed and took a candy-bone. She ate messily, with her mouth open, showing her tartarous back teeth.

She frowned gravely at the Spirit but after some havering she consented to park her considerable butt on the passenger seat. As we drove away, I bribed her with candy-bones, dolefully accepted.

"Gypsy . . . hey, Gypsy? Gypsy?"

Silence. She stared back at me, her eyes full of guarded incomprehension, as if I'd asked her what she thought of deconstructionism or SDI. It was one of those dates. Her tongue sneaked out sideways and licked a crumb of candy out of her gray whiskers.

As we passed a farm dog in the road, Gypsy suddenly gave voice. It was a fine growl, which started with a low bubbling deep in the bronchii and developed into a sound like a car engine from which the muffler has fallen off. I was thrilled.

"Good dog! That's a *good* dog!" I put my arm round her neck and stroked her shoulder. She tilted her nose to the roof and sniffed sadly.

Back on the highway, we overtook a car with another labrador sitting up in the back seat. As we drew level, Gypsy planted her forepaws on the dashboard and ululated like a dinner gong. It was music in my ears. I fed her a candy-bone with the solicitude of a newly infatuated lover.

The telephone was ringing when we reached the cabin. Gypsy, nose to the ground, padded off on a tour of inspection. I picked up the receiver.

"Bri, you mad at me or something?" A woman's voice.

"I'm not Bri—" The phone clattered to the floor out of my hand; Gypsy had found an interesting tidbit in the corner of the room—a poisoned ant trap on a square of card. I threw myself at the dog and wrestled her away from the glob of clear syrup toward which she had already begun to extend her long, pleasure-seeking tongue. It was like trying to shift a Welsh dresser. There was a great deal more black labrador than met the eye. Her frown darkened. For a moment, she tolerated my pushing and shoving as a boisterous game. Then she drew her lips back round her teeth and snarled.

"Gypsy—oh, Gypsy. I'm sorry, Gypsy. Sorry, dog."

I produced the last of the candy-bones from my pocket, and handed it to her on my open palm. She disdained to take it and sat, quite silent now, with an expression of fierce wounded dignity in her eyes. When I moved my hand closer, there was a warning growl deep in her throat.

She watched me as I gathered up the ant traps. I flushed them down the toilet bowl and washed my hands. When I came back into the living room, Gypsy was standing beside the door, tail tucked tightly between her legs, motioning at the door handle with her nose.

"I'm sorry, Gypsy. You don't understand. Please, dog?"

I filled her bowl with Canine Maintenance and rattled it enticingly at her. She didn't move. I presented her with a soup plate of water. I laid the red candy-bone at her feet.

"Please? Come on, Gypsy."

But she had eyes only for the door. She gave me to understand that the only way in which she wished to communicate with me in future was through her lawyer. I thought, I have been here before. I got down on my knees and talked to her, saying that I was sorry, that it was all a big misunderstanding, that I'd make it up to her in any way I could. She stared me down. I hadn't known that dogs were capable of looking so implacably righteous, so *I've done everything in* my *power* and *it's not* my *selfishness we're talking about here.*

The moment required some dramatic concession on my part. I held out no great hopes for the strategy, but I got out the remaining three-quarter-pound tranche of rib-eye steak from the fridge and unwrapped it from its cellophane-and-cardboard tray.

"Gypsy?"

She frowned, stared, slowly unglued herself from her position at the door. I cut an inch-square cube from the steak and held it out to her. She took it, chewed, and was transformed. She began to prance. Her tail was drumming on the door of the Frigidaire as she flung herself from side to side, tongue lolling, hindquarters executing a series of froglike vertical jumps. Throwing rheumatism and injured womanhood to the winds, Gypsy reverted to puppydom. I cut up the rest of the meat and carried it in scooped handfuls to her bowl, where she vacuumed up every last scrap in less than a minute. The moment she was through, she came back to the Frigidaire, laid her jaw on the carpet between her forepaws, rolled her eyes back and moaned devoutly at the closed door.

"No more." I showed her empty hands. She studied the gesture cross-eyedly and moaned some more. The scything motion of her tail gradually slowed, and she rose, a little stiffly, to lick the hands that were still bloody from the holy meat.

We drove back to town, to Food Land ("Home Folks Serving Home Folks"), where I bought five pounds of chuck steak. It came to about the same price as a bouquet of roses. Back at Polecat Hollow, Gypsy shouldered her way ahead of me into the cabin and stationed herself at the Frigidaire as if we'd been doing this for years.

At sunset, when the dog-telegraph began, Gypsy stood out on the porch and bayed on cue; a gruesome eldritch tremolo that echoed through the woods and over the darkening water. She was doing me proud. I scribbled a marginal note on the page of a book I was reading for review, feeling as snugly domestic as any householder in the hollow.

Both the dog and I needed exercising. On the levee next morning, Gypsy, fueled by a large steak breakfast, went lolloping ahead, nose down, ears out sideways, her creaky hindquarters a little out of sync with her plunging front end. Her record as a guard dog so far was patchy. She had slept through two spook calls during the evening, but an hour ago she'd summoned me from the house with an urgent, gravelly snarling. I had braced myself for an encounter with one of Bri's business associates, and found Gypsy bravely standing her ground against a floppy yellow butterfly in the dogwood tree.

Even though I'd disconnected the phone at midnight, I had had little sleep. To begin with, the dog had curled herself up

meekly on the floor at the foot of the bed, but at 1 A.M. I woke
half-suffocated by a ton of dog sprawled full-length against me on
the coverlet. Afraid of another scene of mute recrimination and
suitcase packing, I let her stay. She was not a considerate bedfel-
low. She snored, she hogged the bed, she dribbled copiously.
Twice she thrust her muzzle into my face, and not gently, because
she wanted to go and pee in the yard. When, at 5 A.M. I switched
on the bedside light and tried to read, I saw us both reflected in
the mirror tiles on the ceiling: a large black dog in a state of
luxurious abandon; a haggard man with bags under his eyes,
living, like the dog's household pet, in a state of resigned subjec-
tion.

On the levee, Gypsy looked as if she'd slept well, eaten well,
and was now eager for a day of concentrated research; I lagged
behind, tired, crapulous, wincing at the terrible brilliance of the
water. She scrambled down the bank, guilelessly making friends
with anyone she could find, while I, hands in pockets, stared
blankly into the middle distance, feeling too fragile to face even
the most glancing social contact.

"This your dog, mister?"

"Oh—yes, I'm sorry . . . *Gypsy!*"

"Gypsy. Gypsy. Oh, she's such a pretty dog."

Gypsy? Pretty? The two ideas seemed impossibly disconnected.
I looked doubtfully down at the dog, who was now wantonly
flirting with her new conquest, a woman in a wide-brimmed
straw hat who was sitting on a rock with three fishing rods
stretched out over the water in front of her. In the manner of old
husbands worn down by their spouses, I grudged Gypsy's claim
to be considered beautiful.

"She's pretty fat," I said.

"Oh! She ain't *too* fat, are you, Gypsy?"

"She's old—"

"That's a pretty dog," the woman said conclusively, as if I was
being a complete heel to carp at my dog in front of strangers. I
tried to make good by asking her what she was fishing for.

"Catfish . . . crappies . . . about anything I can catch."

She was fishing on the lake-bottom with night crawlers. Each
of her rods had cat-bells on their tips to signal when she had a

bite. Her husband, twenty yards further along, in an identical straw hat, was tending a whole armory of rods. She said that they'd driven up from Birmingham for the day's fishing. They'd left the city at six, reached Guntersville at seven-thirty, and already had two good "cat" for the pot.

"Are you Jewish?" she said.

"No—I'm English, from England. Why did you think I was Jewish?"

" 'Cause you speak funny. You speak real funny. I thought you musta been Jewish or somethin', speaking that way." She chucked Gypsy under the chin; the dog's eyes rolled in my direction—this was the kind of treatment she would expect from me in future. The woman said, "You like it here in Alabama?"

"This is only my second day here, but yes, I think I do. Do *you* like it?"

"Well—I don't know. I never been noplace else."

Walking away from the couple, I saw that one aspect of Southern life was laid out in diagrammatic form around the lake. The people who fished from the banks were all black, while the people who quartered the water in aluminum bass boats with thirty-horse Yamahas on their sterns were all white. Most of the blacks were husband and wife teams, some with a string of children; all the whites were male. The blacks wore straw hats, some made of real straw, some of plaited plastic; the whites wore cotton baseball caps. The blacks fished with worms, on the bottom; the whites were continually casting out and reeling in lures—silver spinners and painted wooden plugs that were easily lost to snags and cost two or three dollars apiece, at least. The blacks were fishing for the table, while the whites fished competitively, pound for pound, and returned their catches to the water.

Everyone stuck to these rules; along more than a mile of levee, I failed to spot a single exception. It was as if two tribes were proclaiming their separate identities by observing a strict totemic system. Wherever I looked it was bank/boat, marriage/buddy-dom, worms/synthetic imitations, straw hat/baseball cap, bottom/surface, food/sport. I wondered what would happen if you broke the rules: could I get run out of town if I sat in a boat wearing a straw hat and fished on the bottom with a worm? Quite possibly.

Gypsy took a dip, lowering herself cautiously into the water like a pantalooned Edwardian gentlewoman emerging from a bathing machine on Brighton beach. When she looked back at me, the expression on her face was one of gratification mixed with suffering in equal parts. Unadulterated pleasure came only with the business of shaking herself dry, to which she devoted more than a minute of solemn, introspective concentration, spraying my shirt and trousers with a potent solution of mud, dog and Tennessee River water.

From the levee one could see how Guntersville must have been before the TVA flooded the valley. The lake still looked like a temporary accident, the levee like an improvised barricade. At any moment the water might begin to shrink away from the trees, slowly uncovering the miles of black soil over which it had risen, and go back to its old life as a big bad river.

"Gypsy!" Truffle-hunting, she had discovered something sweet and gamy in the grass: a catfish corpse, its wrinkled skin cobble-stoned in blowflies. The dog and I wrangled, matrimonially. She agreed to leave the dead fish to its squatting tenants, but threw a heavy sulk on me for the next twenty-five yards or so—a distance that appeared to exhaust her memory span.

Guntersville had started up as Gunter's Landing, a trading post and crossing point on the narrow, southernmost bend of the Tennessee. By the Civil War, it had grown into a plump and comfortable small town. The local farmers mostly grew cotton on the rich bottomlands close to the river. The farms themselves tended to be small—sharecropping outfits, not slave plantations—but they added up, and Guntersville was their big city. It sent cotton downstream, by flatboat, barge and sternwheeler, on the looping fifteen-hundred-mile voyage to New Orleans (from where it was shipped to Liverpool and Manchester); wheat and corn came upstream to Guntersville from the Midwest. Standing proud of the river on its spur of low hills and woody hollows, the town was safe from the floods that regularly marooned the farms in its hinterland, and whenever the river devastated the valley, Guntersville did well out of the catastrophe. It had the second-biggest store in the whole of Alabama (the biggest was down on the coast in Mobile).

But by the beginning of the 1930s the place was dying on its feet. It was Walker Evans territory—bare boards, sunken jaws, jute-sack dresses . . .

"Gypsy!"

. . . dogs that were no more than gimcrack assemblies of bones and mange. The price of cotton had dropped to five cents a pound. The farmers had stripped the hills of timber and their topsoil was blowing away. Only the mosquitoes were doing well. In the boggy ground near to the river, the mosquitoes, at least, were having a fine time of it, and the valley families were wasted and shaky with malaria all summer long. In 1932, more than half the farms in the valley had a net income of less than five hundred dollars, against a national average of more than eighteen hundred dollars. Even by the standards of the Depression, Guntersville and its surrounding farms were depressed: they had sunk into that lightless basement of American life which, in one form or another, is always kept ready and furnished to accommodate people who fail. In its time, the valley had been like the night shelters of Manhattan in the 1980s: a dump, full of half-starved no-hopers posing listlessly to have their grainy portraits taken by photographers from the national magazines. They were so poor that they had passed into the realm of the picturesque. The Alabama sharecropper was a *subject,* along with the pot-bellied African child and the naked Amerindian in his war paint with a peg through his nose.

In the presidential election of 1932, the valley was a campaigning issue. Roosevelt proclaimed that "The problems of the Tennessee Valley are the problems of the United States," and when he was on the stump in Montgomery he talked of "planning for the generations to come" in a speech that the *New York Times* called "a folly." The word *planning* was just an alternative spelling for the word *socialism,* and Roosevelt's great federal project for the resuscitation of the valley was clear evidence that the man was a Red of the deepest and dirtiest hue. For the government to build a five-hundred-mile-long chain of hydroelectric dams, to reforest the hills, irrigate the farms, sell electricity on the cheap . . . it wasn't just un-American, it was Soviet-style Marxist-Leninism.

The United States Chamber of Commerce, the private power companies, the entire Republican party stacked themselves against the passing of the TVA bill in 1932. But it went through. Within eighteen months, the TVA had a work force of over twelve thousand people, and from Knoxville, Tennessee, to Paducah in Kentucky, the giant dams were going up. Six miles downstream from Guntersville the site was being cleared for the construction of a dam a mile long and nearly one hundred feet high. I had seen a photograph of the work—it looked like a Hollywood studio's version of the building of the pyramids, the antlike streams of laborers, the concrete cliff emerging from its industrial chrysalis of scaffolding.

In January 1939 they closed the sluices, and the river began to spill over its banks. For eleven days, the water went on rising, drowning the bottomlands, closing over the tops of islands, running through the fields in long tongues. By the end of the month, Guntersville had been turned into a club-shaped peninsula, lapped by water from side to side and end to end. The new lake squeezed it tight: at its narrowest, two and a half miles south of the bridges over the river, it was connected to the rest of Alabama by a neck of land only a quarter of a mile wide. Rip-rap causeways now carried the roads east and west and south out of the town. Self-containment had been thrust on Guntersville: it was a working American city that you could almost completely encircle in a four-mile waterside walk with the dog.

She was paddling in the shallows under the trees by the Kiwanis Pier.

"Gypsy!"

She tried to cannonball across the grass, but her rheumatism was getting to her, and what started as a brave gallop finished as a limp hip-hoppiting, as if the spring in her clockwork was winding down. When she reached me, she was scowling with the effort and her eyes were big with a kind of generalized, aphasic remorse. She had, said her eyes, done a hundred and one things that she ought not to have done, but at this particular moment she couldn't quite put a name to any of them. No wonder people were such suckers for dogs, with their genius for self-abasement. For a pound of chuck steak, you got supplied with more flattery and contrition than you knew what to do with. Plus, you had the twenty-four-hour services of a resourceful dinner hostess. Gypsy had made it plain that she could wangle me an entrée into every level of Alabama society. She might be a lousy guard dog, but her social skills were in the Lady Diana Cooper class. She was a heart-melter; all I had to do was to tag along behind.

Like so many of their citizens, most American towns were seized by the chronic itch to get up and go. They roamed thuggishly over the countryside, struck out across green valleys, and, on a sudden whim, carted their main streets off to replant them in some scented shopping mall on the nearest interstate. No sooner had they got themselves incorporated than they started to dissolve and go on walkabout until, as Gertrude Stein said of Oakland, there was no *there* there.

The lake had stopped that nonsense dead in Guntersville. Main, once Broad Street, had been rechristened Gunter Avenue, but it was still the living spine of the town, built wide enough to turn a train of ox-drawn cotton wagons in; now grandly colonnaded with veteran oak and maple trees. It bulged with civic self-regard. Wherever one looked one saw the lick of new white paint, repointed brick, neat flowerbeds, turf freshly trimmed. You could see how well the place was doing by counting the lawyers' names, picked out in gold leaf on the windows of their offices on the street; by the unplated Grand Ams, Park Avenues and Celebrities drawn up around the Bob Hembree Buick Chevrolet dealership; by the pressed and laundered look of the lunchtime crowd, the good color in their cheeks, their unhurried, loping tread on the sidewalk. Guntersville people looked as if they ate well and slept soundly. I thought, an address in Guntersville ought to carry with it a whacking automatic discount on any health or life insurance policy. After the swivel-eyed Valium poppers who hung out on Third Avenue, with their ricepaper skins and sparrow-claw wrists, these Gunter Avenue guys looked like some new brand of immortal. The only trouble was that on Third

I felt part of the crowd; here I felt uncomfortably like coffin bait.

People were being familiar with Gypsy.

"Hello, puppydawg!"

"Hi, pooch!"

She simpered politely, bemusedly at all comers. I gruffed out her name on request. Her silence, her sticking-out ears and dopey grin must have made Bri's friend snigger contemptuously behind his hand if he was watching from the wings.

The big houses, set back from the street behind painted picket fences, were in the Southern vernacular style of Confederate Doric, with tall pillared porches and closed shutters that gave them a remote, abstracted air, like old men in white suits still chawing over their favorite tags from Aristotle and Cicero. The banks were as serious as churches, while the churches were surprisingly jolly: the United Methodist was a turreted castle, in brick the color of dried blood; the First Baptist, much the biggest and swankiest church in town, could have been mistaken for a great white German opera house.

"Well . . . I see you took the first step to becoming a paid-up resident of Guntersville—you got yourself a big black dog."

The man was a realtor to whom I'd spoken two days before. It was easy to remember his name as it was posted on giant signboards hung in the trees around the entrances to town. They said, HAPPINESS IS—ED NEELY REAL ESTATE.

The love-dog was doing her stuff with Mr. Neely, giving him the rolled eye, the lolling tongue, the shy grizzled smile.

"That's some dog."

"She's just borrowed. Her name's Gypsy."

"Gypsy . . ." he crooned in a pillow-talk voice. She brought her tail into the action and gazed at him, evidently under the impression that he might well turn out to be a wholesale butcher.

Ed Neely had avid eyes. He was a collector. When I'd gone to his office in search of somewhere to live, he'd said that he collected "just about anything I can pick up," and had filled the desk between us with photographs of steamboats, Indian arrowheads, beads and bits of pottery; now he added the dog and me to his collection and swept us off down Gunter Avenue.

"Seen my new lube?" He pointed to a drive-in service station on a side street. "I just bought that land. It's kind of like a philosophy with me: I like to try and own a piece of every block in town."

I remembered the graveyard on O'Brig. Certainly the Neelys had cornered a fine piece on that block: a dappled glade under the trees where the Neely dead lay on a south-facing slope. Their weathered memorial slabs formed a compact little village on the edge of the cemetery. The Neelys were one of the First Families of Guntersville.

"We do go back," Ed Neely said. "First Neely in this town came here as a missionary. That was in the eighteen and twenties. We're kinda proud of him."

Mr. Neely had a fine stride for a man pushing seventy; the dog and I were hard pressed to keep up with him as he loped down Gunter, showing off his fiefdom. He carried himself with the bounce of a man who still expects to draw admiring glances from women. His powerful shock of sandy gray hair was oiled like a boy's, and his face had kept the knuckle-jawed and pointy look of adolescence. It was easy to see that face looking out of a high-school football team photo of around 1938—the face of a sexy quarterback, eyeing the world as if he meant to eat it.

I was bidden to join Mr. Neely for lunch. When I locked Gypsy up in the Spirit under the shade of a white oak, she treated us both to an eloquent stare of baffled exasperation and laid her head on the steering wheel as if she was submitting herself to the ax.

"I could *use* a dog like that. That's a *good* dog. I like to see obedience like that. You ever get through with her, you be sure and let me know."

We crossed the street to the pillared veranda of the Glover, once the town hotel and now the headquarters of an industrial corporation with a restaurant on its ground floor.

"Alabama!" Mr. Neely said as we went in, spreading his hands to include the patrician splendor of the place. And it was true—everything had been designed to confound your idea of what to expect in rural Alabama. It was royal: marble tables in the lobby . . . carved chiffoniers . . . stiff white napery, heavy silver, goblets of jade-green blown glass.

The quality were at table; the FFGs, hunkering down over broken *baguettes* and bottles of Sauvignon. Ed Neely led me on a social tour of the room, formally announcing me as a man who'd borrowed a big black dog. I stood politely by while he sang Gypsy's praises to Mr. Bob Hembree, the mayor, of Bob Hembree Buick Chevrolet, to Chief Jerry Gamble of the police department, to Mr. Claude Herbert Smith and Mizz Ida Will Smith.

"May I ask if you're buying property in these parts, sir?"

"No. Just renting. In Polecat Hollow."

"You better watch that Ed Neely; mind where you sign your name. He'll sell you the whole of Georgia Mountain, and that's only by the *soup.*"

Mr. Neely modestly hung his head. As we sat down, he nodded at his cronies and said, "We're all Anglo-Saxons here. This is an Anglo-Saxon town. I don't know why that is." He spread his napkin across his knees. "No Jews. No Hispanics. No Italians. No French, excepting Bob Hembree's wife. She's French." The way he said "I don't know why that is," and the faintly crooked smile that went with it, suggested that he knew very well why it was, and that if I was half smart, I'd know why it was too.

"I guess they just don't like it here . . ." He looked at me across the table, sizing me up. I could imagine what was coming next. In a society that dwelled obsessively on fine distinctions of ancestry and race, my Old Testament first name and my odd patronym marked me out as a dubious character. "Now *Rayburn,* that's an old Guntersville name. General Samuel King Rayburn—he was mayor here back in the eighteen and eighties . . . Maybe you'd be related?"

"No. Rayburn's Scottish; my name's English. It's a corruption of a place-name in Shropshire." I felt shabby at laying so meek a claim to Anglo-Saxondom; it would have been morally better to have lied boldly and said I came from Lodz or Warsaw. Nor did "Anglo-Saxon" seem quite the right term to describe the Lowland Scottish, Ulster Protestant and potato-famine Irish names borne by nearly all the FFGs. The Lusks of County Dublin . . . the O'Brigs of Kerry . . . the Neelys of Belfast, once the McNeillys of Galloway . . . The names of the FFGs stood clearly for that wave of early nineteenth-century immigration by the rural poor of Scotland and Ireland. Their route was well established—from Virginia and the Carolinas, through Georgia and Tennessee, following the steadily declining price of an acre of uncleared land. Trading with the Indians, planting small holdings of cotton, corn and tobacco, they swung south of the Appalachians on the westward trail, leaving behind them towns like Guntersville much as mountaineers leave camps equipped with supplies on a Himalayan climb.

"You never know," Ed Neely said. "You could be kin. It sounds an awful lot like Rayburn."

"It's a nice idea," I said, seeing a definite possibility here. Forget Bri. Be John Rayburn . . . *lives out on Polecat Hollow with his black lab. Goes way back.* William the pharmacist had already called me by that name. It was the identity that Guntersville had been keeping in readiness for me, and all I had to do was to slip into it as gracefully as I could.

"Tell me," I said, "about how you remember the town before the dam was built."

"Before the lake came up? Oh—that was the difference between Hell and Heaven. Hell and Heaven," Ed Neely said, putting five vowels into *Hell* and eight into *Heaven* for emphasis. "Gosh, people used to *hate* that Tennessee River. It did so much terrible destruction. In flood time, you go down to by the bridge, and, oh, the things you'd see! It was like a procession . . . whole barns'd go by, dead hogs, dead chickens, dead dogs . . . That river, it'd rip right through a farm and take away everything that was in it . . . man's entire livelihood. You could get things out of that river, too, sometimes. Once, we hauled out a dozen oil-drums that were floating down from some refinery place up by Chattanooga . . . free gasoline! We supplied just about every automobile in Guntersville with that stuff for weeks. Made a few bucks out of it, too.

"Then there was the malaria . . . Hell, it was just *swamps* round here before the lake came up. Whole lot of people died of it every year. You had to take quinine against it . . . start taking the quinine around March, by June that quinine, oh, it would get to you. You'd be dizzy, headachey, seeing double—the quinine was near as bad as the malaria, but you had to go on taking it, else you could die. That was how bad it was. It was Hell. Then the lake came up . . .

"That was Heaven. Did away with the floods, did away with the malaria . . . It brought electricity. Gosh, I remember seeing mountain people putting their new Frigidaires and washing machines right out in their yards, just so everyone could see they were on electricity. *Hey, man! Look what we got here!* And you could make a decent living; when before the lake came up, you couldn't hardly get money at all. You look around now, isn't it just about the prettiest town you ever saw?"

Ed Neely had made a splendid living out of the lake. Before the lake came up, people were scared of water, and with good reason. It was wild; it could wash out the work of a decade in an angry night. Now it was tame, its level controlled by the dam to the nearest inch, people wanted to live right on it. They wanted waterfront lots with piers and boathouses. In 1947, the young Ed Neely opened the first real-estate office in town, selling flood-free, malaria-free life on the lake.

To begin with, land was hard to come by. Most of the lakeside was owned by the TVA, and it was earmarked for "industry and unborn generations" (in Ed Neely's words, sarcastically pronounced). But when Eisenhower won the presidency in 1952, he took up the old Republican line that had been used against Roosevelt twenty years before. The TVA was "creeping socialism." It must be systematically weakened and humbled. Eisenhower installed an army general of his own political color as chairman of the Authority, and the general ordered the T.V.A. to sell off land in three-monthly auctions.

At the first auction, Ed Neely was bidding. He collected acres like stamps. "Oh, that was *good* business. I'd keep ahold of as many of those waterfront lots as I could. At any one time, I'd have sixty lots. Prime land. I'd just sell off as many as I needed to buy what I wanted when the next auction came around. You could count on that land. It was punctual. Every four years, it'd double in price. Twenty percent. Per annum." Affected by the memory, he wagged his big boy's head over the *rosettes de veau.* "That was *something* in those days. Now there's nothing to sell."

Nothing?

"I have to disappoint so many people. Retirees come here, see round the town, and they look for the lake. They'll spend a week looking at waterfront properties, maybe two, before it hits them that they just don't have the dough for that kind of lifestyle. Then they settle on a house in town. Lake view, maybe. But on the lake . . . that's out of sight now for most people. Like, do you have property back in England?"

I owned up to a low-ceilinged cottage in the Essex marshes, sixty miles out of London; a box of four small rooms, roughly as big in total as the summer cabin on Polecat Hollow. Describing it, I found that it didn't sound at all like home; it was more like an inconvenient piece of luggage that I'd left behind somewhere on my travels. I remembered its shaggy patch of grass, its mice in the larder, its flaky paint, its iciness in winter, without a twinge of nostalgia. It was not a happy place. It continued to belong to me by negligence rather than by choice, like the old clothes in its closets from whose linings and pockets dozy moths fluttered every time I pushed them further up the rail.

Ed Neely had expected something better than this from me. He chuckled, in a commiserating way, and said, "How much would *that* fetch, in England now?"

I told him.

"Oh, gosh."

"I come from an overcrowded island."

"Why, that's better than a hundred forty thousand dollars!"

"About that. It doesn't buy much in England, at least not within commuting distance of London."

"All right," Ed Neely said. *"All* right." And he began to sketch for me a house, a life, in Guntersville. It would be *waterfront.* He had just the place in mind. A cedar and stone rancher on the lake. Pier. Boathouse with electric hoist. Garage. Three bedrooms, two bathrooms. Den. Stone fireplace. Central heat and air. Cable hookup. Gravel drive and breezeway . . .

I filled in the spaces between the realtor's words with details of my own. My typewriter was set up on a table by the window in the den. Beyond the glass was a bird-feeder where goldfinches, tufted titmice and chickadees wrangled aerobatically over the sunflower seeds. From where I was sitting, I could look down to the sailboat tethered to the dock, to the wide-open miles of the lake, like thumb-scored tinfoil, to the floating bluffs and solitary islands where the bald eagles were. From round the corner of the porch, Gypsy sauntered, yawning, into the foreground of the picture.

Smell: pine needles, creosote, ground coffee.

Sound: a mockingbird singing, like a Bartók record stuck in a groove; the nip-and-tuck noises of wavelets breaking on a gravelly shore; wind in the branches; the surprisingly weighty double splash of a leaping bass beyond the boathouse.

It was a life worth waking early in the morning for. Up at six-thirty; at the typewriter by eight; work till noon, then walk the dog; at one, take the five-minute drive into town for lunch at the Glover . . .

"And you'd still have close on fifteen thousand dollars left over," Ed Neely said, and I could almost feel them in my pocket already—plenty to put a secondhand car in the garage and make a good start on furnishing the rancher.

"You want to take a look at it, it'll be my pleasure to run you round there this afternoon . . ."

Watch it.

How easy it sometimes seems to walk out on one's life and into a new one. You reify your marriage, your mortgage, your job contract, the appointments in your diary—those precious chains that make your life seem merited, inexorable, yours. Yet put a thousand miles or so between yourself and home, change your clock by a few hours, feel a more indulgent climate on your skin, and the view alters. From here, home looks makeshift and arbitrary, a sandcastle on a distant beach. The tide could wash the whole thing away in no time at all. Given one drink too many over lunch, a trick of the light on the water, someone's smile, and you could be shot of it. *It wasn't much of a life anyway,* says your old demon, that unreconstructed addict of risk and roulette. *Why not?*

The realtor smiled across the table.

The mayor, on his way out, said, "That rascal not sold you a house *yet?*"

"Very nearly. We're only an inch or so away."

Safer to stick to the rented life and the borrowed dog.

"Let me think about it," I said to Ed Neely.

"Call me any time," said this blandly charming, pearly-suited Mephistopheles.

Later, with Gypsy barreling lopsidedly down Lusk Street, I was thinking *den . . . private dock . . . breezeway* (whatever a breezeway was). There was a half-written page in the typewriter, a skirl of wind on the lake. Was there a ghostly someone in the "family room," leafing through a magazine or putting a CD on the stereo? I rather imagined so.

The Rayburn place.

It was a pretty Southern town with murder in the air. Within the last ten days, the bodies of two young women had been found in the lake. The *Gleam* carried details of the latest corpse:

- Part of a concrete block had been tied to the woman by a rope around her neck.
- There were several deep lacerations to the head, apparently made by some blunt instrument.
- The woman was wearing a diamond ring and a ruby ring, as well as a Caravelle watch.
- Most of her hair was missing, leading to an initial belief that her head had been shaved. But investigators are now inclined to think that the long time in the water had caused the body to decompose to the point that the hair simply fell out.

The fisherman who found the body told the *Gleam* that "I had just baited my hook when I looked down and saw what appeared to be legs and feet . . ."

The whole tone of the report, and its relegation to a mere half-column on the right-hand side of the front page, suggested that Guntersville had grown pretty much accustomed to news of violent death. The *Gleam* took strange things in its stride. A back page story was about a recent Rotary Club meeting at Hartselle, thirty-five miles west of the town, where a psychiatrist, late of Guntersville, had given a talk about devil worship.

Dr. Twente said a teen-age girl abducted from another state was taken to south Morgan County where she was "drugged, gagged and then she was split open. They drank her blood, ate her heart and her liver," he said.

". . . The closest place I know where a human sacrifice has taken place is up the road from here at Crybaby Hollow," he said.

. . . He said that what he has learned "has made a change in my life," and that "there is no other way to deal with this" except through Christ.

On this sunny afternoon, on these smiling, respectable, middle-aged streets, the nasty tales seemed preposterous. They simply didn't fit the architecture, the people, the modest family sedans cruising through town at twenty-five, the sleepy calm of the lake as it showed round every gable-end and through every gap between the pines. I was inclined to put them out of my head, but wherever I went something happened to put me in mind of them again.

With Gypsy on the lead, I went into the Guntersville Tackle Co. to look at fishing rods. The building was a breezeblock bunker, its door heavily barred. Inside, strip-lighting gave it a forever–3 A.M. air. It was a deadly serious place. Beyond the childish playthings of the fishing tackle section, the big boys' toys were chained up to the walls—carbines, automatic rifles, enough firepower for a small war. Handguns were displayed in illuminated cases around the store counter, like so many watches or necklaces. I made a show of weighing a twenty-dollar spinning rod in my hand, but it was the guns that held my eye.

"Need any help?" The store owner was seated at the till—a heavy-lidded, heavy-jowled man. A lifetime of natural suspicion had given him the face of a snapping turtle.

I bought the rod I was holding, together with a reel, some line and a couple of bass plugs, just so that I could draw the man out on my real interest, guns. What was the cheapest handgun in the shop? He opened a cabinet and took out a 9mm automatic pistol. $77.95.

"That's what you might call a Saturday Night Special. May I ask how much experience you have in handling guns?"

"None at all."

"Then my advice to you is don't buy an automatic. Unless

you're real used to handling a gun, an automatic—she's liable to jam up on you at the critical moment. You just want personal protection, I'd recommend a revolver. You're going to have to pay a little more, but you're going to sleep a whole lot easier at night, is the way I look at it."

I said I was asking only out of curiosity. I wasn't an Alabama resident; I wasn't even a U.S. citizen. So there was no way I could actually buy a gun.

"Oh, you won't have no difficulty finding someone to come in and pick one up for you," he said. "Now, something like this . . ."

The gun made a leaden clunk on the counter. I felt shy of touching it. It wasn't a phallic symbol, it was a black steel phallus: the wrinkled grip a scrotum, the dimpled chamber, the absurdly virile barrel. Far more craftsmanship had gone into its making than its function warranted. It was as finely finished as an Etruscan cup.

". . . Smith & Wesson .38. That's *foolproof.* But she'll set you back around three hundred fifty dollars."

She? I'd never in my life set eyes on anything less female than this gun.

I said, "Do a lot of people carry guns round here?"

"Put it this way. You stop twenty people in the street out there, you can bet twelve of 'em will be carrying a gun."

"Do you?"

"Damn right I do." He reached into the back pocket of his trousers and brought out his equipment with a flourish. It was a big one.

"Loaded?"

"Damn right it is." He broke it, exposing the six brass cartridges snug in their beds. "Every time I go to sleep, that gun's sitting on my night table. My wife has another gun on hers. Just like most folks round here."

"Is that necessary?"

"Well, the police can't do nothing for you 'til you're *harmed,* and the way I look at it, after you're harmed is a piece too late. So I'd say you ought to get yourself a gun. Look after your own protection."

"I've got the dog—"

Snapping Turtle peered over his counter with an expression of satirical disbelief. "Yeah." Gypsy, under the scrutiny, began to simper at him. Her tail brushed the floor in slow, friendly strokes. "I got two dogs like that. They might just *lick* somebody to death . . ."

"She's got a good bark."

"I'm serious. If I were you, I'd get myself a gun."

Looking, thinking *should I really?*, at the Smith & Wesson, I picked up the parcel of fishing things.

"Be sure and come back now," said Snapping Turtle.

Rayburn's gun.

Returned to the cabin, I watched him living in the third person.

It was after dark, and a gothic Budweiser lantern hung on a chain over the long trestle table in the porch, lighting the first blank page on the new typewriter. Papers, maps and books were spread on the table: a sheaf of stuff from the Guntersville Chamber of Commerce, *The History of Marshall County, Alabama*, *Peterson's Eastern Birds*, *I'll Take My Stand*, *Battle Cry of Freedom*, *The Mind of the South*, Allen Tate's *Essays of Three Decades*, *A Piece of My Heart* by Richard Ford. Just inside the screen door, Gypsy was asleep on a dusty folkweave vinyl mat, probably a relic of the same vacation that had produced the hideous Puerto Rican wall-hanging in the living room. An hour earlier, she had thrown a happy fit over her evening ration of chuck steak, and she occasionally stirred in her sleep to let out a whimper of reminiscent pleasure.

Across the water, there were friendly lights on the neighbors' private docks and behind their screened porches. A big bass crashed somewhere out on the lake and, homing in from the far distance, came the hornet drone of a returning outboard.

Seated at the table, elbows planted on either side of the typewriter, his chin cupped between his hands, beads of sweat showing on his skull, he was trying to work; at least, he was putting a good deal of effort into the business of acting the part of a man trying to work. His surroundings were too new, too insistent on having notice taken of them, for him to concentrate. In an hour he had done no more than type the title, author and publisher of the book he was supposed to be reviewing at the top of the page, and even the keys of the typewriter felt strange, disconcertingly squishy, under his finger ends. He wasn't looking at the paper on the platen in front of him; he was looking out through the porch screens and he was seeing things.

A few minutes ago he had noticed a small witch, or afreet, riding on a hang-glider. It had banked sharply between the trees, cruised in a low swoop over the dock, banked again and come flying back over the porch roof. To begin with he'd taken it for a bat, but on its return flight he saw that it couldn't be a bat; it was too full in the belly, too queerly humanoid, too slow and deliberative in its flight pattern to be a bat. Nor was it a bird. It was something more in the incubus/succubus line.

He would have sniffed at an idea like that in England or Manhattan, but in Polecat Hollow it didn't seem so easy to say where nature left off and the supernatural began. Alone at night in this spooked cabin, he had found himself losing forty years and going back to those nights when a candle used to burn in a saucer on the bedside table, and beyond the candlelight lurked those invisible muttering malevolents who made floorboards and door hinges creak into the small hours. Even ordinary nature, by daylight, made him jumpy here. Making a few practice casts with his fishing rod from the dock that afternoon, he'd been within three or four feet of a cottonmouth or water moccasin—a creamy electric wriggle in the water, as it headed out from under the dock toward the fallen beech tree where the snapping turtles basked. The small deadly snake, rocketing away just an inch beneath the surface, looked more like something out of an allegory than a creature to be seen at the bottom of everyone's garden.

So it was with these hang-glider things. The more he looked, the more he saw. If he stared at any dusky gap between the trees, another one would show up in the course of a minute or two, a silent, furtive night visitor on rigid skeletal wings. Then one flew within inches of the screen, and the Budweiser lantern lit it clearly: its pointed face and black button eyes, the membranous web stretched taut between its forepaws and hindpaws. It was definitely a squirrel, but an Alabama squirrel, exotically equipped, like a griffin, with the means to fly.

His forefinger drummed against his lips as he tried to think about his damned *review*. The dog snuffled in her sleep. Slowly he typed *In the bland climate* and immediately pressed the erase key on it. *Bland* wasn't the word for it.

At least he had a wonderfully portable occupation. He could as well hang up his shingle on Polecat Hollow as anywhere else on the face of the earth. All he needed was paper and something to make marks on it. When he was through with this piece (if he was ever through, which at this moment seemed unlikely), he could take it out to the Guntersville Holiday Inn where there was a fax machine in the lobby. He was mystified by how the thing worked, but in two minutes it could place the Polecat Hollow review on the desk of a literary editor in London. By the time he got back to the cabin, the phone could be ringing, with the editor's review of his review. Thinking of his other house, his three-bedroom ranch, he added a fax machine to the amenities of the den, and thought of himself looking at the chickadees through the window while his typescript zapped across the Atlantic to the cold and rainy city that was no longer home.

He typed, *In the emollient climate of American* . . . The phone rang. The dog didn't stir at the sound. He went into the living room to take the call at the breakfast bar.

"Hullo?"

"Bri?"

"No one called Bri lives here—"

"Who is this?"

"John Rayburn—"

"Sorry. Must've got a wrong number." The caller hung up.

He came back to the typewriter, cheered by the sound of his own voice. His real name was a tricky gallop over seven consonants, and no one ever got it first time. His new name was a leisurely, Southern slide down three long vowels. It made him sound, for the first time, as if he had rights around here.

He squared up to the typewriter again. Trying not to pay attention to the flying squirrels, he wrote . . . *political journalism today,*

Christopher Hitchens is a refreshingly corrosive agent.

It took him a couple of hours to tap out his eleven hundred words. By a quarter of ten, he was finished. There was still time for a drink. He woke the sleeping dog and drove to the Holiday Inn. At about 4:30 A.M., London time, his book review showed up in the empty offices of a Sunday newspaper, a few seconds before he perched himself on a bar stool and called for a vodka martini, dry, straight up with a twist.

"There you go, John," the barman said.

How quickly people learned one's name in Guntersville.

It took me a little while to discover that many of my neighbors lived much as I did, doing jobs that were dependent on the baroque economy of a distant capital city. The encircling water made Guntersville look self-contained, a tight little *polis,* rooted to its own green island; and so it still was to people like William Benefield and his partner at the drugstore, to the FFGs with their family businesses, to the old people who drove into town from their mountain farms. But the town was not really half so self-contained as it seemed at first glance.

The lights would come on in the newest and biggest waterfront homes shortly before dawn. At 6:45 A.M., the electric-eye doors of their garages would unveil the '89 model Bob Hembree Buicks and Bob Hembree Chevrolets as they rolled slumbrously out over the wet gravel. At seven, the northgoing bridge over the river was loud with commuter cars making the thirty-eight-mile trip through the hills to Huntsville. What people did up there— what nearly *everybody* did up there—was curious. They made rockets.

When the lake came up, the giant turbines on the dams began to generate electricity at an astounding rate and at a price far lower than that charged by the private power companies in the North and West. This was Electric Valley. Nothing sopped up electricity so hungrily as the missile-development wing of the armaments industry, and so, during World War II, the backwater town of Huntsville grew into one of the most important weapon-manufacturing sites in the United States. Redstone Arsenal on the

Tennessee River was like the Krupp factory on the Ruhr—and the water that lapped so prettily outside my porch was the direct cause of the experimental bombs and warheads that were being assembled just a few miles downstream. By the 1980s, Huntsville, still growing fast, was into the space program (NASA was there), into the doctrine of MAD, SDI and all the other terrible acronyms. Something about the place's general character might be guessed from the fact that Huntsville's civic center was named in honor of Wernher von Braun.

So it was that the Arcadian peace of Guntersville—the lawn mowers and potted plants outside Hammer's, the backslapping over morning coffee in the Northtown Country Cooker, the silver bass boats on the lake, the lunchtime recitals by the Methodist Choir, the Garden Club, the Huck Finn children's fishing derby—was actually sustained by the Cold War. Gunter Avenue answered directly to the mood swings of Washington. If the incoming president made a slash in the defense estimates, Ed Neely would soon find himself lopping some thousands of dollars off my waterfront rancher; if Russia snarled, the Glover would be taking a few extra reservations for dinner. There were people who were eating their fingernails behind their mosquito screens at the thought of what *glasnost* and *perestroika* might come to mean for Guntersville. To the morning commuters on the bridge, the idea of Mutually Assured Peace was just the thing to spoil a perfectly good breakfast: MAD meant full employment, guaranteed up to the moment of the final bang, for guys with college degrees in engineering and physics, while MAP would mean—it would mean that you'd have to start thinking about the unthinkable. It would be real dangerous.

So much for rural self-containment. Inside the town, some of my neighbors did work at jobs that would have earned the approval of the Agrarians, with their ideal of an economy based on the land and on trade arising from the produce of the land. The town wharves were lined with elevators stacked with soybeans, wheat and chickenfeed, and every day there was a steady shuffle of grain-barge traffic on the water. Out on the neck of Polecat Creek there was the Gold Kist broiler processing plant . . . though it was hard to imagine Allen Tate warming much to the idea of the oven-ready frozen chicken. The cotton gins that had once dominated Guntersville were gone now, but the Lee blue-jeans factory at the south end of town stood as a reminder of the fading power of local cotton, the staple of the Agrarian dream.

But the clean, well-paid jobs that most people wanted were in industries that would have spelled the death of the South to the contributors to *I'll Take My Stand*, had they been able to conceive of their existence in 1930. The old cotton spinning mill now housed Comptronix, a firm that made printed circuits and had a $30 million turnover. The upstairs floor of the old hotel, above the Glover restaurant, was now the head office of Kappler Inc., manufacturers of germ-proof, fire-proof, chemical-proof, radiation-proof Teflon suits of the kind that were supposed to have magically protected Ronald Reagan during his presidency.

I'd heard people talk about George Kappler at the bars of the Holiday Inn and the Dime Store Deli. He wasn't *from around here; came from some place out in Mississippi, but he married an Alabama girl, from Decatur.* This Alabama marriage was important; it claimed him as a regular guy. For Kappler was popular: he paid *a dollar, dollar-fifty above minimum;* and gave good bonuses too—one of his employees said that she got an extra $150 a month for turning up punctually.

"And for around here, hell, that's real money."

He was young, *only around forty.* He'd started small: *I remember when he just had, oh, six or eight girls working for him in a little-bitty shed there.* Now he was big, *he's even got a factory over in England, where you come from.* Kappler's success story, with its youthfulness, its local girl, its modest beginnings, was of a kind that everyone could applaud and identify with. The Comptronix business was too arcane to grasp, especially after a couple of Miller Lites, but Kappler had got where he was with, as it were, some bits of colored PVC and a needle and thread. He was the town's favorite millionaire.

I lunched with him at the Glover—the restaurant he'd opened in order to entertain his clients from out of state in a style designed to take them aback.

"Guy flies in from New York . . . or Nottingham, England . . . this is just a little different from what he's been led to expect,

huh?" His proprietorial smile took in the French menu, the English antiques, the immaculate table linen and the wine waiter,
standing deferentially at his elbow.

Ed Neely had said almost the same thing two days before.
People in Alabama knew the stigma that was attached to the
name of their state. It was like saying you came from Gomorrah
or Sing Sing. Strangers instantly got the picture. They saw flat-
lands, cotton fields, Klansmen, blacks in tarpaper hovels, redneck white supremacists talking loose and dirty over quarts of
Jim Beam, George Wallace, Bull Connor . . . the body of a man
swinging by his broken neck from the top branch of a tree. For
the Alabamian, the worst of it was that there were still things in
this picture that were true—or at least not so untrue as all *that*.
So he had to go in for extravagantly dramatic gestures to wipe the
shameful image from the stranger's eye. In Guntersville, the lake
and the mountains went a long way toward breaking the picture
up; the Glover wiped it clean. Bracing yourself for an Alabama
catfish sandwich, you were faced—praise be!—by *Filet de Boeuf
en Chemise*. I'd been told that Kappler was losing money every
day on the restaurant, but money wasn't the point. The point lay
elsewhere, in the region's recent past, and in the lengths to which
the Deep Southerner had to go to controvert his history.

One saw immediately why people liked Kappler. His voice was
in no hurry. It was one of those sitting-here-in-my-rocker-shoot-
ing-the-breeze voices, an instrument to be picked and strummed
at leisure, and not forced into the military march time of the
business lunch. His face wrinkled easily into a chubby smile. He
seemed modestly amused by his success.

He'd come to Guntersville as an employee of the Monsanto
Corporation; when Monsanto moved on, Kappler, then twenty-
nine, had stayed. He'd hired eight women and eight sewing machines. The Du Pont Corporation supplied him with precut panels
of polyethylene, and he and his girls sewed them up into safety
garments for use in industry.

"Like a sweatshop on the Lower East Side," I said.

"Kinda," he said. Then, "Hardly." Then, "No, not like *that* at
all."

Kappler had graduated as a chemist. He began to improve on

the materials he was working with, laminating polymers together to make new fabrics that could withstand acids, toxins, carcinogens, viruses. He patented new methods of thermal welding to make his weird-looking clothes seamless. Clad in sky-blue Kappler space suits, people handled the nastiest by-products of the twentieth century, touching pitch without being defiled.

I listened as he spoke of how his garments *protected, repelled, retarded, resisted.* One of the materials he worked with had the trade name of "Barricade." The vocabulary was fortuitously apt. Kappler's war against the penetration of foreign bodies fitted well with the embattled, conservative spirit of the small town holding out against the city.

Why Guntersville? I asked. Hadn't he been tempted to go home to Mississippi to start his business there?

"Talent," Kappler said. "There's so much *talent* around here. People in Mississippi, they just don't seem to have the ambition. Don't have that get-up-and-go. I don't know why that is."

That phrase again. "They're—black?" I said.

"Oh, I don't want to sound racist about this, but where I come from, yes, you got near eighty percent black."

The reason why Guntersville had so much "talent" was very simple. Few of the cotton farmers of Marshall County had been able to afford slaves, for their holdings were too small, hilly and unproductive. It was father-and-son country. In 1860, sixteen percent of the county's population were slaves, a low percentage by Alabama standards—so low that the county representatives to the state convention in January 1861 held out against immediate secession from the Union, but were outvoted by the big slaveowning interests from further south in the state. What had once been the measure of Marshall County's poverty was now its major asset. Labor here was not just cheap, it was—*talented.*

I'd seen surprisingly few black people in town. In the chamber of commerce statistics, twelve percent of the population were listed as "non-white." Yet the face of Gunter Avenue was almost uniformly Caucasian. There were the fishermen on the lake shore, the black women who worked in the Food Land supermarket and Hardee's hamburger joint—but these were one in fifty, not one in eight.

"You haven't been to the Hill? Turn right at Kentucky Fried Chicken—that's where they all live. They seem to like to keep themselves pretty much to themselves up there. I don't know why that is."

Kappler and Guntersville seemed made for each other. He liked to keep things small, and had the countryman's mistrust of big cities, big government, big corporations. When I talked about the goings-on at Macy's, his cheerful face colored with contempt.

"Ell Bee Owes!" he said, washing his mouth out with a tumbler of iced water after he'd said it. "That's just fancy talk for *scam*. They're scams. Half of those New York bankers, best place for them is jail. Some of them are there already. No, when I invest my money, I put it into things I can see, things that are *real*. I invest in my own company. I invest in real estate. I don't trouble with stocks on *Wall Street*."

Yet surely, I said, bigness was an inevitable consequence of success? The Kappler Safety Group was hardly a corner grocery. *Wrong*, Kappler said. It had the philosophy of a grocery. As each division of his business grew, so he snapped it off and replanted it as a separate company. From the factory in England to the Glover restaurant, every one of his enterprises had its own board of directors, own management, own budget. They were all self-sufficient. *Exactly* like groceries.

"Intra-preneurialism. Not entrepreneurism. Intrapreneurialism. What you got to watch is the critical mass, and every company has one. Say you have a company with nineteen employees. Runs like clockwork. You hire the twentieth guy, and you exceed the critical mass. So—that's when you know you got to start another company."

He weighed in against the economic gigantism of the North, the decay of social relations in the industrial city, the unreasonable power wielded over the South by Washington and Wall Street. In everything he said there was an echo, strong if distorted, of that old Southern conservative platform on which Allen Tate, Robert Penn Warren and the Fugitives had stood in 1930. It interested me that someone so deeply involved in hi-tech industry should sound so like a contributor to the Agrarian manifesto.

" 'Only a return to the provinces, to the small self-contained centers of life, will lay the all-destroying abstraction America to rest'?" I said.

Kappler squinted at me, suspicious that I was putting him on. His hair was chopped, Roman emperor-style, over his forehead, a Southern classical haircut to match the stepped and columned facade of the building we were sitting in.

"Sounds a little flowery to me, but yes, something like that."

The big difference between Kappler and the Fugitives was that he could see himself riding the contemporary tide, not struggling to swim against it. His belief in the small, controllable, human-sized industry rooted in a correspondingly small local commu-nity was endorsed by the business schools; and the North was littered with megalithic ruins to prove him right. One only had to think of the cities of the Rustbelt, the Daytons, Akrons, Spring-fields, Peorias, looking like the burned-out insides of old radio sets, their valves blown and condensers locked solid, to warm to Kappler's idea that Guntersville was the coming thing.

"You know, this country is getting to be a whole lot less mobile than it was. People want to stay where they were raised. You look for the community first and take industry to it, not the other way around."

After lunch, he took me upstairs to his HQ. A Confederate flag and a cavalry sword were hung over his desk. In the boardroom an imperial portrait showed Kappler, apparently barely out of his teens, gazing confidently ahead at the financial heights that still remained for him to conquer. In the passage, he stopped beside a florid oil painting of a marine battle.

"This means something special to me."

Blobs of red paint on the ships' gunwales were cannons in action. The gray smoke of the engagement was joined to the darker gray of the storm clouds overhead. It was a boys' painting, all rigging and adventure. It was a cut above the works of Burton, the John Copley of Macy's, but it belonged to the same 1980s school. Varnish, laid on thick and fast, was responsible for its appearance of rosy antiquity. It was already beginning to look as cracky as an unrestored Van der Velde. It rendered history as "heritage"—a harmless confection of noble deeds and quaint technology. *Those were the days,* it said; those were *our* days.

"You ever hear of the *Alabama?*"

The CSS *Alabama,* Kappler explained, had been the most famous rebel cruiser in the Civil War. Under Captain Raphael Semmes, she had destroyed or captured sixty-four Union merchant ships before she was sunk off Cherbourg by the USS *Kearsarge* in 1864. In the painting, she was breaking through a Union blockade. Her two Yankee pursuers were under sail alone; she was outflanking them with a combination of full sail and steam.

Kappler prodded at the *Alabama*'s funnel with his forefinger. "See? *Innovation.* Southern innovation."

It looked to me as if things were all the wrong way round. Could the industrial North really come up only with obsolescent sailing ships, while the agrarian South raced ahead with its new machinery? Steam wasn't even new; there had been screw-propeller steamships in service for at least twenty years before the Civil War (Brunel's *Great Britain,* the transatlantic liner, was launched in 1843). What the painting enshrined, or so it seemed to me, was a fond lie about the 1860s—a lie which had become a believable truth, at long last, in the late twentieth century. The painting showed a small, nippy, Southern industry, like Kappler Inc., or Comptronix, showing a clean pair of heels to the Rustbelt; and, if your historical memory was shaky, it told you that things had ever been thus. "Yankee know-how" was a flash in the pan; Southern know-how was bred in the bone.

Kappler was politely impatient with my *ifs* and *buts.* He was treating me to the guided tour that he always gave his clients. We were in a realm of rhetoric and mythology in which actual history was a mere pollutant. He waved at a passing secretary. "She runs things around here. She's my boss. She makes out my paycheck; she tells me where I have to be every day." *You see? I'm not spoiled. I'm still the country boy from nine miles south of Vicksburg.*

Nor was this just a contrived mask. All through our lunch, I had been reminded of another businessman, Edward Finkelstein of Macy's. Finkelstein had seen himself as a general in his bunker, planning "strategy," far removed from "the people down in the trenches." Kappler's metaphor for himself was no less martial, but it was cast in a fundamentally different style. He was at the wheel of a ship, close to his men, in the thick of the battle. He would outwit the bigshots with his charm and dash. It was a good metaphor. It set the tight ship against the great, topheavy corporation, province against city, New South against Old North.

It also said something more subtle, about the changed meaning of the Civil War for Southerners of Kappler's generation. For one hundred years, the defeat of the Confederacy had been a lingering humiliation. The South went on defiantly flying its own flag (every morning, the Stars and Bars was hauled up alongside the Stars and Stripes over the statehouse in Montgomery, despite regular black demonstrations against the practice); but the values the flag stood for were anachronistic ones—romantic gallantry, outmoded piety, regional patriotism, the hard-boiled conservatism of the briar patch.

These reactionary attitudes ran so counter to the prevailing current of America that in time they came to seem picturesque, part and parcel of the antebellum home/hominy grits/historical marker/*you-all*/down home/Heart of Dixie version of the tourist South. To see the Confederate flag—symbol of the South's broken nationhood—flying was kind of cute; no more.

Then something happened. It was hard to put a date on exactly when it happened. Barry Goldwater's presidential campaign in 1964 ("In your heart you know he's right") was a premonitory symptom of it. When George Wallace, running as a third-party candidate in 1968, took four million votes, it was clearly under way; and Wallace's support outside the South, among industrial workers in big Northern cities, might be seen as more interesting, more of a true victory, than the election that year of Richard Nixon. In the campaigns of 1976 and 1980, and the presidencies of Jimmy Carter and Ronald Reagan, it was clear that the something—a great shift of national feeling—had taken place.

Wallace, Carter, Reagan? Their parties, their natural constituencies, their policies on race, social welfare, public expenditure were as different as could be; but there was a deep kinship of style and temperament between the three. They each proclaimed themselves against "big government." They tried to make their assaults on Washington look as much as possible like the coming of James Stewart as Mr. Smith in the Frank Capra movie. How they loved their hometowns! Plains, Georgia, and Dixon, Illinois, were not the boondocks or the sticks—places from which any smart adolescent would escape at the first possible opportunity; they were the nurseries of Civilization and Community, of that lost order in American life which might, even yet, be restored by a good-hearted hometown body. How they loved Jesus!—and loved Him on first-name terms, in a public way that would have struck earlier generations as tasteless and embarrassing. The Church of the Disciples, in which Reagan grew up, was an exact Northern equivalent to a Southern Baptist congregation: Calvinist in its inspiration, fervently dry, much given to dramatic "revivals" and baptisms by total immersion in the local canal.

In each campaign, the divine plan for America was seen through a glass, and darkly. Jesus had foreordained racial segregation; He had foreordained racial equality. He made manifest His approval for, variously, the free market economy, the welfare state, détente and a holy war against the great anti-Christ, Russia. The candidates weren't offering to make any bold intervention in American affairs (as presidents from FDR to Johnson had done); they merely saw God's intentions more clearly than their rivals, and they submitted themselves to the people as humble instruments of His will. In this theological context, Jimmy Carter's liberal vision of American society was as deeply conservative as the bigotry peddled by George Wallace. (It was Carter's great bad luck that his religious beliefs went so deep as actually to make him humble, and true humility has only been tolerated in American statesmen when practiced on the heroic scale that Benjamin Franklin famously prescribed for himself, *Humility: imitate Jesus Christ and Socrates.*)

If one was looking for a geographical capital in which these attitudes were centered, it would be in the Calvinist South. It would not be a city like Atlanta or Memphis, but a small town, bigger than Plains, smaller than Dixon. It would be a town like Guntersville. And if one wanted a flag to hoist over them, the Stars and Bars of Jefferson Davis ("We are not revolutionists—we are conservatives") and the Confederacy was the flag of godliness, honor, resistance to change, hearth and home—values that were riding higher in the 1980s than at any time since the Civil War.

Southerners had good reason to feel smug at the unlikely turn taken by the nation toward the end of a predominantly liberal, secular and Northern century. I tried to imagine what it might be like to be George Kappler: to be born in rural Mississippi in the 1940s, to go through a segregated school system, to see one's home territory identified on TV and in the national press with everything in American society that was regressive, poor, stupid, cruel and out-of-date—and then to look out, in one's own forties, to a world in which small-town conservatism, Southern religion, all the forces that had once conspired to make one feel irremediably provincial, were now held up as examples of the best that America had to offer. No wonder he seemed so chipper. As his favorite painting put it, the CSS *Alabama* was steaming safely home through the blockade.

I turned right at Kentucky Fried Chicken, parked the car on Rayburn Street, and let Gypsy out to pursue her lumbering, nose-to-the-ground researches on the Hill. The name of this part of town had gone through several uneasy mutations. First, it had been known to whites as Nigger Hill. Then, in the 1960s, it became Colored Hill. In the 1970s it was rechristened Church Hill, on the feeble but well-meaning pretense that its handful of peeling clapboard chapels were its most noticeable feature. Calling it *The* Hill was a misnomer too, since it was only the southernmost of the four distinct hills that formed the Guntersville peninsula.

What I noticed first was not its negritude but its prettiness. Its narrow streets twisted and turned along their contour lines like European country lanes. Where gardens in the white quarters of town were kept mown, pruned, chopped and weeded to within an inch of their lives, gardens here ran wild, in thick tangles of greenery and drifts of blossom. Lapped in honeysuckle and dogwood, the cabins of the Hill people, with their bleached timbers, open doors and shady porches, might have figured in a Ralph Lauren catalog as every urbanite's dream of the delights of the country cottage.

The picture would need some cropping. You'd have to remove the ten-year-old tan Datsun from outside the gate, also the rusting cylinder block from the center of the lawn. You would airbrush out the intruding top corner of the neighbors' house, a trailer propped up on piles of bricks. You would make the most of the bluebird, the straggling wild rose, the antique rocker, its back spread with a lace antimacassar.

The rocker's occupant lowered her *Gleam* to watch me go by. I nodded to her and was met with a stare of mild but firm interrogation: was I a Welfare snooper? A loan shark? A bail bondsman? The entry of Gypsy, with her broad sycophantic grin, only compounded the puzzle. Though the Hill was only a hundred yards away from Gunter Avenue, it was a world set apart from the rest of the town. The sight of a white man walking his dog here was a radical disturbance of the Guntersville order of things.

From every porch we passed came the same stare. I would have liked to have stopped and talked with people, but their baffled expressions deterred me. The afternoon hush was heavy in the air, and my footsteps sounded loud, too loud, on the sidewalk. It is a good thing for whites to be made to feel their own skin color as a brand; in the green and peaceful suburb of the Hill, I felt my whiteness more keenly than I'd felt it when I'd strayed from the East River Drive into a housing project in the war-torn hundred-and-thirties.

According to the chamber of commerce figures (which were almost as old as the tan Datsun), 1,244 people, nearly eighteen percent of the town's population, had incomes that were "below Poverty." The Hill was below Poverty. Yet what the Hill represented was not Poverty as a threat to public order, or a scar on the good conscience of the community, but Poverty as something useful—an asset to be included in the prospectus sent out to businessmen who were thinking of setting up shop in the town. You could look at the pleasant streets of the Hill, and see there a convenient labor pool of potential maids, janitors and odd-job men.

Gypsy was taking a pee on a patch of grass outside the African Methodist Church, her head tilted to the sky in prim disdain at the functions of her netherparts. From behind a tousled hedge there stalked a light-heavyweight black chow. The chow stared at Gypsy; Gypsy rolled her eyes blamefully back at me—*look what you got me into now!* The chow lowered its head, bared its teeth, shook its mane of dreadlocks. It was a Rasta dog. It strolled up to Gypsy with the casual sure-footedness of an accredited street king. Locking her eyeball to eyeball, it let out a long snarl of warning.

You better get your ass outa here, and fast, *scumbag!*

In a second, my guard dog had positioned herself behind my legs. Her answering growl was a whimper. I snapped her lead onto her collar, and did what I could to appease the sneering chow.

"All right . . . Okay! Okay!"

The chow made a feint of going for Gypsy's throat, glowered at my ankles, sized us both up for the kill. My skull was sweating badly as I backed off and marched my dog toward the car, with the chow swirling round us in a continuous black circle of abuse.

Muh-fuh! Shithead! Corksacker! Fruit picker! Meatball! Fade!

My legs kept on getting tangled up with the lead as Gypsy dodged from left to right, trying to get out of the way of this flying bomb of hair, teeth and vocal cords.

Twat! Booger! Marshmallow! Honey bucket!

"Okay! *Okay!*"

I bundled Gypsy into the Spirit, scrambled in beside her, and slammed the door in our persecutor's face. The moment she hit the passenger seat, Gypsy's blood suddenly ran red again. She began to bark back, on a note of fierce wounded pride. The chow planted its forepaws on the door and reared at us against the window—a blazing, frizzy hairdo enclosing a pair of close-set, piggy eyes and a furious mouth. I inched the car backward, scared of catching the chow under the wheels. It would make a hell of a headline in the *Gleam:* Rubberneck Slays Dog on Hill.

The chow followed us for a few yards, then turned and ambled back toward the church. It had the air of rubbing its hands over a job well done, while my feeble companion, gorged on prime beef, sat beside me growling in a fit of bold *esprit d'escalier.*

When night fell on Polecat Hollow it revealed a dozen small illuminated theaters strung out along the waterside. On each raised and pillared porch, an exemplary life was put on show, an advertisement for serene and civilized domesticity. If people hereabouts had screaming marital rows, cuffed their kids around the ears, or hit the bottle, they took good care not to do it on the porch. In the art-movie soft focus of the screens, they mounted decorous conversation pieces; and always the onlooker's eye was drawn to the object in the center of the frame, the rocker.

The rocker was to Guntersville what the elevator was to New York: the fundament of social life. It was a mark of honor to usher the senior guest to sit in the rocker where, easing himself back, tinkling the musical ice in his glass, he could begin his sentences with *Nowadays . . .* and *I remember when . . .* and *I was just reading in the paper . . .* The rocker was the great fount of reactionary wisdom. The rocker harbored a deep mistrust of the modern world, was skeptical of strangers and gravely memorious. In houses crammed with VCRs, freezers, CD players, cordless phones, computer games and all the rest, the plain wooden rocker (preferably granpappy's rocker) was a testament to the idea of the sound, unfickle Southern heart.

At the Rayburn place, the rocker was not much of a rocker. It was a slatted bench, suspended from a beam by two creaky chains. It was, to be frank, only a porch swing. But it served. Swinging gently, turning the pages of the *Gleam,* my dog sleeping at my feet, I found it easy to drift into that crusty, Guntersvillian state of mind in which almost anything that happened beyond the local scuttlebutt was to be either ignored completely or chawed over with incredulity and disapproval.

I had pretty much given up on watching TV. In New York, one scanned the screen to see what was happening in the street outside; here, the pictures were of a world so remote from Polecat Hollow that they were a mere flickering irrelevance. For one thing, the weather was all wrong. Reporters in Washington (where House Speaker Jim Wright was fighting an unseemly battle to stay in office) were seen to be still in the early spring of the year, where Guntersville was blossoming into high summer. They looked weeks out of date, as if CNN had been digging out footage from the archives. In New York, a jogger in Central Park had been gang-raped and beaten unconscious; the park was still in the grip of winter. England was famous for a day, when ninety-five spectators at a football match in Sheffield were crushed to death. The overcast half-light, the pinched and bony faces of the survivors, the Liverpool accents, so foreign to America that they had to be accompanied by subtitles, made my own country look, not weeks or months, but several decades old, grainy, black and white. In the Dime Store Deli bar, I had a hard time trying to explain why the British authorities had to lock up football fans in barred cages, like animals in a slaughterhouse pen. When I admitted that the kids had actually paid to be herded behind the wire like this, the Dime Store Deli crowd wagged their heads in disbelief.

Our news—the news that counted—was of a different order. Nancy Larson (Gypsy had made friends with the Larsons' red setter on the levee) called me to say that Mrs. Bob Hembree, Jr., was expecting her first baby. "They've been wanting a baby for so long, and I am just *so* excited for them . . . I *knew* you'd want to hear the news."

And so I did. I'd never met Mrs. Bob Hembree, Jr., but she sounded a lot more real to me than Speaker Jim Wright, the Central Park jogger or the Hillsborough Stadium disaster.

The big news in the *Gleam* was a story that figured in every issue, about hydrilla weed. It was interesting, too. If you read the *Gleam* right, you could see that nearly every story that it ran was, in a way, about hydrilla weed.

Hydrilla weed was a foreign substance that had come to plague Guntersville within the last couple of years. It was a tough and fecund variety of water weed. It grew in great rafts on the lake, where it interfered with navigation, smelled bad in the hot weather and was a breeding ground for mosquitoes.

It had been introduced, so people said, by bass fishermen visiting Guntersville from Florida and bringing the spoors of the weed to Alabama on the bottoms of their boats. "A lot of folks here have real hard feelings about Florida, since this hydrilla business started up," said one of my bar cronies. He was serious. If you asked him, he said, the state of Florida ought to pay for this. Hell, it was *pollution,* and everybody knew that that damned hydrilla had come up here from Florida. So why was it down to the people of Guntersville to put their hands in their pockets to pay for cleaning up the mess made by them Floridians? Why, it was just the same as if they'd dumped their shit in your back yard. Who was responsible for cleaning the shit up? *Them*—that's who.

The best way of ridding the lake of hydrilla was by releasing large numbers of grass carp to eat it. Fifteen grass carp could clear a weed-infested acre; some hundreds of thousands of grass carp, munching their way through several long summers, would leave Lake Guntersville hydrilla-free. A single grass carp cost between $2.50 and $6.00.

This was serious. The *Gleam*'s front page headlines managed to convey the idea that hydrilla was a disease very much like cancer. TWO RAYS OF HOPE IN THE FIGHT AGAINST HYDRIL-LA, said one.

Congressmen Tom Bevill and Ronnie Flippo are flying here Monday to take a look at the weed problem first-hand. Many think a lasting solution to the problem may require a good bit of federal money. The congressmen will arrive at the Lurleen Drive pavilion by helicopter about 11:30 . . .

There were unexpected reversals of policy (T.V.A. PLANS DRAWDOWN—MORE HERBICIDE, NO CARP) and disappointments (FIRST FOUR THOUSAND CARP WERE STERILE). The last had a significant twist to it:

Save Our Lakes President Leamon Jarman said the group just found out that the first 4,000 they released were the sterile kind, also known as triploids.

"We bought them from a man at Brooksville, who had gotten them from a hatchery in Arkansas," Mr. Jarmon said.

Mr. Jarmon should have known that you do not use Arkansas grass carp to eat Florida weed in Alabama. So the next big occasion, pictured in the *Gleam*, was the tipping of a further two thousand grass carp into the lake. These were native Alabamian fish. They "came from American Sports Fish, which grew the fish in their hatchery in Montgomery."

It was not the weed itself that interested me, so much as the language in which the fight against the weed was couched. Hydrilla was described in the same terms that Guntersville applied to cocaine (the police department's new sniffer-dog was the grass carp of the drug world) and to crime (which came to the town, or so the town liked to claim, "from the cities," meaning Birmingham and Huntsville). Sitting in your rocker on a quiet evening, you could feel that you lived in a community beleaguered by aliens. The wagon train was drawn up in a circle; armed vigilantes were staring out into the darkness, waiting and watching. You had to be perpetually on your guard. The aliens were out there, plotting. If there was a chink in your defenses, the aliens would find it.

Alien ideas were the worst. Their spoors, like the spoors of the hydrilla weed, were so small as to be invisible; but if you allowed them once to take root, they could destroy a whole town.

Chain-smoking, fast-talking, wheezy Dot, whom I'd met one day in the public library, had run into trouble for importing an alien idea. She was a dabbler in the liberal arts, with half a degree from a college in Virginia. For a while she'd taught at Guntersville High School, but had been reported by her pupils for "teaching Evolution."

"Oh, they raised *hayull!* And all I was saying was that this was what *some* people believed, and how there was two sides to the argument. I never did say Evolution was the truth. Though it *is* the truth. I know it."

"Do you really mean they still teach Creationism here?" I said.

"Oh—no, they don't teach Creationism, neither. The thing you better learn about people in Guntersville is they don't like to go to extremes. Me, well, they thought I was *extreme.*"

"If they don't teach Darwinism and don't teach Creationism, what do they teach? The Big Bang?"

"They've worked out their own kinda middle way, you understand."

A day or two later, I met Les Click, the high school principal, a big, genial young man, with a face full of laughter lines and outsize teeth. He was no bigot, and I guessed that Dot's run-in with the authorities must have happened years before his time.

I asked him if he had problems with the censorship of school textbooks.

"It's a funny thing. You'd expect people here to be hot on *race.* But that's not the issue. Well . . . we did have a brush with it, a year or two back . . . some parents from the Hill complained about *Huckleberry Finn* and 'Nigger Jim.' But that wasn't mostly about the book. That was mostly about the teacher. She came from Arab," he said, as if this was sufficient explanation.

"Oh?"

"Arab people have a reputation for being prejudiced."

Arab was a town ten miles west of Guntersville. Later I was told that until recently a sign had been posted at the Arab city limits which read, "NIGGER—YOU LET THE SUN SET ON YOUR ASS IN THIS TOWN, AND YOU'RE A DEAD MAN."

"It didn't amount to much. We took the book out of the class that year, put it back the next. Nobody complained since. No, what we have to look out for here, it's not race, it's Women's Lib."

"You mean there's a strong feminist lobby?" I was pleased and surprised by this breath of unexpected radicalism.

"Oh, *no!*" Les Click roared with high humor at the thought of such a thing. "No, it's the other way around. You know about the Eagle Forum? That's a women's group, kind of like the DAR. But fiercer. They keep a kind of an eagle eye on every book that goes into school. Like, you bring in a book with a picture of a man in an apron washing the dishes . . . boy, you're in trouble there. Or a woman in a business suit, driving to work in a car . . . hoo!" He sucked his breath noisily in between his teeth to indicate the heat of the water in which a hapless high school principal could land if he dared to cross the Eagle Forum.

Feminism, hydrilla weed, drugs, Darwinism, crime . . . they were *out there,* like so many water moccasins, rattlesnakes, vultures, coyotes and all the other creatures of that jungle from which the small civilization of Guntersville had originally been hacked out. The town saw it as its business to keep them out, to hold them off at gunpoint, cut them down wherever they showed their ugly heads, bring in dogs, grass carp, censors to harry them in their holes.

This siege mentality had powerful roots. There was the wildness of the surrounding nature, always threatening to encroach on your hard-won domestic territory. There were dozens of specific local images, from the river marauding through the farms on the bottomlands to the fire ants killing William Benefield's friend in his back yard, that gave substance to people's fear of what lay *out there.* There was also the fact, in this town with an unusually long memory, that it had been besieged, in January 1865, when the USS gunboat *General Thomas* had landed a crew of marines who set the town alight. Guntersville, described in a Union memorandum as "that nest of treason and rendezvous of guerrillas and bushwhackers," was efficiently burned down. Only seven buildings survived intact. The rest of the town was a heap of smoldering timber and rubble.

That was the story that granpappy had told from his rocker. So it was not surprising that Guntersville people had got into the habit of reaching for their guns, or for their red pencils, at the first rustle of the alien in the woods. *You want protection, you better get yourself a gun . . .* Or, as Bill Perryman, commodore of the Guntersville yacht club, said, "Remember—we're a long way south of the Smith and Wesson Line down here."

It began as justifiable small-town pride, the decent desire to look after your own. But it could tip over, and quite often did, into small-town xenophobia of the most paranoid and brutal kind.

Beside my typewriter as I work now is a Xeroxed copy of a cracked eight by ten photograph. It was given to me in Guntersville by someone who said, "I thought you might just be interested in this." It has held my interest ever since. It was taken at night, on a creek, perhaps Polecat Creek. A blaze of light somewhere behind the photographer turns the water to silver and dramatically illuminates the event on the far bank—a mass rally of the Ku Klux Klan. In their sheet-and-pillowcase gear, the Klansmen form a band of solid white across the center of the picture. Ranked four and five deep, as if for an end-of-term school photo, they are too many to count accurately. I calculate that there are about 320 men in the shot, with more out of sight of the camera.

The Grand Wizard, seated in the middle, is in black. American flags are being waved from within the ranks. The light source must be either a bonfire or a gigantic burning cross. The photograph is inscribed, "Guntersville, Alabama, September 7th, 1925."

The Klan started up on Christmas Eve 1865, in Pulaski, Tennessee. They took their name from κυκλος, Greek for circle, plus a cod-Germanic spelling of clan, thereby combining the Old South's twin obsessions, with Ancient Greece and with their Saxon heritage. They stated that "Our main and fundamental objective is the MAINTENANCE OF THE SUPREMACY OF THE WHITE RACE." Their nightriders, patrolling the countryside in white robes, were meant to frighten black freed men into believing that the Klansmen were the avenging spirits of the Confederate dead, returned from the grave to reclaim their lands.

In the 1880s, the Klan petered out. It was revived in Georgia in 1915 with a new brief. This time it was as hostile to Catholics and Jews as it was to blacks. It rampaged through the 1920s, reaching a climax at about the time of the Guntersville rally. Then, for a while, it sank out of public sight. Its most conspicuous revival was in the 1960s, when the Klan headquarters had shifted to Tuscaloosa, 110 miles southwest of Guntersville.

Gail, a woman of my age, said, "Oh, I remember the Klan. When I was a kid. Some nights you'd wake out of your sleep and hear the screams. When they were giving a man a beating. I'd look out my window, and I'd see it . . . the, you know, like the fiery cross burning there? And hear the nigra screaming? It was terrible. I'd have nightmares . . .

"And then, we'd go play hide-and-seek in each other's homes. You'd be It, hiding there in a closet, in a strange house? I'd be crouched down there, with all the clothes and stuff on hangers? And as you got used to the dark, you'd see, like a dress . . . hanging in with all these men's clothes? That was his Klan robe. They was in so many people's closets . . . That was so spooky!"

This must have been in the 1940s or early '50s. I said, "I wonder how many kids now, when they play hide-and-seek, find themselves snuggling up to Klansmen's robes?"

In the excitement of telling her story, Gail had forgotten she was talking to a stranger. Now she remembered. Her face clouded, shut on me like a door.

"Oh, I wouldn't know. No, I wouldn't know nothing about that. At all."

Sunday morning: and in the airy temple of the First Baptist Church, I felt a sinner. I had a hangover from drinking too long and too deeply aboard Bill Perryman's fifty-six-foot motor cruiser the night before, and every time I raised my eyes to look around, I had to wince. The electric pastels favored by the Guntersville Baptists for morning service would have been hard to bear at the best of times. Women went in for crisp white perms, men for golf jackets of terrible laundered brightness. I made a note to buy a pair of dark glasses at the drugstore before I next went church-going.

The organist seated at the Yamaha was idly wandering from one cloying, holy chord to the next, vamping for Jesus. I made a solemn pretense of studying the church accounts for March, which had been handed to me along with the order of service.

The First Baptist was a medium-sized business by Guntersville standards. Its annual budget was for $550,000. Turnover in March, at only $30,000, had evidently been slow. The bass fishing season probably had something to do with it; but even on this brilliant—too brilliant for me—morning, there were more than 150 people in the pews, and the First Baptist was only one out of 19 churches in the town. Total expenditure on religion must run into the millions here. I tried to guess it. Say, $2.6 million . . . that'd be . . . close to $400 a year for every man, woman and child in Guntersville, which sounded about right for a region of the country where Christianity was still a growth industry.

Certainly the First Baptist looked in good financial shape. Its front end was a half timbered Tudor theater, full of microphones for the star performers, several portable organs, a Moog synthesizer, banks of fresh-cut flowers.

Everybody was standing up. I stood up, several seconds late, and tried to cover my tracks by joining enthusiastically in the hymn.

"I was sinking deep in sin, far from the peaceful shore, very deeply stained within, sinking to rise no more . . ." The tune was jollier than the words. But my voice came out as an unnatural double-bass—a voice stewed in a mixture of Jack Daniels and pipe tobacco.

The pastor, a bank vice-presidential type, in bow tie and gold specs, announced the fun events for next week. I decided to skip the hamburger cookout, along with the softball championship and the recital by the youth handbell choir.

I let the service roll along over my head; but I was having Sunday thoughts, about theology, and the reason why this kind of bland, well-heeled Calvinism had taken such a strong hold on the imagination of the South. Calvin's European followers, with their strictness, their detestation of ornament and show, would have been shocked by the flashy style in which the Southern Baptists conducted their affairs. So much melodrama! So much soupy music! So much blatant salesman's insincerity! It was all so un-Calvinistic.

The pastor had started his sermon. His theme for this week was the Bible itself, the Word of God. There was no discernible argument in what he was saying. Rather, he was delivering himself of a series of ten-second sound bites. He had a product, a good product, and he was selling it, just like he was on TV.

"How'd they get it all together? One author. The Holy Spirit. That's how!"

There was in Calvinism one doctrine that the South needed for its own secular purposes. When Southerners cast around trying to find some intellectual justification for the peculiar institution of slavery, they lit on predestination. If the world-as-is existed by His will, everything in it was intended.

"You got poetry! You got songs! You got history! You got *origins!*"

If there were slaves in it, then God must surely intend that there should be slaves, just as He intended that there should be male and female, or that there should be a serpent in the garden. Slavery was not a creation of man's; it was a creation of God's. To meddle in it was vainly to attempt to deny His will.

"It's always timely. Because it's timeless. That's why!"

So the Confederacy embraced predestination as a political necessity. In this skew-whiff version of Calvin's teaching, the slaveowner became the custodian of the Divine Will. He was a "conservative" because he was defending God's own intended Order against the blasphemous depredations of the godless armies of the North.

"Reach out and be a blessing, in His precious name!"

We ask only to be let alone had been Jefferson Davis's final declaration on the eve of war. There was no need to mount a rational defense of the slaveocracy. That it existed was sufficient proof that it was good. Let it alone! If you could bring yourself to swallow the theology of this position, just hypothetically and for a moment, you could begin to feel in yourself that moving spirit of righteous indignation which took the South into the Civil War.

"Friend! I'd like you to spend at least as much time with the Bible every day as you do with your daily newspaper. The *Wall Street Journal*. Or whatever. Because, Friend, if you haven't got time for God, if you're too busy . . ." The pastor was glowering at me through his specs. He'd got to the hellfire stage, and was looking for a suitable sinner on whom to vent his wrath. I could see that I was the prime candidate for the job. I let it ride over me.

The South had needed Calvin, but it had never really been in tune with Calvinism. It was too much in love with decorative ritual, with Greek columns and the novels of Sir Walter Scott. So it had created this strange crossbred religion in which Calvin's severe doctrine of predestination went hand in hand with a great paraphernalia of indulgently fancy stuff: splendid robes for the choir, lush orchestrations, colored glass, and the extravagant, artificial language of Madison Avenue.

Listening to the preacher's words breaking on my head, I thought of Jonathan Edwards and that other, Northern tradition of American fundamentalism. *The God that holds you over the pit of hell, much as one holds a spider, or some loathsome insect over the fire, abhors you, and is dreadfully provoked: his wrath towards you burns like fire; he looks upon you as worthy of nothing else, but to be cast into the fire . . .* That was real and came from the heart. Edwards, preaching in Northampton, Mass., in 1741, would have reduced me to mortal terror. But Southern Baptism . . . I looked the First Baptist pastor in the eye, and thought, *I bet you don't know why you believe in predestination, but I do, Friend.*

I was first out of church and down the steps before the Baptists could get at me. Crossing the street, I saw a forlorn-looking figure in a black cassock coming out of the Catholic church on the other side. I went up to him and remarked that a Catholic priest in Alabama must have a pretty hard row to hoe.

He laughed, gauntly. "Oh, ain't so bad," he said, "ain't so bad." He was from a long way out of state; his voice had the dry, granular sound of the Northwest in it. Since he seemed pleased to talk, I fell in step beside him. "I'm a Benedictine," he said. "I'm just the visiting fireman here." He came from an order based somewhere up in Tennessee.

There were around two hundred fifty Catholics living in and around Guntersville. "Most of 'em are foreigners like me. They're down here from places like Milwaukee and St Louis. I'm just getting to know 'em. Nice people. It's been one hell of a blow for them to take . . . Father Craven dying like that." He shook his head. "Everybody's in a state of shock over him getting killed."

"Killed?"

"You don't know? Yeah. He was murdered. Just a coupla months ago. Over in Tuscaloosa."

Tuscaloosa.

"Pig valves!" said Katherine Duncan; "that's what they're keeping me running on now—pig valves!" She pointed at her heart. "I got a pacemaker in there, too. But, praise God, I've been healthful all my life. My doctor now, he's just a boy, know what he said to me last week? This *boy,* he says, 'Oh, Mizz Duncan, but you are just a *tough* old chicken!' And I guess he's right. That's what I am. A tough . . . old . . . chicken."

At eighty-four, Mizz Duncan was the Guntersville town memory. She'd long outlived her husband and her only son. The living room in her bungalow on Big Spring Creek was a bright modern box, filled to bursting-point with family heirlooms: a spindly whatnot, its shelves laden with whimsical Victorian china figurines; a gothic brass candlestick; needlepoint cushions; a cornucopia of fruits cast in black bronze; old oil lamps converted to electricity; enough high-backed, overstuffed armchairs to seat a full meeting of the Daughters of the American Revolution. Mizz Duncan sat, ramrod straight, on the stool in front of her harmonium, with "Liebestraum" on the music stand. A side-table held a silver tray with a sherry decanter and a single glass.

I was looking at two Mizz Duncans. One was the tough old chicken, in her acrylic slacks and pink tank top; the other was seated immediately behind her, framed in gilt, lavishly varnished and fifty years younger. The painted Mizz Duncan was a striking beauty in billowy, off-the-shoulder, marigold chiffon. The artistry of the picture was flat and amateur, but it captured the sitter's headstrong eyes, the frank and determined set of her rouged lips. The young woman, a honey blonde, gazed out over the blue rinse of her future self with admirable equanimity, as if she'd long had it in mind to become a tough old chicken.

"This is no fly-by-night town," Mizz Duncan said. "This is an old-moneyed town. We go back."

She went back further than anyone now alive. Three of her four grandparents had been living in Guntersville before the Civil War. They were almost here with us in the room. Why, "Daddy Jim," her maternal grandfather, Jim McKinstry, he'd been badly wounded in the War between the States; shot in the thigh and in both shoulders, and Mizz Duncan still had his pants and vest with the bullet holes in 'em, to prove it. Daddy Jim had recovered, gone on to be a civil engineer and Guntersville's first real-estate agent (so much for Ed Neely's claims in this department), and died in 1922, when Katherine Duncan was in her late teens. So, as a clever young adult, she had talked with officers in Jefferson Davis's army, with survivors of the Guntersville firestorm in 1865, with freed slaves. She had been brought up in the gossip and the mores of the antebellum South.

"I was raised old-fashioned. Like my grandma used to tell me? 'Always do, and always say, the nicest thing in the kindest way'? I was just a little wild, though. Why—I used to talk to the McWhirter girls . . . "

I quizzed the young Katherine over the old Mizz Duncan's head.

"The McWhirter girls? They were our ladies of the night. Lived at McWhirter Hollow, by the old steamboat landing . . . Some of 'em were McWhirters, some of 'em had other names, but we used to call them the McWhirter girls, and I knew every one of them. My mother used to say I was a scandal. To be seen talking to the McWhirter girls!"

"There was a lot of that round here, was there?"

"Cathouses? Oh, yes. The McWhirters had it about all sewn up here in Guntersville, but Decatur was *famous* for it!"

Katherine Duncan taught high school ("I look at those old men running the town now, and they're just the boys in my class, to me"); for years she wrote the weekly "Chatter" column in the *Gleam;* in her sixties she took to teaching children suffering from autism. On pig valves and pacemaker, she was still burning brightly, a fervent woman, all spark and vehemence.

I asked her about the time the lake came up.

"We were so arrogant in Guntersville—we just thought we were ruined! When we lost our farm economy to the TVA . . . we didn't think much of this newfangled water economy. All we could see was fishin' and boatin'. You take the Henry family; now they had sixteen miles of good bottomland on the water. Old Mr. Henry, he had his blacks, he had his own boat to take his cotton to Liverpool . . . Well, for him it just was tragedy. And all the small farmers . . . When the TVA came along, they went into their shells. They wouldn't sell up. They sued the government. Why, the federal government had to establish a big law office in town, to handle all the lawsuits against them. They were being sued on every side. Some of the farmers took the compensation and lit out for Tennessee; others of 'em, well, they just took to the bottle and turned their heads to the wall. It was only some of the young ones could see the advantage in it. The rest—they thought it was a *ruination."*

She chuckled over the sharecroppers' shortsightedness. "But ain't it turned out fine! There was a whole lot more in the water economy than any of us could see at the time. But in nineteen and thirty, oh, it was weeping! It was gnashing of teeth! It was just the end of the world!"

"I suppose it must have put a lot of blacks out of work, too, when the lake came up?" I said.

"Yes, we lost a lot of our Negroes then."

"And you felt it as—a loss?"

"Oh, but our Negroes in Guntersville, they were *outstanding*. I don't know why that is. They evidently came from a better part of Africa . . . that's the only way I can explain it. They were more like the kind of Negro you got over in England, I believe. You don't have a Negro problem in England?"

"Not exactly. Not quite in those terms. But—"

"That's because you got in there first," Mizz Duncan said. "You've been able to get the very choice ones of the crop.

"Here in Alabama, what we got mostly was what I call the Gold Coast corn-field nigra. You know—with that flat nose and the thick lips? And from what I read . . ." —she shook her head—"that man has always been a slave. Over there, he is a slave today, to the other blacks.

"One thing I've never been able to work out is where our Guntersville blacks came from. John Gunter, he left fifty slaves in his will, to his children. But where he got 'em, that's a mystery to me. Then Judge Wyeth—now, he did not *believe* in slavery. He had a *very* few, only about sixteen or twenty, something like that."

Though she was talking in contradictions, her tone was perfectly even.

"Don't mistake me," she said. "I know that a black person is just as good in the sight of God as I am. I know that. And segregation—in the buses and restaurants—I have no patience with it. Never did."

"So you were for the Civil Rights movement?" I said.

Mizz Duncan stared at me for a moment. I was being a dull student.

"Oh, *no!* Those people, they had just no understanding of the deep-bedded love of the Southerner for the Negro. There was such mutual love . . . The way I was raised, it was my job to *see* to that nigra. I loved him, and he loved me. That was the way it was between the whites and the nigras, there was trust, there was responsibility, there was love there, real love. And Civil Rights . . . they destroyed that. Now—oh, it's so unhappy. Where there was love, now there's just bitterness. The nigras and the whites now, they're living together in a state of armed truce. That's how bad it is."

"But—"

"We were created *different*. For instance. When I go to my church, I want to sit quiet and listen to the preacher. That's in my nature. When the nigra goes to church, he wants to take part. He wants to clap and holler—that's *his* nature. And that's his right, and I respect it.

"A while ago, in my church, that's the First Baptist, they invited some Negro families from the Hill to join with us. We welcomed them. We did all we could to make them feel at home. But their ways were not our ways. They were not *happy* there. It didn't work out: after just a few Sundays, they went back to their own church where they could worship in the way that was in their nature.

"That's why I will not tolerate to see a black boy walking the street with a white girl; that is a thing I *hate* to see. That boy and that girl, they are going against their own natures. And I have seen those poor children . . . They are the most misfortunate children on this earth. No one will have anything to do with them, black or white either; it makes me just so sad."

Listening to Mizz Duncan, I heard so many different voices in each sentence that it was like attending a crowded seminar on race relations in the South. She contained multitudes. The voice of Daddy Jim was in there; so was the voice of the corrupted Calvinist preacher, banging on about foreordination; so was the voice of Katherine Duncan's own instinctive liberality and independence of mind. She was kindly, intelligent, fair—and trapped in the language into which she had been born.

This language was a maze of mirrors and dead ends. The people of the Hill were *nigras*—no, *Negroes*—no they weren't, they were *blacks;* but somehow, whatever you said, it always came out sounding wrong. Reason told you that segregation on a bus was just plain silly; but Religion told you that segregation in a church was sanctioned by "nature." Of course all men were equal in the sight of God; but Civil Rights were wrong. Slavery was wrong, too; and a man could express his disbelief in the institution by owning fewer slaves than his fellows.

As a listener, I could feel Mizz Duncan's difficulty as she tried to talk to me in this peculiar Southern dialect that only a fellow Southerner could be expected to understand. "You were with us in the war," she said; but that was not true, either. The organized industrial working class in Britain had strongly supported the Northern interest; the agricultural landowners, together with the cotton manufacturers, had been on the side of the Confederacy; the government of Lord Palmerston ("Those who in quarrels interpose/Will often get a bloody nose") had sat cautiously on the fence through the hostilities. Yet the myth of a special relationship between the British and the South still survived; and that was why Mizz Duncan was speaking to me as she might not have spoken had I come from Boston or New York.

"I will *not* celebrate the birthday of Martin Luther King!" she said. "When they put that bill through Congress, oh, it made me mad! That was Jefferson Davis's birthday. They were putting that man over Jefferson Davis. That was a mortal slap in the face for the South!"

I was the only afternoon drinker in the downstairs bar of the Holiday Inn. Chaz the bartender was squinting professionally at the water through the long picture window; when he wasn't tending the bar he worked as a commercial fisherman, laying trotlines for catfish from his aluminum skiff.

"Father . . . Francis . . . Craven," he said slowly. "Yes, everybody liked him. Not just Catholics, but most everybody in town. He was a good man."

"Somebody didn't like him," I said.

"That was a tragedy."

"When did it happen?"

"January. He was meant to be taking an afternoon service. Just never turned up. They waited there in the church for him; thought he'd been caught in the traffic . . . he was coming back from his vacation in Florida. Then, a week later, they found his body, what was left of it, in a remote place outside of Tuscaloosa. He'd been clubbed to death, then they'd bound him to a pair of railroad ties and burned him. Only way they could identify him was by his teeth."

"Why was he in Tuscaloosa?"

"Don't nobody know. He used to work in Tuscaloosa, before he came here to Guntersville, but Tuscaloosa ain't on the route from Florida. They reckon he must have been *lured* there. Lured to his death."

"Was the Klan involved?" *Were the two railroad ties a flaming cross?*

"I don't know about that," Chaz said. Then, "There been *theories*. Nothing definite, though. Ain't no evidence to prove nothing."

"You think there was a Guntersville connection?"

"Maybe. But I don't know nothing about that. Don't nobody know, I reckon."

Silence. Long silence. I could hear the squeak of the cloth on the glass as Chaz wiped an imaginary speck from it.

I said, "How's the fishing?"

"Oh, the fishing . . . that's getting to be pretty good."

"How big do the catfish run round here?"

"The *record*, it stands at 103 pounds, and that's a big catfish, but that ain't nothing to what there *is* down there. There's catfish there that are *big* big; bigger'n you could imagine. Why, when they were putting down the piles for the new bridge, there was a diver working there, he felt the ground move under his feet . . . That was a cat. He saw it with his own eyes. He was scared. He said that cat had a mouth so big it could have swallowed a man alive. And that ain't *doubtful!*"

Even the dog led a secret life.

When I went out to dinner, I usually left her in the cabin, where she seemed happy enough, dozing, watching TV and snacking on her pellets of Canine Maintenance; or so I imagined. An evening of *LA Law*, Johnny Carson and David Letterman would have driven me to the edge of despair, but Gypsy appeared to like it. She was not an intellectually demanding dog.

I came back one night after supper at the Larsons' and was met at the screen door by Gypsy in a state of ecstatic possession—prancing, barking, tail throbbing like a pistonrod.

"Hey!"

She was a dervish. Hurling her elderly bulk from side to side, she capered, panting, at my feet. The cabin looked wrecked. The standing lamp in the living room lay on the floor. Bits of laundry were strewn in heaps in the center of the room. My first thought was that Bri's friends had been round and done the place over.

"Gypsy!"

Towels from the bathroom; dirty shirts from the closet in the bedroom; a pair of trousers from the back of a bedroom chair; a half-eaten sock; my facecloth. The typewriter on which I had been working held a raggedly torn strip of paper; the rest of the page had gone. The dog had gone from room to room, gathering everything of mine she could find and assembling it into a trash pile.

I shook out the trousers. A soggy twist of paper fell out of the folds. I smoothed it flat:

There were the Street People and there were the Air People. Air People levitated like—

"Oh, dog!" I searched for the continuation of the paragraph, but it seemed that Gypsy had swallowed it. The only remaining words on the typewriter were *sociable gulls swooping.*

"What *happened?*"

It had never occurred to me that dogs could be so complicated. How long had it taken her? What did she think she was doing? The whole mess looked as if it had been elaborately planned—the product of many long, solitary evenings, dreaming of love and revenge.

"Gypsy?"

She laid her head between my knees. Her eyes rolled back in their sockets. I stared into them, trying to figure out just what kind of emotional turmoil you could be *in,* if you were a dog. But the eyes gave nothing back, just blank doggy complaisance. It was like looking into the lake, windless at sunset, and trying to guess at the monster catfish forty feet down in the mud.

On the TV screen, Letterman batted a ghostwritten witticism to his bald straight man in the studio band.

"Dog?"

But she'd forgotten. Wading through my tumbled clothes on the floor, she ambled across to the refrigerator and drummed on the door with her tail.

"Man, I'm telling you. That was the damnedest battle I ever did fight in all my life—"

Mayor Bob Hembree knew what he was talking about when it came to battles. Under an upstanding quiff of oiled gray hair, his big, mottled, meaty face had been in the wars. We were lunching at the Glover. I'd asked for a glass of Sauvignon; the mayor had hesitated, then, with some rue, settled on a gallon jug of tap water.

"Trying to lay off the sauce just now," he said. "Well . . . trying to lay off the sauce at lunchtime is more like it." He broke open a pack of Marlboros. The cigarette looked oddly delicate and vulnerable in the mayor's bunched fingers. His gold cufflinks were monogrammed RLH; so was the buckle on his rawhide belt.

The monograms seemed hardly necessary, since no one in Guntersville was likely to forget for a moment who Bob Hembree was. His name was emblazoned in red letters on half the car plates in the town. The signboards for BOB HEMBREE BUICK–CHEV-ROLET were the biggest and boldest in Marshall County. To own an automobile dealership was a big thing in any small town; and the Hembree power base, right up behind the county courthouse, was a big dealership, a real big deal. RLH had commandeered the best commercial site in Guntersville, with land on both sides of Blount Avenue. You could barely squeeze between the new se-dans and pickups that were lodged, shoulder-to-shoulder and nose-to-tail, on the Hembree lot. His service garage was a little larger than the hospital; and its bays were equipped, like operat-ing theaters, with the latest in hi-tech auto-surgical equipment.

His son, Bob Hembree, Jr., now looked after the day-to-day running of the dealership, while RLH sat in his office in city hall, a hundred yards away, and ran the town. He was the Boss Crump of Guntersville, a mayor in the old-fashioned, autocratic American mold.

He had been telling me about some of his battles. In the fifties, he'd smuggled truckfuls of blacks from the Hill down to the courthouse, under cover of darkness, to register them to vote.

"Swore 'em in before Judge Clayton by the dozen . . . then we trucked 'em back up to the Hill again . . ."

"Was that dangerous?"

He sucked on his Marlboro, shrugged, exhaled. "You call a posse of men out there with shotguns dangerous?"

There was the time when "I one-wayed the streets"; that was a good battle. There was the time when "I raised the sales tax to three percent—boy, you haven't lived!" In that battle, RLH had faced a meeting of angry local merchants. "I walked in that room, I'm telling you, man, I was *a-lone*. I couldn't get only one person to shake hands with me?"

The big battle, the damnedest battle he ever did fight, was when "I took the town wet." There were two key dates in the recent history of Guntersville. The first was "when the lake came up"; the second, also liquid, was "when we went wet." That had happened in September 1984, and it was the end—not so much of a battle as of a protracted war, in which RLH had fought the Baptists, the Church of God, the Church of Christ, the bootleggers, the legal liquor merchants over the county line, the Methodists, the Presbyterians, George and Lurleen Wallace, the Assembly of God, the Pentecostalists, and RLH had won.

Since 1920, when the Eighteenth Amendment became law, Guntersville, like most small cities in Alabama, had stayed dry.

"Don't get me mistaken, now," Bob Hembree said, "they *drank*. Even the ministers—they drank. They just liked to keep it locked away in the closet. Didn't want their children to get at it. Didn't want nobody else to drink, but, man, yes, they *drank*."

He was eyeing my wineglass as I tipped it on my lip. It seemed a grave pity to me that this liberating hero should currently be off the sauce, even if it was only at lunchtime.

"They bought the stuff up in New Hope" (which was eighteen

miles up the road to Huntsville) "or they could get it off a bootleg-ger here in Guntersville. We had thirty bootleggers in town, and the city wasn't making a dime out of 'em. Thirty bootleggers, and forty vacant stores. That was how it was."

So, along with the town bosses of Decatur, Florence and Scottsboro, RLH had driven the Local Option bill through the state legislature. The idea was that any city with a population of more than six thousand could take the "local option" and vote itself wet. There had been mass demonstrations by ministers in Montgomery, a tied vote in the House of Representatives, two gubernatorial vetoes. The bill had been thrown out, re-presented, thrown out, re-presented; finally it slipped through, on a majority of one. Then the real battle began, to talk the people of Gunters-ville into taking the option.

The Catholics and Episcopalians backed the mayor; in the rest of the churches, Sunday after Sunday, Bob Hembree was cast as the Devil's disciple.

"They had to preach against it, for publicity. That was their job. Just like I was looking for revenue for the city, they were looking for revenue for the church plate. The way they looked at it, a dollar spent on beer was a dollar lost out of the Sunday collection. So that made 'em preach pretty hot."

I'd had a taste of this hot preaching, in the files of the *Gleam* in the public library. "Which way would Jesus vote if he were a citizen of this city?" inquired the Concerned Citizens of Marshall County. "Just remember, Mr. and Mrs. Voter, when you walk in behind that curtain and vote wet, you have disagreed with God," wrote a Baptist pastor. From Brasher's Chapel:

> *"Wine is a mocker, strong drink is raging: And WHOSOEVER is deceived thereby is not wise."—Proverbs 20:1*
>
> *If you vote yes you oppose the churches, so remember this and VOTE NO!*

From the Open Door Baptist Mission:

> *Let every man hear this statement. If the lower link goes to hell and the upper link does not, if the poor old drunkard goes to hell and the Churchman, who voted for the saloon that made him,*

doesn't go with him, then the drunkard can stand on the black-crested waves of damnation and cry: "Unjust, unjust, unjust," until he tears down the pillars of Heaven.

From the Church of Christ:

Liquor causes trouble, strife, sorrows, woes, pain, deaths and will weaken and cause many to stumble.
   IT IS NOT OF GOD! IT IS OF THE DEVIL!

From T. Euclid Rains of Albertville:

God pity the women and children, who're under the scourge of rum,
And hasten the day when against it, neither heart, voice nor pen shall be dumb.

I thought myself that the Concerned Citizens of Marshall County made a tactical error with their picture of how Guntersville would develop if the wets won:

There will be beer joints, night clubs, dance halls, etc., alias lounges, just like other towns where alcohol is legal. Soon that won't be enough. Then we'll have gambling casinos, bookie joints and houses of ill repute etc. There will be "Exotic Male Dancers" at the Lush Pony Lounge, "Wet Tee-Shirt" contests and "Female Mud-Wrestling" at the Red Dog Saloon.

"Oh, yes," said Bob Hembree; "there was going to be honky-tonks, and hookers, and drunks lying around in the streets . . . maybe that got us a few votes, I don't know."

The most affecting piece of dry propaganda was a poster, which showed up one day on all the roads leading out of town. It showed a car speeding drunkenly away into the distance, leaving behind it the broken body of a small girl, her bicycle a twisted wreck in the gutter. In the immediate foreground was a bottle with a black cross over it and the message "VOTE DRY FOR ME."

"It took me a while, but I traced that one back." It had been paid for by the owner of a big liquor store across the county line, in Kilpatrick. "And that was a *personal* thing for me," Bob Hembree said; "that guy, he's got the *dealership* out there, and I ain't never going to forget it.

"Where did all the church groups get the money for their advertising? It was from the liquor merchants over the line. They were funneling it down to the dries in thousands. Even the bootleggers here, the little guys, they were reaching deep in their pockets to give to the Church of Christ!" He laughed appreciatively. He was a man who clearly thrived on shenanigans.

When it came to the vote, the preachers were routed. One thousand and sixty-three people voted to stay dry; 2,149 voted to go wet. A celebratory ad appeared in the *Gleam:*

FREE ICE COLD BEER. 20 KEGS!

Today, Saturday, September 15

FALL FESTIVAL BBQ

11 A.M. TILL AFTER MIDNIGHT!

1ST LEGAL PARTY SINCE

PROHIBITION!

Four days later, notice was given that a liquor license was being sought to convert the old Church of God building at Blount and Henry into a restaurant and lounge. In the first fifteen days of legal sales, revenue to the city, in taxes and license fees, was $35,070. "The pace may not keep up," said the *Gleam.*

"Going wet was the best thing this town ever did," Bob Hembree said. "It gave people confidence. I drive around now, I don't see any vacant stores. We got three new motels. It helped the economy, no doubt about it—*and* you don't fall over drunks in the street. Everybody said that DUIs'd go up. Hasn't happened. DUIs are down . . ." He beckoned to the waitress. "Hey, get me a glass of that Sauvignon, will ya?"

"So you've run out of battles to fight?" I said.

"You think? No, what I want now . . . I want a *dawg* track."

He'd been . . . doing some thinking . . . said RLH. Lot of revenue in dog tracks. Cities all over America were going in for 'em. He'd got a site picked out. Perfect site for it. Bring in a whole lot of tourist dollars.

"What on earth do the townspeople think?" I said.

"*Wayull* . . . they're kinda . . . *afraid* of it," Bob Hembree said, limbering up for his damnedest battle yet.

"Hammer's? That was just the grandest place to scratch!" Mizz Duncan had said. What had she scratched for, I asked. "Underwear!" she said. "Sterling silver. Oh, any old thing I could pick up."

It was still a grand place to scratch. I scratched around the bargain basement ("This Table of Adult Clothing Items $3.98"). Upstairs, I kitted myself out in a salmon pink, silk-lined summer jacket ($39.95) and a U. of Alabama baseball cap in crimson.

Its style of what Macy's called "visual merchandising" was the tantalizing heap. You went up to a trestle table and tugged at things that looked interesting. The atmosphere was neighborly. "Hey, John, you look real good!" sang out a passing salesclerk as I stood in front of a tarnished mirror, inspecting Rayburn in his new Guntersville uniform. "How's Gypsy?"

"Oh, she's just *fine?*" I said, finding my voice involuntarily lifting, Southernly, into that question mark at the end of the sentence. I'd noticed my vowels had begun to stretch lately, too. For anyone of a naturally imitative nature, it was impossible not to drift into the Guntersville way of saying things. I'd noticed that people who'd come down from Ohio, Michigan, Minnesota (usually to work in the space industry at Huntsville) nearly all spoke now in distinctly Southern accents. I was pleased that my own voice was taking this southward turn; I was *getting assimilated*, to a degree that I'd never felt assimilated in New York.

Hammer's had been going since 1942, wandering up Gunter Avenue as it got bigger. It was now run by Al Fant, whom everyone called "Mister Fant" in deference to his seniority in the town.

"Mister Fant, he must be a millionaire times over, but you'll still see him first thing every morning outside his store, filling up that Coke machine. He's still got time for every little detail. And that's why he got to where he is."

I found Mister Fant in a dusty cubbyhole at the back of the store. The door was open. He had no secretary to defend him. Bespectacled, clerical suited, seventyish, he was sitting at a battered desk, dealing with a sea of bills and dockets. The ballpoint he was holding looked as if it should have been a quill pen.

He raised his eyes over his halfmoons. "Sir?"

I told him that I'd spent a lot of time in Macy's, New York, but that Hammer's struck me as an infinitely preferable place to scratch.

"Why, thank you, sir. I do sincerely 'preciate that."

How, I asked him, did he manage to keep things so cheap? Hammer's prices belonged to another time zone; they seemed miraculously stuck in about 1972.

"I don't do terms," he said, pronouncing the word *terms* like *drugs.* "They say to me; 30 days . . . three months . . . and I say cash. The moment I take delivery, that's the moment they get their money. They got to know me pretty good by now. There's one price for every other store, and there's another price for Hammer's. Know what the sound of that is? That's cash talking."

It was also—to the letter—the sound of Rowland H. Macy talking, in 1858. I left Mister Fant to shell out his cash on the nail, bought a pair of docksiders ($4.98) and untied Gypsy from the No Parking sign outside the store, where she was mooching caresses from a stranger.

"Oh, hi, John," the stranger said.

"Why, hi?" I said, and tugged the brim of my U. of A. cap politely at her.

These days, Bill Perryman, in lumberjack shirt, jeans and scuffed Nike trainers, dressed out of Hammer's and dined at Burger King. Six months before, he'd been making a quarter of a million a year from his insurance and real-estate business in Birmingham; now he was a boat bum.

"You know what they say?" He was stretched out in an armchair in the bright empty drawing room of his saloon. Water lights from the lake chased each other up and down the paneled walls. Bill Perryman had a skinned and knuckly look; weighing too little for his height, he had the build and nervous quickness of a heron. "Boats, broads and booze. That's me." But the phrase was colored with melancholy irony. He crumpled the empty can of Bud in his fist and lobbed it accurately into a bin on the far side of the room, where it clanked into a lot of other empty cans of Bud.

He consulted his watch. "I've been divorced for eight months, nine days and seventeen hours. Hell, I *still* love that girl. You want a beer?"

I looked at my watch. "It's too early in the morning. I'll stick with coffee."

On the way to the refrigerator in the galley, he stopped to talk with Gypsy. "Hey puppydawg? How you doin', gal? What you want? A cookie? Could you use more water?"

Gypsy was in love with Bill Perryman. At the yacht club, she would bullet out of the car along the pontoons to *Musette*, clambering aboard, claws scrabbling, with indelicate forwardness. Then she'd flounder down the stairs from the bridge deck to find him. When he chucked her under the ears, she crooned long and softly, a thread of drool leaking from her graying muzzle as he called her "puppydawg" and "my girl."

"Hey," he called from behind the fridge. "I got a name for the boat. I dreamed it up last night. I want to know what you think . . ."

He'd bought *Musette* in Chicago and piloted her to Guntersville two weeks before, taking ten happy, obsessed days to wind the thousand miles down the Illinois and Mississippi rivers and up the Ohio and the Tennessee. The big twin-engined cruiser, more ship than boat, still had the mildly desolate air of a vacated house. Voices echoed in it. The beams of sunlight in the saloon were thick with motes of old Chicago dust. Bill was working twelve-hour days on it, cleaning out its previous owners and trying to turn it into home.

He emerged with a fresh beer for himself, another coffee for me. "Circe," he said. "How does it sound? Circe—the enchantress?"

"She turned men into swine," I said.

"Yup!" He pulled the ring-cap from the can. "You know that, and I know that, but I betcha you won't find too many people in the yacht club know it. I kind of like that . . . hidden meanings? Little ambiguities?"

"I like them, too. It's a good name."

"Circe. She and Ulysses, they had a kid together. Son. He killed his pa in the end and shacked up with the widow. Greek family life. I guess it's pretty much like family life today . . ."

Bill was a year younger than I was. At forty-five, he'd come home to Guntersville to nurse his wounds. He was sick of the city, sick of the woe of marriage; but his sudden freedom hung heavily on his hands. In Birmingham, he'd had a mansion, had been a deacon in the local Presbyterian church and the scoutmaster of the local troop—a solid Doric pillar of society. Within a few weeks, he had sold up his business and his house, resigned his civic offices, established his wife and youngest daughter in a condo block, and lit out for the town where he'd spent the best days of his childhood. From the saloon of *Musette* we could see the islands where Bill had camped out alone as a boy, the brush-wood thicket where he'd killed his first rattlesnake, the private dock where his first skiff had been kept moored. Through the trees across the water, we could see the glint of the long window of the Perryman family house on Buck Island, a rancher on massive timber stilts that faced south over the bend in the river. His mother lived there now, with his stepfather; his father had been killed in an aircrash, a few minutes after Bill had seen him onto the plane. His life aboard *Musette* was haunted and mourn-ful, but it was laced with tough humor, and he was healing fast.

Every day he got up at dawn and set to work furiously on his boat, scrubbing, painting, carpentering, pulling the engines to bits and putting them back together again. He had chronically active hands. The ship's ashtrays were packed solid with ciga-rettes from which he'd taken a couple of impatient puffs before mashing them out. When he crumpled a beer can, it folded up in his palm like a used Kleenex. Armed with an electric screwdriver and a hacksaw, he chased "rascals."

"I'm going to *get* that rascal! He's been bugging me all day—"

Rascals were pumps that didn't pump, lights that didn't light up, windows that wouldn't close, short-circuits, leaks, glitches. *Musette* was an animate world; it crawled with rascals.

"I *fixed* that rascal." Then, one cigarette later, "Hell!—you see that rascal?"

It would take a year, and thirty thousand dollars, to turn *Musette* into *Circe*. Reconstructing the boat, Bill would reconstruct himself; that was the plan. When she was restored to glory, the new Bill Perryman would take off in her, first for the western rivers, then for the Gulf, the Bahamas, the West Indies. . . . He was vague on destinations: *travel* for him was an intransitive verb, a state of being. If only he could exorcise his ghosts by meditation and hard labor, then, with grace, he could be afloat on the surface of the world again.

He was talking lyrically of the America he'd never seen, of the Red River, the Arkansas, the Missouri, when he shook his head sadly. "I couldn't do it, not without somebody to share it with. There's no point, without you have somebody to share it with."

"I think the only way to travel is to travel alone," I said. "It opens you up to the world. It puts you in the way of luck and chance. Maybe you'll only find her if you're going alone up the Missouri . . ."

He laughed. "Me, I'd just be looking for her along every inch of the bank all the way from Guntersville. And that's no good for navigation."

"Don't look too hard. You'll find her."

"You think?" He grinned at his own wanness. "I'm going to fix this little rascal."

The best thing about all this fixing was that *Musette* required constant sea trials out on the lake. We'd pick up anyone else who was at a loose end from the dock, shed our lines and head downstream for the lock and dam. Clyde from the *Suzy Q* was usually at a loose end; a burly type, with a twenty-five-year start on Bill and me.

"You ever been divorced?" Clyde asked me.

"Yes, once," I said.

"Me—twice," he said, admitting me, somewhat grudgingly, to the good-old-boy club.

"Look at that red neck on him!" Bill said, when Clyde was standing up forward, prodding the pontoon with a boathook. There were a few remaining tufts of hair sticking out from under the strap of his plastic baseball cap; below them, the skin on the back of his neck was creased in puce turkey wattles. "Looking at that neck, would you ever guess that he was one of the top space engineers in the business?"

Musette crept out onto the lake, barely rippling the still water as Bill steered her for a raft of loons.

"When the loons leave the lake, that's the official start of summer. If the loons are still around by the end of April, guys go out with carbines and frighten 'em off, to improve the weather."

The loons clattered away from the boat, looking like incompetent water-skiers as they struggled to get airborne. Part of *Musette*'s job was to be a floating bird-watcher's hide. Bill was a nature man. He named every bird that came our way: blue heron . . . pintail . . . coot . . . teal . . . black vulture. He closed with the shore, scanning every lightning-blasted tree through binoculars in the hope of finding a bald eagle. But the eagles were not at home today, and *Musette* slewed off over the water with the log showing 15 knots and climbing.

I took over the wheel while Bill went below to rummage in his fridge. Planing on the rigid muscle of its own wake, the fifty-six-foot boat answered to the least movement of one's fingertip. Bows rearing up ahead, we flew down the buoyed channel, leaving a tow of a dozen barges standing.

"Beautiful," Clyde said at my elbow, talking of the even churr of the engines under our feet.

"Isn't it beautiful?" Bill said. But he was looking at the landscape round us, and the question was not rhetorical. It demanded an answer.

I said, "It's like Lake Como or Geneva must have been a hundred years ago, before they spoiled them." It was true, too. The water was enclosed by solid walls of unpeopled forest.

Bill named the trees. Pine, oak, hickory. The woods were broken by sheer limestone bluffs, the pale rock elaborately cross-hatched with cracks and fissures. Squint, and the bluffs turned into mirage-Manhattans, skyscraper cities, like the view from

Alice's room, perversely imitated in wild nature.

"I thought up a name for her," Bill said to Clyde. *"Circe."*

"Circe? That some kind of Greek goddess or something?"

"Kind of. She was an enchantress."

"Bill—I tell you, you can't get that ex-wife of yours out of your head, can you? Admit it."

We sat in line on the couch in front of the bridge console: three men in a boat, all past their best, suckling ruminatively on their beers. We were a line out of a song—*drinkin' whisky 'n' rye, singing "That'll be the day that I die"* . . .

"You love that woman."

"I admit it. I've been divorced for . . . eight months, nine days and twenty-one hours . . ."

"Yeah. I used to be that way too."

The white ferro-concrete of the dam wall was sliding out ahead of us from behind the woods. The dark water, molasses-smooth, was scored with fine lines made by the quickening river current.

"You know, something happens to women after forty? They just change, *snap!* like that."

There was a dipping flash of wings beyond *Musette*'s bows.

"Blue jay," Bill said out of habit.

"My last, hell, she got so goddam *materialistic,* it was unreal. Every time I came home, I'd look in the closet and there'd be another pair of shoes. She never *wore* those shoes? A year later, they'd still have the price tags on 'em. I wasn't living with my wife; I was living with Imelda Marcos."

"She was a country girl. I spoiled her." Bill spun the wheel. The broad fan of our wake lapped the dogwood blossom on both banks of the river. The three cans of Bud were lifted to our faces in perfect sync.

"When I think of the alimony I'm paying . . ."

"It's a connection, though, isn't it? You *like* to pay it. It means that you've still got . . . *control.* So long as you're paying, you know where she is and what she's doing—she's still *yours* . . . know what I mean?"

"Bald eagle!" Bill said, and grabbed the binoculars as he throttled back. He peered into the forest. "Shoot. I lost him."

We hung around, drifting limply on the water, waiting for the eagle to show.

"You pay much alimony, John?"

"No. It's different in England. Anyway, we were only married for about five minutes."

"You know we started dating in high school?"

"Look—up there," I said.

"No. He's just a plain old turkey vulture. See that vee he's making with his wings?"

Dark clouds were building over Georgia Mountain and there was a chill in the air. As *Musette* got under way again, the first drops of rain made circles on the water like rising fish.

"Twenty-seven years. That's how long that girl and I were together. Twenty-seven years."

"Hey Bill—what was the name of that guy . . . used to be in the club . . . from Huntsville . . . had to sell his boat when he got divorced? You know—that Hatteras 40?"

"You got me there. Was he Billy-something or Jimmy-something? I remember the guy. I can't recall his name, though."

"We're all headed for Alzheimer's," I said.

"Not me," Clyde said. "I got CRS."

"Sorry?" I was cursing myself for having been flippant. Clyde's face was deadly serious.

"The CRS disease? Yeah." He nodded sadly. "Cain't Remember Shit."

The loons quit the lake a few days later. There was no need for carbines. Guntersville sweltered in the nineties under a tropical sky, and at the weekend the yacht club filled with the *haute bourgeoisie* of Birmingham and Huntsville clad in shirts from Hawaii and shorts from Bermuda. The smell of grilling human flesh mixed with the smell of steaks from the barbecue pit. Gypsy groveled for tidbits.

On the Saturday afternoon a convoy of twenty Bertrams, Hatterases and Chris-Crafts left the pontoons and set off across the lake for Short Creek. "For the Sacrifices," Bill said. "It's a tradition. You'll see when we get there."

Up on the flybridge, Bill had company. Jennifer, a sophomore at the U. of A., was the daughter of a friend who was captaining the boat behind us in the convoy. In bikini and dark glasses, her skin glistening with suntan oil, Jennifer was alarmingly like Lolita.

"What are you going to *do,* Jennifer?" Bill was asking.

"Oh. You know. Like they say, I guess. Marry a guy for money, then live with another guy for love."

"You're too young to be cynical," Bill said sternly. Jennifer smiled a smile calculated to make one miss a heartbeat, sipped at her Coke, exposed the insides of her forearms to the sun.

"What are you majoring in?" I said.

"Psychology."

Short Creek was a deep wooded bay a few miles east of Guntersville. When we reached the middle of it, Bill, the club commodore, dropped his anchor, then the other boats tied up alongside us. The wide line of roped white cruisers, fenders sighing, sashayed gently round the single anchor. The stars and stripes at our backs fluttered sleepily in the baffled light airs from the hills.

Bill made an announcement. "I know that the Sacrifices are traditionally made from the commodore's boat, but on this occasion I have to ask you to choose another boat. I repeat, no sacrifices from *Musette.*"

His voice was earnest. I remembered that he'd been a deacon in his church in Birmingham; and I saw why he'd been so solemnly insistent in his prohibition when the Sacrifices began, on the bow of the boat next door.

A man mixed a rum and coke in a curious imitation, half parody, half pastiche, of a priest at a communion service. He then stood at the boat's pulpit, holding the glass over the water.

"Friends and visitors! We are assembled here in the presence of the gods of Short Creek to make sacrifices today . . ." The priestly gobbledygook went on for a while. It ended with: "To a year of good boating! To a year of safe boating! To the gods of Short Creek!"—and he poured the rum and coke into the lake.

"To the gods of Short Creek!" everyone called from the rafted cruisers, raising cans and glasses. There were Bronx cheers and cowboy whoops from the younger element.

Then, one by one, came the Sacrifices. Someone brought a defunct water pump to the pulpit. "I wish to make a sacrifice. This pump, which has seen long and honorable service aboard the cruiser *Miss Betty Rose,* I now offer up to the gods of Short Creek . . ." The pump made a good splash, and the sacrifice was met with a round of raucous applause.

A woman brought salt; another brought a can of stale peanuts. The gods of Short Creek were appeased with gifts of junk from engine rooms and the back shelves of galleys. Every offering was accompanied by a ritual speech. There was more than a touch of Pascal's wager in these speeches; although this was a mock religious service, it seemed that one couldn't be altogether sure that the gods of Short Creek did not actually exist, and so it was wise to keep on the safe side and show some serious reverence for them, just in case.

When the sacrifices were over and we had settled to some hard partying, I found myself being interrogated by a woman about my own religious convictions. "Are you a believer?" she said; "I'm a big believer."

I explained that I was an agnostic—not that I "didn't know" or "had honest doubts," but that I could not rationally disprove that which, by definition, could not be rationally proved.

"Oh, I know what you mean," the woman said. "I know so many intelligent people who have felt as you feel. And when they've come home to Jesus, they have come back with their faith doubly renewed. I just know it will be the same for you. John, I know you'll come home. I will be praying for you."

She was drinking bourbon and ginger ale. I was on Bud. I waved my can awkwardly in the air. "Well—thanks," I said. "That's . . . awfully kind of you."

Flannery O'Connor called the South "Christ-haunted." In Guntersville, religion was continually bubbling up to the surface of everyday life, in rituals like the Sacrifices, in small superstitions, in natural magic. The most ordinary conversation would suddenly drift into the formal language of evangelism; the grammar and vocabulary of the Baptist Church were engrained in the culture of the town. People *reached out.* They *shared with.* They *gave thanks.* A local bestseller, much in demand from the Huntsville bookstores, was a theological work, written by a scientist for other scientists, called *The Space Program: Does He Want Us There?* Apparently He did.

At cookouts and family suppers there was always a tricky spell for me, when the joshing talk over cocktails would abruptly subside, and the senior man present would say, "Now let's share a little love around . . ." We would join hands in a circle, out on the porch, while grace was said. Grace could go on for a long, long time, as God was chatted to, intimately and without embarrassment; at grace, God was brought up to date with all the details of our day.

"O Lord, we want to thank you for this wonderful weather we've been having . . . temperature up in the nineties and looks like staying that way . . ."

"Amen," said someone in the circle.

"We want to thank you for the bounty of your gifts to us this day . . . for this fine spread . . . for the good cooking of Shirleen here and Mary Belle . . ."

"Amen."

"Lord, we want to thank you for bringing into our lives our guest this day, John Rayburn . . ."

And so it went. God was very close. Ineffable, invisible, He was somewhere here on this porch, listening in, patiently interested in our most trivial domestic affairs. God in Guntersville was a being much like grandpa. You could imagine him living in the rocker, occasionally lowering His copy of the *Gleam* to say a few quiet, well-chosen words.

I was enlisted in the Optimists Club. Everyone in Guntersville had to belong to something—be a Rotarian, a Veteran of Foreign Wars, a Jaycee, a Civitan, a Kiwani. I was an Optimist. We met at seven every Monday morning at Reid's restaurant, where we breakfasted on scrambled egg, sausages and hominy grits, and listened to an uplifting twenty-minute talk to set us up in the right spirit for the week. At my induction meeting, the speaker was a theologian from Snead, the local Methodist junior college. He talked, pithily and well, about the life of Dietrich Bonhoeffer. Our president thanked him and fixed his gaze on a fat man wearing scarlet suspenders who was lighting up a stogie.

". . . if we could learn something from his example, this world would be a better place—*Dan Gullahorn.*"

Dan Gullahorn flapped his cigar and winked back down the table.

The end of the meeting came when the assembled Optimists rose to their feet, turned to the wall and recited the Optimist Creed in grave chorus.

"Promise yourself—" we mumbled—"to be so strong that nothing can disturb your peace of mind.

"To talk health, happiness and prosperity to every person you meet . . .

"To look at the sunny side of everything and make your optimism come true . . .

"To wear a cheerful countenance at all times and give every living creature you meet a smile . . .

"To give so much time to the improvement of yourself that you have no time to criticize others . . ."

I sneaked a look at the visiting Methodist. His lips were not moving with ours. It was clear that he felt about the Optimist Creed much as Bill had felt about the Sacrifices.

"To be too large for worry, too noble for anger, too strong for fear, and too happy to permit the presence of trouble."

Back in Polecat Hollow, which was growing more jungle-like each day as spring turned into summer, I sat at the typewriter trying to figure out exactly how I felt about the pervasive religiosity of life in Guntersville. To begin with, I had been amused, embarrassed, occasionally angered by it. Lately, though, I had felt less confidently alienated from it.

My own materialism was bred in a world mostly man-made, the world of brick, asphalt, fences, green belts. If there were gods in it, they were quiescent, probably dead. There were few obvious contradictions in nature to be reconciled. Death itself, of course; that was the big one—and the well-bred Episcopal brand of Christianity in which I was raised handled death with satisfyingly gloomy pomp. But no twisters blew into our town and shook it to bits. We were not troubled with biblical serpents.

Only the night before, Gypsy and I had been riding with Bill in his pickup when he spotted a diamondback in the road and swerved to kill it. He'd run over it twice. "I do hate to kill a living creature, but when I kill I like to do it good and clean." We piled out of the truck to inspect the dead snake in the glare of the headlights. Gypsy, eager for a run, stopped in her tracks, whimpered and scrambled back into the safety of the pickup when she saw what we were looking at.

It was nearly six feet long, and paunchy. Its glassy patterned skin looked as if it had been painted by a Chinese miniaturist.

"He's a beauty," Bill said, and he was. *Now the serpent was more subtil than any beast of the field . . .* I spent a long time crouched in the dirt road, admiring the creature's brilliant enameled markings.

Here it was easy to believe that one was living in a world of symbols and portents, to slip into William Benefield's way of thinking and see a snake bite or a tornado as *meant.* Nature here was so profuse and violent that only a magical, or a religious, explanation could match up to the weird splendors of one's own back yard. Sometimes at night I lay listening, connecting things up . . . That was the way religions began. I was not about to invent Southern Baptism for myself; my religion would be pagan, pantheistic, with charms and rituals to ward off snakes and spooks.

I was picking up an accent that turned every statement into a question. I was drifting into a habit of mind more instinctive, more irrational, than anything I had experienced since my childhood. If I stayed on much longer, I thought, I would find myself saying my prayers again. Next year, at the Sacrifices . . .

In Guntersville we did not go in much for social kissing, so I was interested to notice that Claude Hundley was the most socially kissed man in town. Middle-aged ladies would rise from their table at the Northtown Country Cooker to kiss him. If he crossed the street, he got kissed when he reached the other side. For Claude Hundley, the seven-block walk up Gunter Avenue between Taylor and Lusk was a gauntlet of ungainsayable women.

I could see his points. He was quite cuddly—a man in his late twenties inclining somewhat to fat, he looked good in his dark three-piece business suit and scarlet bow tie. He was an attorney; and though lawyers were now replacing Poles as the butt of the mass-production joke industry (George Kappler's favorite was "Why are the science labs at Auburn switching from using white mice to using lawyers? Because they're easily obtainable, prolific breeders and the students don't get attached to them"), they still had some cachet in Guntersville.

There was one other feature that marked out Claude Hundley from the generality of men on the Northtown end of Gunter Avenue. He was black. In a town that was still sharply segregated, Mr. Hundley was the exception who proved the rule.

A great deal of head shaking went on over the blacks who lived on the Hill. People never knew why it was, but . . . Somehow "our" blacks just seemed to—well, lack something. They didn't have the *initiative,* a word much overused. "Our blacks, they seem different from other people's blacks . . ." "They're happy to just stay up there on the Hill . . . drinking beer, smoking marijuana . . ." "They just don't have stable families . . . you go up there and try to find a *father,* it's like looking for a needle in a haystack. Those kids have mothers, but, funny thing, none of 'em don't seem to have fathers." Many people attributed the lack of initiative on the Hill to the way "the guv'ment started handing out food stamps." I was told moral atrocity stories about black mothers on welfare "just having to have freezers!" If the town showed no serious signs of desegregation, that was not the fault of the whites. Far from it: they'd fallen over backward to welcome the blacks into their churches, lay on extra coaching for them at the high school, give them all the encouragement they needed—but the blacks simply hadn't *taken advantage. I don't know why that is.*

At this point in the argument, the speaker always introduced the name of Claude Hundley. He was "a wonderful man." He was "my personal attorney." "Now *Claude,* he is a real gentleman." Much courted professionally, much kissed, Claude Hundley was a living tribute to Guntersville's willingness to foster black talent wherever it could be found.

Talking to Les Click, the principal of the high school, I said,

"I suppose Claude Hundley must have been the brightest black student you've had—"

"Oh, no. Claude was never an outstanding student. He wasn't even the best black student in his year. No, the thing about Claude is that the Hundleys are a real solid family. They stood right behind him. He got back-up. That family is *close*. It's not like the families on the Hill . . ."

I lunched with Mr. Hundley at the Glover, between kisses. His manner was unassuming. He spoke with legal care for his words. We talked about his practice. His clients were mostly white. He was proud to represent people from the famously white-supremacist town of Arab—that was how fast things were changing. He dined out at white tables "two, three, four times a week." We talked about how he hoped to go into politics. He felt that the state of Alabama was "just about ready" to elect people like him now. And no, he had never been tempted to go north to realize his ambitions; he was happy in his hometown, he was accepted here, it was a fine base. His family were here, and he put his family high on his priority list.

"But why do *you* think that the kids from the Hill are such underachievers?" I said. "They're not going to college in anything like the numbers that they should. Most of them aren't getting anywhere."

"I think federal money has a lot to answer for," Claude Hundley said. The people on the Hill had been cosseted with "welfare and food stamps." They didn't have stable families. There wasn't enough "parental pushing."

I could see why people kissed him.

I thought that Guntersville must be a numbingly dull town to be young in. Walking the dog, I would run into knots of high school students kicking their heels around the Kiwanis Pier or in the parking lot of the Jitney Jr. convenience store. They were to be seen in church and in the plastic alpine chalets of McDonald's and Arby's; but they had the air of supernumeraries. William's soda fountain was the exclusive province of these kids' grandfathers, and there was no disco, no cinema, and all the best public places in town were hung with NO MINORS signs.

Going through back issues of the *Gleam,* I had lit on a puzzling statistic. At the end of October 1988, just before the presidential election, Guntersville High School had organized its own secret ballot. Four hundred sixty-eight votes were cast, and George Bush flew home with seventy-four percent, against twenty-six percent for Michael Dukakis. That the children of the town, in a yellow-dog Democrat state, should be so overwhelmingly for the conservative Republican, seemed a sad thing to me. There was plenty for them to vote against, and if they could not make some show of radicalism in their teens, what depths of reaction might they sink to in their forties? I tried to guess at what they talked about down at the Kiwanis Pier. Were they, too, growling censoriously about "federal spending" and the evils of welfare?

Their school was most peculiar. It stood on the edge of Sand Mountain, and it looked like a giant model of some kind of molecular structure: a dozen interlocked concrete hexagons, from which all natural light had been excluded in the interests of academic concentration. The hinterland of Guntersville was full of poultry batteries, and I suspected that the school's architect had only recently graduated from chickens to children. Driving past this windowless, beige-colored hatchery, I grew increasingly curious about what was going on inside. I was invited by Les Click to spend a few sessions with a senior English class.

Most of the graduating twelfth-graders were bound for college in the fall; they were cleverer and more ambitious than the Guntersville average. Even so, I was surprised by the ease and quickness of their talk, by their readiness to take hold of a strange idea and make something of it. Their grim classroom with its bald blue lighting and processed chemical air was full of laughter. They were gentler with each other than the urban students of their age whom I was used to meeting; they had inherited their parents' Southern country manners.

Nor did the black students at all resemble the dismal no-hopers of Guntersville lore. LaTanya Rhines (voted "most intellectual senior" in the yearbook) was a flautist, president of the Literary Club, class valedictorian, and wanted to major in political science at the University of Alabama. Baron Lowe ("most talented") had the most serious eyes I'd seen in town and was trying for medical school.

I told the class that they were conspicuously failing to measure up to stereotype.

"That's *old people,*" a white student said. "That's our parents' generation. A lot of them, they grew up in the sixties, went to segregated schools and all? Some of them, they still can't handle it. But Baron and I are friends. I go around to his place, he comes around to mine . . . Baron and I are pretty integrated, aren't we, Baron?"

Baron agreed. "Yes, there's racism here. But people of my age now . . . well, it's *getting* to be so that you can be accepted for what you are. It's changed a lot from when I was a kid."

"There's racism in the *town,*" LaTanya Rhines said, "but I don't sense racism here in school . . ."

Perhaps the strange hermetic design of the building did have a point.

Several students, black and white, said that they did feel segregated from the mainstream of popular American culture by their provincial Southernness. They switched on TV and saw Dallas, Los Angeles, New York, Miami . . . never anywhere like Guntersville. I asked them if their English classes had introduced them to books set in the South—to writers like Carson McCullers, Truman Capote, Walker Percy, Eudora Welty, Flannery O'Connor, William Faulkner?

"*Absalom, Absalom,*" a boy said. "We read that. That was by William Faulkner."

"Yes, but that was *historical,*" said a girl. "Anyway, it was about Mississippi. Mississippi's different."

I led a discussion on the rival merits of the big city and the small town, and when the bell went I asked the class if they would write me an essay on the subject. I sweetened the assignment with a twenty-five-dollar prize for the best effort. The papers came in a week later. In class, the students had been prevailingly sunny about life in Guntersville; on paper, they were far cloudier. Inter-

estingly, the most enthusiastic endorsements of the small town
came from the two black students. Baron Lowe wrote:

When I cross that bridge coming into Guntersville, I feel so
secure, as if I'm being cradled in my mother's arms. . . .
    When I walk through the store or wherever, someone always
says Hi. I sense openness in the people.
    There is a lot of conformity which leads to narrow-minded-
ness. This has improved, though. There is not as much racism
here as there used to be. Now the people treat me in the same
way that I act toward them. . . .

LaTanya Rhines wrote:

People are close. Everyone knows their neighbors and have the
opportunity to become friends without being afraid . . .

A more typical entry came from a boy who confided that:

To tell you the truth, I'll be a much happier person as soon as
I leave Guntersville behind.
    People are persecuted for expressing different ideas. You
can't be your own self, if that's not what everybody wants. People will reject, threaten and hassle you, just because you're different. . . .

A girl, who acknowledged that in Guntersville "you can call your
next-door neighbor to help you in your time of need" and that
there was something to be said for "a town in which moral values
are put into practice," complained:

Being in a small town, you have to fit into a social category.
Guntersville just happens to be the world's worst town for man-
dating a position status.

Of her contemporaries, she wrote, "The sad thing is, these kids
are just miniature re-enactments of their parents."
    There was a good deal of predictable boredom. From a boy:

In a small town, it's the same day-to-day routine as long as you live there. You could come into this town, never having been there in your life, and know every twist and turn within two days.

It's hard trying to find things to do on the weekends. The Police won't even let you hang out at a local parking.

In a city I could just cruise over to the closest mall and see all kinds of weird and neat people. There is no mall to cruise to in Guntersville . . .

I gave the twenty-five-dollar palm to a pained and thoughtful piece by a girl who, I noticed, had clocked up relatively few accolades in the school yearbook. She wrote:

People who live in real big cities seem to depend more on themselves. But they have an inner core of excitement and suspense that country folk don't have. I mean, they never know what's around the next corner. . . .

You're more cautious, and even a little frightened of the people you meet in the city. You don't know who they really are, and for that matter they don't know who you are. . . .

If you're tired of your family *[she wrote, then crossed it out and began the sentence again]* If you're tired of your job, you can quit to start again at a new job in a new environment without much damage to yourself in terms of personal acceptance. You can't do that in a small town. Everything you do eventually finds you. You can't escape your past in a small close-knit society. It's always there.

It's simplicity itself to make a mistake in a small town that will follow you for the rest of your life. There's an invisible set of rules in every small town that permits people to exist so closely. Eccentrism is not tolerated as it is in the cities.

Often someone who is different or just doesn't fit in with a certain lifestyle will find himself isolated or politely placed out of the way of the majority. It might seem cruel, but it is one of the ways a small town organizes their society. Without it, the people will turn hostile and shut themselves off from one another. A friendly small town will turn into a small armed camp. . . .

She distinguished—subtly, I thought—between the "violence" of the city and "the personal violence" of the small town. She felt safer with the impersonal kind; and I knew what she meant, although her syntax had begun to crack up at this point in the essay.

Everyone, including those essayists who seized on the assignment as an opportunity to stab their hometown in the back, had a go at some rhapsodic nature writing. I tired of the glorious sunsets, the sparkling lake, "cheerful chirping birds," "freely floating clouds," the "swift cool breeze," the "crisp clear blue sky." I agreed with the writers that our local landscape was beautiful, but we seemed to be living in two separate landscapes. Mine had fire ants, vultures, snakes, flying squirrels; theirs was tame and parklike, with nothing wilder in it than the odd tufted titmouse. Mine had tornado watches; theirs was fanned by cooling breezes.

Their landscape was derived from sentimental hymns and filler poems in local newspapers which, in their turn, looked back to Whittier, to Emerson, to Wordsworth in his daffodil mood. There was something of Massachusetts in it; there was more of England. I had grown up in a countryside that did look a bit like the one the students were describing. But there was no connection at all between this decorous, literary nature and the real landscape of Alabama.

There was a particular pathos in this, since the students were living in the region of the United States that was richer in descriptions of itself than any other. Ignorant of their own literary tradition, they looked at Marshall County and saw there a tenth-hand version of Sussex or Shropshire. They were—orphaned.

—like the motel owner who was writing a novel. He came round late one night, after he'd closed up his bar, to discuss the first chapter, which I'd read. (Gypsy slept through the noise of his car pulling up on the road above the cabin; she slept through the creak and shuffle of his footsteps in the loose gravel of the drive, and through his call—"John?"—as he opened the screen door on the porch. When I was offering him a drink inside, she woke and let off a volley of admirable barks.)

There were good things in his sheaf of pages. It had the fluency of the compulsive kitchen-table writer; many excited small hours had obviously gone into its making. But there were problems. The story was set in California, a state to which Tim had never been; in the advertising business (in which he'd briefly worked, in Huntsville); and in the movie industry, about which he knew nothing useful. His twenty-nine-year-old hero (Tim was twenty-nine) was a handsome and guiltless sexual athlete. The landscape (Hollywood Bowl, Sunset Boulevard, Pacific surf) came from television.

"Well? What do you think?"

I praised the fluency, the relaxed and accurate phrases, of which there were many. Then I said, "But it's not real, not yet, anyway. You don't know enough about movie producers and Los Angeles to make them plausible."

"That comes through?"

"It does."

"But is it good enough to send to an agent?"

"I wouldn't, if I were you. You're going to have to bring the whole thing much closer to home to make it work."

"How do you mean?"

"Can't you write about what you know? Write about Alabama? At present your characters are behaving unreally because they're not living in a real landscape. They'd behave quite differently if they were living here in Guntersville."

"*Guntersville?*"

"Couldn't you take a deep breath, rethink the story, and set it in a northern Alabama town where you can get all the details right?"

His face, which had been wearing an expression of injured but still hopeful authorship, cracked into a derisive laugh. I was, after all, a hopeless critic; I didn't know the literary ropes at all.

"You think a New York agent would *touch* a book that was located in *Guntersville?*"

Like Tim, the high school students betrayed their anxiety that the world in which they lived was not as real as places where they'd never been. New York was real, California was real; but Guntersville lay beyond the pale of reality as it was laid down by imaginary Hollywood producers and imaginary Manhattan literary agents. I knew the feeling. Everyone who lives in a province is sometimes prone to suspect that the real world is somewhere else. But in Guntersville the feeling was sharpened by the enormity of the United States. If we were real, then what we saw on CNN was fiction; if it was real, then we must be tricks of the light. Mostly we were real. But when called to put our lives on paper, or conceive of a *Dallas*-style TV series called *Guntersville,* we were assailed by sudden doubts.

If the young were far less deeply stained by racism than their parents, they were also far less adequately buoyed up by the history and mythology of the Old South. They could not take the same wounded pride in the Confederacy; for them, the Civil War was as remote as Agincourt. They could not feed on literature for a definition of themselves: even Tim the would-be writer had never heard of either Eudora Welty or Flannery O'Connor, the authors whom I suggested might be most help to him. There was no Southern television: the kids watched *The Cosby Show, Growing Pains* and *thirtysomething*—a body of fiction hardly less remote than the Confederacy itself. They were culturally lonely, adrift, in a way that no European, no New Yorker or Washingtonian, could possibly be. In Guntersville, Southern religion enjoyed a cultural monopoly. We went to Baptist yard sales, Baptist cookouts, Baptist covered-dish lunches, Baptist showers, Baptist volleyball tournaments. It seemed to me that the town was very seriously in need of a fiction to give it a keener sense of its own reality.

One sentence from the prizewinning essay kept on coming back to me. *It's simplicity itself to make a mistake in a small town that will follow you for the rest of your life.* I liked being John Rayburn. I had fallen into a routine that felt like a good life. I liked working on the porch in the morning, walking Gypsy on the levee, lunching at the Glover, dining out with the Larsons, talking late with Billy Perryman. But I knew that if I stayed much longer,

I would make that one mistake. Scratch John Rayburn, and he'd confess my own thoughts on politics, books, religion—thoughts that wouldn't wash in Guntersville.

Late one night, back from *Musette*, I packed Rayburn's life into my case. Gypsy stood by, doubtfully wagging her tail, trying to figure it out.

"Back to Janet," I said.

Her eyes were full of deep, doggy misgiving. I assuaged it by giving her a midnight feast of chuck steak.

At ten next morning I parked the Spirit on the animal hospital lot. Gypsy lumbered cheerfully out of the car. She remembered the way to the door.

"Hi, Gypsy!" said Janet Potocki.

I had hoped for a joyful reunion, but Gypsy merely shrugged. Dogs are instinctive pessimists, and she'd seen it coming; a girl can't go on eating chuck steak all the time, and now it was back to Canine Maintenance.

I walked to the car, blinking a little faster than usual. In the last few weeks some sort of entropy had taken place; Dodge engineering had been swapping about with elderly black lab, and the Spirit was now more kennel than automobile. The seats, which had been vinyl, were now dog hair. Gypsy had eaten my seat belt in another act of secret, nighttime revenge.

I wound down all the windows, to mix the smell of dog with the smell of pine woods, switched on the ignition, eased the Spirit out onto 69 West and flat-mashed the gas pedal.

FIVE

The Friendly Sky

OUR FLIGHT'S DELAYED. For the last two hours it has been raining. The fields of oily turf between the runways have turned as dark as moleskin; the runways themselves look windlessly deep, like ship canals. The cowled landing lights along the edges of the tarmac burn so violently white in the surrounding murk that it hurts one's eyes to look at them from half a mile away. The planes keep coming. There is something comic about the way they lumber in so self-importantly from the sky—their imperial obesity, their thunder and ado. They make their entrances like Tamburlaine the Scourge of God. Then, minutes later, you see them shackled up to yellow tractors, being led around the inner reaches of the terminal like great blind boobies. Each Boeing wears the same coy grin on its face—the grin of a dolphin in a zoo that has just done something clever with a beach-ball in return for a herring. Standing in line at their gates, plugged in to concertina walkways, fuel pipes trailing from under their wings, baggage spilling from their opened bellies, the jumbos don't inspire trust. I wish I was flying at night, when I wouldn't have to see them in this state of helpless deshabille.

This is an American airport. I mean, it is a particular airport in the United States. It has its own name—Logan, or Bates Field, or William B. Hartsfield, or Sky Harbor, or O'Hare—but in my fear of flying I've forgotten what it's called. As for where it is, anyone can see that it is just *here;* a place with a character more powerfully redolent and oppressive than any of the cities to which the airport might be nominally attached.

Entering *here,* you must abandon almost everything you have. The cheerful Spirit was dumped long ago at one of the place's eggbox concrete outposts; the black zippered bag containing my traveling life went off on a journey of its own down some long dark tunnel at Check-In; my groin and armpits have been immodestly fingered in a search for firearms; my shaving kit has been X-rayed, and a uniformed woman here now knows (if she cares) that I'm down to my last two Ativans. Maybe she read a few lines of my manuscript too, when it went past, and gave it a derisory thumbs-down.

At every point, I have managed to meet reproof. At the car rental office, I tried to amuse a man called Wayne with the story of how the driver's-side seat belt had been eaten by a jealous dog. He fined me one hundred dollars, told me the incident would be reported as an act of malicious damage, and said his company kept a blacklist of customers like me.

Checking in, I said, "Window seat in smoking, if there is one, please." A woman named Marsha sniffed and made a face. Now that I'd confessed, she could smell my habit on me, and intended to make me feel the stink of my own polluted clothes in her nostrils. "There *is* no smoking on domestic flights," she said, her expression warming sharply into a vindictive smile.

The phrase had kept on coming back to me during these last two hours. A cat is a domestic animal. A saucepan is a domestic utensil. To Marsha, jetting across a continent in a 747 was just pottering tamely about the house. I marveled at the size of Marsha's house.

Ticketed, disencumbered, searched and cleared for boarding, we are babyishly dependent on the controllers of the place. Sometimes they tell us to do things; mostly they leave us to fret. Every ten minutes I go and stare morosely at the nearest VDU display. An hour ago we were due to board half an hour ago at Gate B6; now we're due to board in forty minutes at Gate C14. As I watch, one of the invisible controllers adds an extra twenty minutes for luck.

I spend a lot of time anxiously listening to the announcements over the loudspeaker system. In almost all respects, these summonses and bulletins are enunciated with extreme clarity, by women speaking in the painfully slow and fulsomely stressed tones of infant teachers in a school for special-need children. It is only when they reach the flight number of the plane concerned or the name of the passenger who must immediately report to the United information desk that their voices go into misty soft focus—a sort of aural astigmatism in which a flock of pigeons can be mistaken for blooming crocuses, or vice versa. I keep on hearing that I am urgently wanted, but sit tight, fearing paranoia. They don't want me. They can't want me. They want Josephine Rubin, or John A. T. Horobin, or Sean O'Riordain, or Jennifer Raymond, or Jonah the Rabbi or Rogers and Braybourne.

When I first arrived here, I fed three quarters into a newspaper dispenser and took out a copy of the local broadsheet—the *Post-Dispatch,* the *Courant,* the *Plain Dealer,* the *Tribune,* the *Herald,* or whatever it was. It was an unhappy diversion. It spoke too eloquently of the world one had left behind by coming here—that interesting world of School Board Split, City Cop on Take, Teamsters Boss to Quit, Highways Commission Probe—Official. It made me feel homesick for reality: the only news that interested me now was the depressing stuff on the displays. *Canceled. Delayed.* Did the controllers ever get to write *Crashed, Missing, Hijacked* on these screens?

What puzzles me is that I seem to be entirely alone in my frustration and distress. Almost every flight is going out late, and there must be several thousand people in this airport, switching their departure gates, phoning home, putting another Scotch and soda down on their tab in the cocktail lounge. The men's neckties are loosened, their vests unbuttoned. They sit with open briefcases, papers spread in front of them as if this place was a comfortable home-away-from-home. I watch one man near me. He's got a can of Bud, a basket of popcorn, and he's two-thirds of the way through a sci-fi thriller by Arthur C. Clarke. The bastard hasn't got a care in the world. His eyes never drift up to the display; he never cocks his head anxiously when Teacher starts talking through the overhead speakers. He's on a domestic flight. He's a domestic flier.

An hour and a half later it is still raining, but we're getting somewhere here—at least I thought so fifty minutes ago when I buckled in to 38F and began looking out through the lozenge of scratched, multiplex plastic at the men in earmuffs and storm gear on the ground below. Since then we haven't budged. We've suffered faint, pastiche imitations of Scott Joplin, Count Basie and Glen Miller on the Muzak system. My neighbor in 38E, who is careless of the usual rules of body space, has worked her way slowly through four pages of the *National Enquirer,* moving her lips as she reads. In the seats ahead, there has been a good deal of scuffing and refolding of copies of *Business Week* and the *Wall Street Journal.* Still no one seems much disconcerted except me. The inside of the plane is hot and getting hotter. The stewards, flirting routinely among themselves, are proof against any damn fool questions from me.

The Muzak clicks off. A voice clicks on.

"Hi!"—and that seems to be it for a good long time. Then, "I'm, uh, Billy Whitman, and I'm going to be your pilot on this flight here to . . ." I think I can hear Mr. Whitman consulting his clipboard. ". . . uh, Sea-Tac this morning. Well—it was meant to be morning, but it looks to me now to be getting pretty damn close to afternoon . . ."

He's read *The Right Stuff,* and he's doing it—the entire cow-licked, gum-shifting country boy performance.

"I guess some of you folks back there may be getting a little antsy 'bout this delay we're having now in getting airborne . . . Well, we did run into a bit of a glitch with Control up there, getting our flight plan sorted . . ."

We haven't got a flight plan? Is Mr. Whitman waiting for someone to bring him a *map?*

"But they got that fixed pretty good now, and in, uh, oh, a couple or three minutes, we should be closing the doors, and I'm planning on getting up into the blue yonder round about ten minutes after that. So if you all sit tight now, we'll be getting this show right on the road. Looks pretty nice up there today . . . no weather problems that I can see so far . . . at least, once we get atop this little local overcast . . . and I'm looking for a real easy trip today. Have a good one, now, and I'll be right back to you just as soon as we go past something worth looking out the window for. Okay?"

Click.

After the video and the stewards' dumbshow about what to do in "the unlikely event" of our landing on water (where? The Mississippi?), Captain Whitman takes us on a slow ramble round the perimeter of the airport. We appear to be returning to the main terminal again when the jet takes a sudden deep breath, lets out a bull roar, and charges down the runway, its huge frame shuddering fit to bust. Its wings are actually flapping now, trying to tear themselves out at their roots in the effort to achieve lift-off. It bumps and grinds. The plastic bulkheads are shivering like gongs. Rain streams past the window, in shreds and gobbets, at two hundred miles an hour.

This is the bit I hate. We're not going fast enough. We're far too heavy to bring off this trick. We're breaking up. To take this flight was tempting fate one time too many. We're definitely goners this time.

But the domestic fliers remain stupidly oblivious to our date with death. They go on reading. They're lost in the stock market prices. They're learning that the human soul has been proved to exist and weighs exactly three-quarters of an ounce; that Elvis Presley never died and has been living as a recluse in Dayton, Ohio. These things engage them. These guys are—bored. The fact, clear enough to me, that they are at this moment rocketing into eternity is an insufficiently diverting one to make them even raise their eyes from their columns of idiot print.

Somehow (and this Captain Whitman must know a thing or two) we manage to unpeel ourselves from the obstinate earth, which suddenly begins to tilt upward in the glass. An industrial outskirt of the city shows as an exposed tangle of plumbing; there's a gridlock of cars on a freeway interchange, their headlights shining feebly through the drizzle. The airport beneath us is marked out like a schoolbook geometrical puzzle of tangents, sines and cosines. Then, suddenly, we're into a viewless infernal region of thick smoke, with the plane skidding and wobbling on the bumpy air. It's rattling like an old bus on a dirt road. In 38E we're deep in the miracle of Oprah Winfrey's diet. In 38F we're just beginning to suspect that we might conceivably survive.

My ears are popping badly. The noise of the engines changes

from a racetrack snarl to the even threshing sound of a spin dryer. On an even keel now, we plow up steadily through the last drifts and rags of storm cloud and the whole cabin fills with sudden brilliant sunshine. It's exactly the same light that Florentine painters used to employ for religious epiphanies and revelations. We're in the clear and in the blue; aloft, at long last, over America.

As a European child I used to think that Americans were somehow possessed of a lower specific gravity than we were. I envied them for it—for the way they seemed to be able to detach themselves from the ground with so much more ease than anyone I knew. Distant members of my family had occasionally been known to travel by aeroplane; and each of these ascents was spoken of for weeks beforehand, remembered for years after. "That was the year that Uncle Peter *flew* to Geneva." Americans were different. They took to the sky with hardly more forethought or apprehension than swallows launching themselves from a telegraph wire. "Going up in an aeroplane," in British English, was quite a different venture from "taking an airplane" in American. *Aero-* retained the Greek dignity of the word, gave it a dash of Icarian daring and danger. To my eyes, *airplane* always looked impertinently casual on the page; it robbed the amazing machine of its proper mystery.

Flying did mean something different to Americans—even though the aviation industry was at least as much a European as an American creation. It was Louis Blériot who first crossed the channel by plane in 1909; it was two Englishmen, John Alcock and Arthur Whitten Brown, who first crossed the Atlantic, from Newfoundland to Ireland, in 1919. In the design and manufacture of aircraft, Germany, France and Britain were as active as the United States, and in the early days of passenger flying it was a British firm, Imperial Airways, which commanded the longest and richest routes in the world.

Yet none of our nations learned to fly—not with the insouciance of these Americans who had managed to absorb the whole alarming business of airports, flight numbers, take-offs and landings into the ordinary fabric of their daily culture. In 38F, and hardly a novice in the scary tedium of long-distance air travel, I feel leadenly European in the company of these natural fliers.

38E's elbow is in my ribs. She is shouting into my deafened left ear. *"She* says you want a cocktail?"

The steel bulk of the mobile ice-and-drinks canteen has always bothered me. Suppose we hit an unexpected pocket of turbulence . . . suppose that thing takes wing from the aisle and hits the ceiling of the fuselage? Suppose a sharp-angled hundredweight truck of miniatures of Jack Daniels, London Gin, Stolichnaya, Californian Cabernet and Chablis, plus ice, tonic, soda, *etcet* slams into the roof of this elongated eggshell . . . ?

But the steward's waiting, and not conspicuously patiently. I settle, sadly, for a mineral water. I've learned the hard way about high-altitude dehydration. Trying to work out the controls of a strange car at the entrance to a strange city, with a fox-fur mouth and a blinding headache, cured me of my old game of trying to see just how many empty splits of champagne it was possible to secrete behind the airline magazine and the Emergency Procedure card in the netting pocket on the back of the seat in front of you. Eight was my record. Now it's mineral water all the way. Plus, there's no smoking on domestic flights. I have to make do with the consolations of history.

When Charles Lindbergh scooped the Orteig Prize of twenty-five thousand dollars for the first non-stop flight between Paris and New York on May 21st, 1927, he did something that would, almost certainly, have been done by someone else within the next few days—or hours. Two rival planes, the *Columbia* and the *America,* were waiting in their hangars on Roosevelt Field when Lindbergh took off in *The Spirit of St. Louis.* Two weeks before, a French contender, *L'Oiseau Blanc,* had been lost somewhere over the Atlantic; and in September 1926 a big three-engine Sikorsky piloted by René Fonck with a crew of three had crashed on take-off at the end of the Roosevelt Field runway.

Despite the crashes, the technology of aviation in 1927 was clearly up to the challenge set by Raymond Orteig, a French national who owned two New York hotels. Alcock and Brown had flown the Atlantic (by a much shorter route) eight years before; America had been crossed coast to coast; planes with a cruising speed of around 130 m.p.h. and a fuel capacity for forty hours of flying were being built on both sides of the Atlantic. Someone was going to do the thing, and it happened to be Lindbergh.

It was the aftermath of the flight, not the flight itself, that was extraordinary—the transformation of Lindy, the Lone Eagle, the Flying Fool, into the American hero who, for a few years, would shine in the popular imagination as the greatest American hero in history. His fame was majestically out of proportion to his actual achievement; and it is that disproportion which makes Lindbergh so fascinating a figure.

Here one has to forget about the facts and read the newspapers. By the time that Lindbergh arrived back in New York on June 13th, to be showered (they said) with eighteen hundred tons of tickertape, all the essential ingredients of the Lindbergh Story were in place. He was "the lanky demon of the skies from the wide open spaces," a solitary country boy (forget that he was born in Detroit), from Little Falls, Minnesota, on the banks of the Mississippi. He was a child of nature, raised in woods by Fenimore Cooper, on water by Mark Twain.

Like Huck, Lindy ran away from school (correct: he flunked out of the University of Wisconsin, Madison); but he never smoked a corncob pipe or touched a drop of liquor. In bootleg America, Lindy was incorruptibly teetotal and (like this damned plane) smoke-free. He was also chaste. Mother was his only girl.

Even the most admiring of Lindbergh's later biographers have left a picture of a priggish and sexually backward young man with a questionable taste in male roughhousing and practical jokes (he is supposed to have placed a live poisonous snake in the bed of a roommate who'd been dating a girl). In 1927, this sort of thing may, I suppose, have passed for cleaner fun than it does now. Certainly Lindbergh the Virgin Boy was the Lindbergh that America then wanted, and his irritable shrugging-off of the girls who tried to cling to him at parades was a famous part of his charm.

The skies had been billed as "the new frontier" and Lindbergh was groomed by his image-makers into the most perfect of old-fashioned, literary-sentimental frontiersmen. His truest ancestor was Natty Bumppo, wise in the woods, innocent in towns. Natty's aliases—Hawkeye, Pathfinder—fitted Lindbergh beautifully; and the best-known alias of all—Leatherstocking—has a spooky aptness when one looks at photographs of Lindbergh in his triumphal year. In flying gear, Lindy *is* Leatherstocking, from the coonskin hat of his undone airman's helmet down through the trapper's leather coveralls to the fur-lined boots. Leatherstocking's sole concession to technology is his trusty musket; Lindy's is *The Spirit of St. Louis*, in front of which he stands, one hand behind his back resting gently on the plane's propeller.

In the spirit of Leatherstocking, Lindy, in the Lindbergh Story at least, walked alone. Not only was his flight a singlehanded one, in contrast to the two- and four-man crews of most of the rival planes, but he represented the unaided individual talent, battling against the syndicate and the corporation. He was the barnstormer, employed to take folks up for a spin at five dollars a ride at country fairs; the lone pilot, flying the night mail to Chicago for a tinpot outfit in St. Louis. As the house poet of the *New York Sun* put it:

> . . . no kingly plane for him;
> No endless data, comrades, moneyed chums;
> No boards, no councils, no directors grim—
> He plans ALONE . . . and takes luck as it comes.

This was to forget rather a lot, including the backing of the St. Louis *Globe-Democrat,* and several individual members of its board, a St. Louis bank, a St. Louis insurance company and a St. Louis aviation business, along with the services of an enterprising PR man called Dick Blythe, who was assigned to promote Lindbergh by the mammoth Wright Aeronautical Corporation. In fact, Lindbergh was impressively efficient at persuading the various boards, councils and directors of St. Louis that his attempt on the Orteig Prize would bring glory to the city, and managed to raise $15,000 before commissioning a plane from the Ryan Aircraft Company in San Diego at a price of $10,580. But it's true that these sums were small compared with the $100,000 spent on the *America* by Admiral Byrd, and Lindbergh's corporate loneliness rang with at least metaphorical conviction.

Alone (or rather ALONE, *New York Sun*-style), tall, young, pure, a creature of the Heartland and the wide open spaces, the very incarnation of the folk-hero of the frontier, Lindbergh made flying an airplane into something that America had been doing all through the sweetest and best years of its own history. It wasn't something new, like driving an automobile or dancing the black bottom; it was something old, and Lindbergh was teaching America to remember it.

As John William Ward showed in his essay, "The Meaning of Lindbergh's Flight" (1958), the myth of Lindbergh effected a magnificent reconciliation between the new machine age and the tradition of self-reliant American individualism. At a moment when the one was seen to be the inevitable destroyer of the other, the Lindbergh Story told the nation how it might be possible to have both at the same time. "We did it," Lindbergh is supposed to have said when he touched down at Le Bourget, and his book of the flight was simply called *We*—man and machine, nature and technology.

Yet in Lindbergh's time, the airplane was a very special kind of machine, itself a strange hybrid between ancient craft and new technology. It relied on the internal combustion engine, but it did not roll off the end of a Ford assembly line. In an era of steel, the airplane was largely made of wood and natural fabric. It had the motive force of an automobile, the bone structure of a gull and the rigging and joinery of a yacht.

When William Boeing started up his Seattle airplane factory in 1916, there was a telling poignancy in his choice of site on the Duwamish River, a few miles short of its confluence with Puget Sound. For "$10 and other considerations," Boeing bought the tiny shipyard of Edward Heath, who'd built Boeing's personal yacht, the *Taconite*, in 1910. Heath was bankrupt. World War I was a vile time for the wooden yacht business. Boeing bought Heath's premises, tools and stock of timber, rehired his work force, and set to building planes in the same shed. It was shipbuilders' work, on the delicate scale of a lightweight racing canoe. The stringers and steam-bent frames were made of oak, ash and sitka spruce, lapped with hand-sewn fabric and coated with banana oil. This was not the province of the industrial factory but of the chisel, fretsaw, gluepot; a pine-dusty *atelier* where craftsmen, who might otherwise have been done out of their jobs by the machine, instead found themselves, improbably, making the very latest, fastest, most fashionable machines of the machine age.

No love of twentieth-century technology was needed to admire their work. It was intimate handicraft of the kind that could be immediately seen, smelled and understood. The engines of the planes were newfangled, outlandish, incomprehensible except to their mechanics, but their wooden propellors were carved, turned and sanded down to a sculptural finish. You could see through the taut, opaque skin of a plane to a structure as painstaking and delicate as that of a matchstick cathedral. People who still shuddered at the sight of a Ford car or a steel-frame skyscraper could be seduced by a Curtiss Jenny or a Beechcraft . . . as indeed they were by *The Spirit of St. Louis,* Lindbergh's endearingly dumpy and forthright Ryan monoplane.

The Atlantic flight established the myth, but it was later in the summer of 1927 that Lindbergh drove America wild with the domestic flight of all time. He took *The Spirit of St. Louis* on a 22,350-mile tour of all 48 states, and led grand parades in 82 cities. Leonard Mosley, in *Lindbergh,* writes:

> He was paid $50,000 for making the tour, but he did it less for the money than because he earnestly believed that showing himself and the *Spirit* to the people, and always arriving on time no matter what the weather, would prove to them that the air age had arrived and they should become part of it.

Showing himself and the Spirit *to the people* . . . These were the manifestations of a god making himself flesh. His robe was touched, as souvenir hunters snipped away fragments of the sacred fabric from the fuselage.

In that summer, Lindbergh knitted the land mass of North America together in a great web of intercity air routes. Until now, flying had been a sport, a method of warfare, a means of carrying mail. There were a few passenger services—the earliest had been started in 1914, when the Benoist Company set up regular flights between Tampa and St. Petersburg in Florida. Even in the middling-to-late 1920s, though, passengers, insofar as there were any passengers, were usually expected to fit themselves between the mailbags and muddle in as best they could. Lindbergh's second, domestic flight articulated a vision of the whole of the United States seen from the air. He connected up a mass of scattered dots and made a thrilling picture of them.

Here, resting in its molded beige niche, under a silky veil of polythene, is something that the airline, in a shaft of facetious wit, calls breast of chicken. 38E has already wolfed hers down and has started in on the red Jell-O. My bit of bird yields to the prodding of a baby plastic knife and fork with unbecoming cowardice. It goes to pieces. It seems to be as bad at air travel as I am myself. I lunch like an anchorite on a sprig of cold broccoli and a saltine. Face pressed against the chilly perspex of the window, I count the disintegrating jet trails in the sky; four of them, shredding to bits like tufts of wet cotton wool. Below them lie some thin, violet streaks of cirrus, and below the clouds, a land too witchy-dark to make much sense of. Is that a mountain or a city? I'm not sure. The occasional fuse-wire glints are rivers, I think. From six miles up, in hazy visibility, the earth unspools without incident, without much interest, like an underexposed home movie.

After Lindbergh, the big money poured into American aviation. In 1928, C. M. Keys, the asset-stripping, merger-making president of Transcontinental Air Transport, paid the flying god two hundred fifty thousand dollars for—being the flying god, having the ear of President Hoover, and allowing his name to be associated, if vaguely, with TAT. The terms of the agreement between Keys and Lindbergh were made public in 1934 when, under Roosevelt, the Black Committee was investigating graft in the allocation of government mail contracts to the airlines. It appeared that Keys was mainly interested in explaining to Lindbergh what he need *not* do in return for his quarter million down and ten thousand dollars a year.

> You will not, until you express a desire to do so, become a director of the company. It is not my desire or intention, nor is it yours, that this work shall prevent you from carrying on other activities for the general advancement of aviation in which you have so deep an interest. Nor will it prevent you from carrying on other business activities not competitive with those of Transcontinental Air Transport Inc . . .

What the money essentially represented was the price set, in June 1928, by a tough businessman, on the picture painted a year before by the Leatherstocking of the skies. Keys's advertising men set out to educate America into calling TAT "The Lindbergh Line."

The speed of events from then on can be measured by the advance order books for the Boeing 247D, which came into production in 1933. The 247 was the first twin-engined, all-metal airliner. It carried ten passengers, a pilot, co-pilot and one flight attendant. It flew at two hundred miles an hour and had a range of a little over six hundred miles. Before the mock-up stage of the aircraft had been completed, sixty orders had been placed for it by U.S. airlines. It went coast to coast (with refueling stops) and shuttled between cities like New York and Chicago and Los Angeles and San Francisco.

It is, I imagine, a Boeing 247 in which the first chapter of Scott Fitzgerald's *The Last Tycoon* is set, and in which two distinctively new types of American make their appearance. One is Monroe Stahr, the movie producer closely based on Irving Thalberg. The other is Cecilia Brady, the novel's narrator and a rather self-consciously precocious junior at Bennington College in Vermont. Her newness resides in the fact that she is going back to her parents' Hollywood home at the end of a semester, and she is flying.

"The world from an airplane I knew," she says, and the grammatical inversion is a nice Bennington-girlism, just this side of arch.

Father always had us travel back and forth that way from school and college. After my sister died when I was a junior, I traveled to and fro alone, and the journey always made me think of her, made me somewhat solemn and subdued. Sometimes there were picture people I knew on board the plane, and occasionally there was an attractive college boy—but not often during the depression. I seldom really fell asleep during the trip, what with thoughts of Eleanor and the sense of that sharp rip between coast and coast—at least not till we had left those lonely little airports in Tennessee.

This is post-Lindbergh geography, beautifully phrased: the mere "sharp rip" between coast and coast, a black and lonely canyon, barely inhabited, between the two bright points of American civilization. Here is *flyoverland*—that region of disregarded spaces where the lesser mortals live.

In the novel, a brewing storm in the Mississippi valley forces the plane to make an unscheduled landing at Nashville. ("Nashville!" says Wylie White, a Hollywood scriptwriter and fellow passenger. "My God! I was born in Nashville.") During the descent (" . . . going down, down, down, like Alice in the rabbit hole . . ."), Cecilia looks out of the window at the distant city and meditates on airports and on her own grandeur as an airborne American:

I suppose there has been nothing like the airports since the days of the stage-stops—nothing quite as lonely, as sombre-silent. The old red-brick depots were built right into the towns they marked—people didn't get off at those isolated stations unless they lived there. But airports lead you way back into history like oases, like the stops on the great trade routes. The sight of air travellers strolling in ones and twos into midnight airports will draw a small crowd any night up to two. The young people look at the planes, the older ones look at the passengers with a watchful incredulity. In the big trans-continental planes we were the coastal rich, who casually alighted from our cloud in mid-America.

Grounded in the small hours, the Californians might as well have been suddenly tipped into Thailand or Tuscany. They are innocent tourists in their own country. A railroad line, a highway, would have prepared them for Tennessee, but the high night sky has equipped them with no clues or presentiments. They commission a taxi driver to take them to the Andrew Jackson home, the Hermitage; a drive that takes longer in the book (two hours, or thereabouts) than it looks on the map (eleven miles). On the way, they see a Negro driving three cows (the South!); Cecilia is impressed, even in the darkness, by the lush green of the Tennessee woods. They reach the Hermitage at dawn, when, not surprisingly, it turns out to be closed to the public. They go back to the airport, leaving one of their number behind to take the Andrew Jackson tour. Within six pages of dialogue, and back into darkness again, they are landing at Glendale airport, returned to the real, important, coastal world.

The Cecilia Brady approach to Nashville is a prophetic model of a new kind of relationship between Americans and their landscape. Casually to alight from a cloud, to taste a city in a spirit of lofty and alienated connoisseurship, was to become *the* American way of traveling, and it was to have enormous consequences for the social and family life of the nation.

As the planes got bigger and ticket prices went down, air travel stopped being the prerogative of the coastal rich. One of the perks of the job for almost every middle-class corporate employee was to fly, several times a year, to the trade fair, the sales conference, the professional convention (Funeral Directors of America . . . The American Society of Anesthesiologists . . .). The airport cities built Convention & Trade Centers in their moldering downtowns and leafleted the country with extravagant advertisements for themselves. Lifeless dumps rechristened themselves with the names of precious stones (The Ruby City, The Emerald City, The Sapphire City) or proclaimed that they were the Gateway to the Great Lakes, the West, the Orient, the Sunbelt. Color photographs of a recently cleaned-up slum showed gas lamps, cobblestones, a gallery, an open-air café ("Shoppers take a needed break to enjoy Blandville's world-famous *croissants* and *latte*").

In corporate offices high over New York and Chicago, marketing directors and their assistants went into conference. "We gave the beach people Miami back in January; now we owe the golfers one. How about Phoenix? You got anything on golf in Phoenix?"

For the corporate tourists, the nature of cities abruptly changed. Now they swam up to meet you from below the cloud ceiling, out of context, exotic, phenomenal. Their only hinterland was the pale speedway that linked them to their airport.

In the crowded program of the conventioneer there was no time to find out the *why* of *here*. Cities had to make themselves instantly memorable by means of some totem or icon. St. Louis was that place where the Arch was. Philadelphia was the Liberty Bell. In the one-hour guided tour, you needed a single novelty or monument to put the city on your private map of the United States. We went to sales conference there—that was the Alamo; *that* was the Paul Revere House; *that* was the Space Needle; *that* was the Grand Old Opry; *that* was Astroworld; *that* was Preservation Hall.

Touting for custom, the cities were marvelously resourceful at dreaming up ways to imprint themselves on the memories of these jaded and blasé air travelers. In chambers of commerce, fiction writers were set to construct local-color "regional cuisine" recipes. Where no ready-made icons existed, the city fathers raised money to build them—constructions so tall and bizarre that (like the Public Services Building in Portland, Oregon) they would figure in the subsequent nightmares of even the most absentminded of short-stay visitors.

This constant jetting about between convention centers had created an extraordinary body of misleading knowledge. Almost every American I knew who worked for a large company seemed to have visited almost every American city I could name for a period of, on average, about thirty-six hours. Wherever I was going, they knew it.

"Oh, but you *have* to try those tiny oysters there, more flavor than food . . . you *have* to go to the Pike Place Market . . . you *have* to take the elevator up to the top of the Space Needle for the view . . . and there's a hotel there (I didn't stay in it myself) where you can fish right out your window . . ."

"But what's the *place* like?"

That was the trouble. They hadn't been to a place. There hadn't been time for that. They had dropped out of the sky in order to be shown a tight cluster of artfully manufactured symbols.

Yet there was something very different in all this from the usual tourists' whirl through the Great Cities of Europe. These were domestic flights, and these were domestic fliers, beating the bounds of their enormous home patch. If you flew, coast to coast and Lakes to Gulf, as often, and as indifferently, as these people, the experience would eventually give you a landowner's sense of possession. All the cities you have nibbled at, as if each one was an éclair, they are *yours*. Maybe one day, when you're shown the swing door, or the kids are in college, you'll come back and take up your inheritance for a while, in the Topaz City or the Gateway to the Rockies.

It is a thought that comes easily, and comfortingly, at six miles up. You are not really half so heavy as you feel. You think of the house and garden, the neighbors (you never liked their cats, or their children)—that brick albatross with its leaky roof and un-mended fence. On the ground, *home* is a word like *fate;* it's what you've got, what you probably deserved. In the air, it has a differ-ent ring. It's a disposable asset. *I quit the office, sold my home and my car, and took the plane . . .*

My seat-back's on full tilt. I'm indulging myself in American thoughts, looking sleepily out over my great estate. The land below has brightened up since the last time I inspected it. It's agribusiness territory, in some Midwestern state; a flat checker-board, the colors burned out of it by the sun. We're flying over the close crosshatching of a town, and I can pick out its water tower, a silver button-mushroom, and the heliographic wink of what I take to be the herded pickups on the lot of the local auto dealership.

We're sustaining the right height. There's a war on down there—silos full of unsold corn, debt, foreclosures, repo men moving in on family farms. From here, the unhappy heartland still looks orderly and fat, but the news is bad. I remember (in this detached, Cecilia Bradyish way) the story of a respectable Iowa farmer who got out his old Remington shotgun one morning, blew his wife's heart clean out of her body, drove down to the bank and shot his personal banker, killed a neighboring farmer with whom he was in dispute, then, sitting in his pickup, pointed the gun barrel at his own chest and pulled the trigger. This story, or so it was said at the time, fairly represented the despair in the farming communities of the Midwest in the 1980s. Dale Burr of Lone Tree had only done what thousands of farmers like him were on the brink of doing now.

I search the landscape for signs, but find none. I think of the farmers' sons and daughters, booking their flights out.

I think, dozily, of how the Boeing 747 is a machine designed to sprinkle Americans thinly across the breadth of their country like so many grains of pepper. On every flight, I suppose, there's a man or woman who never gets to use the return half of their ticket. *In town for the ABA, I got talking with this guy who . . .* and back in New York, there's another vacancy advertised in *Publishers Weekly.*

So the American family gets atomized. Father's up in Portland, Maine, with his new wife from Minneapolis (they met in Europe). Mother's down in Sarasota, Florida. She's playing bridge. There's a brother out in San Diego, a sister in real estate in Tucson, and Grandma still lives over in Baltimore. We're a real close family.

And they are. At Thanksgiving, the airport is a bee-swarm of people coming home and people going home. They cross each other in the skies—millions of bits of families trying to reunite for the holiday. There is a moment, at around 7 P.M. on the third Wednesday of every November, when more Americans must be up in the air than are down on the ground. It is an hour when thoughtless strangers shoot questioning looks at each other on the streets: is there a curfew? Has the Alert gone out? Was it on TV? It does not last long. Local time zones stagger the effect. Between the jam on the freeway out to the airport made by the homegoers and the jam on the freeway back from the airport made by the homecomers there is an absence, a vacuum, like a missed heartbeat, as America takes wing.

I think of the far-flung families, and imagine trying to draw their family trees. Instead of vertical trunks, angular branches and = signs, you'd have curving Great Circle routes, with little diagrammatic drawings of jet planes, to join them up. An extended American family would look exactly like the flight-path plan at the back of the United in-flight magazine. Degrees of cousinship could be instantly measured by the number of times you'd have to change planes to get from Sam to Delia. Divorce would be signaled by a rerouting. Death would consist of dotted lines.

In the crabby little dim-bulb toilet I shave and—painfully—change my shirt. Returning to my seat, I stumble over the knees of 38E.

"Sorry. I'm so sorry—"

"You're welcome," she says, and I notice for the first time that her English is phrase-book new. When she was moving her lips over the sentences in the *National Enquirer,* she must have been trying quietly to pronounce them to herself. A language lesson. *Sorry.*

Flying west, racing against the sun, the afternoon stands still. The hard light over the Midwest is the same hard light that shines on the mountains below us now, where the tender crust of the earth has broken out in boils. The plane is almost grazing the tops of the tawny craters. The whole place looks like a phase of Satan's exiled journey in *Paradise Lost. Rocks, caves, lakes, fens, bogs, dens, and shades of death* . . . But it is only Wyoming, or Idaho, a fleeting distraction in the window, gone almost as soon as noticed. Few of the domestic fliers even bother to look out at this appalling geological calamity. Long hardened to the extravagance of America, they'd sooner check their engagement books, do sums on pocket calculators and brood over the funnies.

Twenty-five hundred miles on, we've managed to find the same weather we set out in. The sky is lightless, the body of the plane is lapped in feathery gray. The beams of our individual overhead reading lights stand out as sharp yellow cones. We're going down. I've got ear trouble again, and a baby is screaming somewhere back in the forties. The fuselage creaks and slams. There's nothing to see, and only the alarming change of pitch in the engines to listen to. They rev up, drop to a purr, rev up again, as the Boeing shyly feels its way down from cloud to cloud. It is an interminably slow way of falling, and a gristly tumor of fear has taken hold in my guts—a tumor so familiar that I can almost laugh it off now; almost, but not quite. This is still a scary adventure for a foreign flier.

Shouldering through the dark and lumpy nimbus, I can hear the clunk of the wheels coming down, but there's still no sign of land. Like a sick white whale floundering in a muddy sea, the plane keeps on going deeper, way past the point where, by my reckoning, we should have touched bottom. Then, suddenly, the ground is there, right under the wing and sickeningly close: the boxy, two-story houses of a raw suburb, cars with their lights on in a wet street. The tarmac slick is flying past under our seats—and still no touchdown. I keep my eyes tight shut for the crunch, which comes, goes, returns, and is met by the comforting roar of the engines going into reverse thrust.

It's over. In the middle distance, men in storm gear are shunting about in yellow tractors. We're back in the real world. It's raining. Perhaps it never stopped.

SIX

Gold Mountain

I T'S DARK and deathly quiet in here. The sheets of the bed are cool and laundry-smelling, but there's a niff in the air, sweet and sickly, like dead chrysanthemums. Sleep has disassembled the self: it will take patience to rebuild a person out of the heap of components in the bed. The dial of a wristwatch looms in front of a single open eye; its luminous green hands say that it is either twenty-five after midnight or five in the morning. The spare human hand goes out on a cautious reconnaissance patrol through the darkness. It snags on a sharp corner, knocks over a bottle of pills, finds a solid, cold, ceramic bulge. Fingers close on the knurled screw of the switch and the room balloons with light.

It's a conventioneers' hotel room. The waking eye takes in the clubland furniture in padded leatherette, the Audubon prints, the thirty-six-inch TV mounted over the minibar, the heavy cream drapes across the window. The room is painlessly impersonal, artfully designed to tell the self nothing about where it is or who it is supposed to be. It looks like its price. It is just a seventy-five-dollar room.

The nose sources the bad smell to a toothglass of Scotch and tap water on the bedside table. The time is five o'clock, but feels later.

Does seventy-five dollars buy twenty-four-hour room service? The shallow drawer below the telephone ought to yield a hotel directory, but doesn't. It contains two books of the same size and in the same binding: a Gideon Bible and *The Teaching of Buddha*, in English and Japanese, donated (it says) by the Buddhist Pro-

239

moting Foundation, Japan. This is the room's first and only give-away. The hotel where Jesus and Buddha live side by side in the drawer is on the Pacific Rim.

The text is printed on thin crinkly paper.

A true homeless brother determines to reach his goal of Enlightenment even though he loses his last drop of blood and his bones crumble into powder. Such a man, trying his best, will finally attain the goal and give evidence of it by his ability to do the meritorious deeds of a homeless brother.

There's no reply from room service on 107, so, sitting up in bed, long before dawn and *Good Morning America,* I read Gautama for the first time, and find his teaching interestingly apposite to the situation and the hour.

Unenlightened man, said the Buddha, was trapped in an endless cycle of becoming—always trying to be something else or somebody else. His unhappy fate was to spend eternity passing from one incarnation to the next, each one a measure of his ignorant restlessness and discontent. In the search for Nirvana, man must stop being a becomer and learn how to be a be-er.

It is profoundly un-American. Here in this travelers' room, in this nation of chronic travelers and becomers, *The Teaching of Buddha* has the same note of disregarded truth as the health warning on an emptied pack of cigarettes. The idea that the whole of the external world is a treacherous fiction, that the self has no real existence, goes right against the Protestant, materialist American grain.

No wonder that so many Americans have looked across the Pacific to Buddhism to provide an antidote to the American condition. Emerson and the New England Transcendentalists, Whitman, T. S. Eliot, the Dharma Bums, J. D. Salinger, Robert M. Pirsig's *Zen and the Art of Motorcycle Maintenance,* in every phase of postcolonial American history, Buddhism has offered a rhetoric of dissent; and on the Pacific coast it has colored the fabric of the culture.

I look at the advice I've failed to follow—

... in the evening he should have a time for quiet sitting and meditation and a short walk before retiring. For peaceful sleep he should rest on the right side with his feet together and his last thought should be of the time when he wishes to rise in the early morning.

—and copy it into my notebook. It sounds like a good tip; far better than pills and whiskey.

Fiction or not, the external world is beginning to make its presence felt now. The drapes open on a city still blue in the half-light. Lines of cars on the wet streets a few floors below the window are making a muffled drumming sound; the morning commute from the suburbs is already under way. Yet even at this sore-headed hour, no one is slamming on the brakes, hitting the horn or dodging from lane to lane to beat the neighbors to the parking lot. By the louche standards of the American city, this place seems disconcertingly silent, serious and polite, as the cars roll smoothly past, keeping their distance, like a giant funeral cortege.

Seven o'clock. It's time to shave and shower; time to put Buddha back in the drawer and become someone else.

On that particular morning, in hotels and motels, in furnished rooms and cousins' houses, 106 other people were waking to their first day as immigrants to Seattle. These were flush times, with jobs to be had for the asking, and the city was growing at the rate of nearly forty thousand new residents a year. The immigrants were piling in from every quarter. Many were out-of-state Americans: New Yorkers on the run from the furies of Manhattan; refugees from the Rustbelt; Los Angelenos escaping their infamous crime statistics, their huge house prices and jammed and smoggy freeways; redundant farm workers from Kansas and Iowa. Then there were the Asians—Samoans, Laotians, Cambodians, Thais, Vietnamese, Chinese and Koreans, for whom Seattle was the nearest city in the continental United States. A local artist had proposed a monumental sculpture, to be put up at the entrance to Elliott Bay, representing Liberty holding aloft a bowl of rice.

The falling dollar, which had so badly hurt the farming towns of the Midwest, had come as a blessing to Seattle. It lowered the price abroad of the Boeing airplanes, wood pulp, paper, computer software and all the other things that Seattle manufactured. The port of Seattle was a day closer by sea to Tokyo and Hong Kong than was Los Angeles, its main rival for the shipping trade with Asia.

By the end of the 1980s, Seattle had taken on the dangerous luster of a promised city. The rumor had gone out that if you had failed in Detroit you might yet succeed in Seattle—and that if you'd succeeded in Seoul, you could succeed even better in Seattle. In New York and in Guntersville I'd heard the rumor. Seattle was the coming place.

So I joined the line of hopefuls. We were everywhere, and we kept on bumping into each other and comparing notes. At breakfast in the hotel dining room I noticed that the woman at the next table was doing exactly what I was doing myself: circling ads on the Real Estate page of the *Post-Intelligencer* with a ballpoint pen. I was on *Downtown;* she was roaming round the city, going from *University* to *Queen Anne* to *Fremont, Magnolia* and *Capitol Hill.* She had the old-money equestrienne look—the boots, the khaki slacks, the hacking jacket, white silk blouse and gold chain that I'd once coveted for myself. Her expression, as she plowed through the small print, was avid: she was rolling the telegraphese of *3-bed, 2-ba* round in her head as if it were lines from Wallace Stevens.

"I got to find somewhere fast," she said. "Flew in last night. My furniture's all in store in Denver, Colorado, and that *costs.*"

For a minute or two, her eyes went back to the paper. She sucked on the end of her pen. Then she looked up from the advertisements in order to deliver a non-stop ten-minute advertisement for herself.

Yesterday was her birthday, her thirty-first birthday—she'd always said she was going to change her life when she was thirty-one—and it was on her chart; an astrologer had told her—she was a Scorpio—Scorpios were great decision makers—she'd had her own business back in Denver—real estate—and a big house—and a car, a silver BMW 520i—she'd sold the business—and the house—and the car—and just *come to Seattle*.

She was the heroine of an adventure story, and she was telling it like the Ancient Mariner.

"I was up here five days last year—I got friends over in West Seattle. I took one look at this city and I knew. Right then I said, 'Susan, here's where you're going to spend your thirties.' I had this gut feeling. Well—here I am."

It was hard to slide a word in edgeways, but there had to be some as yet unconfessed reason for this audacious and arbitrary move. Love, maybe? If so, why was she spending her first day here alone in a hotel?

"Susan . . . tell me. I still haven't got it. Why here? Why Seattle?"

I was violating her right to tell her own tale. She blinked at the question and shook her head in an impatient swirl of lacquered chestnut hair. "Oh—the quality of the lifestyle, the good environment, the real-estate values; *you* know."

I had misjudged her. She was just a typical domestic flier with a low specific gravity.

Half an hour later, I was lodging a jacket and a pair of trousers with a dry cleaner's a block away from the hotel. The face of the man who took charge of them was a worried knot. He gave the clothes an empty, shell-shocked smile and said, "No problem." Then again, holding up the trousers by one leg, "No problem."

"Don't you want to make out a slip for them?" I said.

His gaze was distraught. "Thank you. Thank you. Yes, thank you."

A woman came out from behind the carousel of hanging garments and said something to the man in what I took to be Chinese. He scarpered.

"Oh, I am sorry," she said. "He is only in America two weeks. He not understanding English good. He learning very slow."

"Where is he from?" I asked.

"Inchon, in Korea. He start work yesterday. We train him as presser. But do not worry! We not let him loose on your pants yet, not this week." She laughed and touched her temple. "Jet lag. No 'on the ball.'"

"You're from Korea, too?"

"Yes, Seoul. But I am in America thirteen years. August 28, 1976."

The greenhorn was listening, peering out at us through a fringe of skirts and dresses. He was close to my own age, but his infancy in English gave him the facial expression of a fractious toddler. When I caught his eye, he ducked out of sight.

"And you like it here?"

"In America? Oh, yeah! It's good. It is so big! So green! So wide—wide—wide!"

Looking for somewhere to live, I quartered the city at the wheel of a new rental—a cherry-colored Spectrum with California plates and a painfully weak stomach. The steep little hills of Seattle made the car break wind with a sickly rumbling in its bowels. When I floored the gas pedal, the engine gave a shuddering sob and stalled.

The realtors turned up their noses at me. *No way*, they said, with lordly smiles, when I described what I had in mind. This was a sellers' market; house prices were up thirty percent on last year; the realtors didn't have time to talk even to *buyers* with less than a quarter million, cash in hand, and they certainly had no time to waste on me.

"Do you know where you're at here? This is Boomtown, U.S.A."

I drove on, through a cloud of pink dust. One could tell that Seattle was on a winning streak by the number of men in cranes who were trying to smash the place to bits with wrecking balls. The pink dust rose in explosive flurries over the rooftops and colored the low sky.

Pitched on a line of bluffs along Puget Sound, with Lake Washington at its back, Seattle had ships at the ends of its streets and gulls in its traffic. Its light was restless and watery, making the buildings shiver like reflections. It felt like an island and smelled of the sea.

It was a pity about the wrecking balls, for the city they were knocking down was an American classic; a survivor of the Theodore Roosevelt age of boosterish magniloquence. Where the high-toned buildings of Alabama had been cotton planters' daydreams of Ancient Greece, Seattle looked like a freehand sketch, from memory, of a sawmill owner's whirlwind vacation in Rome and Florence. Its antique skyscrapers were rude boxes, a dozen to fifteen stories high, fantastically candied over with patterned brick and terracotta moldings. Their facades dripped with friezes, gargoyles, pilasters, turrets, cornices, cartouches, balustrades and arabesques. Every bank and office block was an exuberant *palazzo*.

The whole thing was an exercise in conscious theater. All the most important buildings faced west, over the Sound, and Seattle was designed to be seen from the front. You were meant to arrive by ship, from Yokohama or Shanghai, and be overwhelmed by the financial muscle, the class (with a short *a*), the world-traveled air of this Manhattan of the Far West. If you had the bad taste to look at Seattle from the back, all you'd see would be plain brick cladding and a zig-zag tangle of fire escapes.

Until very recently, it seemed, Seattle had gotten along well enough with its turn-of-the-century Italian Renaissance architecture; but now the terracotta city was beginning to look dingy and stunted beside the sixty- and seventy-story towers that were sprouting over its head. Some were still just steel skeletons, with construction workers in hard hats swarming in their rigging like foretopmen. Some were newly unsheathed, with racing clouds mirrored in their black and silver glass. More were in the chrysalid stage, protected in rough shells of scaffolding and tarpaulins. Then there were the holes in the ground, the wrecking-ball jobs, the molded garland going into smithereens.

I was having little luck. A "furnished executive suite" turned out to be a low-ceilinged room, as small as Alice's, on a new block, at a rent of $1,400 a month. *No way.* A promising one-bedroom apartment on First Hill at $550 was for nonsmokers only.

"Even if I do it out the window?"

"Even if you do it out the window."

I asked around the bars. It was possible, apparently, to rent a room in a rooming house in the International District for $60 a month.

"But they're kind of funny. They're Vietnamese. I don't think they take Caucasians."

I was told about the Josephinum Residence at a bar, where it was variously reported to be an apartment block, a Catholic shelter for low-income families, an old people's home and a hotel. But it was generally agreed that, whatever it was, the place was so big that it must have empty rooms.

The building was a richly encrusted pile on Second Avenue, three blocks back from the waterfront. Inside, it looked like the Medici Tomb. Its vaulted ceiling, forty feet up, was tricked out in flaky gold; huge veined marble pillars supported a balustraded cloister on the mezzanine floor. A fifteenth-century merchant prince might have found it homely, but it was hard to fit this heroic essay in the architecture of power and money to the people who now occupied the Josephinum's lobby. Shrunken, bald, leaning on sticks and planting walking frames ahead of them, they limped and clicked across the marble hall. Crayoned notices, in big round letters, advertised Bingo, flu shots, the arrival of the Bookmobile and Mass at 3 P.M. in the chapel. It had the institutional smell of Lysol and overboiled cabbage.

At the desk I apologized for making a mistake; but no, said the manager, there was indeed a vacant room, and she'd be happy to show it to me. No, you didn't have to be old—it was just that at this time of day most of the other tenants were at work. Nor did you have to be a Catholic, nor a non-smoker; she was neither herself.

We stepped into the elevator with a spry centenarian whose black wig was a little askew on her head.

"She's as old as the state of Washington, aren't you, dear?" the manager said. "And you got a special telegram on your birthday from the President, didn't you?"

"Sure did," said the woman. "From the President."

"Mr. Bush."

"Lot of wind out there today." She tugged at her wig, bringing it down over her eyes.

"Oh, she could tell you a few things about Seattle; she's seen it all in her time, haven't you, dear?"

"Huh? Maybe," the woman growled. Being one hundred looked like a job that she had long grown bored with. As the elevator climbed the shaft, I watched her going through her flight-check routine: *wig*—okay; *afternoon paper*—okay; *specs*—roger; *room key*—where's that tarnation key? Yup, you got it. It's in your other hand.

On every floor we stopped at, a robed figure was waiting at the elevator doors. The first time this happened, I mistook him for a resident, then saw that he was St. Francis, with bluebirds, cast in plaster in the school of Dante Gabriel Rossetti. The centenarian got out at Joseph the Carpenter; we went on up to thirteen, Christ of the Sacred Heart. His beard was chipped, His blood had oxidized to chocolate; He was blessing the brassbound rococo Cutler mail chute.

A long dark corridor led to an enormous room, empty of furniture but full of light. The air tasted as if it had been left to cook for many months, and there were some curious stains on the yellow shag carpet, but the view from the uncurtained windows was serene. The room looked out over turreted flat roofs to Puget Sound: beyond the cowled air vents, plants in tubs, fire escapes and satellite dishes, ships were on the move in Elliott Bay, whose wind-damaged water looked like knapped flint. A car ferry was coming in to dock from a suburban island; a big container vessel, flying a Japanese flag, was being taken in hand by a pair of shovel-fronted tugs.

"You want to see the bathroom?"

I was busy with the fishing boats over by the West Seattle shore, the shipyards, the line of buoys pointing the way in to the Duwamish Waterway. At this window, one could spend all day far out at sea, with the city laid out under one's feet. It was a cormorant's perch.

"If you want a phone, the point's right here."

The light was changing, the water turning from gray to a pellucid iceberg green. The ferry sounded its diaphone. The note, way down at the bottom of the tuba range, reverberated in the glass of the windowpane.

"It's a hell of a view."

"You'd better enjoy it while it lasts. It probably won't last long. We're lucky here. We're saved. They were going to pull us down, but we just got our official designation. We're a historic landmark as of last month."

The building had been put up in 1906, at the height of the craze for Italianate magnificence. It had been the New Washington Hotel, Seattle's grandest. Theodore Roosevelt himself was one of its first guests—and the gilded swank of the New Washington, its triumphant Americanism, was a perfect embodiment of the Roosevelt presidency. It had stayed in business as a hotel until 1962, the year of the Seattle World's Fair, when Elvis Presley had lodged in a suite on the penthouse floor. Then it had been taken over by the Little Sisters of Mercy, who'd run it as a home and hospital for the elderly.

Although the Josephinum was still owned by the archdiocese, it had caught the 1980s virus of free market economics. As the old died in their rooms or were packed off to nursing homes, younger and richer people were being recruited to fill their places. New tenants had to pass a means test to prove that they earned at least sixty percent of the "median income" of seventeen thousand dollars a year, and some well-heeled out-of-towners had begun taking rooms in the Josephinum as their Seattle *pieds-à-terre*. It was still a cheap place to live by middle-class standards—this big studio, with dressing room and bathroom, cost $425 a month— but the building was steadily hoisting itself out of the reach of the people it had housed for the last quarter-century.

When I went down to the lobby, all conversation stopped. Walking frames came to a squeaky halt; dog-eared magazines were lowered and eyes raised over the tops of halfmoon specs. I was shaken to see that on every face there was an expression of frank antipathy to the appearance of the latest cuckoo in the Josephinum nest.

I saw—and saw too clearly for comfort—the man who was reflected in the old people's eyes: a guy in a loud pink denim suit, with a foreign accent and money to burn. He was a sign of the times. When the papers talked about the great Seattle boom, about clogged freeways and massive rent hikes, this was the man they had in mind: a paunchy stranger waving a checkbook and driving a car with California plates.

Booms in Seattle had always been triggered from a spot a long way off. It was not so much a place where things happened in themselves as a place that was intimately touched by distant, often very distant, events.

The city had boomed in 1897, when it had the good luck to find itself used as the main base camp for the Alaska gold rush. Yet Nome, Alaska, was more than 2,200 miles away by sea, and the long foul-weather voyage through the Bering Sea and the Gulf of Alaska tended to put a sobering perspective on things. Up in Nome, men were going crazy, gunning each other to death in bars, jumping claims and hitting the bottle; down in Seattle, the hoteliers, store owners, meat packers and shipping agents went about the quiet business of making money out of the madmen.

By 1910, the gold had run out and the boom towns had gone bust. (In 1923, E. B. White sailed from Seattle, where he had been sacked from the staff of the *Post-Intelligencer*, to Alaska; at Teller, the next port up from Nome, he found "about a dozen white men" left out of a gold rush population of ten thousand.) Yet Seattle, with Scandinavian patience and rectitude, continued to make money from its Alaskan connection. It was still doing so. In the Bon Marché department store on my first day, I had been puzzled as to why a city with such a famously gentle climate should need so many thermal space suits, fur-lined parkas and arctic boots. It took a little while to relate this curious display of winter fashions to the fact that every time I went to the hotel bar I met another resident of Fairbanks, Nome or Anchorage, in town on a flying business visit. Seattle had never given up the habit of thinking of Alaska as its private client-state, dependent on Seattle, to Seattle's considerable profit, for its clothing, victuals, liquor and Rest and Recreation.

In 1939, the city boomed again; and as with the gold rush, the cause was distant but the effect on Seattle was of a tremendous shot of adrenaline in the urban system. Over in Europe, the RAF was in urgent need of bombers. The latest, most devastating bomber was Boeing's B-17, the "Flying Fortress." At the outbreak of war, 4,000 people were employed at Boeing Field; by 1941, when the United States joined in the war, the number was up to 30,000; and in 1944, Boeing had a payroll of 50,000. The city swelled with immigrants from out of state and refugees from Europe.

Just as Seattle kept up with Alaska long after the gold rush, so it stayed in the aviation industry long after the war, when many big airplane factories went bankrupt. Since 1945, Boeing had faltered several times, and in the early 1970s a slump in orders at Boeing sent Seattle into depression. By 1989, around 110,000 Seattle people worked for Boeing, and the company was lording it over the international market, with a $30-billion turnover and nearly 700 new planes a year.

The present boom was of a piece with its predecessors. It had been triggered from far away, when the Tokyo stock market supplanted Wall Street as the fulcrum of world financial power. As the dollar ailed and the yen climbed even higher, Seattle flourished, on America's economic weakness, because, as everyone said, it was so close to Asia, the new New World.

Listening to people talk in New York or Guntersville, one might have supposed that Japan lay just beyond Bainbridge Island, a ferry ride across the water. From Seattle to Tokyo was a voyage of 4,276 sea miles; and by that measure, New York was conveniently close to Lagos, Nigeria, a rather distant sort of proximity.

In fact Seattle was close to the Far East in exactly the same way that it had been close to Nome and close to the European theaters of war—close enough to get the benefit of the action and plenty far enough to feel provincially detached from it. Tucked away in its fastness, deep down on Puget Sound, it was remote from all those great upheavals in foreign parts which brought money to the city and made it fat. Gold prospectors might get royally drunk; bomber crews might get shot out of the sky; Wall Street bankers might take the big leap from the fortieth floor window—but Seattle would get on with the daily business of making and counting its wealth. It had never been a boom town in the ordinary sense of the term. Its booms were so muffled and so long-drawn-out as to be almost inaudible.

Even now, the evidence of the latest boom was scant. Several of the new glass towers were being built with Japanese money. There was *The Teaching of Buddha* in the bedside drawer. The hotel lobby, when I arrived, had been blocked by a line of identical black suitcases with J.A.L. tags. On First Avenue and Seneca, six umbrellas in single file were raised over the heads of the six Japanese businessmen who were crossing the street in the drizzle. Each one carried a crocodile-skin document case with gold snaplocks.

The Japanese businessmen did not look at all like economic imperialists conquering a city. Like Seattle itself, they looked damp, serious and introspected, as if the city was well on the way to conquering them. In strict order, they shortened sail, scandalized their umbrellas and disappeared into the funeral-parlor oak paneling of McCormick and Schmick's Grill.

The whole temper of the city was mild. The weather was mild. The driving was mild. There wasn't a horn to be heard and everyone made room on the road for everybody else. Even on empty streets, pedestrians waited in polite knots for the sign to flash WALK before they crossed. Life here, in daylight hours at least, seemed to be conducted according to the unwritten rules of an old-fashioned gentlemen's club. Even the street people had the air of members in good standing. A shaggy derelict, looking like the prophet Isaiah, was panhandling on Third and Pike. "Any chance you might have some loose change on you?" "Sure," I said, and dug out fifty cents. "Thanks, pardner. Have a good one." He was a world away from the desperate supplicants of Manhattan Island.

From a stool in Oliver's Bar, I watched the shoppers on Fourth Avenue. They were tacking, in ones and twos, between Bon Marché (Seattle's Macy's) and Frederick & Nelson's (Seattle's Bloomingdale's). Ralph Lauren would have been appalled to see them. He had barely gotten a toehold on this city of crumpled dark suits, baggy corduroys, home-knit sweaters, plaid lumber jackets, thick golfing socks, dirndl skirts and sensible shoes. The men went in for beards and rubber-banded pigtails, the women for long, fair, frizzy tangles, as if they'd just come back from swimming. Nobody seemed to be dressing for show, or snobbery, or sexual conquest. The fashion in Seattle was to make yourself comfortable in quantities of wool and flannel.

Nowhere in the United States had I met such an air of gentility and reserve. Seattle, on first sight, was punctiliously dull. It was as if the city had come to believe in the legend of its own architecture; it seemed to think that it really was centuries old, a wise and ancient survivor in a flighty world.

Even the rain was subtle. It had been falling for hours, as light and finely sifted as talcum powder. It didn't splash or drip; you couldn't—quite—feel it on your skin. It was a spontaneous liquefaction of the air, and it imparted an authentic antique gleam to the gargoyles, sculpted nymphs and cornucopias of summer fruits. It muffled, even further, the sound of the boom.

In an art shop above Pike Place Market, I was riffling through a stack of prints, searching for pictures to civilize the high bare walls of the room in the Josephinum. The woman who ran the store was an immigrant from the Midwest. "We like it here. It's so quiet after Chicago. Nothing ever happens. That's why we like it."

I chose a Georgia O'Keeffe poster, of blue and purple pansies enlarged to the size of giant sunflowers, and a big Hockney, half map, half picture, of Sunset Boulevard. The woman rolled them up and fed them into a cardboard cylinder for me.

"Well—" she said. "How long do you think it'll be? Before you die of boredom in Seattle?"

In my absence my name had gone up on the door. The strip of Dynotape read RAINBIRD, which sounded like a useful alias.

It took a couple of days to furnish Rainbird's quarters. With Sandra, the Josephinum's manager, I looted the Presley suite on the fourteenth floor. The rooms had been left as they were in 1962, when Elvis and his entourage moved out; not because the archdiocese revered them as a shrine, but because the plumbing had seized up.

"You mean, Elvis wrecked the toilet?"

"I don't know—he always looked kind of constipated to me . . ."

The place was dusty-sad, its stale air laden. It made 1962 seem a long, long way back. Exposure to nearly three decades of grimy sunlight had robbed the furnishings of their color. What had been the height of hotel opulence at the time of Camelot and the New Frontier was now bleached and woebegone. Even in 1962, Elvis had gone to fat and old-time religion. He must have sat here glumly, pouch-faced, taking pills, already blown at twenty-seven. I salvaged his gold-painted writing desk and matching chair, his six-seater couch upholstered in gilt and crushed velvet, his twin table lamps of turquoise glass. I would have liked to have asked for Elvis's bed, but that seemed to smack too obviously of necrophilia.

The maintenance men fitted my room with blinds and curtains. A bookcase came up from the library on the second floor. I bought an electric cooking ring from Woolworth's. With flowers from the market, a bowl of fruit, a television (lent by Sandra), plus the Hockney and the O'Keeffe blue-tacked to the walls, Room 1327 looked like home. A glance at Rainbird's quarters showed that one important thing was missing from his life, but I'd studied the tenancy regulations of the building and they were firm on the point. *Only caged birds and aquarium pets permitted.*

On my first morning in residence I was woken by the indignant chirrup of a firetruck down below. After the truck had passed, the city was silent except for the wind, which piped and moaned under the cornice, making the Josephinum sound like a ship on passage through an empty sea. I listened carefully. It was blowing Force 5 or 6, from the northeast. I put the kettle on to boil and raised the blind over Elvis's gold desk.

The dawn was cold and clear. For the last three days, Seattle had been smothered in banks of low cloud, the tops of its tallest buildings lost in swirls of pinky-gray. Now the ceiling was gone, and the city, which had seemed so elderly and substantial before, appeared in a quite different light. The keen wind and the rising barometer had restored it to its proper place in the enormous landscape of the West.

Beyond the Sound and its archipelago of low islands, the

Olympic mountains showed as a razored serration of the horizon. At the south end of Second Avenue, Mount Rainier had sprung into view, its creamy fifteen-thousand-foot bulk looming over the city from fifty miles away. Seattle was ringed all round by snowy mountains, thick green forest and violet early-morning water. This morning, the city looked humbled. It squatted modestly on its bay, a man-made scratch on an epic natural landscape. Set beside the sea, the steep woods, the black rock-faces and the snowcaps, Seattle was hardly more than a collection of temporary sheds.

Twelve blocks south of the Josephinum, the roof of the Smith Tower, a white pyramid like a folded paper hat, was outlined against the great white peak of Mount Rainier. The tower had been Seattle's great landmark. Built in 1912, its forty-two stories made it the tallest building west of the Mississippi, a title it had held for more than thirty years. For days on end, as long as the cloud cover lasted, you'd be fooled by the Smith Tower; then, one day, you'd wake, as I had woken, to see that it was not a landmark at all, but a thumbnail parody of the natural landmark that lay in hiding behind it.

Seattle had certainly tried hard. It had caked itself in a crust of historical makeup, had spread as far across its boggy hinterland as it could go, had levered itself up into the clouds; but it still bore the marks of a raw settlement in a new territory.

Once upon a time, New York, Chicago, Boston must have looked like this—as tentative encroachments on a world still wild. Where nature makes everything human look small, a small human can feel that he's in with a chance, here where the big humans haven't completely sewn up the place for themselves.

My window looked out over a city of uncrowded streets and untenanted spaces. There were lock-up stores for rent, vacant lots ripe for development, NOW HIRING placards on building sites. There was the bracing smell of possibility down there; even now, this late in the game, a guy could make a living out of such a provisional and half-built landscape—could arrive out of nowhere, set up shop and become an *alrightnik* in the classic immigrant tradition. As the first wave of commuter cars began to roll funereally down Second Avenue to the glass money-boxes of the business district, I thought: if I were seeking a fresh start in America, I'd go to Seattle.

Of all the new arrivals, it was the Koreans who had made the biggest, boldest splash. Wherever I went, I saw their patronyms on storefronts, and it seemed that half the small family businesses in Seattle were owned by Parks or Kims. I picked up my trousers from the dry cleaner's at the back of the Josephinum, stopped for milk and eggs at a Korean corner grocery, looked through the steamy window of a Korean tailor's, passed the Korean wig shop on Pike Street, bought oranges, bananas and grapes from a Korean fruit stall in the market, and walked the hundred yards home via a Korean laundromat and a Korean news and candy kiosk.

For lunch I went to Shilla, a Korean restaurant, where I sat up at the bar, ordered a beer, and tried to make sense of the newspaper which had been left on the counter—the *Korea Times,* published daily in Seattle. The text was in Korean characters, but the pictures told one something. There were portrait photographs of beaming Korean-American businessmen dressed, like many of the restaurant's customers, in blazers, button-down shirts and striped club ties. Several columns were devoted to prize students, shown in their mortarboards and academic gowns. On page three there was a church choir. There were a surprising number of advertisements for pianos. I guessed that the tone of the text would be inspiratorial and uplifting: the *Korea Times* seemed to be exclusively devoted to the cult of business, social and academic success.

"You are reading our paper!" It was the proprietor of the restaurant, a wiry man with a tight rosebud smile.

"No—just looking at the pictures."

He shook my hand, sat on the stool beside me, and showed me the paper page by page. Here was the news from Korea; this was local news from Seattle and Tacoma; that was Pastor Kim's family advice column; these were the advertisements for jobs . . .

"It is very important to us. Big circulation! Everybody read it!"

So, nearly a hundred years ago, immigrant Jews in New York

had pored over the *Jewish Daily Forward,* the *Yidishe Gazetn* and the *Arbeite Tseitung.* They had kept their readers in touch with the news and culture of the Old World at the same time as they had taught the immigrants how to make good in the New. To the greenhorn American, the newspaper came as a daily reassurance that he was not alone.

"You are interested?" the restaurateur said. "You must talk to Mr. Han. He is the president of our association. He is here—"

Mr. Han was eating by himself, hunched over a plate of seafood. In sweatshirt and windbreaker, he had the build of a bantamweight boxer. The proprietor introduced us. Mr. Han bowed from his seat, waved his chopsticks. Sure! No problem! Siddown!

His face looked bloated with fatigue. His eyes were almost completely hidden behind small cushions of flesh, giving him the shuttered-in appearance of a sleepwalker. But his mouth was wide awake, and there was a surviving ebullience in his grin, which was unselfconsciously broad and toothy.

He gave me his card. Mr. Han was President of the Korean Association of Seattle, also owner of Japanese Auto Repair ("is *big* business!"). He had been in America, he said, for sixteen years. He'd made it. But his college-student clothes, his twitchy hands and the knotted muscles in his face told another story. If you passed Mr. Han on the street, you'd mistake him for a still shell-shocked newcomer; an FOB, as people said even now, long after the Boeing had made the immigrant ship redundant. He looked fresh-off-the-boat.

It had been the summer of 1973 when Won S. Han had flown from Seoul to Washington, D.C., with four hundred dollars in his billfold and a student visa in his passport. He had come to study psychology—that, at any rate, was what his papers said—but what he really wanted to major in was the applied science of becoming an American.

In Korea, he had been brought up as a Buddhist. Within two weeks of his arrival in Washington, he was a Baptist.

"Yah! I become Christian! I didn't go to church to believe in God, not then, no. I go to church for meeting people. Yah. Baptist church was where to find job, where to find place to live, where to find wife, husband, right? In America, you gotta be Christian!"

His voice was lippy, whispery, front-of-the-mouth.

He'd soon fallen behind in his psychology classes. He couldn't follow the strange language. Through the church, he found a part-time job in a gas and service station. He learned the work easily. While the American workers were content to lounge and smoke and tinker, this university-educated Korean gutted the car manuals and took only a few weeks to qualify as a full-fledged auto mechanic.

"We are hot-temper people! Want to do things quick-quick-quick! Not slow-slow like in America. Want everything all-at-once, but in America you must learn to wait long-time. Quick-quick is the Korean way, but that's not work here. America teaches patience, teaches wait-till-next-week."

This must have been a hard lesson for Mr. Han to take to heart. He'd done a major reconstruction job on the American language to give it a greater turn of speed, lopping off articles, prepositions, all the fancy chromework of traditional syntax. His stripped-down English was now fast and fluent. With its rat-a-tat hyphenations and bang! bang! repetitions, it was a vehicle custom-built for its owner—a Korean racing machine in which Mr. Han drove with his foot on the floor, without regard for petty American traffic restrictions.

Working as a mechanic by day, he'd gone to school at night. This time his subject was real estate, and it took him six months to qualify for a Maryland real estate license. He gave up the car business and sold suburban houses, mostly to Korean customers.

"You know, when Korean guy come to this country, he has *plan!* In two year, must have own business. In three year, must have own house. Three year! Four at *maximum.* So must work-work-work. Sixteen-hour-day, eighteen-hour-day . . . okay, he can do. But *must* have business, *must* have house."

Mr. Han himself had run ahead of schedule. By 1982, when he left Washington and headed for Seattle, he was a man of capital with a wife and two young daughters. To begin with, he patrolled the city from end to end by car, casing the joint for opportunities.

"And you liked what you saw?"

"Yah! I like the mountains! Like the water! Like the trees! Is like in Korea, but not too hot, not too cold. *Nice!* No people! Green!"

Everywhere he'd gone, he'd checked in with the local Parks and Kims and got the lowdown on Seattle's social structure. Beacon Hill, just south of downtown, was where Korean beginners started their American lives; as they succeeded, so they moved further north across Lake Washington to Bellevue, across Lake Union to Wallingford, Morningside, Greenwood, North Beach. They measured the tone of a neighborhood by the reputation of its schools. The top suburb was the one with the best record of posting students to famous American colleges like Columbia, Yale and MIT.

On his first day in Seattle, Mr. Han had learned that the Shoreline School District was "much better, no comparison!" than the Seattle School District, and that the Syre Elementary School was just the place for his daughters to set foot on the ladder to academic stardom. So he bought a house in Richmond Beach. He had no Korean neighbors. The closeness of the house to the school was all that mattered.

Then he set up his business.

"Must be *specialist!*" Mr. Han said. Detroit was sick, and more and more Americans were buying Japanese cars, so Mr. Han established his hospital for Japanese cars only. "No American cars! No German! No English—sorry! Must be Japanese. Toyota, Nissan, Mitsubishi, whatever. So long as it made in Japan—bring it in! That is my specialism."

The climax of this success story had happened two years ago. Mr. Han had always dreamed of having a son to carry on the Han dynastic name. In Korea, it was a woman's highest duty to give birth to a son. Mr. Han himself was the only son of an only son—a man genetically programmed to produce a male heir. But it seemed that he could only father daughters. This was, he said, a heavy fate for a Korean man to shoulder.

"So, in 1986, I go to my wife. I say to her, 'One last try!' And we try. And—*home run!*" For the first time, Mr. Han's eyes were wide open, his pride in this feat of paternity matched by this rich nugget of all-American slang.

"Home run!" He smacked his lips around the phrase and

laughed, a joyful *Hoo! Hoo!* that made neighboring diners look up from their tables.

"Now the name of Han goes on!"

With his business in the city, his civic honors in the Korean community, his big house in a wooded, crimeless suburb a spit away from the sea, his straight-A daughters and his precious son, one might have expected Mr. Han to have grown expansive and complacent in his New World estate. Yet his eyes closed as quickly as they had opened; he fell back into hunched vigilance; he looked, as I had first seen him, like an anxious greener who fears that someone, somewhere, is hard on his heels.

He was frightened for his children.

"They see the American TV . . . of this I am scared. I turn off the news. There is too much immorality! Violence! Drugs! Sex! When the news comes up—'Turn that TV off!' "

He had tried to turn his home into a Korean bubble, sealed off from the dangerous American world outside. In the house, the family talked in Korean. Twice a week, the girls went to a Korean church school to take classes in Korean grammar and composition.

He dreaded the day when one of his daughters would bring home a white American boyfriend.

"What would you do?"

"Any kid of mine, I'd stop her marrying another race."

"Stop?"

"Maybe could not *stop*. Maybe. But not *like*. You heard of 'GI Brides' . . . They were not normal average Korean woman. They were—I not say exactly what they were, but you know what I mean." Mr. Han watched me across the table through his nearly closed eyes, "Whores," he said, making the word sound biblical.

I said that the Jews in New York at the beginning of the century had felt much as he did. But they had had the protection of the ghetto. In the Yiddish-speaking world of the Lower East Side, with its all-Jewish streets and all-Jewish schools, it was possible to regard the *goyim* as unmarriageable aliens. In Richmond Beach, a Korean girl would be a Christian, like most of her classmates, and her skin-color would be hardly less pale than theirs. How, growing up in English, could she hug "Koreanness" to herself as the essence of her identity, while all the time her parents talked Columbia, talked medical school, talked her up the path that led to membership of the white, professional, American middle class?

"Ah," said Mr. Han. "This is what we are wondering. Wondering-wondering all the time. *How long?* is the question. In near future, next generation, we got to be serviced by English. We have example of Chinese. Look at Chinese!—in two-three generations, the Chinese people here, they cannot even read the characters! Chinese is only *name.* Is nothing. Now, Chinese . . . all in the melting pot!" He drew out this last phrase with solemn relish. The way he said it, it was a *mel Ting pot,* and I saw it as some famous cast-iron oriental cooking utensil, in which human beings were boiled over a slow fire until they broke down into a muddy fibrous stew.

"But my kids grow like Koreans," Mr. Han said.

"With American voices, American clothes, American college degrees . . . ?"

"Like Koreans."

On the street across from the restaurant I could see a rambling black-painted chalet surmounted by a flying billboard which said LOOK WHAT WE GOT! 30 NUDE SHOWGIRLS! TABLE DANCING! It was a sign to chill the heart of a Korean father of young daughters.

Since so much of American culture was clearly a Caucasian affront to Korean ideas of modesty, industry, piety and racial purity, I wondered why they kept on coming—from a country that was being touted as the economic miracle of the decade.

Mr. Han guffawed when I said "economic miracle."

"Guy in Korea make three-four-hundred dollar a month. No house his own, no business his own. *This* is country of opportunity. No comparison. Chance of self-employment: maybe one thousand percent better! Look. '73. I am in Washington, D.C., with four hundred dollars. Now? My business is worth one million dollars—more than one million. Heh? Isn't that the American Dream? And I am only a small! Yes, I am a *small.*"

Minutes later, I watched him as he crossed to his car. The millionaire was walking quick-quick-quick, shoulders hunched, head down, his skinny hands rammed deep into the pockets of his workpants. He looked like a man who had taken on America single-handed and, in the ninth round, was just winning, by a one- or two-point margin.

The news of the boom in Seattle had drawn all sorts and conditions of immigrants to the city. As Mr. Han said, there were "opportunities for everybody!," and, in this great democracy of opportunity everybody came to Seattle with his or her own distinctive idea of how best to take advantage of the place.

I quickly learned that the two-hundred-yard stretch of Second Avenue between the Josephinum and Pike Street was thought of as a no-go area after dark by most respectable Seattleites. The parking lot where I stabled the Spectrum was an unlit half-acre of bricky open space which emptied of cars after 10 P.M. and turned into the parliamentary center, occasionally the battle-ground, of twenty or so black kids, most of whom sported red baseball caps. They appeared to spend their time kicking cans across the rutted ground, wrangling over metaphysics, and sweetening the night air with blue zephyrs of marijuana smoke. They paid no attention to me as I coasted past them, my car window rolled down, trying to look more blasé than I felt. I suspected that the Spectrum was my salvation. If that short-winded cookie tin was the best that Rainbird could muster, then he had to be a lousy touch. Shake Rainbird by his heels, and all that would fall out would be a few wooden nickels.

Across from the parking lot was the ruinous flophouse of the Hotel Forest. It could not have amounted to much even in its prime, which must have been in Grover Cleveland's day. Now it was mostly boarded up, but the ground floor harbored a few small businesses, like Scandal XX-Rated Video Store ("Nude Dancing—25¢ Peepshow") and its next-door neighbor, the People's Market Grocery, an open-at-all-hours black establishment, whose checkout clerk always gave me a questioning smile when I dropped by for a late carton of milk or a tin of peanuts.

The lee side of the Josephinum, on Stewart Street, gave shelter, of a sort, to a bunch of Indians. They sprawled in a bricked-over doorway, under a fine scrolled entablature, in broken boots, torn plaid coats and grease-caked blankets. Each morosely nursed his own bottle. None of them bothered to look up when a stranger passed; they seemed too far gone in introspective misery even to notice the existence of people outside their desperate *galère*.

I never heard anyone speak of these poor Indians. Before the settlers came to Puget Sound in 1850, the Salish nation had lived quietly off the fat of the land. No great shakes as fighters, they used to hide in the bushes when the fierce Kwakiutl Indians came down on raids from Vancouver Island. When left unmarauded, the Salish went fishing for Chinook salmon, dug clams, ate blackberries and wild grapes, and stalked deer with bows and arrows. In 1854, the governor of Washington Territory, General Isaac Stevens, talked them into selling two million acres of their tribal lands at a price of seven and a half cents an acre, payable, in kind not in cash, over twenty years. They were then hustled into reservations, from where they had the honor of seeing the rising city of Seattle take its name from Sealth, the most complaisant of the Salish chiefs.

The Second Avenue Indians were bottle-babies. They fell asleep wherever they happened to stumble. They were the only people in town who ignored the *Don't Walk* signs, and would sometimes seem to be trying to offer themselves up as voluntary sacrifices to speeding teenagers in pickups. They were very rarely to be seen panhandling: to make the effort to beg would, perhaps, have been to betray too unseemly an interest in staying alive. Shamed passers-by would sometimes plant a bag of food or a handful of coins at their feet.

At night, they lay outside the building like sacks of garbage waiting for collection by the early-morning truck. I tiptoed past them, as one walks needlessly quietly in the presence of the dead.

Returning to the Josephinum just past midnight, after dinner with a Seattle novelist and reviewer in a Capitol Hill restaurant, I found my way to the door blocked by a fight. A man was dragging a woman across the sidewalk by her hair. A knot of kids stood on the touchline, going *Heh! Heh! Heh!* in a chorus of humorless derision. The woman locked her teeth into the man's calf.

"Suck your *asshole,* bitch!" The man planted his boot in her face. There was a smudge of blood on the pavement like a Rorschach inkblot. It might have made you think of a spider or a flower, depending on your mood.

"Heh! Heh! Heh!" went the chorus.

She was on her feet now, going for the man's eyes.

"Motherfuckin' shit!"

I felt as if I was perfectly invisible, a secret witness, like a hidden electronic eye. The principals in the scene were too engaged in their own drama to notice me, but it seemed that the chorus couldn't see me either. In New York, it was the Street People who were invisible to the laundered classes; in Seattle, it appeared to be the other way round. I had the comforting, if not quite trustworthy, conviction that it would be possible for a man to step straight through the middle of a murder without being seen, provided he was properly dressed in jacket and tie.

I brushed past the chorus, avoiding the woman's flailing leg, and stepped up to the Josephinum's front door. It took a minute or two for the night doorman to abandon his Ed McBain paperback and walk, without hurrying, across the marble to let me in. At my back, I heard a sucking, squelching sound, like a gumboot going into soft mud up to the knee, followed by an electric scream. I didn't dare to turn my head.

"Out late tonight," the doorman said. His smile was routinely polite, his tone neutral, as if all he could see behind me was the blue glow of a city fast asleep.

I wriggled hastily through the double plate-glass doors. "There's too much street life out there for comfort," I said.

"Oh . . . *yeah.*" What he actually seemed to be saying was *Oh, so you noticed that too, did you? You* must *have sharp eyes!*

Together, we stood looking out at the street beyond the glass. The smudge of blood was now a pool. Someone in white sneakers ran through it, leaving rusty tracks. A man was shouting, out of sight.

"Oh, yes . . ." the doorman said. His tone was warm, as if he rather approved of the mayhem outside. Yet he was in his sixties;

a tall, gray, courtly man, with a slight stoop. I would have expected him to be shocked. Not at all. He nodded at the glass.

"That stuff goes on pretty continuous now, from around midnight to four, five in the morning most nights. Quite a show. Used to be real quiet out there. You'd be here all night and you'd never see nor hear a thing. That was up to around last April, when the drug gangs moved in from L.A. Yes, they're all here in town now. The Crips. The Bloods. The Black Gangster Disciples . . ."

He might have been saying the Beatles, the Rolling Stones, Fleetwood Mac. Seattle was evidently playing host to the real big stars of the drug world.

"Now the Bloods, I bet you've seen them: you can tell them by the way they always wear something in their clothing that's red, like a red hat, or a red patch on their jeans, or something. While the Crips, they go for blue; that's their color. If a Crip writes a message on a wall, he's under oath never to use the letter *B* because *B* stands for Blood. And the Bloods, well, they never use the letter *C*. Same reason. That's why when you see a graffiti up there over in the parking lot, it prob'ly won't make no sense to you, because either it's in Crip code, else it's in Blood code . . ."

As he talked, a faint bell was ringing in my head. I couldn't place it, then, suddenly, it came back to me. It was the middle of the 1950s. I was visiting my grandmother, who was hooked on a TV serial called *Emergency—Ward 10.* As we watched, she would talk exactly as the doorman was talking now, treating me to a running commentary on every scene. *That's the doctor I like—last week he had to do a very difficult amputation—and that nurse, the one over there . . . no, she's gone now . . . well, she's got a crush on him, but I don't trust her; she behaved very badly to another doctor, one we haven't seen yet. Oh, and Nurse Gibbs—you see Nurse Gibbs?—well she's had such a trying time with her father, who's got shingles, and Dr. Marsh (I told you about Dr. Marsh) has been telling her . . .*

So the glass doors of the Josephinum were a screen on which a nightly soap opera was being performed for the entertainment of any idle insomniac in the building. You could come down to the lobby in your dressing gown and slippers, park yourself on a leaky horsehair sofa, brass spittoon conveniently to hand, and sit back and enjoy the unfolding drama. The people on the other side of the glass were creatures of fiction; characters in a wild adventure story that was every bit as remote from the Bingo and the flu shots and the church services of the Josephinum as anything that happened in Ed McBain.

A white stretch limo coasted slowly past.

"Drug car," the doorman said, in his pleased voice. "Boss man, checking out his territory."

A kid in a puffy windbreaker with a thornbush of hair glanced in at us for a moment, then crossed the street to the Gibson Bar & Grill.

"Samoan," the doorman said. "They use the Samoans a lot, to make the street deals. Them Samoans, they're not scared of *anything*. And they've got legs. You see a Samoan running, it's like he's in for the Olympic hundred meters . . ."

"What about the Gibson Bar?" I said.

"Oh, that's some place, too. Had a shoot-out there, a little while back. Guy walks in, pulls a gun, shoots the bartender. Dead."

"And you still bother to read Ed McBain?"

"Oh, he's a good author. That's pretty exciting stuff he writes about, out there in New York."

The coca tycoons of Los Angeles had probably read the brochure put out by the Seattle Chamber of Commerce, designed to wheedle businessmen into relocating their industries here ("Growth in nearly every sector . . . Seattle-area communities offer something for everyone. Pursue any lifestyle . . ."); and it was easy to see how the city was ideally placed for an expansion of the crack industry. It had a virgin police department. There was plenty of money to spare for recreational use. There was a ready-made work force of eager young immigrants, like the Samoans, who were the poorest and the wildest of the newcomers from Asia.

So, like the rest of us, the Crips and the Bloods had succumbed to the charms of Seattle, pursuing their particular lifestyle with that "adventurous entrepreneurial spirit" which the chamber of commerce brochure writer had nailed as the chief characteristic of the city at large.

*   *   *

Next morning at nine, still more asleep than awake, I lay in bed listening to the brass band which was having a rehearsal somewhere out near the waterfront. They were bad. They were the worst brass band I'd ever heard. They appeared to be trying to play "God Bless America," but were hideously out of tune and out of time. They'd get as far as "God . . . bless . . ." competently enough, but when they hit the descending phrase of the next four notes, they went to pieces and had to go back to the beginning again. It was murder.

I raised the window-blind. Puget Sound was lost in a brilliant silver fog, and the diaphone orchestra came from the sightless ships in the Bay, poking their way slowly about the water like old men with white sticks. Had they consented to hire me as their musical conductor, I could have got them to play "God Bless America," and "Hail to the Chief" as well, in perfect tune, *con brio.*

Below the window, Second Avenue was restored to uneventful legality. Looking down on the orderly drift of the traffic, the country-clad shoppers with their paper sacks of groceries, I began to wonder if the doorman had been winding me up. Maybe prolonged exposure to McBain's 37th Precinct had led him to endow his own home street with more criminal glamour than it really possessed.

When the *Seattle Times* came out at noon, the front page bore out the doorman's story. While we'd been talking in the lobby, there had been a murder on East Marginal Way. Witnesses spoke of a car chase down the length of Boeing Field, of shots exchanged at 100 mph. One of the cars had eventually crashed into a wall, the body of the driver honeycombed with slugs from a .38. The dead man, Fiaai Taulealea, was a twenty-year-old Samoan. The police were looking for a named suspect, known to be a member of the Crips.

"In America, everything is temptation, is pleasure, is *fun . . .*"

When Pastor Kim said *fun,* he spat the word out as if it was a putrid oyster. Fun was the poison in the bowels of Pastor Kim's

America, and he was doing all he could to stop his community from having fun.

I had driven out to see the newspaper agony-uncle at his head-quarters, the Korean Presbyterian Church of Mountlake Terrace, fifteen miles up the interstate, where Exit 177 led to a deciduous green suburb of irreproachable dullness. Boxlike frame houses, all in a state of good repair, stood on identical rectangular lots: their lawns were shaven, their shrubs grimly barbered into shape by amateur topiarists. Nature here was expected to live up to the same strict conventional standards that governed the rest of life. Outside every kitchen window stood a hummingbird feeder, but it was some weeks now since the violent-tempered humming-birds had forsaken Mountlake Terrace for their winter vacations in more exciting places. They were living it up in Acapulco, San Salvador, Managua and Panama.

You needed only to glance at Mountlake Terrace to see that its school system would be good, that everyone owned a Black & Decker home handyman outfit, that the high points of the week would be the PTA meeting and the visit of the life-insurance salesman. Though my own private sympathies were with the hummingbirds, I could see that Mountlake Terrace was a lot of people's idea of the American Dream come true.

The Korean Presbyterian Church had been built as a college, and it looked like an over-extended motel; inside a corral of high chainlink fencing, a complex of classrooms and assembly halls was arranged around a central grass quadrangle. For the church was a great deal more than a place of worship: it was a counseling center, a crèche, an old people's club, a night school, a labor exchange, a sports stadium, an embassy. It was a comforting enclosure. For the bruised FOB, here was a safe Korean space, a world away from the bewildering foreign territory of Seattle.

Meeting Pastor Kim, the newcomer would set eyes on the kind of man he might dream of becoming himself. Daniel So Kim had been ten years in America, and he had the air of having mastered the country and the language without conceding an ounce of his essential Koreanness. He was bandbox-spruce in conservative Frederick & Nelson tweeds. His confident beam and bold hand-shake were those of a successful American corporate executive, but what he preached was severely, proudly Korean. His whole style announced that Pastor Kim had discovered the great immigrant secret, of how to get the best of both worlds at once. The wall of his study was lined with sociology books, and his speech was littered with the fruits of his reading. Where Won Han's grasp of the American language had been signaled by phrases like "home run!," Pastor Kim went in for less colorful Americanisms like "status anxiety," "role model," "ego threat," "peer pressure."

"When the Korean comes to this country, you know, he has what we call a 'blue hope.' Like a blue sky—wide, open. 'I am going to *be* someone here!' But then comes the culture shock. No one welcomes him. Things are strange. There is the language barrier. He gets scared. He is a trained engineer, but he can't get that job. Where is his English? What is *for* him? Maybe only to be janitor in a building, *custodian!* And I am speaking of very proud man. In Korea he *is* someone; in America, where he go to *be* someone . . . here he is *nobody.* It is only to his children can he turn. *'I* couldn't get that job—*because! because! because!* But *you . . .* Do that on behalf of me!' That is crux of situation."

Here Pastor Kim began to draw from his story a very different moral from the one I would have drawn myself. I saw children painfully burdened with the unreasonable ambition of their thwarted parents. What Pastor Kim saw was children diverted from their proper filial duty by the lax standards of America. It was not the parental pressure that worried him; it was the failure of the second generation to succumb to that pressure as good Korean children should.

"In Korea, we are a very competitive people. At school, we have not just one lunchbox, we have two. One for the lunch, one for the supper. In the ninth grade, we go 8 A.M. to 6 P.M. Then is private study. Then from 8 P.M. to 10 P.M. is special tutoring. Fourteen hours. You see? Look at me—that is why I am not tall. I am too busy to grow tall! Too much study! Too much stress! Must get scholarships!

"In America, my daughters go to school, but 8 A.M. to 3 P.M. only! Oh, their grades are good. All A-plus—very good points— but I am not satisfied, I am all the time complaining about lack of homework. Is too much free time; time just for pleasure, pleasure, pleasure. Time for *fun.* What can a child learn in this free time? Only bad things! He listen to music, and I am not talking *music* music, I am talking 'heavy metal,' I am talking 'rock and roll.' He use the telephone, he call up his friends, chat-chat-chat all the afternoon. He watch TV. *Bad things!* For *fun* only! Why is this violence in America? Why is this premarital sex? Why this substance abuse? *Because here is too much free time!*"

From Pastor Kim's puritan fastness in Mountlake Terrace, America stretched away below us, a nation of backsliders, lazy and corrupt. Twice a week in his newspaper column, he exhorted Korean parents to stay true to the values of the old country and not give in to the degenerate practices of their new compatriots.

"In Korea, society is up-down, top-to-bottom, *vertical.* Like the Bible say, 'Wives *obey* your husbands, children *obey* your parents!' But in America now, society is flat like a table, *horizontal.* Here parents and children, they are like friends only. Father say to son, 'I am your buddy,' right?

"So we see our children being westernized by this American school system. It is the peer pressure, it is very very hard. And human is human . . . The child say to the father, 'I am taller than you are, I speak English better.' In one generation the child, he is talking down to his parents! This is big problem with us. We must make our children very busy, with schoolwork, with social life, with church. I tell the parents, 'You must *supervise!* You must be *model!* You must be *spiritual authority* to your children!'"

Pastor Kim was straining to say more than he was able, his emphases and exclamations betraying his impatience with a language that he could not yet quite work to his will. I saw what he meant more in the fierceness of his eyes, the flash of his white teeth, the jerky fervor of his gestures, than in the words he actually spoke.

To Pastor Kim, America was the wilderness and the Korean immigrants were the chosen people. Like the *Mayflower* pilgrims, who had drawn deeply on the same biblical myth, the Koreans had brought to the new country a godfearing zeal, a strict code of family relationships and a passionate belief in the spiritual value of labor. In the twentieth century, the Protestant work ethic had become a limp history-book phrase; but to the

Korean Presbyterians, it was still an idea of tremendous motive force.

Korean Presbyterianism was a religious hybrid whose vigor derived as much from its root stock of Confucianism as from the engrafted Calvinism brought to Korea by (mostly) American missionaries. The cardinal Confucian virtues of filial piety, duty, honor, loyalty were stern in themselves; combined with the teaching of the Christian fundamentalists, they evolved into a steely and purposeful religious system. It was a system that placed a crushingly heavy stress on the responsibility of the individual, on work and on obedience to authority. This was not a sensual, indulgent and self-dramatizing religion, like native American born-again Christianity. It had a great deal of the hardness of seventeenth-century New England puritanism; and, like that original strain of puritanism, it was a religion of immense practical results.

There had been Christian missions in Korea for well over a hundred years, but the great mass of Christian conversions had happened during the period of Korea's tearaway industrial growth. In 1970, there were three million professed Christians in Korea; in 1988, more than ten million. Most of these were Presbyterians. In the age of *Work! Work! Work!* Korea had lit on the religion of *Work! Work! Work!*

For Pastor Kim and the pious ones in his congregation, there was a devastating irony in all this. They had come to the country from which they had imported their own brand of puritanism with, as he said, "a blue hope." They had found there a fallen land, given over to licentiousness and easy living, where their tender young were being led astray by American schoolfellows hooked on *substances* and *fun*.

So it was the immigrants who, in Kim's terms, were the true guardians of American values. Their hard work, their dutiful religious observance, their thrift, their respect for education and the family were in the American mainstream, while America itself had drifted off into a lazy backwater.

"God called me to stay in America," Pastor Kim said, and it occurred to me that, if you were a Korean Presbyterian, you might well feel that God was calling you to restore this lost-sheep nation to its proper path by your own good example.

A few days later, I happened to be reading Cotton Mather, lamenting America's lapses from godliness in the late seventeenth century. *Idleness, alas! idleness increases in the town exceedingly; idleness, of which there never came any goodness!* It seemed to my ear that Mather was writing in a strong Korean accent.

Rainbird's thirteenth-floor window had a panoptic view of the fun. Below the hovering firefly lights of the shipping in the sound were other lights that raced and flashed on trip circuits—lights of pleasure and temptation. Down on First Avenue, the Midtown Theater was showing *Depraved Innocent* and *Interlude of Lust*. The Champ Arcade ("The Adult Superstore") advertised LIVE GIRLS—50 BEAUTIFUL GIRLS—& 3 UGLY ONES! Another sign alerted one to the fact that Nina Deponca, the XXX STAR, was playing Seattle LIVE IN PERSON!

Every so often a car would detach itself from the drift of traffic down Second and cruise up to the edge of the pool of light cast by the People's Market Grocery. A tropic-island kid, quick on his feet, would nip out of the store, check the street with a single swivel of his neck, like a garden bird on the lookout for cats, and attend the driver's window. The deal was over in seconds: the tail-lights of the car lost in the downhill stream, the kid slouching back into the safety of the gang.

One quiet night, while I was sleeping with the window open, I woke to what sounded like a scene of religious dissension.

"Jesus," said a voice. The tone was firm. "Jesus *Christ.*" Some point was being insisted on.

"Whurrawhurrawhurra, man?"

"Jesus Christ," said the Anabaptist.

I went to the window. Under a street lamp, the Anabaptist had his arms raised high and he was preaching loud and long at a man in an ankle-length overcoat, who was prodding him in the stomach with what I at first took to be a finger, then, as it glinted in the light, turned out to be a handgun. A third man, a Scandinavian type, with shoulder-length fair hair, in T-shirt, jeans and ragged sneakers, was prowling round the other two in a slow circle. He looked underdressed for this below-forty-degree night.

"Okay, okay," said the guy with his hands up. "Go ahead. Okay. Kill me."

There was now a telephone installed in Room 1326. I could have called the police department. Yet, from thirteen stories up, the scene in the street was just a scene. These people were play-acting. I thought, for a moment, about going to the phone, but it would have been like rising from the balcony in the middle of *The Mousetrap* in order to fetch a policeman. So I went on watching.

The man with the gun was backing the Anabaptist up against the wall of the building across the street, a 1900-ish Italianate affair, now gutted and converted to a multi-story car park. It was empty, except for a single pickup truck on the roof, where the parking spaces were marked out on the black creosote in Mondrian-yellow paint. The gun was winking in the man's hand. I thought, this is where a writer should instantly identify the caliber and manufacture of the thing. If someone's going to get killed, it is, for some reason, important to know whether he will fall to a Colt .45 or a Smith & Wesson .38. This gun was just a gun. For all I could see, it might have been a starting pistol or a child's cap-gun, but the man against the wall seemed to be taking it seriously.

The Scandinavian type now moved in. He kicked at the Anabaptist's knees, using the flat of the sole of his running shoe until the knees gave and the man began to slide down the wall, his hands still up. Now that he was down on his haunches, continuing to protest the name of God, it was somehow clear that this was where the scene ended. The gunman shoved his pistol into the pocket of his overcoat. He spat, quickly, and without any discernible volume, into the upraised face of the man, who was now revealed by the lamp to be a crying boy. He was hardly of an age to shave yet. Later this morning, he should be in school.

Overcoat and blond ambled back up the street to the Gibson Bar. They had the leisured complacency of men who've done a useful job for the common weal. The boy picked himself off the ground, shrugged at the sky, and went jogging north up Second, his feet slapping on the sidewalk.

It wasn't a slaying. It wasn't even a hold-up in the ordinary sense of the term. It was just an everyday, or everynight, encounter on Second and Pike.

This was, after all, the city from which the phrase "skid row" had made it into the American language. In the 1850s, Skid Road was the steep mudslide that led down to the Henry Yesler sawmill on the waterfront. The Scandinavian loggers who hauled the timber to the mill had managed to turn Skid Road into a national byword for melancholy dereliction. While its north side was the official edge of the business district, its south side was lined with vomit-smelling bars and the insanitary working premises of the local prostitutes. It was, clearly, a place that lingered in the memory with quite exceptional nastiness. That people in Chicago, or Boston, or Washington, should associate the sight of an incapacitated homeless alcoholic with the name of a street in Seattle was an impressive measure of Skid Road's power to nauseate the unwary nineteenth-century visitor.

Its name was changed, to Mill Street, then to Yesler Way, but Skid Road had taken on the qualities of a natural frontier. Even in the late twentieth century, Yesler Way divided Seattle like a river. As one crossed it, the whole temper of the city changed. Rents dropped. Streets darkened and narrowed. The architecture shrank in size, and Italian Renaissance and Japanese Croissance suddenly gave way to bare smoke-stained brick.

To the filled-in tideflats south of Yesler had been relegated the Kingdome stadium, the marshaling yards, Union Station. Where the land began to rise eastward up to Beacon Hill, the International District occupied a four-by-four-block grid of morose, rust-colored tenements whose crumbling stucco balconies were looped with lines of hung-out washing.

In another city, this quarter would have been posted for tourists as Chinatown, and it would have been whimsically decorated with painted-dragon archways and plastic-pagoda telephone booths. In Seattle, it was just the part of town where the Chinese lived, and where subsequent refugees from Vietnam, Laos and Cambodia had come to find their first footing on American ground. These newcomers from Southeast Asia were moving out of the grid; going north as far as Yesler, heading east up Jackson, under I-5, and into territory that until now had been exclusively black.

Inside the grid, the looming tenements blotted out the sun. The buildings seemed too weighty and overbearing, their residents too short and skinny, to match up. Many of the restaurants were grand, tricked out with fountains, statuary, and floor-to-ceiling fish tanks; but the offices of the Chinese dentists, optometrists and lawyers looked threadbare and hungry for trade.

Here you could still rent a room for $60 a month: a cold-water walk-up, with a bathroom down the hall, in the kind of rooming house that I thought had disappeared from American life. Families would take three rooms, paying from $90 to $150 for their lodgings. It was a start. You could speak your own language to your neighbors, and for some jet-shocked immigrants, the International District was like a walled city; America, *real* America, didn't begin until you crossed Yesler or walked under the thundering overpass that carried I-5.

A grimy-windowed pet shop in an alley offered companions, of a sort: bullfrog tadpoles 75¢; garter snakes $2.50; mice $2; nothing in the black lab line. On the brick back of one building, six-foot letters held out an invitation to CHOP SUEY, CHOW MEIN, DANCING, but the paint had flaked off to leave only a pale photographic print of the message.

The Chinese had been the first Asians to make a new life in Seattle. They called America "The Gold Mountain," and were eager to take on the hard, poorly paid jobs that were offered to them in the railroad construction gangs. For as long as it took to build the railroads, they were made welcome, in a mildly derisive way. Their entire race was renamed "John," and every John was credited with an extraordinary capacity to do the maximum amount of work on the minimum amount of rice. As soon as the railroads began to lay off workers, the amiable John was reconceived as "a yellow rascal" and "the rat-eating Chinaman." During the 1870s, the federal legislature began to behave toward the

Chinese much as the czars Alexander II and Nicholas II behaved toward the Jews in Russia. At the very moment when the United States was receiving the European huddled masses on its eastern seaboard, it was establishing something cruelly like its own Pale, designed to exclude the Chinese from white American rights and occupations. The Geary Act prohibited the Chinese from the right to bail and habeas corpus. In Seattle in 1886, gangs of vigilantes succeeded in forcibly deporting most of the city's Chinese population of 350 people—persuading them, with knives, clubs and guns, to board a ship bound for San Francisco.

For the immigrant from Asia, the Gold Mountain was a treacherous rock-face. No sooner had you established what seemed to be a secure foothold than it gave way under you. The treatment of the Seattle Chinese in 1886 was matched, almost exactly, by the treatment of the Seattle Japanese in 1942, when hundreds of families were arrested, loaded on trains and dispatched to remote internment camps.

Now, if you came from Asia, you could not trust America to be kind or fair. This particular week, if you went to an English class at the Central Community College, you would see spray-gunned on the south wall of the building SPEAK ENGLISH OR DIE, SQUINTY EYE! Peeing in a public toilet, you'd find yourself stuck, for the duration, with a legend written just for you: KILL THE GOOKS!

In the ghetto of the International District, there was at least safety in numbers. There was less pressure on the immigrant to get his tongue round the alien syllables of English. Even a professional man, like the dentist or optometrist, could conduct his business entirely in his original language. In the bar of the China Gate restaurant, I sat next to a man in his early seventies, born on Jackson Street, who had served with the USAF in World War II. He was affable, keen to tell me about his travels, and almost completely incomprehensible. *Yi wong ding ying milding hyall!*

"You were in Mildenhall? In Suffolk?"

"Yea! Milding Hall!"

So, painfully, we swapped memories of the air base there. He didn't understand much of what I said, and I didn't understand much of what he said; yet his entire life, bar this spell in wartime

England, had been passed in Seattle—or, rather, within the Chinese-speaking fifty-acre grid.

The Chinese, the Japanese, the Vietnamese, Laotians and Cambodians all had established solid fortresses in, or on the edge of, the International District. There were few Koreans here. There was the Korean Ginseng Center on King Street; there was a Korean restaurant at the back of the Bush Hotel on Jackson; some Koreans worked as bartenders in the Chinese restaurants.

In Los Angeles, there was a "Little Korea": a defined area of the city where the immigrant could work for, and live with, his co-linguists, much as the Chinese did here in the International District. For Koreans in Seattle, though, immigration was, for nearly everyone, a solitary process. The drive to run their own businesses, to send their children to good schools, to have space, privacy, self-sufficiency, had scattered them, in small family groups of twos and threes, through the white suburbs. They didn't have the daily solace of the sociable rooming house, the street and the café. For many, there was the once-a-week visit to church; for others, there was no Korean community life at all.

It was this solitude that drew me to them. The Seattle Koreans knew, better than anyone else, what it was like to go it alone in America; and although I came from the wrong side of the world, I could feel a pang of kinship for these people who had chosen to travel by themselves.

Everyone could name the date on which they'd taken the flight out from Seoul. The beginning of their American life was at least as important to them as their birthday.

"August 29th, 1965," Jay Park said. He owned a plumbing business up on Beacon Hill and drove a pearl gray '88 Mercedes. In 1965, he'd been twenty; and on that August afternoon he'd stood in the Seoul airport being hugged by every aunt, cousin, uncle, friend.

"Everyone envy me. It was like I'd won the big lottery, you know? I'd got the visa! Wah! They were seeing me off like I was some general . . . like I was going into paradise!"

Park knew America. He'd "watched it through the movies." On

the streets of Seoul, he'd seen "U.S. soldiers, spending money like it was going out of style. Wah! I tell you, the U.S. was like a paradise. You feel like you're going to dreamland. Everything's going to work out okay!"

It was a Northwest Airlines flight; Jay Park had never been on an airplane before and he had "not one word" of English. The stewardess showed him to an aisle seat, next to an American who was reading a book.

"He don't look at me. I felt shy. Suddenly I was kind of scared, the excitement was overwhelming. This guy was reading his book, so I read the in-flight magazine. I mean, not *read,* but made out like I was reading. I was just looking at the pictures of the U.S., but I was taking a long time over every one, so this guy would think I could read the English."

The plane took off. "No problem." But Jay Park wished he could see out the window. He didn't dare to lean across the body of his American neighbor; so, holding the magazine close to his face, he'd sneaked glances—seen jigsaw-puzzle bits of city and mountain slide past the wedge of perspex as the plane banked.

A meal was served. "That was real great! American food! I was in the U.S. already!"

At Tokyo they had stopped to refuel. Jay Park was in an agony of impatience. Other Koreans on the flight were buying watches and radios at the Tokyo duty-free shop, but Jay Park sat fretting on a bench during the stopover, his mind full of America.

Then came the long haul across the Pacific. They left the sunset behind—Park could see it gleaming gold on the trailing edge of the plane's starboard wing—and flew into the night. He remembered the blinds being pulled down for the projection of the movie. With no headset, he could only watch the pictures—more postcards of America. "Oh, boy! *Dis* is where I'm goin'! I'm in the movie!"

Exhausted by his excitement, he fell asleep. When he woke up, the quick night was already over. Time itself was whizzing by faster than the clouds below, but the plane was still a long way from America. The morning lasted forever. Then—"They were saying something through the speaker, but my ears were blocking up. *Seattle!* That's all I hear. *Seattle!*"

There was nothing to see. America was a huge gray cloud, through which the plane was making its unbearably slow descent. When it touched down, Jay Park was high, in a toxic trance.

"Wah! Man! The airport! When you're walking through, your mind is set, *'This is America!'* Everything is *nice! Great! Fantasy!*"

The air inside the terminal was magic air. It smelled of cologne and money. There were advertising posters for things—"I don't know what they are, but, boy, they look good to me!"

The two hours he spent standing in line, waiting to be processed by the immigration officials, were precious, American hours. "No, I don't care! I just think, 'Wah! I'm in the U.S.!'"

His sponsors were waiting for him in the arrivals lobby, a Korean-American couple in their forties who had been friends of his parents back in Seoul. Jay Park had never met them before; but they were holding up a sheet of cardboard with his name on it.

"Oh, but they'd done *great!* I was expecting them to take me in a bus, but they got their own car! A Chevy. Blue. Musta been a '63, '64 model. Yeah. Nice long sheer, box-type, really fancy! You sitting in the back seat, looking out, it *astounds.* Wow! All the freeways, all the cars!"

The blue Chevy drove north, up the I-5 toward Seattle.

"*'Whassat?* Hey, goddam, *whassat?'*"

Jay Park saw a great factory—but it wasn't a factory, it was a supermarket. He loved the huge pictures raised over the six-lane highway, the smoking cowboys, the girls in swimsuits. *Wah! America!*

"Then, passing the downtown, *goddam!* The Smith Tower! The Space Needle! Godawmighty! You gotta *look* at that! But so few people! There was hardly any peoples was there! *No people, hardly.* You feel uneasy. *What's going on? Is the people all gone home?* This is real strange, not having people around. In Korea, people everywhere; in America—no people!"

The Chevy left the I-5 and headed up Aurora Avenue, along the wooded edge of Lake Union. It crossed the high bridge over the ship canal and entered the northern suburbs.

"It was the cleanness! The cars parked neatly! Just like the movies! And the lawns . . . No fences, no walls. In Korea, it was all high stone walls round every house. Here, is all open, all lawns, lawns, lawns. Looking out the car window, I see people's bikes left out front, just like that . . . like, here you can just leave things out overnight. No thieves! I think, *everything is coming true! What the movies say is true! This is like paradise is supposed to be!*"

His sponsors lived in a neat frame house in Greenwood.

"They had tables and chairs, the American way, not all on the floor like in Korea. Wah, man! I was cautious, then. Like, first thing, I want to use the toilet, you know? They show me where it is, and I spend a long, long time just looking around in there. Like, *if I use it, where's the smell going to go? Oh! I get it! There's the fan!* Stuff like that. Little things. Then they show me the bed where I'm to sleep? I never slept on a bed before. I think, *how you sleep on a bed without falling off?* I fell out of that bed a few times, too."

That evening, his sponsors took Jay Park to the local super-market.

"Wah! The steaks! The hamburgers! To eat a *whole* piece of meat! Even chickens! And they're so *cheap,* too!"

He slept on the strange bed in a state of delirious wonder, his dreams far outclassed by America's incredible reality. In the morning, he ventured out into the back yard. A man—a white American—was pottering in the garden next door.

"He said to me, 'Hi!' and then he said *something.* I didn't say anything. I think I give him a smile . . . I *hope* I give him a smile . . . then I go back into the house. *They speak English out there!*"

But "I was ready to tackle anything, anyhow." With his spon-sors' help, he enrolled for classes twice a week at the Central Community College. He got a job as a porter at a dry-ice factory. It paid $1.25 an hour—"great money!" He found lodgings, with an Italian woman who worked at a downtown grocery and mothered him. Bed and board cost him $35 a week; but as soon as work was over at the factory, Jay Park was out mowing people's lawns. If he put in a sixteen-hour day, he could make $120 in a week—a fortune. In his new Levis and his long-brimmed baseball cap, Jay Park was living the movie as he toted ice and mowed grass.

"Downtown, though, that was a big shock for me. You look—wah, godawmighty!—really strange people! Those poor whites, down in skid row? You never expecting skid row to exist in a country like this! I never seen *that* in the movies."

He was having a hard time with the language. He went to his classes. He sat up late every night, slogging over his homework. He studied the programs he saw on television, treating *Hogan's Heroes* as a set text. "I want something, I get it," Jay Park said, but he couldn't get English.

"There was such pain building up inside of me . . . People say things at work, I can't answer back! There's no *language* there! Nothing in the mouth! So you must make physical movement, you know? You get *violent!*"

So he punched and jabbed to make himself understood. Lost for a word, he socked the American air and laid it flat.

He was *making out.* He was saving. After a year of lawn mowing and digging out borders, he was able to bill himself as "Jay Park—Contractor and Landscape Gardener," but he was still traveling across Seattle by bus. It took him until 1967 before he'd put away enough to buy his first car.

"It was a 1960 T-Bird. Light blue. Electric windows and everything else. *You* owning own car, wah! That was a thrill, man."

Now he drove his Italian landlady everywhere. She was chauffeured to work, chauffeured around the stores. Waiting for her, parked on the street, Jay Park, Contractor, Landscape Gardener, Ice Merchant, American, sat behind the wheel listening to the music of his electric windows buzzing up and down. "Boy, I loved that car!"

It was something in the disposition of the landscape, the shifting lights and colors of the city. *Something.* It was hard to nail it, but this something was a mysterious gift that Seattle made to every immigrant who cared to see it. Wherever you came from, Seattle was queerly like home.

The Scandinavian fishermen and loggers who had formed the original backbone of Seattle's working population, and who still held the suburb of Ballard as a Nordic fastness, had felt immediately comfortable here. It was fjord country, with wooden houses reaching down to the edge of half-wild, half-tame water. On Puget Sound at night, looking across to the lights of Winslow and Suquamish, one might easily be on the Oresund at Hälsingborg, with Elsinore twinkling on the far shore. The forest, the sea, the lakes were things that were already memories in the imagination of the rawest newcomer. In Seattle for the first time, he knew that he'd been here before.

Koreans kept on telling me that they found it "just like Korea." Japanese immigrants looked up at Mount Rainier and saw Mount Fuji there. Out on Fourth Avenue under my umbrella, I walked through London rain, at a London temperature. In Guntersville, I had mentioned to George Kappler that I was thinking of going to Seattle. He said, "You may laugh now, but I bet, when you get there, that Seattle will remind you of Guntersville." Now I saw exactly what he meant: its wateriness, its green hills, its bridges, its houses hidden in the trees *were* like northern Alabama, but a kinder, gentler northern Alabama, without the sleepy heat and the poisonous snakes.

It was an extraordinarily soft and pliant city. If you went to New York, or to Los Angeles, or even to Guntersville, you had to fit yourself to a place whose demands were hard and explicit. You had to learn the school rules. Yet people who came to Seattle could somehow recast it in the image of home, arranging the city around themselves like so many pillows on a bed. One day you'd wake up to find things so snug and familiar that you could easily believe that you'd been born here.

I noticed that my life and Rainbird's were beginning to diverge. While I spent my days roaming round the city, a restless and provisional first-person, more *eye* than *I*, Rainbird was making himself at home.

Every time I returned to the room at the Josephinum, I was surprised by the accumulation of litter there. There were more books on the shelves than I remembered borrowing or buying, more dismembered and bathwater-splashed copies of the *Nation*, the *New Republic* and the *New York Review of Books*. In the spiral-bound notebook on the desk under the window, there was more writing than I remembered doing myself. I kept on coming across half-read novels, left face down at page 64 or 77, but the names of their characters meant nothing to me at all. Who was this guy Robie Lindqvist? Scratch me.

It was Rainbird, not I, who left the half-drunk bottles of Washington State Merlot on the top of Sandra Taschman's television; Rainbird who was running up the bills (on my Visa card) at the Elliott Bay Book Company, 101 S. Main; Rainbird who was sometimes to be found at midnight, shooting pool in the studious upstairs barn of the Two-Eleven, in the company of a painter friend he'd met at Oliver's bar, or, worse, shooting the breeze over brandy in the piano bar of the Edgewater Inn with a writer who had once reviewed Rainbird for the *Seattle Times*.

My *alter ego* was trying to turn Seattle into the kind of inky, bookish city he knew best. Charmed by the view, by Seattle's seeming ease and openness, he was seriously wondering if he could make a convivial living here.

With a population of more than a million and a half, the place was certainly big enough to use the skills of almost anyone, however eccentrically qualified. If you happened to be a restorer of clavichords, an armature winder, a gold blocker, a Rolfer, a marbler, a holographer, a flock sprayer, you could find a market in Seattle. Yet the city was sufficiently small and remote to tolerate strangers and beginners; it wasn't like New York, where the practitioners of odd crafts were so numerous that the newcomer was likely to meet only blasé smiles and closed doors.

Surely there was room here for a Rainbird? His reputation was slight, but he was a hard worker, he could meet deadlines, he was a naturally gregarious type.

On Rainbird's behalf, I fixed lunch dates with Donn Fry, the book editor of the *Times*, and with Roger Sale, professor of English at the University of Washington, plus supper with Rick Simonson, the bookstore manager.

Rainbird sat up by the window. Scribble, scribble, scribble. An emptied Planters Peanuts tin housed a growing collection of dead ballpoint pens. Stuck for words, he watched the ships slide past on the Sound and listened to the somber music of the diaphones.

Leaving Rainbird's room at midmorning, I closed the door quietly, glad to leave Rainbird to the literary life while I went about my business in the real world.

Their experience had turned the immigrants into compulsive storytellers. Much more than most people, they saw their own lives as having a narrative shape, a plot with a climactic denouement. Each story was molded by conventional rules. Korean men liked to see themselves as Horatio Alger heroes. Once upon a time there had been poverty, adversity, struggle. But character had triumphed over circumstance. The punchline of the story was "Look at me now!" and the listener was meant to shake his head in admiration at the size of the business, the car, the house, at the school and college grades of the narrator's children, and at the amazing fortitude and pluck of the narrator, for having won so much in this country of opportunity. The story, in its simplest form, was a guileless tribute both to the virtues of the Korean male and to the bounty of America.

I preferred to listen to the stories of the women. They were closer to Flaubert than to Alger; their style was more realistic, they were more complicated in structure, they had more regard for pain and for failure.

Insook Webber took the flight for Seattle on April 23, 1977.

"I'd never been in an airplane before, but I loved—I absolutely adored—the idea of flying. I loved to see the planes in the sky. For me, they were flying into—like a fantasy world? A world of possibilities. And I had this premonition. It was always inside me, that somehow, someday, I'd leave Korea."

She was in her thirties now, fine-boned, fine-skinned, her hair grown down to her shoulders in the American way. Her English was lightly, ambiguously, accented. In silk scarf and chunky cardigan, she looked dressed for a weekend in the Hamptons, of the kind that was featured in the Lauren catalogues. She was married to an American, a Yale philosophy graduate who chose to work, unambitiously, in an accountants' office. She herself was a hospital nurse.

In 1977, Insook's elder sister had already been in America for five years, and Insook was flying out to help look after her sister's children.

"I didn't know what to expect. I was totally open, totally vulnerable."

"What did 'America' mean?"

"America? It was a place in novels I'd read, and films I'd seen . . . It was Scarlett O'Hara and *Gone with the Wind.* I was going to live at Tara and meet Rhett Butler, I guess. . . ."

The flight itself was thrilling. Insook had a window seat; looking down on the clouds was how life was meant to be.

"I was breaking out all over with excitement. I was totally tired, but I couldn't sleep for a moment in case I missed something."

It was after dark when the plane approached the coast. The sky was clear, and Insook's first glimpse of America was a lighted city.

"Like diamonds. Miles and miles of diamonds. I couldn't believe it—that people could afford so much *electricity!* We were having to save electricity in Korea then. I knew America was a rich country, but not *this* rich, to squander such a precious thing as electricity . . . I'd never dreamed of so many lights being switched on all at once."

The plane landed at Sea-Tac, and it wasn't until past 2 A.M. that Insook was in possession of her green card, her ticket to becoming an American. Out in the concourse, she spotted her sister waiting for her, but her sister didn't recognize her.

"I was only fifteen when she left—still a kid. I was twenty now, and I'd grown. I had to *persuade* her I was me."

Insook's scanty luggage was put aboard the family car, and they headed for the suburbs.

"Those huge wide roads, and huge lit-up signs . . . it made me feel very small . . . it was like being a little child again . . . everything so big, so bright . . ."

She was describing the shock of being born.

Her sister's house was quiet. "Too quiet. It was like the inside of a coffin. It wasn't like the real world . . ."

Nor was America. Insook was astounded and frightened by the extravagance of the country in which she found herself. When she went to a McDonald's, she wanted to take home the packaging of her hamburger and save it—it seemed criminal simply to throw it away in a litter-bin. A short walk on her first day took her from a rich neighborhood into a poor one. "On this street, these Americans live like kings—and on that, they are beggars! I thought, *My God, how can people* live *like this? How can they live* with *this?*"

Most immigrants were able to enjoy a few weeks, or days at least, of manic elation in the new country before depression hit them, as they woke up to the enormity of what they'd done. For Insook, the depression came at almost the same moment as she touched ground.

"It would have been different if I'd come to be a student. I would have had clear goals, a program to follow . . ."

With no program, she sat in the vault of her sister's house, staring listlessly at television.

"I was terrified. I felt locked in that house for an entire year. I hated to go out. I was cut off from all my friends. I could read English, not well, but I could read it—but I couldn't speak it . . . hardly a word. I felt I was blind and deaf. My self-esteem was totally gone. Totally. I was in America, but I wasn't part of this society at all.

"I was a huge mess of inertia. I was *stopped*—you know? Like a clock? I slept and slept. Sometimes I slept eighteen hours a day. I'd go to bed at night, and it would be dark again when I woke up."

During that year, Insook's whole family—parents, brothers, cousins—came to America by separate planes. They were scattered across the land mass, between Washington State and Detroit.

"There was no going back. I had no home to return to. I had come here to *live,* and I felt suicidal. That sense of homelessness . . . you know? You have no past—that's been taken away from you. You have no present—you are doing nothing. *Nothing.* And you have no future. The pain of it—do you understand?"

Yet even at the bottom of this pit of unbeing, Insook saw one spark of tantalizing possibility. On television, and on her rare, alarmed ventures onto the streets, she watched American women, with wonder.

"Oh, but they were such marvelous creatures! I would see them working, driving cars, talking; they were so confident! Free! Carefree! Not afraid! And I was . . . *me.*"

The prospect of these women made English itself infinitely desirable. Korean was the language of patriarchy and submission, English the language of liberation and independence. Insook had school English. It worked on paper; she could write a letter in it, even, with some difficulty, read a book. But its spoken form bore hardly any relationship at all to the English spoken on American streets. She followed the news programs on TV (she was through with fictions), and parroted back the words as the announcers said them. She practiced, haltingly, in the stores.

I said that I marveled at her articulacy now. "You're saying things with such precision, and complex, emotional things, too. You're making me feel inarticulate, and I've spent forty-seven years living inside this language."

"Oh, it is so much more easy for a Korean woman to learn than for a Korean man. She can afford to make mistakes. When a man makes a mistake, it is an affront to his masculine pride, to his great Koreanness. He is programmed to feel shame. So he learns six sentences, six grammatical forms, and sticks to them. He's safe inside this little language; his pride is not wounded. But when a woman makes mistakes, everybody laughs. She's 'just a girl'—she's being 'cute.' So she can dare things that a man wouldn't begin to try, for fear of making a fool of himself. I could make a fool of myself, so it was easy for me to learn English."

It was still three years before she felt "comfortable" about leaving the house, and four before she began to make her first American friends. She had gone to stay at the family house of a cousin in Bellingham, at the north end of Puget Sound, where she went to college to study for a diploma in nursing.

At Bellingham, Insook began to go on dates with American men.

"My brothers came to see me. They felt betrayed. Korean males—you must know this—are the most conservative on this earth. For me to be seen alone in a café, talking to a white American man, that was a deep, deep insult to them. I was insulting their maleness, insulting their pride, insulting everything that 'Korea' meant to them. They threatened me . . ."

A year later, Insook announced her engagement, to an American.

"My father said, 'I will disown you.'" She smiled—a sad, complicated shrug of a smile. "So I said . . ." For the first time since we'd been talking, she produced a pack of cigarettes and lit one. "I said, 'I'm sick and tired of this family. Okay, disown me. *Please* disown me!'"

The brothers came round, with a fraternal warning.

"They promised me that they would bomb the church where we were getting married. We had to hire security guards. One of my brothers said he would prefer to blow me up, blow me to pieces, than see me married to an American."

"And you really believed that he meant it—that he'd make a bomb?"

"Oh, yes. My brothers weren't doing well. They were struggling in America. They were just fighting me with what little ego they had left."

The wedding went ahead, with security guards. At the last moment one of the brothers turned up, shamefaced, with a gift.

Her marriage was "absolutely democratic," and it was, thought Insook, the prospect of this democracy that her father and brothers had so feared and hated. "For the Korean man, everything that he is, his whole being, is in direct conflict with what this society is about."

A little Korean culture had survived in Insook's American marriage. She and her husband left their shoes by the front door and went around the house barefoot or in stockings. They lived closer to the ground than most Americans. "He has a naturally floor-oriented lifestyle." She sometimes cooked Korean food. "He likes to use chopsticks." Her husband had "a few phrases" of Korean.

"But I seldom feel my identity as a Korean now. I forget that I look different—"

"You think you look 'different'? Look at all of us here—" We were sitting in a booth at the Queen City Grill on First, a favorite lunch-spot for Seattle's wine-drinking, seafood-eating, stylish middle class. We had melting-pot faces: at almost every table, you could see a mop of Swedish hair, an Anglo-Saxon mouth, an Italian tan, Chinese grandmother eyes, a high Slav cheekbone. In this company Insook's appearance was in the classic American grain.

"No, you're right. It's when people know I come from Korea, I sometimes get deadlocked in arguments. The moment someone knows I am a Korean, then I'm framed in their stereotype of how a Korean ought to be. Like, if I'm shy for some reason, then it's 'Of course you're shy—that's so *Korean.*' But then again, if I am outspoken, if I get angry in a discussion, that's 'being Korean' too. Whatever I do, it must be 'Korean.' I do get mad over that sometimes."

Yet Insook's attachment to Korea still went deep. It would sometimes take her by surprise. Shopping in the Bon, she felt "shame" (that most powerful of all Korean words) when she saw how Korean products were almost always shoddier than their Japanese or American counterparts.

". . . they are made to fall apart in a few months, and I think, *this is my country.*"

"But your country is America now."

"No. I still identify with Korea. I do still think of myself as a foreigner and of America as a foreign country. Not on the surface. In a profound way, which I can't change. I think, too, that my sense of roots is beginning to return. Just lately, I've been taking up calligraphy again. And I'd like to do something for the Korean community here. When I see other Koreans in Seattle, I know that we've all been through the same pain, the same suffering, and I feel good that I went through that pain; it's very important for me."

She was doing what she could. For Korean patients in the hospital where she worked, she was translator, legal advisor, counselor, kind heart. That morning, she had been trying to find a lawyer who would take on the case of a Korean who had been injured at work and whose employer had refused to pay him compensation.

"But I do feel uncomfortable with other Korean people.

There's so much suspicion and resentment. To so many of them, I am not *me*, I am a girl who married an American. As soon as I tell them my American name, I see it in their eyes. I am *one of those."*

"But you still go on trying—"

"I feel compulsion—compulsion? compassion? I don't know, I suppose both—for Korea. You know? It's like having two friends . . . There is the rich friend, who's doing very well in life. You're always glad to see him, you're happy in his company . . . But you don't need to worry about him. That's like America is for me. Then I have this poor friend. Always in some kind of trouble. It depresses me to have to meet him. But . . . he is the friend who needs me. That is Korea."

Some days later, I was talking to Jay Park again. A year after he'd arrived in Seattle, he'd met a Korean girl (at the Presbyterian Church), and they'd married in '67, driving off in the pale blue T-Bird with electric windows. They now had two sons and a daughter.

It was odd, Jay Park said, that while nearly all of his sons' friends were Korean, "eighty percent" of his daughter's friends were American. "She just seem to like to hang out with white Americans."

I could hear Insook's voice, talking of "marvelous creatures."

"How do you take to the idea of a white American son-in-law?" I asked.

Jay Park laughed. "I deal with that one awready. I tell her, 'Day you bring home American boyfriend, that's the day you dead meat, girl!' "

It was a joke. He was hamming the role of heavy Korean father, but there was enough seriousness in it to give it an uncomfortable edge.

"Dead meat!" His laugh faded into a deep frown. "I see these intermarriage families, and always is some . . . *unsatisfied . . . life.* You get what I am saying now? I am thinking our kids got lost somewhere . . . somewhere between the cultures."

*   *   *

The Central Community College, gaunt and white as a hospital, straddled two long blocks high up on Capitol Hill. It was the people's university of Seattle, a landmark visible from far downtown, an institution where almost anyone could enroll to learn almost anything, from elementary accounting and business practice to courses on Foucault, Derrida and Lacan. The SCCC figured importantly in the biographies of nearly all the immigrants I had met.

Early one wet Monday morning, in Room 4168, I sat at the back of the class in Survival English, feeling belittled. The bentwood chair was too small and I had to do an origami folding job on my legs to make them fit under the low desk.

There were a dozen of us; six men, six women. I was the oldest by a year or two; the youngest was in his early twenties. We came from Vietnam, mainland China, the Dominican Republic, Mexico, Hong Kong and England. Everyone bar me had been living in the United States for less than six months. This was a course for FOBs.

The instructor was a slight woman with thunderflash eyes and a smile that could find its target at a hundred yards. From her first "Good *morning!*" and "Are you *ready?*", she radiated the idea that learning English was an exhilarating adventure. She was, I guessed, from the Philippines, and her own English, though grammatically faultless, was still a long way from newscaster-standard American in its pronunciation. She carried with her the warming message of *If I can do it, so can you;* but even if you ever managed to speak the language exactly as she did (an improbable achievement), you would still sound like a foreigner in America.

We began with a spelling bee, recapping on hard words from last week's lesson. Four students stood at the blackboard, chalk at the ready. It was a competition.

"Toothbrush," said the instructor, waving a toothbrush and miming the action of cleaning her teeth with it.

Armando from Mexico, a solemn janitorial figure, his face deeply channeled with worry-lines, wrote TOEBUS in slow and wobbly letters that climbed the blackboard like ivy ascending a wall. Sylvia from Dominica stood back from her effort, which read TOOF BROPHUS. Armando looked defeated by this; he'd known all along that he was a letter or two out. To his surprise, it turned out to be Kuan from Shanghai who'd got it right. Kuan, clapped by the class, returned modestly to his seat. The champ.

The four Chinese students were always the quickest off the mark. They sat together, a mutual aid society, whispering and passing notes.

"No Chinese here!"

"Sorry, lady!"

After the spelling was over, the instructor produced a cardboard box full of plastic fruits and vegetables: an eggplant, a squash, some nuts, an artichoke, a green pepper, peas, beans, two figs, a cucumber, oranges, apples and bananas. She held up each object in turn and the students yelled out the names, tumbling over themselves to get in first.

"Airplan!" "Squish!" "Artichoker!" "Grin peace!" "Figure!"

Next, the box was turned on its side to represent a refrigerator, and the students had to place the fruits and vegetables in relation to each other in or on various parts of the make-believe fridge. It was an exercise in the use of prepositions.

"Please put der grin paper on top of der fridge," said the instructor. "Now put der grin binz *behind* der grin paper . . ."

The students clapped, giggled, shot their hands up *("Me!" "Me!" "Me!")*. Failures were met with *oohs* and *ahs*, success with whistles and applause. The students, infants in the language, had reverted to the social behavior of a happy, squealing infant school. They were six years old again.

Yet they were husbands, wives, breadwinners. Within the last few months they had made the most important, most grimly adult, decision that they would probably ever make in their lives. Coming to America had made them far too old and far too young all at once, and I trembled for them, these helplessly newborn grown-ups.

"Yes, please? You know this word?"

I was in the line of fire of the long-range smile. I'd drifted off. The class had moved on to looking at the picture book in front of me. It showed a bedroom, and we were naming the furniture and fittings.

"I think there is another word the British use for this. Not *bedspread,* but something else. I have forgotten it. Will you tell us, please?"

It had always been a recurrent nightmare of mine to find myself back in school. I gazed stupidly at the picture, as blank-minded as I'd ever been at six and seven.

"Uh . . . eiderdown?" I said.

"No. I do not think so. Some other word."

I went rambling around inside my head, in search of what she wanted. The damned thing looked like a bedspread to me, and only a bedspread.

"Ah—*counterpane!*"

"Correct! If you are in the U.S., you say 'bedspread.' If you are in England, you say 'counterpane.' "

The four Chinese students turned simultaneously to give me an encouraging smile. I was coming along—I was doing just fine.

The instructor kept the class moving with a continuously changing menu of activities. She brought out a sheaf of drawings made by the students and projected each one on a screen. In the darkened classroom, his artwork embarrassingly enlarged and illuminated, the student had to tell the story of what was going on in his drawing.

Nearly all the drawings might as easily have been done by real six-year-olds. The people in them had balloon faces, stick bodies and banana-bunch fingers. They had been executed in childish crayons.

"Is my . . . familee. *Walking. Shopping.* My brodder . . . he work . . . going by car."

In picture after picture, one object kept on showing up. In the top right-hand corner of the page, where the sky was meant to be, was an airplane—the vehicle that had brought the artist to America. The odd thing was that, while the human beings in the drawings were blobby and vestigial, the planes had been done with careful regard for proportion and perspective. The students dwelled lovingly over the details of the 747s as if, in drawing them, they were both limning the tremendous distance they had traveled to get here and reminding themselves that there was, still, a way to go home.

To begin with, I had taken against the infant-school style of the teaching, but as the class went on I grew increasingly to see its point. America had made the immigrants feel very small indeed, and in the crèche-like atmosphere of Room 4168 they were being encouraged to behave as they felt, like children. In less than an hour they'd be returned to the harsh adult stuff of hustling a living down in the streets of Seattle, but for now they were being mercifully babied. The instructor knew her job.

When the lesson was over, I waited for the elevator in the company of a Vietnamese man who'd put on twenty years in the last five minutes. He and his family had been in America for nearly two months now. He'd found a job, in a shipyard, and was due to start work next week. In the meantime, he was frantically practicing his English with anyone who'd speak to him.

"How long *you* come to U.S.?" he said.

I totted up the bits and pieces of time that I'd spent in the country.

"Altogether, about three years. Maybe less."

"Years!" His voice was forlorn, the news far worse than he'd expected. *Years*—and I was still taking courses in Survival English.

Rainbird's chief crony in Seattle was the novelist Michael Upchurch, another refugee from another battleground city. Upchurch had been wounded in the daily war of New York City, and had come to Seattle to start life over again in a kindlier place.

In 1986, he'd been thirty-two, the author of two books, *Jamboree* and *Air*. Both novels had had good reviews, but too few of them, and they'd shown a disappointing reluctance to shift themselves out of the bookstores. The best that Upchurch had been able to manage in the way of a publisher's advance was five thousand dollars. In New York City, you couldn't rent a decent shoe closet for five thousand dollars. An apartment for four hundred dollars a month would come with a guarantee of limited life-expectancy.

Trying to buy time to write, he'd worked as a sales clerk in a bookstore, watching the Stephen Kings fly out of the shop on winged feet while the Upchurches stood roosting on their perch.

He'd worked night shifts as a typesetter. As his rent rose, so his hours of paid employment became longer and his writing time got shorter. It was fast getting to the stage when a good day's writing meant penning a subordinate clause with just enough time left to close it with a semicolon.

Upchurch shared a small apartment with his lover, but the relationship went sour. They agreed, sadly, to break up.

It's usual, when couples split, for one of the pair to move out, but in a New York rental, with two people on modest earnings, that custom was becoming an unaffordable luxury. There was a solution, said the lover. On separation day, they would have to draw an imaginary line down the center of the room. The lover would stick to one end, Upchurch to the other. Problem solved.

The novelist packed his bags and took flight to Seattle.

The best thing about the city was that it was a long way from New York. He knew one couple here. He came with no job in view, a manuscript that had jammed solid on him and a rankling soreness of the heart. Listening to him talk of his escape, I thought of him as a fleeing Cambodian (definitely not a dollar-hungry Korean), a Cambodian with a brush-beard, thick specs, a disorderly laugh and a wary, self-ironizing smile.

In three years, Upchurch had put together exactly the kind of life in Seattle that Rainbird might reasonably dream of leading for himself. He'd finished—and published—the jammed novel, *The Flame Forest,* and was writing to live, and living to write, in possession of that small, shabby independence which Dr. Johnson held to be the freelance author's claim to standing in the world.

He lived in a warrenlike apartment building on the three-hundred-foot-high brink of Capitol Hill. On seeing Rainbird's magnificent view over the Sound, Upchurch had coughed and said, "Yes . . . but like most things around here, views in Seattle tend to be pretty democratic"; and his own view was of the city falling away below his window in a deep bowl. The waterfront was a mile off, and on clear days he could rest his eye on the deckle-edged Olympics fifty miles to the west.

Rainbird took in the essentials of the Upchurch life. The tight little apartment was a magpie's nest. There were books shelved, books stacked in toppling heaps, books open, books fresh from their publishers in army-khaki jiffy bags. Words were spilling from the word processor on the dining table. There was an enormous gray-eyed video and a miniature Moog synthesizer, together with the kind of sound system that requires a degree in Japanese to learn how to operate it.

In this dusty den of communications technology, Upchurch sat, furiously communicating.

Mornings, he worked on the novel with which he'd been battling for more than two years now. The characters, Rainbird gathered, were getting out of hand, leading Upchurch down unfamiliar streets that kept on turning into blind alleys. Somewhere inside the memorious word processor, these recalcitrant people were conspiring against their creator. They clung to life whenever Upchurch tried to kill them off, and died, suddenly and in mysterious circumstances, just when he'd been counting on them to stay alive and well. But they commanded Upchurch's mornings. For four hours every day, he slogged it out with them, trying to persuade them to return to the narratorial straight and narrow.

In the afternoons and evenings, he turned critic. For the *Seattle Times*, he reviewed novels, films, dance and music. It meant living a hard-pressed and hectic imaginative life. On the bus to see the new Scorsese, he'd finish off the new Joyce Carol Oates and get started on the new Craig Nova, while back inside the word processor one of his own characters would embark on an unplanned and highly unsuitable affair. His working days were Koreanly long, and at night he was prone to dream other people's fictions.

But he was—at last, at thirty-five—doing what he had always wanted to do; and it was Seattle that had thrown him the chance to do it. "In New York, no one was ever going to ask me to write about movies for the *Village Voice.*" In New York, too, Upchurch had known very few writers and he'd practiced his own vocation as a secret vice. In Seattle he met other writers nearly every week. Almost everyone with a national reputation eventually passed through town to read at the Elliott Bay Book Company or to give a lecture at the University of Washington. Upchurch, when he liked their work, would collar them in their hotel rooms and write profiles of them for the *Times.*

And how, Rainbird inquired, was the pay?

Jay Park, who charged $75 an hour for his plumbers, would have sniffed at it, but the pay was enough to keep Upchurch, or Rainbird, afloat. The *Times* paid $75 for a full-length book review, and for any "overnight" review of a dance concert, play or movie. Shorter book reviews earned $50 and $25. For a profile of a writer in the Sunday arts section, Upchurch made anything up to $150.

This was just the *Times.* Upchurch sometimes wrote for the *Washington Post Book World* and the *San Francisco Chronicle,* bigger newspapers that paid more. There was also the *Seattle Weekly* to write for ($150 for 2,000 words), plus local magazines like *Pacific Northwest* and *Washington* (which had just established a basic rate of $800 for a feature article of 2,500 words).

Upchurch told Rainbird, "If you were prepared to do the kinds of things that I can't do, like travel pieces, tasting Washington State wines or investigating ski resorts, then you'd be getting five, six, seven hundred dollars a time."

Rainbird reconciled himself to investigating ski resorts.

In the last year, Upchurch's freelance earnings had been just under $13,000. In New York, that would have been starvation wages, but in Seattle, for a single person, it was a competence. His apartment cost him $370 a month. He had no car, but Seattle was safe and small enough for most journeys to be enjoyable walks of a mile or less. The *Times* office on John Street was half a dozen blocks away. Broadway, two blocks east, was not quite Greenwich Village, but it was a civilized strip of movie theaters, bars, restaurants, bookshops and groceries. It stayed open at all hours. Its dominant tone was distinctly but unemphatically gay. In an incurious big-city way, it was hospitable to the dissenting life of the freelancer. Around Broadway, everybody did odd things, at odd times of the day. A man who was to be seen hanging out in the public library on Republican at noon, lunching alone with a book at the Trattoria Pagliacci, spending the afternoon watching a movie at the Harvard Exit, and rattling at a typewriter at 3 A.M., would excite no particular attention here.

What was the title of the work in progress on the dining table? *Peculiar Passions.*

Rainbird looked at the view from the novelist's window; the lights coming on all over the darkening city, the warning flash of the lighthouse off Duwamish Head, the fading bulk of the mountains in the far distance . . . this democratic vista. He could see himself here. He'd be scratching away in old-fashioned pen-and-paper style . . . walking down to the *Times,* copy in hand . . . wrangling with a friend about the new Thomas Pynchon over take-out pizza and a bottle of wine . . .

He said to Upchurch, "You want to trade?"

It was November now. Late at night, every night, crouched over Sandra Taschman's TV, I flipped through the channels, from KIRO to KOMO to KING and back to KIRO again, trying to make sense of what was going on in the far world.

There were two iconic images of the moment. The first was of a young man armed with a domestic hammer, hacking deliriously away at the massive concrete face of the Berlin Wall. The camera zoomed in to expose the rusty and twisted steel ganglia of the thing, then cut to show a great slab of it coming clean away, like a stone being rolled from the face of a tomb. Through the hole were seen the East German guards, looking desperately unsure about whether they should grin for the camera or take aim with their Kalashnikovs and shoot the cameraman.

The second image was of dazed East Germans, clutching their government-issue D-marks, swarming through the aisles of a West Berlin department store. They came toward the camera, solemnly staring, hesitantly prodding at this astounding new world of Giorgio Armani, Estée Lauder, Calvin Klein and all the other *Wunderdoktors* of the rag and makeup trades.

When television in Seattle dealt with issues like a scandal in the Japanese cabinet or the forced repatriation of the boat people in Hong Kong, it was reporting on reality and its stories were generally intelligent and sharp. When it tried to show the mighty crack-up of Eastern Europe, it fell into the genre of pure fairytale.

Freedom and Democracy had broken out all over. We were

witnessing a *fête champêtre,* a triumph of Liberty over Tyranny. There was almost no coverage of events on the far side of the wall, no serious questioning of what might happen to these bankrupt republics with their ancient blood feuds and their lapsed memories about elective, multi-party politics.

For the fairytale which was being told in nightly installments was not really about *them* at all; it was about *us.* It was as if the Statue of Liberty had been removed from its old site in New York Harbor and re-erected alongside the Brandenburg Gate. The Hungarians, Czechs, Poles, East Germans were the people in the Emma Lazarus poem; they were the tired, the poor, the huddled masses yearning to breathe free, the wretched refuse of the teeming shore, and they were coming over to Our Way of Life.

So every image was colored with American self-congratulation. The reporters on the scene made happy play with the cranky temperaments of the old Wartburg and Trabant cars in which the refugees were crossing the border into West Germany. For this was the hour of the Ford, the Cadillac, the Oldsmobile (and, to be fair, also the hour of the Toyota, the Nissan and the BMW).

Out of the blue had come a marvelous vindication of the American Way. After years of bilious talk about "the consumer society," after the grave prophecies of liberal economists like J. K. Galbraith and Benjamin Friedman, here were the European millions endorsing the ethic of consumption which was the fundamental ethic of decent, conservative, suburban America. In the downfall of Honecker and the rise of Havel what we saw, in Seattle, was a victory celebration for the lawn sprinklers and electric-eye carports of Magnolia, Bellevue and Mercer Island.

How was Democracy at work to be best represented? It was easy. You simply showed people going shopping, in stores exactly like Frederick & Nelson and the Bon.

To any immigrant that image would raise a pungent memory of his or her own first birthday encounter with the American Way.

For Mun Hee Han (June 5, 1976), it was the unnatural frigidity of the beige Cadillac in which she rode out of Cincinnati airport. Outside the car, the city was as fiercely hot as Seoul, but the air conditioning made Mun Hee shiver the whole way. They reached her brother's apartment. It too was an icebox. She asked to use the bathroom. "I remember the smell of the soap, the starchy smell of the towels. My sister-in-law had just washed her hair, and the smell of the shampoo was still in the room. It was Helen Jourdain shampoo, and I just stood there breathing it in, it smelled so fresh, so cool, so good. That's what I remember . . . the smell of the U.S. . . . it was so *clean,* and so *cold!*"

For Jay Park (August 29th, 1965), it was the novelty of finding the toilet inside the house and the strange American custom (he did not learn it until he had been in the country for more than a week) of taking a shower every day.

For Young Ho Kim (November 27th, 1976), it was the tin of Campbell's soup with which his first American meal began, and the taste of the cheese that came after it. "I hated it. I'd never eaten cheese before. It tasted bitter, different, strong. It was processed cheese from a tube, and I can taste it now . . . *horrible!*" Later that day, the family went on an outing to the Safeway supermarket. Young Ho, then ten years old, was dazzled. "It was incredible! Huge! And the smell, of meat, fish, detergent, fruit, all mixed up, that was weird. I remember these miles and miles of pieces of meat, all wrapped up in cellophane, like gifts. We filled the trunk of my cousin's car with food. *Filled* it. It cost . . . forty-nine dollars . . . I can't remember the cents."

Seattle liked to pride itself on its liberality of mind. While I was living there, the city, with a black population of less than 15 percent, elected Norm Rice as its first black mayor; and it was—on the whole—impressively tolerant of the immigrants and refugees. Fugitive graffiti writers dirtied the walls with vicious nonsense about *gooks, chinks* and *slant-eyes,* but the language of Seattle public life was clean. It was not a place where people could comfortably get away with the kind of xenophobia and discrimination that were aired freely in both New York and Alabama.

There was one exception to this rule—one group of immigrants who could be openly abused in bars and public places, in the newspapers and on television. *They* were taking our jobs. *They* were buying up our houses. *They* were responsible for the sudden rise in the crime rate. *They* were clogging up our freeways and straining our school system beyond its limits. *They* should go home where they came from. *They* were Californians.

There was the bumper-sticker (more often talked about than actually seen on bumpers) which read, HAVE A GOOD TRIP— BACK TO CALIFORNIA. Within a few days of the first breach in the Berlin Wall, Emmett Watson, the resident grouch on the *Seattle Times,* proposed that Seattle should buy the wall, block by block, and rebuild it around Seattle to keep the Californians out. Billboards advertising a local beer showed a bottle, with the slogan CALIFORNIANS JUST DON'T GET IT.

These Californian jokes were Seattle's chief claim to having a distinct regional humor. They acted as a useful safety-valve, allowing people in Seattle to vent their real disquiet and anger at the effects of mass immigration without being tagged as racist bigots. Californians were fair game. You could happily jeer at a Californian in a way that you would not dream of jeering at a black or an Asian.

Californians in Seattle did not find the jokes funny. One Tuesday, I spotted a notice in the *Weekly,* placed on the back page, at the end of the massage and therapy ads: it announced the formation of a group called UCLA, short for United Californians Looking for Acceptance in Seattle.

I called the contact number (after all, my Spectrum did have California plates), and got an answering machine. My own telephone rang a few moments later. Victoria James, UCLA's founder, said that she'd had to put the machine on because she was getting so many hate calls.

"Such as?"

"Oh, such as 'Get your fuckin' mellow outa here, you slimy-assed bitch.' And that's *repeatable.* That was from a woman. There've been worse."

Ms. James was in deadly earnest. For more than a year, she and her husband had been pointedly ignored by all their neighbors, she said. She had been repeatedly shouldered off the freeway because she drove a car with California plates . . .

This didn't chime with my experience at all. I'd driven all over Seattle, with California plates, and thought that no American city came near to matching it for the courtesy with which one was admitted to the traffic stream.

"What make of car are you driving?"

"An E-type Jag."

I recommended her to trade it in and buy something more humble, like a Geo Spectrum.

The first meeting of UCLA was held a few days later, in a community center in Queen Anne. It was a group-therapy session: thirty of us, seated in a circle in a too-large room, taking turns to tell our hard luck stories. *My name is John, and I am a Californian . . .*

The stories were long, solemn and self-servingly credulous. "My Honda was broadsided," said a man; and that was because he was a Californian. A woman knew of a woman whose husband had died; when the widow had called the undertakers, she'd been told, "Why don't you take him and bury him in California?" People had seen job applications torn up before their very eyes when the employer reached the bit that revealed that they hailed from California.

A portly and sallow young man, with a moth-eaten blond mustache, said that he'd come to Seattle with an MFA in theater arts. He was a fully qualified actor, but the only work he'd been able to find was occasional continuity-announcing at a TV station. For the last year, he'd been forced to resort to house painting to make ends meet.

His story was met with sympathetic headshakes round the circle. Listening to him tell it, in unrelenting monotone, I thought that if I were a director scouting for an attendant lord or second policeman, I'd put him straight down on my *Don't call us, we'll call you* list.

The man next to him said, "This is a big deal. It's not a nice deal. It's not a comfortable deal. We're certainly not wanted in Seattle, and we're getting the deep freeze . . ."

"I'm stressed out," said a woman. "I'm paranoid about telling people I'm from California. I've seen them wince when I've said it. I'm lonelier here than anywhere I've ever been before."

"The money," said a man who evidently had plenty of the stuff, "is real welcome—but the people aren't."

A sullen-faced woman of fifty-five-going-on-sixty said, "I'm going to say something now that I haven't dared to say in five years. I haven't dared to say it even to myself. But I'm going to come out now and say it right here. *I hate Seattle!*"

She brought the house down. The whole room clapped and cheered.

The sadsack Californians represented themselves as a warm-blooded southern people, friendly, outgoing, intimate, spontaneous. In Seattle, they agreed, they had come up against a granitic northern coldness of temperament. Seattle people never invited you into their houses. They had "this quick-distancing thing."

"I don't have one friend here—not a friend like I used to have back in Santa Monica."

Though everyone in the room originally came from somewhere in California, they had lived all over the United States. They'd put in time in New York, Chicago, Atlanta, Phoenix, Denver, Houston . . . They had sampled the cities of America as one might go round sampling well-recommended restaurants. Most of them had come to Seattle because they'd read about it in a magazine. To the horror of the Emmett Watsons of the world, Seattle had just been named as the Most Livable City in America by yet another magazine, and these puffs for the city were drawing thousands of people like the malcontents of UCLA. They had descended on Seattle as gourmands. They demanded that the food should be first-rate, the service attentive and deferential. They had come here, not to live, but "for the lifestyle," and they were comically, insupportably outraged by what they conceived as the poor value they were getting for their money. The waitpersons were so *surly!*

"I come from a world-class city," said a woman from Los Angeles, "and this is my lesson in life—to learn provinciality." Everyone nodded. Seattle was *so* provincial. "But I'm going to give Seattle a chance . . ." This was issued as a serious threat to the city. It had better take heed—or else. "I'm going to give it one more year. And then I'm through."

This woman's contribution was particularly well received. It showed a nobility and generosity of spirit that Seattle had really done nothing to deserve. Seattle, it was generally felt, was amazingly lucky to have people like her—like *us*—who were prepared to give it a chance at this late stage.

I left this sorry assembly while the complaints were still coming thick and fast. At the Two Bells Tavern, someone pulled up a stool so that I could join the group at the bar.

"Where you been?"

"Listening to a bunch of Californians talking about what shits all you guys are."

"You been hanging out with *Californians?* And I was going to buy you a drink. Hey, Steve, don't serve this man. This man has just confessed to fraternizing with Californians."

It showed in the faces of so many of the teen-age children of the immigrants—a taut-skinned, hollow-eyed look, as if all their strings had been keyed up to breaking point. They were vibrant with the tension of trying to be Koreans and Americans at the same time. They had real problems in Seattle.

Many had American names. Some had been christened with them, like Regina, now sixteen, whose father's first job had been in the car insurance business. "He noticed that the people who had the rich stuff, like Olds and Caddies, were all Eugenes and Reginas. So I'm Regina and my brother's Gene." Her friend Christine had been Chu Mee until one day in the eighth grade when she returned from school to announce to her parents that from henceforth she was Christine.

They had American voices, American clothes, American haircuts; they were fans of the Mariners, the Seahawks and the Sonics; but they were Korean children, locked into a family system that was centuries away from modern urban America.

Jay Park, whose daughter was now in her first year at Columbia, heading for an MBA, said, "There is old saying in Korea—'You got to whip a running horse.' " These children were whipped. Every Korean child was designed, in a phrase I heard a dozen times, to become a brain surgeon by day and a concert pianist by night. They had to be on the honor roll, make straight As, play at least one musical instrument, speak Korean as well as English, revere their elders and continue the patriarchy into the next generation. They had to be not only Koreans and Americans, but outstandingly dutiful Koreans while becoming outstandingly successful Americans.

"Like, say you come second in something, you go home and tell your mom, 'Mom, I came second.' An American mother, she'd say, 'Honey, that's great!' But if your mom's Korean, she'll only say one thing: 'Why didn't you come first?' "

This kind of goading often worked far too well for its own good. By the third grade, the child would be top of the class, expert in the American language, while the family patriarch would still be trying to decode a simple newspaper story with the aid of a dictionary, and the only American television program he'd watch with any pleasure would be *Sesame Street.*

When not pinned down to their homework, the children were called into service as translators. Nine- and ten-year-olds had to deal, on their fathers' behalf, with landlords, clients, the I.R.S. One girl told me how her father, a tailor, had been cheated by his American landlord and lost his business premises: at thirteen, she'd gatecrashed a Business Administration course at Central Community College, mugged up on company and real-estate law, found her father a new workshop, fixed the terms of the lease and incorporated him as a company. He was doing fine. Seahawks stars now wore his suits. Yet, still at school, she was the company secretary and accountant while her father, who had only a few shards of English, cut and sewed his way into American prosperity.

America was turning everything upside down. It turned children into adults, as it turned their parents into children. It made proud men, bred to a zealous belief in male superiority, submit to wives and daughters.

"Respect isn't what it used to be . . ." This was from a sixteen-year-old girl, a churchgoer, a good Korean. "We don't see truly devoted Korean children now. Like, that traditional bowing every morning, with everyone younger bowing lower to everyone who's older?—that's going out. I smart-mouth my parents. The translation stuff gets to be a pain in the butt."

The girls were doing best out of the deal. Infected by what Jefferson once called the virus of liberty, they were beginning to enjoy a degree of independence that would have been unthinkable for them in Korea. For the boys it was different. Their parents had promised them that they were the rightful heirs to the estate of Korean manhood. But the Korean girls they knew in Seattle were now far too unabashed and well educated ever to make good Korean wives.

Regina said, "So the boys like to go back to Korea to find a wife. Girls in Korea are nicer, prettier, more submissive than we are." She did not say this with a smile. She said it sadly. She seemed to think that the boys had a real point.

Young Ho, at twenty-two, had been through the mangle of becoming an American. He'd grown to an American height, he walked with a cultivated hipster's lope. When he wasn't studying history at the University of Washington, he played drums with a rock band.

When he came over with his family in '76, they'd had problems at the airport with the Buddhist shrine that his mother had insisted on taking to America. With its candlesticks and framed pictures of the Kim ancestors, it was too fragile to be trusted to the cargo hold, and had been grudgingly allowed on board the plane as hand baggage. During the flight, the family had watched *Skyriders* with James Coburn and Susannah York, and nursed the shrine between them.

In the grocery store at Ballard where they settled, Young Ho's mother didn't "have time to do the ceremonies right." A doorstep evangelist converted her to Christianity, and just last year the local Baptist pastor had taken the precious shrine away ("I think he said some prayers over it and burned it").

In his thirteen years in the United States, Young Ho had grown used to seeing essential bits of his past go up in smoke.

At school in Korea, he'd been marked as a smart child. In the fifth grade in Seattle, he was given first-grade *Dick and Jane* books to work on. He was hazed by his schoolmates. "They called me things like Gook and Slant-Eye, and said I looked real evil. They'd say, *What are you? A Jap, or a Chink or a Viet, or what?* They never said *Korean.*"

He felt dumb. He cried a lot. He couldn't sleep. In the small hours, he would climb into his parents' bed for comfort.

"At school, they encouraged me to draw. That helped. I spent hours doing pictures of what I couldn't say. Then I wrote my first poem in English. It was about the rain—Seattle rain. I was proud of that . . ."

By the sixth grade, Young Ho was "thinking in English, not Korean." By the seventh, he was on the honor roll.

In Scandinavian Ballard, his skin color had been conspicuously yellow; but in high school he was bused, as a white, to a black school in Seattle Central. "That was something. I made friends there, with black kids. Until then, I'd always been obedient and shy . . . always hanging out with squares." He listened to black music and picked up a smattering of black slang.

He was still a dutiful and hard-working Korean son, "on that guilt and shame trip." Home life was conducted exclusively in Korean, but he was stuck with a ten-year-old's version of the language. He could only think and say childish things in it, while his parents were entirely unable to follow where he was going in English.

It was not surprising that the academic subject which he wanted most to study was astronomy. Few distant planets could seem as alien as the one on which Young Ho had landed. He wanted to be an astrophysicist. He fulfilled every Korean parent's dream of what a son should do, and won a scholarship to Columbia. *Columbia* was a word like *please* or *bread;* it was an elemental item of immigrant vocabulary.

In his freshman year, he met Laura, a pre-med student whose family had fled Hungary in 1956. They fell in love, and at weekends Young Ho was made welcome in her parents' house. Immigrants themselves, they, far more than most Americans, could understand the pain of the transition he was making and recognize the enormous distance he had already traveled.

"It shocked me sometimes, the way she used to talk to her

parents, her American boldness. After the honorific titles that we used to talk to each other in our house, in Korean, it seemed insolent. It was engrained in me that you treat older people with respect, and show it by using titles, but Laura just went right in, like she was talking to girls in her dorm. That *irreverence* . . . I mean, I was excited by it, but a little scared of it, too. It seemed part of the way in which white society was bastardized, and the whole English language was a product of that bastardization."

In the summer, heart-in-mouth, Young Ho took Laura back to Seattle and the house in Ballard, to meet his parents. His father bowed to her and was distantly polite. His mother froze her out. "She was completely cold, silent, wouldn't look at her. Whenever they were in the same room, my mother's body language would say, 'I can't see you—you don't exist!' She'd walk past Laura like she was a chair that had gotten misplaced.

"It's bad for a Korean woman to marry a white man, but it's worse, much worse, for a Korean man to marry a white woman. I hated it, but I felt sympathy for my mother, even while she was doing it. I understood."

At Columbia, Young Ho's physics and astronomy were up to snuff, but he was falling badly behind in his math. His relationship with Laura was coming apart at the seams. When he flunked out at the end of his sophomore year, his parents blamed his failure on the evil influence of the white girl.

He came back to Seattle, to live at home and re-enroll, this time as a history major, at the local university. He had discovered the drums.

"It was just something I badly wanted to do. I didn't know why. My parents didn't like it at all—they still won't speak about it. My brothers had taken lessons in the violin, bass and clarinet, but it would have been *unspeakable* for me to ask my parents for a drum set."

Drumming had been his solace for the last two years. "It's not that I'm all that good, it's just that, somehow, I feel most comfortable behind a drum set."

His five-man band was black, white and Korean, a small enclave of harmony between the cultures. They played in bars and at fraternity parties. Seated on his stool, with his line of drums standing between himself and the rest of the world, Young Ho was happy. He thundered away on the skins, building a percussive wall of noise: for as long as the number lasted, he was out of Korean, out of American, out of the fray.

On Thanksgiving morning I was up early. I had a date with a Canadian friend who lived on Vancouver Island, and was due to catch the ferry which steamed daily up the length of Puget Sound from Seattle to Victoria, B.C. I watched breakfast television while the coffee brewed.

They were showing the Macy's Parade, which had started in New York three hours before. It was snowing in Manhattan. The sky looked like mattress stuffing and car lights were plowing slowly through the dim streets. The balloon handlers, in oilskins and woolly hats, looked cold and wet as they negotiated the oily slush on Central Park West. The balloons themselves swam into view on the screen like the faces of acquaintances one has met at a party one didn't much enjoy. I could endure a life in which I never encountered Woody Woodpecker, Bugs Bunny or Big Bird again, but here they came, lolling like drunks through the bare treetops.

I found, or thought I found, the window from which I'd watched the parade a year ago. It was open then, and crammed with wiseguy kids. Today it was closed against the snow, and there seemed to be no faces behind the glass. The picture cut to a gang of frozen revelers on a float and a Missouri marching band.

The view from my own window beat the images on television hands-down. The Sound was still, the water a pale lavender in the misty sunshine. I could see the white funnel of my waiting ferry at Pier 48. Fourth Avenue was holiday-morning empty, except for an Indian in a plaid jacket who was taking an erratic promenade down the center of the street.

I switched off New York. The paraders were welcome to the place. Watching an inbound container ship from Singapore slide over the roof of the Hotel Oxford, I blessed my luck in coming to Seattle.

*   *   *

On the mild Seattle winter afternoons, there was no happier place to be than afloat, alone, on the brackish, stone-gray water of Lake Union. The lake was Seattle's village pond. A mile and a half long, half a mile wide, it filled the valley between the built-up heights of Fremont, Wallingford, Queen Anne and Capitol Hill. It was plumb in the center of Seattle, whose districts, north, south, east and west, took their names from their standing relation to Lake Union.

The concrete viaduct of the I-5 towered over its eastern shore; to the west, suburban traffic surfed past along Aurora Avenue. Big ships steamed along the channel at its northern end, on their way between Puget Sound and Lake Washington, and single-engined seaplanes used the lake as an airport. It was rimmed with noisy shipyards and out-of-season marinas. There was nothing quiet or pastoral about Lake Union, but it was the reflective heart of the city that throbbed and grumbled all around it. Here, you could lie back in the stern-sheets, the brim of your hat pulled low over your eyes, and get Seattle in perspective.

I used to rent an eighteen-foot "catboat" from the Wooden Boat Center. It had been built in 1924, and its single lugsail rattled up the mast on wooden hoops. It was a staid, auntly sort of boat, broad in the beam, placid in temperament, slow on the uptake when it met a sudden shift of wind or brought its head round in answer to the tiller. It was a vehicle constructed less for sailing than for thinking in.

On this particular afternoon, the sky was down to thirty stories and the air was sluggish. Only far out in the middle of the lake was the oil-smooth water frosted over by gusts of wind that were being funneled down from the Sound through the gorge that carried the ship canal. I was sailing on sleepy breaths of wind that came from trucks rolling by on Fairview Avenue. They were just enough to give the boat steerage.

I handed the tiller over to Rainbird.

For more than a week now, Rainbird had been toying with the idea of a novel. Disconnected characters and situations kept on cropping up in his head and finding their way into my notebook. The characters had names (Chester, Ben, Mi Hyun, Woon Soo

Rhee, Piet . . .) but the hero of the book would be the city. You could find Seattle in novels, but there wasn't a Seattle Novel. Rainbird badly wanted to have a stab at rectifying that.

For Seattle was a perfectly novel-sized city. There was something just right about its 1.7 million population. In 1831, when Dickens was nineteen, London had a population of 1.65 million, and there was a relationship (Rainbird was sure of it) between the demography of the city and the plot of the nineteenth-century London novel. A city of less than two million was big—plenty big enough for people to disappear into it without trace for years at a time. It was also small enough to ensure that chance meetings, coincidences, would continually happen in it, unexpectedly and out of context. Twentieth-century critics had sometimes complained of the way in which Dickens's plots were kept moving by these surprise encounters, with X and Y suddenly bumping into each other around the next corner. Yet that was always happening in the real life of late twentieth-century Seattle, just as it must have happened in the real life of early nineteenth-century London. There was an inherent *plottiness* about Seattle now, a plottiness unmatched in Rainbird's experience of other cities. It was various, sprawling, a place full of secrets and dark corners; and yet it was contained . . . it would fit inside the covers of a book.

The luff of the sail began to tremble as we ran into a steady exhalation of real wind. I tightened the sheet. The wake was bubbling behind the rudder now as we headed off on a beam reach toward the University Bridge end of the lake.

So . . . the main character would be this lumpy, drab-colored, marine city. Rainbird saw it as being like a sponge—and maybe there was more to that metaphor than immediately met the eye. Seattle did sop people up, like an enormous bath sponge; but if you carried the life of the sponge back to its previous existence in the sea, the parallel still held good. A sponge was an elastic skeletal structure; a labyrinth of ducts, canals, chambers, as complicated and multifarious in its arrangement as any city. All sorts of creatures found their dwelling places in its chambers: shrimps, crabs, mussels, snails. A single sponge could act as host to several thousand other animals, most of whom lived peaceably inside it, swimming, scuttling and slithering about their proper business.

It was also beset with parasites, like the rotifers, mites and sea-slugs who were bent on eating away the sponge from the inside. Everyone knew who were the rotifers, mites and sea-slugs of Seattle: they hung out on the corner of Second and Pike and they went in for running gunfights along East Marginal Way.

Seattle. Genus: Porifera. General Character: Porous.

The boat ran along the edge of a street of frame-houses built on floating pontoons. Small yachts were moored up at their side doors. One could see through the picture windows of their lounges and watch the racing waterlights play on the furniture inside. It was extraordinary—this capacity of the city to mimic the homescapes of so many of its immigrants. Here, just off Fairview Avenue East, a Dutchman could think himself back at Aalsmeer or Dordrecht. This was where Rainbird would place the house of Piet Keijzer, the divorced marine engineer.

A truthful Seattle novel would have to be about the newcomers. Few people over the age of forty had been born here. There were the old-money Seattleites in Magnolia, the Ballard Swedes, the encrusted Pacific Northwest upper middle class with their rambling timber houses on Capitol and Queen Anne Hills ... but they had long been outnumbered (as Londoners had been outnumbered) by the people who had descended on Seattle during its wartime and postwar booms.

Rainbird needed a person, a central *he* or *she,* a good swimmer, on which to hang this story of a sponge. He'd be an American, with one of those first names that might as easily be a second one: a Calvin or a Chester. His patronym would be that of a half-forgotten president, like Harding, Harrison, Garfield or Hayes. *Chester Hayes* ... a distant descendant. He'd be gay. He would have fled New York within the last few months for Upchurchy reasons, and would live in a rented apartment on Capitol Hill; an apartment with Upchurch's view over Seattle.

He couldn't be a writer, though. Make him an actor, with a BA in English and an MFA in theater arts . . . Age: twenty-six or twenty-seven, old enough to have been pricked by failure, young enough to hope for a thrilling breakthrough. He'd be getting some continuity work out of KIRO TV, and be auditioning for parts at the Empty Space, the New City Theater and the Seattle Rep. He'd be awkwardly tall for an actor; good voice (though in private conversation he'd be afflicted with a mild stammer); bad at moving gracefully. He'd need to take dance classes to keep his not-too-gainly body limber. When resting, which was more often than not, Hayes would be enlisted in that volunteer army of part-time English teachers who were coaching the immigrants in their new language.

This was how he'd know the Korean woman. *Mi Hyun Rhee.* Six years in America, she'd be an advanced student, able to stumble, insecurely, through basic literature texts. Hayes's class would be reading Salinger, short stories by Malamud, poems by Theodore Roethke and Elizabeth Bishop.

Mi Hyun . . . head down, shy, but tough and avid. She would have come to Seattle (June 14th, 1984) with her husband, Woon Soo Rhee, and her two-year-old son, Kwang Chung (now *soi disant* Ben). Now she and her son would be on their own. Watching her American neighbors, first on Beacon Hill, then in Greenwood, she'd learned the astounding temerity that had at last enabled her to walk out of a Korean marriage.

For her, America meant liberty—a frightening liberty, with nightmares of pursuit and flight, but for the first time in her life she was embarked on the exhilarating experiment of trying to be *her* self and not someone else's. For her husband, Woon Soo, America meant humiliation. Seattle had affronted his manhood, had stolen from him *his* wife, *his* son, and he was going to take his revenge on the city, on the nation *(Wah!),* for this unconscionable assault on his male dignity.

Rainbird was keen on Woon Soo. His face would be a reef-knot of bunched muscle. His furious hands would fill the gaps in his fractured, FOB American English. His body would be like the kind of steel spring that tough guys use to strengthen their hands. Woon Soo would be a creature of tragic aggression.

Supercharged with anger, Woon Soo would be making it, in the classic American way, out of pure hatred for America. He'd begun small, with a rented candy kiosk in the lobby of a building much like the Josephinum. Now he owned a chain of the things. He scoured the city for locations. Every time a new office building started to go up, he'd see another candy kiosk in it. The rest of the city would see seventy stories of black glass; Woon Soo would see only a closet-sized space—six feet by six would do fine—in the lobby. He meant to perpetuate the name of Rhee as a Seattle trademark, like Starbuck or Nordstrom.

Pride and *shame*. Woon Soo Rhee would get his own back on America by riding in American cars, each one flashier and more expensive than the last. Every time he showed up in the book, it would be in a different car. He'd go through Dodges, Chevies, Olds, Caddies, trading them in at chapter ends.

His head would be full of dreams of custody and kidnapping. Mi Hyun would be kept on the run. Court orders and injunctions wouldn't stop Woon Soo; and so his wife would move from chamber to chamber, hill to hill, a shrimp evading the attentions of a red snapper.

Scenes from the story were writing themselves in Rainbird's head. He saw Hayes, Mi Hyun and Ben on a Sunday excursion to Bainbridge Island on the ferry. They looked a mismatched family: the man an inch or so too tall; the woman an inch or so too short; the mother with her questing, uncertain English; the son with his manically fluent fourth-grader's American slang.

Hayes was watching the Seattle skyline diminish across the water. Mi Hyun was studying the American women on the boat. She was anxious as to whether she'd dressed right for the occasion, and feared she'd overdone it; holidays were a novelty for her. Ben was trying to interest Chester Hayes in last night's football game, when the Seahawks had lost 7–17 to the Cleveland Browns (BUMBLING SEAHAWKS BROWNED said the headline in the newspaper-dispenser window). Seattle, a winning city, had a losing football team.

Chester Hayes hated football, but was acting the part of a serious fan. It was not one of his better roles.

"Hey, you hear the one about the guy with the dog who's a real big Seahawks fan?" Ben said. "It's kind of neat. Guy's telling another guy about this dog he has. Guy says, 'I'm telling you, he's a real smart dog, understands every move of the game. Watches every game the Seahawks play on TV. And when the Hawks score a field goal, that dog, he'll flip right over, do a somersault . . .' This other guy says, 'Hell, what's that dog do when the Hawks score a *touchdown?*' " Ben was already sniggering at the thought of the punchline to come. "Hey, Chester, you listening to me?"

"Oh, yeah," Chester said. "So w-w-w-w-what does the man say? What does the dog do when the Hawks score a touchdown?"

"This'll kill you. This'll really kill you. Guy says . . . 'Well, I wouldn't know about that. You see, I only had this dog the one season.' You get it? 'I only had this dog the one season!' " Ben was doubled up. "That really freaks me out."

Mi Hyun said, absently, "So the dog scores the goal . . . ?"

"Oh, Mom! You're crazy! Look. Like, there's the *field goal* and there's the *touchdown,* and . . ."

In another scene, Chester Hayes was caught in the late-afternoon gridlock on the I-5, heading north for the University exit. He drove (Rainbird thought) a many-times-pre-owned tan Plymouth. He was window to window with a '90-model red Caddie. *Woon Soo.* The passenger window of the Korean's car buzzed down. He shouted something that Hayes failed to catch.

"What?"

"You *meat,* man!"

The traffic in the lane to Hayes's left began to budge, taking the Cadillac away with it. Fifteen minutes later, half a mile further on, the red car appeared on Hayes's right. The driver's window buzzed down. Hayes sat, staring straight ahead, but Woon Soo Rhee was rapping with his fist against the passenger window of the Plymouth.

"What the hell?" He had to lean across the Plymouth to wind the window down by hand.

Speaking quietly, his pronunciation ludicrously exaggerated, as if he was parodying a teacher of English-for-immigrants, Rhee, the candy millionaire, said, "Fuck—wife—you—meat," and pressed the button on his electric window. The grid unlocked, the Cadillac sailed away, leaving Hayes shaken, pink, stammering at the wheel.

Yet one would have to learn to like Woon Soo; or, if not quite to like him, at least to feel sympathy for him, his violated pride, his longing for his stolen son. Maybe, at some point, Hayes could yield the tiller of the narrative to him, and we'd see the city through his eyes. In his American voice, he might seem a thug with the language of a retarded child; but in his interior narrative, he'd be dolefully eloquent.

In my own wanderings inside the sponge, I'd met a Korean who played me a tape of a Korean song, translating it for me line by line. After it was over he said, "Koreans have more tears than any other Asians. They love dramatics. In Korea, all art ends in tears."

Rainbird could use that in his story. Whatever car he drove, Woon Soo Rhee would always be playing the same tape on the stereo.

> *Love is going away, before the end of the day;*
> *Love is crying.*
> *The farewell is before our eyes, which will never return.*
> *Love is going away.*
> *Even as I die, I will never forget you.*
> *Love is going away.*

He'd be out on the site of a half-finished skyscraper in the business district, wearing a hard hat, trying to negotiate a lease in his whispery, sticky, monosyllabic English, while at the back of his head he'd be thinking in sad musical Korean.

One day, with fog in the Sound, each of the main characters would hear the diaphones playing a different tune.

It seemed to Rainbird that there was at least the germ of something here. Start with the newly arrived American and the broken Korean family, and move out to include a cast of immigrants in a plot that would take one all over the city, from the Kingdome to Ballard and the northern suburbs, and from Pike Place Market over the hills to the Lake Washington shore . . . The book, like the city, would absorb its people, soaking them up as it went along. How much, he wondered, would he need to write of it before he could persuade a New York publisher to stump up a five-thousand-dollar advance?

I was back at the tiller of the catboat now, wearing it round before the wind off Gasworks Park. At only four o'clock in the afternoon, it was already beginning to get dark. I remembered how one of the Californians at UCLA had complained, in a voice of the utmost seriousness, that Seattle had caused him to fall victim to SAD, or Seasonal Affective Disorder. The rain! The long dark winters! "Medical scientists," said the Californian, "are now recognizing SAD as a genuine physiological disease." Rainbird could use that, too.

I'd been living in Seattle for just over two months now. I had a circle of friends, a room with a view, a growing library, and a part of me ached to stay on. It was all right for Rainbird: he could sit up at the gold-painted desk under the window and get on with his story; he could write reviews for the *Times.* His evenings were increasingly spoken for, and when things went badly he could grumble comfortably about the writing life with Michael Up-church. But I was rather differently placed. I had my own book to write. It needed one more location; a final chapter. Then, per-haps . . .

I packed my two suitcases. Gently closing the door of the room with Rainbird's name on it, I left him to his fiction.

SEVEN

Land of Cockaigne

The houses were made of barley sugar cakes, the streets were
paved with pastry, and the shops supplied goods for nothing.
                    —thirteenth-century French poem

Duval Street, Key West, is as far removed from the mainstream of American life as is Queen's Landing Road, Hong
Kong. So removed that in terms of economics, sociology and
politics we could no less comfortably be stationed in Karachi
as Key West. In my opinion this office is a hardship post of
duty.
                    —memorandum (1980) from Supervisory
                    Customs Patrol Officer, Key West,
                    to director of Miami District Patrol
                    Division, U.S. Customs

On a Wednesday afternoon in early April, I was looking for
the end of America. I knew roughly where it was—somewhere around the southern tip of U.S. 1, where Florida dribbled
out into an irregular string of coral islands and the temperate
United States stood on the brink of the lax and intemperate
Tropic of Cancer.

Most things came to an end down on the Keys: English drifted
into Creole, religion into natural magic, work into play and
crime. In the industrious north, I had often dreamed of the Keys

as the great American haven of un-American activities. On these islands, loafing in the sun counted as a respectable occupation. Any fool with a boat could turn a few thousand easy bucks by running drugs, arms or aliens across the Gulf Stream. People lived under assumed names and carried false passports. Retirees went there to wither away gently in the heat, like drying prunes; couples with alibis locked themselves into anonymous waterbed motels, for sticky sex conducted behind the shutters under a creaky overhead fan. If there was any place on the map of the United States where the elevated ideology of being an American finally unraveled, it was on the Keys. Morally and geographically, the Keys were *terminal.*

The rush hour traffic was gridlocked in the hot swamp of the Miami suburbs. With the air conditioning on Hi and the radio on National Public Mozart, I was afloat in an icy musical bubble. The overcooked world outside, of broiled Radio Shacks and pan-fried Chevrolet dealerships, lurched slowly past the car windows. Stoplights danced on their wires in a wind that blew in from the Everglades, warm and rank like the breath of a panting hog.

The afternoon commuters, with their Dade County plates, peeled off from the stream, bound for palm-fringed condo blocks with pantiled roofs and security walls of fake adobe. As we coasted past the exits for Monkey Jungle and Leisure City, the traffic steadily thinned into a line of rental cars aimed at the Keys.

The newcomers were painfully conspicuous. They wore the company plates of Avis, Thrifty, Hertz, National, Budget and Dollar, they were dressed in the wrong clothes for the heat, their skins were still winter-white. They looked like cons, out on the street for the first time after a jail term. Staring widely from behind their windshields, they blinked in the unaccustomed sunlight and kept on naming to each other all they saw—the bottle-shaped palms, the roadside sprawls of puce bougainvillea, the circling kites and vultures in the enormous dome of empty sky.

The flat landscape rippled in the heat like a reflection in disturbed water. Cars a few hundred yards ahead turned suddenly wobbly, then were swallowed whole into the haze. It was what people came here for—to lose weight and substance, to disappear. *Last I heard of him, he was down on the Keys* was a sufficient epitaph. You plopped into the silvery liquid air, and that was that. You entered a Limbo between the Americas; a place where social security numbers were in short supply and final demands from the I.R.S. were returned to sender, marked NOT KNOWN AT THIS ADDRESS.

In my late-model blue Alamo I overhauled an elderly couple in a tan Thrifty. They were Bill and Vera types, with the anxious, eager look of house-hunters. I saw them as fresh off the plane from Cleveland, scouting for a cinderblock paradise on a mangrove canal. Bill (hairless, thick specs, with a more than passing resemblance to President Eisenhower) was into fishing; would send himself to sleep dreaming of bonefish and groupers. Vera was artistic. She'd taken a class in Home Jewelry Design and hoped to do something with seashells—string them into necklaces, or glue them together into souvenirs. She saw herself with a trestle table beside the Overseas Highway, selling her work to the winter tourists. Cash only. No checks. Vera's Art of the Sea.

A single man in a white Hertz sloped past me in the left-hand lane. He was doing seventy and had eyes only for the road. Fortyish, with button eyes and a squashed boy's face, he was one of nature's Freds. Fred's plane from Boston had been late on arrival. He was supposed to be sitting tight in his room at the Howard Johnson's in Islamorada, waiting for the telephone to ring. His Keys connection would identify himself as Bluey. Fred was wearing a money belt; had sixty thousand dollars strapped to his waist in used hundreds; a man of means. He was going for eight kilos on this run. But he had to make the Howard Johnson's before seven-thirty. His car melted into the steamy air, just short of Homestead.

The couple in the burgundy Avis were mismatched. She was young enough to be his daughter, but clearly wasn't. His safari suit looked as if it had been living on a hanger in the Summer Casuals department of Brooks Brothers until earlier this morning. Her linen jacket had been crushed on the flight. Her pale hair hung in tight ringlets around her ears. A pair of jumbo sunglasses were fetchingly perched on the tip of her nose. I nailed them as a Schuyler and an Ellen.

I could imagine the breakfast scene at Schuyler's house some-

where in Westchester County. This Florida trip, as he explained
to his wife, was just the last thing he needed right now. He
couldn't wait for it to be over and done with. But there was no
getting out of it. The contract depended on it. The clients were
insistent. He had to prove himself as one of the boys and spend
the long weekend on their goddamned *Chris-Craft.* He hated
fishing. He got seasick at the sight of his own *bathwater.* He just
had to grin and bear it, he guessed. If there was a radio or something on that *boat* (Schuyler dwelt elaborately on its probable
smells and bodily discomforts), he'd try and call. But he was
afraid he was going to be totally incommunicado for the next few
days. It was just—hell.

Reflecting on the scene, on U.S. 1, Schuyler was indignantly
thinking that it was *true.* He *hated* fishing.

Ellen toyed with Schuyler's earlobe.

He put his foot down hard on the gas pedal. The thing with
rental cars, as he now explained to Ellen, was that they were
constipated. You had to give their systems a laxative blast to wake
them up.

Ellen said, thoughtfully: "I could do with a back rub."

Schuyler was getting righteously annoyed with his wife, because *she* was the one who'd made him invent the cock-and-bull
story about the clients and their Chris-Craft. He felt obscurely
cheapened by her.

The burgundy Avis ahead appeared to swell like a balloon
before it tapered, flattened and disappeared, into a territory of
unbridled license.

There was a back road to the Keys that I remembered from an
earlier descent into this nether region; a long straight lane which
branched off U.S. 1 and ran through a boggy forest to North Key
Largo, over the toll bridge at Card Sound. The road was lonely
and deep shadowed by the stands of cypress, live oak, banyan,
pine and mangrove which came crowding to its verges. Many of
the trees were dead, their black frames standing out from the rest
like giant crosses. They were rooted in shallow, tarry pools of

stagnant water, where bubbles of marsh gas broke on the surface in a sickly stream of vegetable farts.

This was dog-eat-dog country. The strangler fig, choking its host tree to death with its twiggy tentacles, was typical of the characters who lived in the forest, where things grew so fast and so profusely that every plant and animal had to fight for living space. It was the last place in the world where a sane human being would choose to leave their car for a spot of nature study: peer through the mosquito cloud into that tangled greenery, and you'd see twining rat and coral snakes, bobcats on the prowl in the poisonwood trees, hungry twenty-three-foot saline crocodiles (far more athletic than the torpid and phlegmatic freshwater alligator). After the insects, the toxic plants, carnivorous mammals and the dozen or so species of deadly reptile had had their fill of you, the vultures would be quick to polish off the balance.

This, more than my Guntersville back yard, was exactly the kind of nature that made Crèvecoeur frightened for America's human future. It set a fine example of stealth and rapine. Properly equipped, in snakeboots and pith helmet, and armed with a hunter's carbine, you could learn a lot in there, about such things as techniques of camouflage, strategic defoliation, the advantages of the pre-emptive strike and the deterrent effects of Mutually Assured Destruction. The ten-mile stretch of mangrove swamp and hardwood hammock was a pretty realistic training ground for the conduct of life on the Keys in general.

I pulled in at Alabama Jack's, a redneck heaven on a creek just short of Card Sound, whose architecture was a fine example of Keys gimcrack. A series of tumbledown shacks along the water's edge had been loosely bolted together with forest logs, bits of driftwood and lengths of two-by-four. The rafters, open to the sky, had been draped with fishnets and floats. Phyllis, the owner, was behind the bar, cashing up at the end of the afternoon. She was feeding quarters from the till into an aluminum tube.

Without looking up she said: "We're closed." Then, "Oh—hi. I haven't seen you in here for a good long while. Must be months. Where you been?"

"It's more than two years," I said.

"That so? There've been some changes here since you've been away."

While I sucked on the cold nipple of a Bud, Phyllis ran through the changes. The crocodile who used to live in the pool under the bar had taken off for a quieter neighborhood; the creature had apparently grown sick of being pelted by the customers with French fries and half-eaten hamburgers. Mumbling, kindly Ernest had gone, too.

"Yeah. He's been on the wagon for best part of a year now. Got a regular job, up in Miami."

Don had gotten into trouble again and hadn't been sighted in Alabama Jack's for some weeks; and Phyllis had finally given her aging boyfriend his marching orders.

"Trouble was, once he got me, he reckoned he didn't have to do another stroke of work in his entire life. Day after day I'd see him, just hanging out in the bar and drinking beer. Oh, that man, he was in *clover.* Till I told him to shift his useless butt outa here . . ."

Phyllis rubber-banded a fat stack of bills.

"And my best friend's husband . . . He's just been sent down. Eight to fifteen."

"What was it?" I asked.

"Cocaine." She made a face. "Those *men* . . . You know, he used to come in here before they took him to the jail, and he'd be crying on my shoulder. Looking for pity. I told him straight, I said, 'I don't feel sorry for you. Why should I feel sorry for you? I didn't have the money, I didn't have the cars, I didn't have the five years of fun. *You* had all that. *I* was working.'" She shook her head. "And he expected my heart to bleed for *him*—for his cars and his boats and his restaurants . . . Poor little *boy.*"

Like most people on the Keys, Phyllis had led a previous life. Once upon a time, in another existence, she had been a teacher, in a Catholic grade school up in Michigan. In Florida, on the run from the stern north, she had acquired a Hispanic second name (though the Cuban husband was long gone) along with her proud proprietorship of Alabama Jack's. The ghost of the schoolmistress she had once been still haunted her manner, and with good reason. The roistering men in T-shirts and oily baseball caps who kept her bar hopping through the long hot afternoons bore a powerful resemblance to a class of unruly six-year-olds. Down on the Keys, as up in Michigan, Phyllis was the solitary grown-up in a childish world.

Now, counting her money in the pineapple light, she looked tireder and sadder than I had remembered.

"Yes," she said. "Good men round here are few and far between."

I drove on. Beyond the bridge over the sound, the gloomy sunset forest was as deep and dark as the forest in a story by the Brothers Grimm. There was no one about. An osprey, nesting on top of a telephone pole, kept the road under surveillance. As the Alamo slid past I watched the bird tracking me with swiveling neck and speculative eye. It had the seen-it-all-before expression of a world-weary policeman.

I stopped for a few minutes at a bizarre ruin. Some years before, a group of developers, backed by a savings-and-loan institution, had threatened the Keys with the biggest and most lavish waterfront condominium complex in the whole of the U.S. It was named Port Bougainville. The site had been cleared and construction begun when the S & L went broke. Last time I'd been here, the score was pretty much even between the ravaging developers and the renascent forest. Now I was glad to see that the forest was winning hands down.

At a little over treetop height, the PORT BOUGAINVILLE sign was on its last legs; bleached and birdlimed, its paint faded to runic stains, its wood cracking apart at the seams like the planks of a wrecked boat. The ceremonial entrance to the site had been blocked off with rocks. Another sign, directing the prospective buyer to the registration office and furnished show-home now pointed slap into dense jungle. A pink adobe archway, like the gatehouse to a Mexican castle, was almost entirely swallowed by the new-growth timber. In a minute away from the car, my wrists and ankles were itching furiously with mosquito bites.

Nature worked wonderfully fast here on the Keys. The busy mangrove, tiptoeing over the ground on its delicate, knobbly stilts, was capable of reclaiming land as fast as man could build on it. The islands were an instructive theater of human rapacity, where most bucks were fast ones, where boy-men sank their drug money into real estate, where people were continually hacking and gouging their way through the limestone and the swamp to make room for jerry-built dream homes and hideous weekend hideaways. But, as developers had found out, there was an answering rapacity in nature here. Release the Keys from human habitation, and in a year or so the mangroves, live oaks, snakes and spiders would get their own back. The strangler fig yearned for nothing so much as to hug a twenty-story vacation community to its bosom and throttle the life out of it, while the punk trees dreamed of marching, in close green formation, through the Mr. Submarines and Burger Kings.

At the point where the back road rejoined U.S. 1, man's temporary conquest of the Keys began, in an unzoned, unregulated ribbon of fast-food outlets, trailer parks, Shell Man souvenir shops, Tom Thumb mini-markets, bald and peeling shopping plazas, Bait'n'Tackle shacks, aluminum marinas, giant billboards, gas stations and antique scabious motels. The evening lights were coming on. Arrows flashed every which way, pointing the weary motorist to land-of-perpetual-midnight cocktail lounges with topless waitpersons, to While-U-Wait muffler shops, to pizzas-to-go. The electric words FUN! HOLIDAY! and PARADISE! repeated each other so frequently down the highway that within a mile they had shed all meaning. Hung, one on top of another, their syllables swapped about and turned into PARAFFIN! HOLOFERNES! PARODY! DISPARITY! The semiotic babble was punctuated at intervals by high-stepping road bridges that linked the islands over straits of darkening water. To the left, the Atlantic; to the right, the Mexican Gulf. The wind had died and the sea looked varnished, its high-gloss finish lightly scored with knifepoint squiggles of current.

On Plantation Key, one sign stood out from the rest for the way it meshed exactly with the theme that was running in my head. It announced that somewhere behind the trees over on the Atlantic side lay the Ragged Edge Motel. It was a chance not to be passed up. I braked hard, slewing the Alamo into the offside lane. I had to spend at least one night in, or on, the Ragged Edge.

A graveled road led through a pocket-sized, pine-smelling suburb to a neat cluster of two-story chalets on the ocean. There was a sliver of beach, more mud than sand, where two egrets were fastidiously paddling in the shallows, a dock, a moth-eaten brown pelican on a tarred post. The owner of the place showed me to a second-floor room, an "efficiency," with a tiled kitchen and breakfast bar and a bed big enough to sleep a family.

The drawer of oddly matched silverware and kitchen things failed to yield a corkscrew to open the bottle of wine that I'd been keeping in my shoulder bag. I went out onto the deck to see if there was somebody around from whom I could borrow one.

On the strip of turf below, a very large young woman was seated on a bench. She was holding out the elasticized front of her white cotton dress and peering inside. I coughed. She looked up without embarrassment.

"Caught it real bad today," she said.

"Looks like you did." Even in the mellow remains of the day's light, her breasts were a mottled raspberry. She began to squirt cream on them from a bottle. "Wow!" she said, and laughed. I laughed, too, engaged by her air of easy candor as she exposed first one nipple, then the other, dousing them with Johnson & Johnson's. I thought that the sheer size of her body had a lot to do with it. It was something like the state of Arizona: a rolling, sun-baked landscape, plenty big enough to accommodate the gaze of many strangers without anyone feeling remotely crowded or intruded upon. Together, the woman and I stared at the red hills and valleys under her dress, and marveled, like the tourists from the north that we both were, at the effects of the fierce sun on that strange and magnificent terrain.

A dented hatchback with Indiana plates pulled into the lot. "Here's Duane," the woman said. Duane brought out a big fish, closely wrapped in tinfoil, which he laid on the grass at the woman's feet.

"Grouper," he said. He was a year or two younger than the woman. She was flesh, he was bone; skinny, straw haired, with the pale shadow of a mustache on his upper lip.

She pulled her halter top down for Duane to see her sunburn. Smiling, he squinted at her enormous breasts with the pride of a landlord who is comforted each day by the sight of his own acres.

"You caught it bad," Duane said.

"I was telling this gentleman . . ." the woman said.

"I was just looking to see if anyone had a corkscrew," I explained to Duane. "I was trying to open a bottle of wine—"

"*We* had wine," the woman said. "Yesterday. We didn't have no corkscrew. Duane opened it. With his thumb. Pushed the cork right down into the bottle. Got wine all over his pants."

"I could go see if there's a corkscrew in the room," Duane said.

"I looked in mine, and couldn't find one," I said.

"You wait right there," Duane said, holding his hand up to me like a traffic cop.

"Duane always finds things," the woman said. As she shifted her weight on the bench, I saw that she was many months pregnant.

Duane came out from their room, beaming vacantly. "No corkscrew!" he said, as if he'd found something. Maybe he just had the manner of a man who was always making important discoveries: as Columbus might have cabled to the King and Queen of Spain, "No America!"

The woman said: "You could open it like Duane did. Push the cork right in. I don't think they bother too much about things like that around here. I get the feeling they don't bother much about *anything* around here. On the Keys."

Back in my room, I got at the wine Duane-fashion, with the blunt end of a fork, then sat behind the shutters, watching. All the doors of the hatchback were now open, with the radio tuned, at full volume, to a country music station. Under the coconut palms, the fiddles and accordions were going at it, hammer and tongs, while a man sang that he'd made a lot of money but it didn't buy him dreams; he'd thought he was rich, but he was only in between; when he'd met his darling, he couldn't resist. Oh! Love couldn't get any better than this!

Duane, standing by the open trunk of the car, was carefully removing a portable barbecue from on top of what first appeared to be a heap of white tissue paper then resolved into a lacy wedding dress, now severely crushed and much the worse for wear from its forced intimacy with the barbecue. Duane set up his instruments on the grass, moving with a deliberation and solemnity that made him look like a young priest celebrating his first communion. His matronly bride watched over him with fond approval as he readied himself with charcoal briquettes and can of kerosene. Finally he raised the silver fish from the grass with both hands and laid it reverently over the flaming coals. Then he joined the woman on the bench, where they sat together without touching, in silence, their mouths both slackly open.

I tried to guess at who they'd been before they came to the Keys. Had they come from Muncie? Indianapolis? I could see them living, on sufferance, in a single room in Duane's mother's house, where Duane's stupendous girl would be spoken of, through gritted teeth, as *her* and *she.* I could hear Duane's mom: "*She*'s finished up the milk"; "*Her* hair's clogging up the shower drain." When I looked into the couple's future, all I could see was diapers and food stamps.

But here and now they were on parole from the real world. The Florida Keys were about as far beyond reality as anyone from Muncie, Indiana had ever dared to go; and in a few weeks' time, with the baby squalling on the foldaway bed, this evening would take on the disbelievable glamour of a sequence from a TV movie about the kind of life that only actors in fictions ever get to live. Duane, gaunt and sulky in his new fatherhood, would see the canopy of palms, the purple water, the great fish on the barbecue. *Unreal.* Somewhere on the foggy edge of the frame there'd be an absurd detail: a man with a foreign accent begging for a corkscrew. *It was unreal.*

I left the Ragged Edge to find something to eat; when I came back, the place was dark and the barbecue had been folded away and put in its place on top of the wedding dress. I stood by the motel dock, listening to the whisper of a feeble tide inching its way up the beach, and watched the buoys that marked the Hawk Channel down to Key West flash red, white and green. The channel was a wide marine highway, sheltered from the real Atlantic by a long line of coral reefs, half a dozen or so miles offshore. The ocean never showed its teeth on the keys. Inside the reefs, it was more lagoon than sea; tame tropic water that went from pretty ruffles to mirror calms. I ached to be out there. A big ship, moving slowly up-channel, showed as a quadrangular patch of mat black against the moonlit gleam of the water, and the night was so still that I could feel the ship's engines drumming under my feet. Close by, a leaping tarpon fell back into the dock with a crash like that of a jettisoned fridge freezer, and the wash of its ripples made the moored boats lurch and saunter on their ropes.

I walked back to my room. The shutters of the room below were lit by the mercurial synthetic colors of the television inside. There was a burst of studio laughter, then the sly, self-preening voice of Johnny Carson telling a story from a cue card. The honeymooners were busy, catching up on the reality they'd left behind.

The people who were most at home on the Keys belonged to the water, not the land—the lobstermen, crabbers, shrimpers, delivery skippers, bonefish guides, charter captains, customs and Coast Guard patrolmen, liveaboard boat bums. Out of sight and out of mind of the Coney Island jangle of U.S. 1, they understood the intricate and devious nature of the place. They could find their way through the labyrinth of unmarked channels, many no more than a boat's width across, which led through the reefs and mangrove swamps. They knew the hidden anchorages where a boat might lie for days without being spotted, and the flats where the water was only a few inches deep. These bruise-colored flats, where big bonefish rocketed away from shadows, were useful places. A skiff with a twenty-five-horse outboard could scoot safely over them, leaving any law-enforcement vessel far behind, its propeller churning impotently in soft, powdery mud. Only the water people could count the islands in the archipelago. The highway between Key Largo and Key West traversed about two dozen separate keys. There were at least 150, maybe 250, more. Some keys were just knotty clumps of mangrove, others were full-blown islands, a mile or so long, with beaches, bays, hills, capable of supporting a varied population of scaly, carnivorous things. Some hadn't yet made it onto the marine charts (the mangroves were continually building new islands out of the floating debris they caught in their tangles of roots); nearly all were unin-habited.

In this warm, wet, mazy world, nothing was what it seemed at first sight. It was a reflection, or a refraction. It was not to be trusted: the little hump-backed islet would suddenly sink beneath the surface and turn out to be a turtle; the dark hole in the sea would reveal itself—too late!—to be a coral head, as it ripped the bottom out of your unwary boat. To be a true denizen of the place, you needed to cultivate the twistiness and liquescence in your own character. You needed to take on the attributes of a water snake.

You needed, first of all, to be able to float.

In the morning I exchanged my unlovely rental car for a char-tered thirty-two-foot sloop. *Sea Mist* was a buoyant white motel room, equipped with two sails and a three-cylinder diesel. With a double bed up front, an alcohol cooking stove and icebox at the back, and a saloon in which to sprawl in the middle, it was not much smaller than Alice's studio in New York. Its oatmeal uphol-stery was faintly permeated with the stains and smells of other people's family holidays; Rorschach blots of Maxwell House and Pepsi, tincture of sunblock and mosquito repellent and the not-unpleasant lingering staleness of a bedroom where, as they say in the divorce courts, intimacy has taken place. For a motel room it was expensive, at just over one hundred twenty dollars a night for two weeks; but in this easy-money country, the dollar, like everything else, seemed to have lost its fixed value and turned viscous and runny. In any case, it was sixty dollars a night cheaper than a single room in the Key Largo Sheraton which lay immobilized, in irons, a few miles up the highway.

I provisioned the boat from the Winn Dixie, filling a cart with peanuts and raisins, packets of spaghetti and bottles of sauce, canned soups, honey bread, cheese, crackers, oranges, bananas, two six-packs of Bud and a dozen bottles of Merlot from Washing-ton State. Pushing my way sweatily past the teak-skinned women of the Keys, in baseball cap and new dark glasses, my knees exposed to the light for the first time in twenty-something years, I keenly felt the stigma of my sickly whiteness. Outside, the shop-ping plaza had been flyposted with stickers that deployed the three-spoked-wheel symbol of the anti-nuclear movement in the service of the slogan: BAN THE TOURISTS, SAVE THE KEYS. Inside, I was jostled sideways at the fruit counter by a creature, more lizard than human, which croaked abusively in my direction as it skewered a bunch of grapes with one of its claws. I was afraid that it would take more than two weeks living aboard a sailboat before I stopped being discriminated against because of the color of my skin.

Soon after noon, the tide was leaking rapidly out of the harbor where *Sea Mist* was tied up in a line of untenanted charter yachts. These were the last few days of the tourist season. The snowbirds were locking up their winter houses and heading back north for the summer. That helped. In the climbing humidity and heat, in a boat grown honorably scruffy after four months of week-and-week-about chartering, I felt I had a sporting chance of passing myself off as a resident of these parts. Racing to catch the tide, I dumped my shopping at the foot of the companionway steps and got the engine started.

It was good to be back, after an age away, at the wheel of a proper seagoing vessel. The boat slid smoothly away from the dock and answered promptly to a touch on the rudder. It was plump and long-keeled, built on the lines of a friendly porpoise. It breasted the water without disturbing it, leaving only a rippling trace of wake. I fed it into the narrow channel that led out to sea. The tide was very low now, and twice the keel jolted on rock as I hugged the line of posts that marked the deepest water.

Beyond the harbor entrance, the water was as clear as that of a mountain brook, and, like a brook, it was studded with boulders that seemed to be almost breaking the surface. Steer One-Four-O, the people at the yard had said, and I kept the lubberline of the compass locked to 140, on a route through an enormous rockpool. It was more like paddling than navigation. With the engine turning slowly over underfoot, hop-hippety-hop, I moved the boat on cautious tiptoe, watching the barnacles on the pink and green rocks, frightening small striped fish with my looming shadow, seeing fronds of weed shiver in the running tide.

Sea Mist needed four feet of water to stay afloat. To my eyes, there seemed to be about four inches. According to the digital read-out on the depth sounder, we were a foot clear of the nearest rocks. 4.9. 5.1. 5.3. 5.0. 5.6. 5.1. 6.2. 4.9. 5.4 . . . A crab was ambling up the scarp face of a boulder, its mottled pincers held akimbo. A fleeing pipefish was making slow progress on the starboard beam, although its pectoral fins were going as fast as a humming-bird's wings.

Slowly the clear water thickened to an opaque and filmy green, like luminous minestrone; a wriggly soup of plankton, on which the laziest fish could comfortably survive simply by open-ing and shutting its mouth. Easy money, easy living. The depth sounder was on twenty feet, but the sea looked bottomless. I let the headsail unfurl from its roller on the forestay, switched off the engine and put the boat in the hands of the light northerly which was blowing off the shore.

The wind was just enough to keep the floating islands on the move while I sat still, listening to the companionable chuckle of water under the hull and basking in my luck. No house, and certainly no other vehicle, grants you such privacy and good solitude as a small boat a mile or more out from the land. It is a meditative space, contained inside a drumskin frame and pitched at a slight angle to the rest of the world. Life aboard a small boat is often anxious and troublesome, and sometimes seriously nasty, but even at its worst it manages to borrow some-thing from the deep and various nature of the sea on which you are afloat. The most timid of amateur sailors is prone to the besetting mariner's conceit, that he can see and think things that are closed to the people on the beach. A mile out, with one sail up on a sunny afternoon, and he's Captain Ahab, he's Marlow, he's Slocum. He has the whole sublunar world in his spyglass, and it looks strangely small to him.

Now, canted over at a ten-degree heel away from the Keys, I had the islands in sharp focus. A Burger King was skulking be-hind the mangroves; a condo block peered over the top of a tall pine forest; a pale fringe of sea oats almost, but not quite, veiled a Texaco station. Along the water's edge, the wall of jungle green was broken at regular intervals to disclose the fat-cat country mansions of the bankers, drug barons and real-estate tycoons who were the backbone of Monroe County's local gentry. The houses (which I knew from the road only by their steel security gates and the warnings of canine patrols that were posted on their trees) were unmistakably aristocratic, both in their contempt for their natural surroundings and their indifference to their neighbors. Here was a *casa grande* from Veracruz; next door, just across a reach of mangrove swamp, was an Elizabethan manor from Warwickshire. I peered at them through binoculars, marveling at what could be done with a few tons of cinderblocks and poured concrete. I looked in vain for a gardener on their lawns or a swimmer in their swimming pools, but there was nobody about. The houses' white cigarette boats were hoisted up on davits, clear of the sea, and their windows were blinded by storm shutters. If you called there for tea now, you'd have to take it with the Dobermans and their handlers, or, maybe, leave your card with a surly Filipino butler carrying a gun.

One by one, the separate keys drifted past, like sods of moss on a swollen stream. I marked them off on the chart as they went by: Windley, Upper Matecumbe, Teatable, Indian, Lower Matecumbe, Long Key. During the last twenty years, the poor islands had been unforgivably battered and abused. The tourist industry, the retirement industry and the cocaine industry had all done their worst. They had been "developed," with the license and ebullient energy that goes with deregulated greed. Yet—astonishingly—they were still themselves; still beautiful, although their beauty now had a ravaged look, as if they'd been hitting the vodka for too long. They had a surviving ebullience of their own. The soft sludge of the swamp was a mercifully treacherous foundation for new buildings; the mangrove was the most unstoppably vigorous creature in the whole vegetable kingdom; and, above all, the Keys were touched at every point by water, with its miraculous powers of healing. It rinsed them, reflected them, bathed them in marine light. None of the islands stood more than a few feet proud of the water, and from the water one could watch them shifting and scattering, inseparable in texture from their own reflections. Had I at that moment chucked a winch handle in the direction of the Caloosa Cove Marina on Lower Matecumbe, the splash would have broken it up into something not far from a thousand points of light.

*   *   *

Stuff had always been coming into the islands from the Caribbean and South America. Their fundamental character had been shaped by their Jamaican, Haitian, Cuban and Colombian connections. When the Keys were bare rafts of limestone, they'd been colonized by spores that blew in on the wind from the Antilles, or came floating up on the Gulf Stream. Their trees and plants, and many of their animals and fish, were immigrants from the tropical, extravagant world that lay to the south of the Keys. Washed ashore on a Florida key, they got their start in North America—Cuban tree frogs, Honduran mahogany, land crabs, fruit bats, reef geckoes, toxic manchineel, black noddies, tree snails, floppy butterflies and lignumvitae trees.

The immigrants kept on coming, and by much the same means. The Gulf Stream, pouring past Key West at three knots (a breakneck speed for water to travel) discharged its daily flotsam of Cuban and Haitian refugees on the beaches. A few came in boats; more arrived on makeshift rafts or wearing old motor tires around their waists. From the Bahamas, on the wind, came the yachts, their illicit cargoes packed tight behind false bulkheads, in false fuel tanks, in hollow spars. With the people and the substances came tropical ideas and tropical codes of conduct. Magic and murder did well on the Keys. The warm soil suited them. Like Cuba libres and hibiscus flowers, they had become part of southern Florida's local color.

It was no wonder that so much of the U.S. government's vigilance over foreign bodies and foreign matter was concentrated on the few miles of water round the Keys. Though cocaine and "illegals" were coming in at almost every port and border crossing in the United States, the Keys were the most tender of America's nether parts. With their long-standing reputation for being lazy, Latin and corrupt, they were the place where you could actually see the South American tail wagging the North American dog. So the DEA, the Customs, the U.S. Coast Guard and the Navy kept the Keys under prominent surveillance. They were a symbolic frontier. On this side of Key West stood the embattled churchgoing American family. On *that* side lay voodoo, communism, banana republics and the unsavory produce of the Medellín cartel. The troops of decency were drawn up along the shore. The Drug War was not really a war against drugs at all. (Had it been so, its generals would have given a great deal more time to the causes of addiction, as to the delicate economics of North American demand and South American supply and to the reasons why the coca plant had become the only profitable crop in a rural economy which had been blighted by the cut-flower and coffee barons in the United States itself.) It was, rather, a high-toned rhetorical war against Alien values and Alien people—and the Keys were the site of its front line.

Sailing down the Hawk Channel on a course of 243°, I could see a tiny white speck, high up in the western sky. Through binoculars, the speck showed as a deep-bellied fish swimming in the blue. Fat Albert was looking after us.

Albert was a dirigible. He was owned by the U.S. Navy, who packed him full of electronic gear and floated him over the Keys on a long leash. Then the navy men, in plain clothes, went from bar to bar, planting tall tales about the tricks their pet could perform.

"Fat Albert, he can look right into your boat and see what you're cooking for dinner," I was told.

"They got things up there that can record your private conversation," I was told.

"They got cameras with telephoto lenses that can take pictures of everything you do," I was told.

"They can crank that thing up to fifteen thousand feet. They can watch people in the streets in Havana, Cuba," I was told.

One yachtsman, recently arrived in the Keys from the Great Lakes, and much impressed, told me an elaborate story about a couple he'd met on a boat in Key West. They'd found a floating bale of marijuana, hauled it on board and turned it over to the Coast Guard. A few days later, a letter arrived from the DEA, thanking them for their public-spirited action. On file at DEA headquarters, said the letter, was a stack of excellent photographs showing the couple's boat maneuvering in circles round the marijuana bale; and, any time the couple happened to be in Washington, D.C., they were welcome to inspect them.

"Well—did they go?" I said.

"No, they couldn't make it. They were heading for the Virgin Islands."

"What a pity."

So the stories of Fat Albert went the rounds. The boat bums of the Keys were, on the whole, a godless crowd, but they were inclined to harbor a deep superstitious belief in the all-seeing, all-hearing powers of Albert. He watched over the fall of every sparrow. He could hear you when you spoke to him.

I was an agnostic. My own intelligence sources reported to me that Fat Albert, like his namesake in the children's comic strip, was a goofball. He was good for plane spotting and not much else. He couldn't track boats, let alone take photographs of them or listen in to pilot-house small talk. His maximum altitude was around three thousand feet, and nowhere close to fifteen thousand. He frequently went AWOL, and had to be shot down by fighter planes to stop him from drifting across to Cuba. (If Fidel got hold of Albert, he might discover, and, worse, tell the world, that Albert's perceptive abilities were more limited than was generally advertised.)

Fat Albert was the *genius loci* of the Keys. In this world of crooked meanings, he lived deviously, by refraction. His power lay not in what he could actually do but in what the rumor-makers could persuade people that he might be able to do. Everything about Albert was supposed to be secret, but the secret of Albert's success was his high public profile. Wherever you were in the Keys, you could see him in the sky. You'd be psyching yourself up to make that once-in-a-lifetime run from a Bahamian cay, when, suddenly, you'd notice Albert giving you his fishy stare, and your thoughts would turn uncomfortably to what it might be like to go down for eight to fifteen.

He had another, rather more straightforward, role. Albert was fighting communism. Right now, he was beaming *The Brady Bunch* at Cuba, winning hearts and minds for the American Way of Life. TV Marti, based in Miami and funded by the U.S. government, fed Albert with game shows, soap operas, Donahue and Geraldo, and Albert sicked them up over the Cubans. He had earned some extravagant praise from President Bush for his efforts. Defending Albert (who had come under attack by the Democrats and by the owners of AM radio stations in the U.S. whose broadcasts were being jammed in retaliation by Castro), Bush said, and, as far as I could gather from the *Miami Herald,* said with a straight face: "The voice of America will not be stilled as long as there is an America to tell the truth."

It was getting late in the afternoon and the wind had turned lazy. It was hardly bothering to even frost the surface of the water as it blew off the land in fitful dog-breaths. The big genoa was spending more and more of its time hanging limp and wrinkled from the top of the mast. Occasionally it came to life with a crack and a bang, and the boat would slide another hundred yards through the sea before it sank back into a lethargic sideways drift. The boat was a registered resident of the Keys and it had picked up the local habits. It knew when it was cocktail hour.

I rolled in the genoa and started the engine. Behind the green and uninhabited peninsula of Long Key lay Long Key Bight, a square mile of sheltered water, almost landlocked by the curve of the highway on one side and the protective arm of woodland on the other. As I pulled in out of the channel, the bottom shelved sharply, with rocks and sponges looming suddenly under the keel. I nosed my way as far as I dared into this shallow tropical aquarium and dropped the anchor, where it lay insolently close to the surface, winking at me as the sun caught its flukes.

Three other boats were already in the anchorage. The first two were white sloops, too waxed and scrubbed to interest me; but the third was a boat after my own heart—a wooden ketch in desperate condition, its dark blue paint flaking away from its planking, its sails hanging in untidy lumps from its spars. It had the mark of serious travel on it, homemade wooden ratlines in its shrouds; and its decks were packed solid with old bicycles, propane bottles, kerosene cans, engine parts and things in colored plastic sacks. A line of washing was strung over the cockpit, and the ship's dog had growled at me when I passed on the way in. No other member of the crew was visible.

I could live like that, I thought. On the Keys, as nowhere else in the world that I knew, you could drift easily into the life of a floating outlaw. Boats like this ketch were cheap here. After a single successful run they became valueless to their owners, and could be bought for almost any offer you cared to make. Five thousand dollars would be an ample sum with which to buy an elderly forty-footer. In this climate, you needed hardly any clothes. T-shirts and baseball caps came free; and a pair of K-Mart sneakers would last you six months, at least. As for food, here fish—and big ones, too—came willingly to the baited hook, while you could scavenge all you needed in the way of vegetables from the shore. There was no rent to pay for an anchor on the sea bottom, though the marine patrol might hustle you along from harbor to harbor down the coast. And when you needed money . . . it was best not to think in too much detail about what you did when you needed money on the Keys.

Every inlet in the mangroves had its liveaboards. They'd fallen as far through the net of American society as the street people of Manhattan. Like the street people, most of them had once paid mortgages and gone to work from nine to five before they'd been hit by divorce, or foreclosure, or simple boredom, or an addiction to white powder or the bottle. Out on the watery fringe of America, they'd found as happy a berth as any misfit could hope for. In the twelve-month summer of the Keys, the liveaboards had struck on a version of life as perpetual vacation. Where the street people spent their days rattling paper cups at strangers, the boat people went fishing over the stern, tied Turk's head knots in spare rope-ends, tinkered with bits of unfinished woodwork, swam to each other's residences for dinner, daydreamed over charts and read Joshua Slocum by lamplight. I'd been on boats in which the saloon was a floor-to-ceiling library, and whose tanned and skimpily clad owner had turned out to be a regular subscriber to the *New York Review of Books.* Anchored off, in the uncrowded quiet of a sheltered bay like this one, you could be a serious scholar; and who gives a fig for tenure on a Florida key?

I went below and put my house in order. Neatness came easily to me in the Lilliputian space of a boat, with its honeycomb of sweetly curved compartments. It took five minutes to transform a chaos of clothes, books and groceries into a swept and tidy bedsitting room. I put a match to the wick of an oil lamp to light me home in the dark, pumped up the inflatable orange beach toy that served as *Sea Mist*'s tender, and paddled ashore.

*   *   *

In the dark corner of a rowdy bar, I dialed the number that I'd scribbled into the flyleaf of a notebook two years before. I didn't know if he was still on the Keys. People here tended to disappear into thin air—particularly people like him. A woman answered the phone. When I said his name, she announced herself as his girlfriend, and, no, he was out, was bringing a boat down from Key Biscayne, but she expected him to be home at any moment. I said I'd call again in an hour.

Few of the men whom I met on the Keys would care to see their names in print. Two of them, at least, were known to me only by *aka*s. Let them all be called Robinson, for their kinship with Crusoe, and let them have color-coded first names. The man I was trying to contact was Red Robinson.

Red was close to my age. We had the sixties in common, when Red had dodged the draft and (we had once calculated) been in the same Amsterdam demonstration as I was when we sat, in our several thousands, on the banks of a canal, chanting "Hey, Hey, LBJ—How many kids did you kill today?"

Down on the Keys in his forties, Red delivered yachts, took fishing parties out to the reef, tended bar for friends during the tourist season, and did a little drug running when his funds ran low. He was strictly a marijuana man; a dropout sixties hedonist, not a millionaire death dealer.

After a grim bar supper of blackened grouper and soggy French fries, I tried his number again. This time Red answered. Sure, he remembered. "Shit, I read your book! You want to drink some cocktails?"

In fifteen minutes he showed up in person; a long, lean creature, all angles, who looked as if he had a lot of eagle in his ancestry. Twenty years on from its heyday, he still wore a Zapata mustache. His long-brimmed cap was caught on top of a thornbush of still-black hair, and his stubble had reached that decisive moment when tomorrow it would turn into a beard.

"Hey, *look* at you, man—double martini, two olives—you look like you just crawled out from under a stone."

He stood back, making a sorrowful appraisal of his rubberneck drinking companion for the evening.

"Oh, we're going to have to make some changes. Now those sneakers . . . they're for real. I bet you wouldn't take five hundred for those sneakers. They're *good.*"

The sneakers, bought four years before in Dieppe, had seen heavy marine service. Odd toes showed between the tartan uppers and the soles, which had developed fjord-like cracks around their insteps.

"But the rest of you . . ."

"Yes, I need a total makeover," I said, thinking that Red had an assignment that was a good deal tougher than the one I had once set Linda Lee of Macy's by Appointment.

"That cap!" He flipped it off my head. "Jesus! Where'd you *get* this? In the mail? from L. L. Bean? Look—" He took off his own cap. *"That*'s a cap." He put them side by side on the counter. "They look kind of . . . different, don't they?"

His was a piebald masterpiece, once white, on which sunshine, diesel, salt and anti-fouling paint had played until it resembled a subdued and moody Jackson Pollock.

"First, you got to have a good crease." He broke the brim of my cap, fore and aft. "See? Then you got to *age* it." He used it as a rag to mop up some spilled beer on the bar counter, then ground it into the floor with his feet. He retrieved it, squinted at it, and shook his head. "You could try shitting in it for a week. That might do *some* good."

For a while we talked innocent shop about boats, routes, anchorages and the unreliable holding power of Keys sand ("like wet talcum powder"). When I mentioned the dope trade, Red said that we had better go someplace else.

We bowled down the crazy light-show of U.S. 1 in Red's pickup. "I'm warning you," he said, "guy at this bar we're going to, he went to the Attila the Hun school of bartending."

"Oh, yeah?"

"You'll see."

And I did. The bar was the back room of a liquor store; a bare concrete box whose only decoration was a nudie calendar which had never been turned beyond the month of January. The lighting was fierce, the air conditioner growled bearishly. Attila was dealing with a lady customer who had walked in just ahead of us.

"Number one," Attila was saying to the woman, "you can get that fuckin' gum outa your mouth."

She giggled and said: "Gimme a Miller Lite."

"You think I'm not serious? You get that fuckin' gum outa your mouth, or you get out the fuckin' door. *Nobody* gets served in this bar with gum in their fuckin' mouths. Okay? So *get that stuff out.*"

Her giggle had turned to an affronted simper. She was looking for help to the other customers, but none came. She reached into her mouth.

"And you better think good about where you're gonna put it. Best place for it is up your ass. I'm telling you, I'm not cleaning that shit out of my fuckin' ashtrays."

Her face looked as if it had been boiled. She wrapped her gum in a twist of paper and put it in her purse.

"Okay. Now, what do you want? Miller Lite?"

When he'd finished with the woman (who was now blowing smoke and staring distantly at the ceiling), Attila turned to me with the same look of pleasurable anticipation as a cobra might have on discovering a jackrabbit in its territory. He took in my greenhorn cap and the T-shirt of which, up to that moment, I had been rather proud. It showed the Brooklyn Bridge and the Manhattan skyline over the words *caveat emptor.*

"He's mine," Red said, tugging at the brim of my cap.

I could see the disappointment in Attila's eyes. "Whatcha want?"

"Scotch and water."

"Brand?"

I raked the line of bottles behind him.

"Johnny Walker. Black Label."

"Wiseguy," Attila said to Red, who was looking across at the gum chewer.

"Hey," Red said pleasantly, "haven't we met somewhere before?"

The woman turned gratefully toward him. "I dunno . . . I . . ."

"Your face sure looks familiar."

"Maybe . . . in Miami?"

"If you took your clothes off, now, then I could be sure."

She stared wretchedly back into her drink.

Attila's bar was a measure of just how bad things had gotten in the war between the locals and the tourists. For the locals to have anywhere to themselves, the place had to be so deeply unappealing that no vacationer would set foot in it. Yet even Attila couldn't keep the tourists out. Tonight he had the woman from Miami and he had me. I could see that he was beginning to smell defeat; and there might be worse yet to come, since, properly promoted, Attila himself might be turned into a first-rate tourist attraction.

Now, without a glimmer of expression, he got a fistful of ice from a bucket and tipped it down the inside of the woman's shirt. She gasped, wriggled and sat tight on her stool. No one laughed.

Red said, "There's a front coming through. The wind's going to go all the way around the clock."

Armed with a bottle of wine from Attila's store out front, we hit the highway, bound for Red's house. Half a mile down an unmetaled road off U.S. 1, it was a suburban cinderblock ranch perched on the lip of a deepwater canal. The window of the long living room framed a light on the dock, and beyond the light a moored white Bertram. Red's bookshelves had a friendly look. Hemingway was there, and Thomas McGuane, and Chapman on piloting, and Herreshoff on yacht design.

Red's girlfriend, also in her forties, passed through in her bathrobe, on her way to make cocoa. On the Keys, people had boyfriends and girlfriends, not husbands and wives, appellations that I found tricky, since these girls and boys would turn out to be aged anything from thirty-five to seventy.

Primrose apologized for turning in early; she had the flu.

Red rolled a joint, plumping it between his fingers. It was an old-fashioned evening, this assembly of mid-lifers settling down to grass and cocoa.

When Primrose had gone to bed, I said that I'd been thinking ... I was toying with ideas about how one might best shift this stuff from, as it were, A to B.

Red, slowly exhaling a lungful of oily-sweet smoke, said, "These books you write, they're not bringing in enough moolah, huh?"

"No, it's not that. I just want to guess at what it might be like to be . . ."

"You want to put it in a—*novel?*"

"Sort of."

I took the joint. It was like sucking on a tube of distant memories. Not many were good ones. I didn't want to fog my head, and kept the smoke in my mouth without drawing it down.

I sketched out what I had in mind. I wasn't going to bother with secret compartments. The false bulkhead was too much of a liability, too easily discovered by an inquisitive customs man with a tape measure. A discrepancy of just an inch or two was enough to get a boat torn to pieces in a U.S. government boatyard, and it seemed to me that there was a far simpler way.

All you needed was a length of nylon monofilament and a weighted waterproof container. Several pounds of cargo could be trailed beneath the hull, at the end of a line which would pass up through an existing seacock. With a loop at the end, it could be secured to a faucet in the galley or the head. At the first sign of interception, you'd note your exact position on the Loran (which should be accurate to within about fifty feet in an area with good Loran reception), then go below and unhitch the monofilament from the faucet. The cargo would go to the bottom—and even if it was found, it should be impossible to prove a certain connection between it and the boat. The worst that could happen would be that you'd lose your investment; probably you could return to the spot and pick it up a few days or weeks later. The inshore waters of the Keys were dotted with the red and white flags of snorkelers and scuba divers, and with a good Loran fix the job ought to take no more than ten minutes of flippering around among the angelfish.

"The little guy's dream run," Red said. "The *just-this-one-time-run,* right? So you can pay off the mortgage and never get your nose dirty again? Okay, it might, it just might, work. People do it. But you're thinking amateur, and I know a whole lot of amateurs who are in jail right now."

"Why?"

"First off, you're talking chickenshit. You're talking fifty, maybe a hundred pounds at most. That's chickenshit to the nice

Cuban gentleman who sells you the stuff on the other side. You're laying out around thirty-five hundred dollars and you're going to sell it here for thirty thousand . . . that's the one-hundred-pound run. It's a lot of money to you, but the Cuban gentleman can't *see* your thirty-five hundred. It's nickels and dimes to him. The only reason he's even talking to you is because he needs a few dumb guys like you to trade. The moment you're off that harbor wall, he's going to be on the phone. To the DEA That's another five grand to him, plus he's keeping things sweet for himself with the DEA.

"You don't see *nothing* on the crossing. No customs, no Coast Guard, no marine patrol—nothing. You get in, you go down—you got a lobster line tangled round your prop, right?—you come up, and suddenly you got company. Company's got you spreadeagled on the dock. That's okay . . . you might get off with only two to five."

So, I got bigger. I started talking in terms of bales.

"*Bales?*" Red said. "You talking *bales* still? Do you know what a pound of marijuana looks like nowadays? Come here, I got something to show you."

I followed him into the den. It was stacked with tinfoil-wrapped blocks, each the same size and shape as a relatively short Sidney Sheldon paperback. There were hundreds of them piled neatly up against the wall. Red picked one up from the top and cracked it open. The dope inside was fibrous, ocher-colored, powerfully scented.

"Steam pressed," Red said. "Here," he snapped a two-by-two-inch corner off the brick. "A souvenir."

"I wish I could," I said; "but I daren't keep it on the boat."

The dry seeds of the marijuana crunched underfoot.

Red said, "You worry me a little, you know, man? I don't know whether I ought to be showing you this stuff, or whether I ought to be finishing you off with this—"

This was a small automatic pistol. It lay on the flat of Red's palm. He laughed and put it back on the table, next to his computer. The pupils of his eyes seemed very large. "I'm telling you, and I am serious, don't go messing like this with the cocaine guys. They're a bunch of crazy shits, and they wouldn't think nothing about killing somebody like you. You could get yourself lunched, like *that*. You want to wind up under six feet of dirt with a coupla nine-millimeter holes in your head? I'm warning you. You be careful, and I'm not joking."

On the ride back to Long Key, Red took the road very slowly. The illuminated signs were getting to him. I was less than halfway to being stoned, but they were getting to me. They came crowding round the highway, shouting their ugly heads off. The pickup snaked its way through them as they bent down on their stalks, going ZAP! and BLAM! at us, in shocking pink and horrible orange.

The dinghy was where I'd left it, drawn up on a boat ramp, its painter tied off to a mangrove root. Red swung the pickup round on the gravel pavement, covering the water with his headlights on full beam. *Sea Mist* was further out than I remembered. If I kept the power-line pylon roughly in transit with the low moon . . .

Red said, "Remember what I just been saying, now. You take care. Stick with the nice guys. Like me."

There was a warm wind now, and an irritable popple on the water. The inflatable had softened with the nighttime drop in temperature, and it slopped and sagged over the waves. It also leaked. I paddled toward the light in *Sea Mist*'s cabin, wishing that I'd had the sense to bring both a flashlight and a hand-bearing compass from the boat. I counted fifty strokes, then another fifty, then another fifty. My trousers were full of water. It took a long while to reach the black shadow of *Sea Mist*'s stern.

I was within six or eight feet of home, lurching on a wavetop, when the dog growled in my ear, a throaty snarl that sounded like a big motorcycle getting started. Wrong boat. I splashed hurriedly away from the German shepherd which began to bark. Then there was a voice, talking, I was relieved to hear, to the dog and not to me.

If people were up at this hour, they were probably up to no good. As I paddled, putting as much distance as I could between myself and the ketch, I thought a lot about getting myself lunched.

Half an hour later, I found a silent white sloop, but it wasn't mine. Half an hour after that, I stumbled soddenly up the swim ladder at the back of *Sea Mist*. I felt a fool. I was at least a decade too old to be living out this kind of boys' book stuff.

The boys' books had a lot to answer for.

American men of my own and Red's generation had been raised on a kind of tribal literature that was a more suitable preparation for life as an Apache brave than it was for husband- and fatherhood in the average American suburb. From the moment they could read, their teachers had fed them with Fenimore Cooper, Mark Twain, Hemingway. Out of school, they were suckled on the mythology of the western and the romance of the frontier. Their ideal of American masculinity was pitched somewhere between the characters of Buck Rogers, Harry Morgan and Huckleberry Finn.

Real life, according to these books and movies, always happened out of doors. It was essentially solitary. It was dangerous. It called for self-reliance above all other human qualities. Woodcraft and seamanship would stand you in far better stead than, say, the capacity to express affection.

The books and the movies heroized the rejection of domestic life that was so memorably made by Huck Finn in the last sentences of the novel:

> I reckon I got to light out for the Territory ahead of the rest, because Aunt Sally she's going to adopt me and sivilize me and I can't stand it. I been there before.

Running away from Aunt Sally was a noble thing to do. Lighting out for the Territory was a mark of true manhood and not, as it was in historical reality, the sign of economic failure, the last resort of the broken man.

Long after the settlement and suburbanization of the West, America was wonderfully productive of fresh territories to light out for. Somewhere in American culture, there would always be a place for Huckleberry Finn, even though the theater of his operations would shift about from age to age. He might be fighting a foreign war, bootlegging, riding the rails, working as an oilman in Alaska. In 1990, he could be found running drugs on the Florida Keys.

Here, he'd meet that curious strain in the national temper which still endorsed the outlaw as a kind of hero. Behind the freewheeling, open air, adventurous and self-reliant life of a man like Red lay a long and hallowed American tradition. The law might frown on what he did, but the buzz of the culture was on his side.

So the smugglers were able to see themselves in glowingly positive terms. I knew someone who'd made a single long-haul run, from a harbor in Massachusetts down to the Caribbean and back again. With two other guys, he'd loaded a sixty-five-foot sailboat with 12,500 pounds of pot and discharged his cargo onto a waiting fishing vessel on George's Bank. He would speak of his trip with the air of a man who has been to a revival meeting and seen the light of the Lord. He hadn't done it for the money. He'd done it in order to get in touch with himself. On the run, he'd met *real people;* he'd put his life in perspective; he'd realigned his body with his mind. It had, all in all, he said solemnly, been a cleansing experience.

Next morning the wind was up and Fat Albert was hidden by the banks of low nimbus that were swarming in from the northwest. I'd breakfasted on black coffee and the voice of Noah. Channel 3 on the marine VHF in the saloon was a continuous weather forecast put out by the National Oceanic and Atmospheric Administration, whose happy acronym came over the air as the captain of the ark. Noah had a distinct Hispanic accent. He issued a small-craft advisory and warned of squalls and dangerous lightning-strikes around the Keys.

Inside the reef, though, everything happened on a reduced scale. The driving seas were no more than two feet high, and their breaking crests toppled harmlessly down their fronts like baby drool. It was no great shakes to be out in a storm on this teacup ocean.

With half the genoa left on its drum and the mainsail close-reefed, the boat shot past Duck Key, the sails molded rigid by the gale-force wind. All the interest today lay in the water. The land was just a greasy stain to starboard, as diffuse in substance as the clouds from which it was inseparable. The curdling sea, green as soapstone, welled up under the bows of the boat and boiled away under the stern. Streaks of sand blew from the wavetops in long straight lines. It was Hurricane Helene in pretty miniature, with every wave showing off its own particular geometry of sweeping curves and crystalline, colliding planes.

It is on days like this one that the sailor is tempted into the conviction of his magical immunity from the land. Just one mile away, though it might have been one thousand, overbroiled Floridians were getting snagged at stoplights, pacing the aisles of the Tom Thumb, hawking real estate at the local Century 21. The landlubbers were unaware that they were within hailing distance of Captain Ahab, plowing the whale's acre. Poor mutts; they inhabited a lesser reality. Their little laws and customs, their judges, cops and jailers, seemed puny, even from this shortest of sea distances.

So thinks the runner, as he works his crabwise way across the Gulf Stream. He's not in the same world as the people who would punish him. Out in his boat, in no one's territorial waters, he is possessed by that easy solipsism which creeps up on people who have a ship's wheel in their hands and a binnacle compass to fix their eyes on. The self alone exists—the self, and the sea.

When the rain came, it hit the water like a tumble of icing sugar, turning the sea pure white under the coal-dust sky. It was followed, seconds later, by a barreling gust of wind that laid the boat hard over, before I hauled in the remainder of the genoa and motored up into the wind's teeth, with the loose mainsail thundering over my head. Wind-whipped, soaked to the skin, I felt touched with mania, laughing aloud to feel so safe in weather so extravagantly wild.

Then the wind eased and shifted round to the northeast, getting behind the boat and shoving it past Marathon. I was able to go below for a few minutes, to light a pipe and grab a Bud from the icebox. Noah was reporting gusts of up to 50 m.p.h., small craft endangered. Not this one, I thought complacently, switching from Noah back to Channel 16.

With the clearing weather came a visitor from the land, a Coast Guard helicopter which dickered up the Hawk Channel at low altitude, then veered off course to hover over me. The downdraught from its rotors confused the sails and roughly tousled the sea. I waved at the pilot to show that I was okay. The helicopter stayed put, and the faces at the window were less than friendly. I realized that it was not my welfare they were interested in. Eventually the thing banked sideways on the wind, in an expressive aerial shrug, and went off in search of a more likely suspect.

Rounding Boot Key, the boat touched bottom more than half a mile offshore. There was hardly any sea running, and it came unstuck on the next wave, but it took it as fair warning. This was a tricky coast. It required diligence to stay afloat. Earlier in the day, the boat might have been slammed hard on coral and suffered a bad spinal injury. For the next few miles, I triangulated my way across the chart with a series of anxious compass bearings. *Forget the Ahab stuff—you're a novice in these waters.*

At the far western end of the drab city of Marathon, I coasted up to a palm-thatched tiki bar, whose owner, seeing me alone, came out to take my bow rope.

"Where've you come from?"

"Just from Long Key today."

"It must've been real rough out there."

"No," I said, feeling the blood of Ahab running in my veins once more, "it was just a bit splashy, that's all," and ambled over to the bar, to order a dry vodka martini, straight up, with a twist.

There were two ways of getting from Marathon to Key West by sea. The quicker one was down the Hawk Channel on the Atlantic side, hugging the populated shore and running in close parallel with U.S. 1. The second route, twenty miles longer, went north, on the Gulf side, deep into the back country of the minor keys, then round to Key West on the far side of the archipelago. I settled for the Hawk Channel, ran into a brisk headwind, turned the boat round and steered for the back country.

The monotonous long march of the Seven Mile Bridge divided the two seas. To the south, the Atlantic was dark and turbid, though the sky was blue. The flood tide was spilling from the ocean to the Gulf, and as I lined up *Sea Mist* with the central span of the bridge, the tide gripped the boat and propelled it downhill, at speed, through the narrow chute of stone piles and rusty girders. I didn't sail into the Gulf of Mexico; I was catapulted there.

Beyond the bridge the sea was flat and—in the nice American word for shallow—*thin.* Small mangrove islands were scattered across it, like pieces of a baffling jigsaw puzzle in which all the bits are the same shade of dull green. Far out from land, gulls and waders were walking on the water, barely wetting their feet as they paddled over the flats. The color of this foreign sea, with the sun shining through it onto soft mud a few inches below the surface, was a streaky violet.

The five-foot alarm on the depth sounder was beeping. 4.9 . . . 4.7 . . . 4.5 . . . 4.8 . . . I switched it off. The mud looked hospitable enough, and the tide was rising. In any case, I was within sight now of the buoyed channel of the Intercoastal Waterway, which meandered through the open water like a lazy river digressing over its flood plain.

Even in the channel, the sea was thin; seven feet was a lot of water here. Tacking from one channel marker to the next, I put a steadily increasing distance between *Sea Mist* and the fading thread of civilization around U.S. 1. Off No Name Key, up Big Spanish Channel, the mangroves closed in on the boat, enclosing it in walls of mossy green. Blanketed from the wind, the water was like glass. *Sea Mist,* ghosting through the islands, ran over trailing fronds of kelp, shoals of striped fish, warty, pillow-shaped brown sponges. Three large porpoises came to join me for a while; they angled in on the bow of the boat, diving over and under, under and over, as they plaited the water into rope. Once, I crossed the black submarine track of a shark. It was on patrol, cruising with languid purpose down a dead-straight line. As it rose in the water, I could see the tender white crescent of its underlip and the raised, serrated ridge between its dorsal fins. It was about eight feet long; not enormous, but big enough to be deadly. Letting the boat look after itself, I got out Kaplan's *Field*

Guide to the Coral Reefs of the Caribbean and Florida, and identified the beast as what I thought was probably a tiger shark, *Galeocerdo cuvieri,* though it seemed to be a bit short of stripes. I tried emptying half a bottle of Bolognese sauce over the stern, hoping to attract it with the smell of meat, but it didn't return.

Fourteen miles out, the islands stopped coming. Ahead, beyond a very shallow mud bank, where spiderlike mangrove roots were trying to establish their last colony, was open sea. A single shrimper was working far offshore; otherwise I was alone, with the United States beginning to shelve away under my feet.

Clear of the Harbor Key Bank marker, I hauled the boat's head round and set it on a course of 248°, running west-by-south to follow the ragged line of the outer keys down to Key West.

This was runners' territory. To starboard lay the empty blue of the Gulf, with all its easy routes to Colombia, Cuba, Jamaica, Haiti and the Bahamas. To port lay something like one hundred fifty square miles of flats and islands, reticulated with hundreds of winding threadline channels. A shallow-draft boat, crossing from blue to green, could vanish off the face of the sea. The Atlantic side of the Keys was exposed and bald compared to the profuse and witchy convolutions of their northwestern flank. If I was trying to sneak a cargo of prohibited substances or persons to the mainland, there'd be no question; I'd come in from the Gulf and wriggle quietly through the mangroves. If I could learn just a few of the hidden paths through the islands, and know them in the dark as well as by daylight, my chances of being found out would be minimal to nonexistent.

The trouble was that the agencies of the U.S. government were making it as hard as possible for newcomers to find their way round here. For thirty miles, between Harbor Key Bank and the bell buoy that marked the entrance of the ship channel to Key West, there was not a single buoy or marker. The chart showed a dozen navigable channels that gave access from the Gulf to the inner labyrinth, but they were all spiked with coral heads, and you'd have to be very sure of your marks before you turned into them from the sea.

Sailing gently downwind a mile out from the line of islands, in twenty feet of lucent blue, I checked every channel on the

chart, looking for a place to anchor overnight. Content Passage
was too shallow; Johnston Key Channel was too serpentine for
me to safely follow; there were three black asterisks of coral at
the entrance to the Barracuda Keys Channel. The only one that
looked possible was the Cudjoe Channel, and that involved finding a quarter-mile-wide gap in a submerged reef.

More urgently, it involved finding the Sawyer Keys which
formed the channel's western bank, and, round here, one key
looked very much like another. I was looking at perhaps twenty
of the things. The mangroves on all of them grew to exactly the
same height. On each one, the same osprey had built the same
nest on the same stump. The same clatter of waterfowl came
from the black roots of the islands as the boat approached. I had
been counting keys off when I left Harbor Key, but had fallen
behind on my arithmetic; that fat smudge over there—was it
Crane Key, Hurricane Key, Raccoon Key or Tarpon Belly Key?
Search me.

According to the chart there was a tide station on the northern
shore of the Sawyer Keys, and if I could get a fix on that I could
easily find my way into the channel. Since I didn't know what a
tide station looked like, I called the Coast Guard on 16 and asked
if the duty officer could give me a description of this useful object.

A voice told me to stand by. Five minutes later, he came back.

"I am not," he said stiffly, as if reading from a script, "at liberty
to disclose any navigational information."

I said, with some warmth, that I had thought the primary job
of any Coast Guard was the disclosure of navigational information. What the hell else was he there for?

"I'm sorry," he said, ad-libbing now, "but the best advice I can
give you is to call up a local fishing boat and ask him."

I should have known. In the last ten years the U.S. Coast
Guard, though still funded by the Department of Transportation,
had changed from being a search-and-rescue organization, the
mariner's friend in need, to being, in effect, a branch of the
military. It was fighting the Drug War, guarding the coast against
the runners, and no longer at liberty to give help to people like
me. Its patrol boats were warships, with anti-aircraft guns
mounted on their foredecks and swiveling M60s on their bridges.

The sides of their bridgehouses were decorated with symbols that recorded their drug busts. A successful marijuana raid earned the ship a picture of what looked like an overgrown lettuce; a cocaine bust got it a white snowflake. A couple of days before, I'd spotted one of these vessels in the Hawk Channel, and been puzzled by its surreal artwork, which appeared to represent a salad in a blizzard. Red had put me right.

The mangrove islands were inscrutably alike. There was only one mark in the landscape that stood out clearly: Fat Albert. His position was a state secret, and there was no mention of him anywhere on the chart. Out of curiosity, though, I had been taking compass bearings on him as I sailed up Big Spanish Channel, and I took another now. The pencil lines on the chart intersected in a neat triangle, deep in the islands, on the northeast tip of Cudjoe Key. Albert's windlass, I was interested to see, was on the same site as a charted tide station.

(Here—as it were, in a sealed envelope—is Albert's position: 23° 42.00′ N; 81° 30.25′ W. Destroy the paper as soon as you've committed this information to memory; you will need it if you ever get lost in the outer reaches of the Florida Keys.)

I watched Albert through the prism of the hand-bearing compass until he bore exactly 145°, then I steered for him, straight down the middle of the Cudjoe Channel. Lobes of coral passed eight feet under the keel; I caught a glimpse of a large and flashy parrotfish; then the water deepened abruptly to twenty feet, and the boat was inside the lagoon.

I found a muddy pool, ringed with mangroves, well out of the way of returning fishing boats, and lowered the anchor into 4.4 feet of water; just enough to stay afloat. I stuck the Velcro-edged mosquito nets to the inside of the open hatches and dined off spaghetti and the sauce that the tiger shark had spurned.

Outside, as the evening darkened, the wildlife turned rowdy. The big Keys mosquitoes sounded as if they were powered by miniature one-cylinder gasoline engines, like model airplanes. Fish splashed. A tuneless string orchestra of cicadas started up. Fights broke out in the mangroves. Angry bass croakings were answered by high monkey-squeals, the warning cry of a bird by the crackling undergrowth of a large mammal. Trying to identify these noises and put names and shapes to them, I found the Peterson field guides less than helpful. The Book of Revelations would have been far more useful; but I hadn't packed it in my boat bum's luggage.

At midnight I crawled out on deck through the mosquito mesh. Only a few throaty gobbling sounds now came from the islands. There wasn't a breath of wind, and the water was full of the night sky. Swollen stars were slopping about in the tide, big enough to fish for with a bucket. Below the surface, firefly shrimp were shoaling, in brilliant disappearing curlicues of light. Up top, Albert flashed green and white in stroboscopic pulses, guiding the runner safe home from the sea.

It was hard to sleep in the close heat of the forecabin. I kept on coming awake to the creak and sway of the boat as it rocked on a muscle of wash from the main channel. I listened, with some apprehension, to the engines of the night fishermen, but none came to my pool. Far into the small hours, I picked up the chirrup of a distant outboard—not in the channel, out on the flats off Happy Jack Key. It was just an early-bird angler, searching for bonefish, probably; but in this landscape suspicions took hold and spread like arching mangrove roots.

In the morning, there was no mistaking the tide station on the north shore of Sawyer Keys, though I had missed it the afternoon before. It was a rough wooden jetty, beside which was now moored a long gray Coast Guard patrol boat. My exit from Cudjoe Channel was being studied through binoculars whose lenses winked in the sun.

The wind was kind; a steady easterly, strong enough to drive the boat to Key West under the genoa alone. Past the reef, *Sea Mist* surged downwind on an easy sea. With the wheel lashed to the compass binnacle with bunjie cord, she sailed herself, with only occasional adjustments from me. I took bearings on Albert to measure her speed (the knotmeter was a goner), and she was making nearly six knots, only a jogger's pace on land but a heady rate of progress in a small sailboat. It put Key West less than five hours away.

Something was happening to Albert. Each time I focused on him, he looked somehow sadder. It took a while to figure out that his handlers were winching him down out of the sky. He came sagging over the mangroves to join a second white blimp on the ground. So Albert had a twin sister. They were only a minute or two together before Albertine (I named her with Proust in mind—Albertine La Grosse) started to rise. She went up without grace, in a series of slow jerks, until, at the end of her tether, she continued Albert's valuable war work, showing Cubans what muppets and teenage mutant ninja turtles were.

In an hour, I had Key West in view. It showed hazily, as a bunch of wobbling chimney stacks, adrift in the sky, high above the fringe of islands. From twenty miles off, it looked like a city in a folk tale, towered and battlemented, unreal. Its name was a makeshift anglicization of the Spanish *cay hueso*, island of bones; and so it looked this morning—bleached and brittle, as if a breath of wind might shatter it to powder.

Far ahead, big ships were moving in the entrance channel. The approach to any big port is a ceremonial affair: you take your place in line, you process slowly down an avenue of seamarks, then you are formally received into the city. The approach to Key West was unusually grand—a broad mall of water, a mile wide and seven miles long, lined on both sides by the wrecks of boats that hadn't made it and by cormorants on timber posts, hanging their wings up to dry. It began with the irregular tolling of the bell on Buoy No. 1 as it shifted on its haunches in the swell, and it opened up on a facade of military spit and polish. The town was fronted by warships and by the restored ruins of Fort Taylor. If you were sailing in to Key West from Granada, Panama, or Nicaragua, you were meant to tremble a little in your boots as you came close to this tropical outpost of American power. Its show of flags and ships and new white paint was there to put you in your place, to remind you of whose back yard it was, where you enjoyed the privilege of squatting.

Under engine, I crept past the naval docks and put into the big, untidy harbor of Key West Bight, where I found lodgings for the boat, tied up to a corrugated iron shed under the striped towers of the power station. Spilled diesel fuel gave the water a rainbow tint. The surface was riddled with metallic scales from dead tarpon and marlin, brought in, by the hour and by the ton, by the charter fishing boats nearby. The temperature was ninety something. The smell was rich and strange.

Taking a shower in the three-by-four-foot toilet on the boat, I was impressed by the appearance of the louche and lobster-colored stranger in the shaving mirror. With his bloodshot eyes and patchy, graying stubble, he looked criminalized. He had green teeth. He was still a long way short of being mistaken for a cocaine or marijuana runner, but he had the air of a man who might make his living by stealing things from unlocked cars. He was, I had to admit, a good deal closer in appearance to Pap than to Huck Finn. Even so, he looked as if he should be able to make himself pretty much at home on the Keys.

Behind its concrete military frontage, Key West was a city of carpentry. It looked as if it had been put together by a ship's chippie on furlough. He had the sailor's affection for small, intricate spaces, bound by the length of a hammock and the width of a ditty box, and had built streets of cabins rather than houses. He had the sailor's weakness for whittling ornaments, for fancy chisel-and-gouge work. On every porch, he had carved flutes, scrolls and entablatures. He was used to decks and guardrails, and to every cabin he had added a planked forecastle and a white picket fence. His taste in flowers was sailor-gaudy and slightly drunken. He had planted the gardens with oleander and hibiscus, jasmine, azalea, bougainvillea and prickly pear.

Reeling a little from the movement of the sea, I walked Key West from end to end in twenty minutes flat. Though it was late in the season, parts of the town were still under occupation by tourist troops in their uniforms of Hawaiian shirts and Bermuda shorts. They held Duval Street and Mallory Square, and had bridgeheads at important strategic places like the Hemingway House and the *ersatz* buoy that marked the southernmost point of the United States. They marched, very slowly indeed, in snatch squads, taking over conch shells, espadrilles and jewelry from the natives as they passed. They read every sign they saw out loud to their companions, who were, apparently, illiterate. ("Oh, look, it says it's Hemingway's house—" "Oh, look, it says it's ninety miles to Cuba—") After the solitude and freedom of the water, it was a cruel fate, to find myself drafted into the service of this noisy multicolored army.

The natives, though, had constructed an exquisite humiliation for their conquerors. They had chained together a series of open tumbrils, pulled by a diesel tractor fancifully disguised as a children's-book steam locomotive (it might have been called Thomas the Tank Engine, or Sammy the Shunter). The tourists were loaded into the trucks and hauled around the town for the cynical entertainment of the residents. En route, they were lectured, by megaphone and with condescending facetiousness, on history, botany, architecture and literature. Every few hundred yards the Conch Train stopped for a session of compulsory photography. The tourists, grinning like frightened chimpanzees, all panned their video cameras along the same arc, before the train led them off to their next station of abasement.

I balked at riding on the Conch Train and deserted from the army, up hot dusty streets too crooked and narrow for the train to follow, to the geographical center of the town: its fifty-acre graveyard. Wiry little geckoes skeetered ahead of me on the bare white rock and busy yellow vireos flew from tomb to tomb. Key West's dead were buried aboveground. Most of them resided in whitewashed stone cottages of almost exactly the same size and shape as the wooden ones they'd left behind. Some were walled up in four-story condo blocks of coffin-sized apartments, with 256 corpses in each long block. The graveyard was a true necropolis, a city within the city, the heart of Key West.

Its streets were named and numbered like the streets outside. You didn't pass away here; you moved house. You checked out of your old place on the corner of First and Catherine and moved into a new, slightly smaller home on the corner of Second and Violet. The dead of Key West were a great deal more alive than their colleagues in most places.

Half a dozen solitary women were visiting their friends and relatives that evening. They were gardening in the backyards of the cottages and arranging flowers in vases at the front doors of the apartments. I wandered through the streets, looking to see if I could find a namesake here. I found a Rabhan, but we weren't close. Then I called at the graves of strangers.

I took an instant shine to a man called Earl Saunders Johnson, who had been in residence since May 1972. He had been sculpted, life size, in plaster of Paris, and stood casually over his own tomb, with his right foot resting on a boulder. He was looking westward and grinning, his eyes wrinkling at the low sun. Even in death, he was dressed for the weather in baggy shorts and a sort of plaster golf jacket. His lace-up canvas boots were real; Mr. Johnson had been wearing them before he moved to the graveyard.

But the man who interested me most was B. P. Roberts, who'd arrived here in June of 1979. With five other people, he shared a fine stucco house—almost a mansion—with a wreath of fresh roses pinned to its oak portal. His epitaph, printed in black capitals on a nameplate of varnished teak, was I TOLD YOU I WAS SICK. It was a wonderful line, as rich in Empsonian ambiguity as any critic could hope for. In one resounding chord, it struck notes of triumph, pathos, accusation, self-pity and high humor. It called at the passer-by from inside the house, in a voice of extraordinary liveliness for someone eleven years gone. I wondered how B. P. Roberts had got away with this lusty yell from beyond the grave. He must have made it an inalienable condition of his will. Was it the planned revenge of a conscious wit—or was he a mild man, meekly voicing a reasonable complaint? He might have intended the chief emphasis to fall on any one of the six words in the line. It was impossible to guess his original meaning now; the sentence had taken on a bizarre and autonomous life which, like all works of literary art, transcended the intentions of its author.

Once met, B. P. Roberts was a difficult character to shake off. He kept on parsing himself in my head as I walked down Passover Lane to Margaret Street. At Caroline, he was still saying, I *told* you I was sick . . . I told you *I* was sick . . . I told you I was *sick*. Sometimes he spoke very quietly, sometimes he shouted, sometimes he whined. He was as close to being an unquiet spirit as I had ever encountered in my life.

*   *   *

Dawn in Key West Bight announced itself with a chorus of marine diesels, over whose sleep-busting din I could hear roosters crowing. The roosters seemed a strangely bucolic touch in a modern American city, and I asked about them over breakfast at Pepe's Bar. Yeah, my neighbor said, without looking up from his scrambled egg and hominy grits. Fighting cocks. Fighting cocks? *Fightin' cocks.* The bartender chipped in, saying that the birds were bred in garages all over town for bloody Latin amusements. Dim in the still-too-early morning, I said I thought such things were illegal.

My neighbor sniggered. "This is Key West you're in," he said. "Mile Zero," said the bartender. "The end of the road."

Swart Robinson was in his office, on the fourth floor of a business block at the industrial, eastern end of Key West. He looked like Red's cousin—the older one, who'd once nearly made it as a pro football player and whose bulk and muscle were still useful in tight corners. He had the gruff family humor and the avid family eyes. His big hands were restless. His bushy, steel gray hair was brushed straight back from his temples in a style that made one immediately see the brawny teenager he'd been in 1952, while his military mustache gave him an official, authoritative air that the rest of his face belied.

Swart was a senior customs investigator. He chased "bad-asses"; but there was enough surviving bad-ass in Swart's own temperament to give him a sense of amiable identity with the drug runners whom he pursued around the Keys.

Where most men decorate their offices with photographs of wives and children, Swart had pictures of drug busts on his walls. There were dozens of them; well-framed ten-by-twelves of yachts, motor cruisers, fishing boats and cargo ships, each with a red Dynotape label glued to the glass. The labels were terse: "14,500 lbs."; "120 kilos"; "2,140 lbs." There was a picture of a plane crash. A single-engined Piper stood askew on a dirt road, its prop buried in mangroves. It was captioned: "2,000,000 Quaaludes."

"See that one?" He pointed at a photo of a handsome white Chris Craft which had been caught with a lot of kilos on board.

"The brown mark on the scuppers? That's *yuman* blood."

"Really."

"Yeah. Ninety k's of cocaine and one dead Cuban. *Them guys* cut his throat before they took off. He was still real warm when we arrived." Swart smiled at the memory; a complicated smile, not unfeeling, which seemed to acknowledge that his own kind of job satisfaction might not be everyone's taste.

Swart was a New Yorker, born in Bay Ridge, Brooklyn. As a kid, he had been happiest kicking cans along the shore of the Verrazano Narrows and on family outings to Rockaway. He loved the water. Joining the customs service was a city boy's route to a life in the outdoors.

He'd begun by going on patrol in New York Harbor. Then he'd angled for a posting to the wilder shores of Long Island, where he'd cruised up and down Peconic Bay in search of bad-asses. In his spare time he fished and raced stock cars; he was a man who needed a lot of adrenaline to feel properly alive. He kept on moving house. Long Island was getting tamer and more suburban by the week, and every time the new neighbors showed up in their Bloomingdale's weekend gear, Swart moved north. When the offer of a transfer to Key West came up, he was almost at Montauk Point.

At some point in his progress up the spine of Long Island, he'd left a family behind. When he drove down to the Keys, he was single again. A life was over and he was looking for a new one.

Swart was happy here. His only grumble now was that he was a hundred miles and more from the nearest stock car stadium, but there was almost enough wildness and excitement on the Keys to satisfy even Swart's large appetite for trouble and adventure in the open air. Nowadays, in his mid-fifties, he wasn't "in the field" as often as he would have liked—but years of riding around in a customs go-fast boat had played hell with his back, and a long sea chase could put him on pain-killers for a week. It is sad but true that even Huck Finn and Deerslayer will, in time, go down with lumbago and slipped discs.

He loved his territory. When he spoke of it, there was still a note of latecomer's wonder in his voice.

"Most places in the world, you have a coastline. This place, there's nothing but coastline. I don't know if they ever computed it, but if you said there was one thousand miles of coastline between here and Marathon, you wouldn't be far wrong. It's a unique game here. Just about every key has a secret little spot, and you could go a lifetime and still not know half of them. Then there's Ocean and Gulf . . . You can get a tip-off; you can know *who* and *what* and *where* and *when;* you can know it's happening at mile 15.5—but if you don't know it's Ocean or Gulf, you're nowhere."

He was possessed by the inexhaustible secrecy and profusion of the islands, and by the criminal ingenuity of their inhabitants. He spilled on to his desktop a sheaf of more photographs, of false keels, false waterlines, false bulkheads, false fuel and water tanks. "Look at that," he said admiringly, of a photo of a hydraulically operated secret wall in the bathroom of a cabin cruiser; "we knew that boat was loaded, somewhere, but it took two years to find it."

I shared Swart's pleasure in this world of semblances and hiding places, secret compartments and secret water. The openness of so much of American life, its frank manners, its way of conducting private business (from one's cholesterol level and the workings of one's bowels to one's job record and the details of one's divorce) in public, was often hard to bear. There were occasions when the country felt like an enormous TV studio, in which the lights were turned on everybody, all the time. America needed the Florida Keys, where, in a warren of sliding doors and concealed chambers, you could hide yourself, as you could hide almost anything else.

"So," I said; "you catch some. What goes wrong? Why do the ones you catch get caught?"

"Greed," Swart said. "It's nearly always greed. Look here . . ." He fished out another picture from his box file of trophies. A sailboat. Two hundred thirty pounds. "We got him on a cold pop. He was *good.* The stuff was packed inside the Zodiac inflatable he was towing. He'd taken that dinghy apart and put it together again like it was new. All the glued seams? They were like factory made. We'd never have bothered to deflate it. It was real convincing. The guy would've got clean away with it, except for one thing . . ."

"Which was?"

"Greed. Pure greed. He couldn't resist going for a little extra. Know where he put it? In the dinghy's canvas bag, right out on the deck. It wasn't even zipped. That's where they fall down, on the last thousand dollars' worth. A pound or a kilo too many. Either it's greed, or someone tips us off."

"Who are your main tipsters?"

"Oh, it varies. Guy has a girlfriend, so we get the jealous wife. Or the jealous girlfriend. Then the suppliers, they turn in a few of their customers to us, for the reward money. Plus, there are the rival groups; they do the best they can to put each other away in jail."

"Okay," I said. "I'm thinking about making a run. I've got the boat. I know someone who can put me in touch with someone. How do I get away with it?"

Swart seemed pleased to be asked. This was not a question that he'd had to answer very often. He gave it some serious thought.

"Well . . . if you're happy with one or two kilos, you'll have a much better success rate."

"Won't my supplier tip you off?"

"You're going to have to choose your supplier. Don't set yourself up as a one-run guy, whatever you do. He'd better believe you're good for a regular series of runs, even though they're all small ones."

"Marijuana or cocaine?"

"From a businessman's point of view, you'd be crazy trying to smuggle marijuana. But there's a lot less violence in it. You don't get to deal with the real bad-asses. You'd be safer with marijuana. A lot of people end up under six feet of dirt in the cocaine trade."

"Anything else?"

"Get a good-looking girl in a bikini. There used to be a smuggling profile—you know: two males alone, grubby people, grubby boat—those are the ones we used to go for on a cold pop. Then they wised up. They all got girls. Well—I'm human. I'd sooner stay up on deck looking at a girl in a bikini than be down sniffing shit in the bilges."

"I'll see what I can do," I said.

"I'll show you my turf," Swart said. "We'll go out on a patrol."

We met next morning, at the marina on Stock Island where the customs go-fast boat was moored. Swart, wearing Polaroids and a uniform plastic cap, was looking younger, cheered by the prospect of a day's hunting in the field. He reversed his cap on his head, then did the same to mine. "We're going to be headed up into sixty miles an hour of wind." Then he issued me with a pair of latex ear plugs. "Know what these boats are called? Blue Thunders. Blue for the color of the customs uniform and thunder for—you'll hear it."

The Blue Thunder was an unmarked white power catamaran, thirty-nine feet long, bristling with radio antennae. Its guts were located in its back end: twin 575-horse Chevrolet gas engines which, even on tickover, sounded like the beginning of Armageddon. I strapped myself into the seat next to Swart's and squinched in my ear plugs. The Blue Thunder, feeling more like a taxiing jet fighter than a boat, stalked out through the pontoons.

Past the entrance channel, Swart gave it the gas. The engines made a noise that had me fearing for the fillings in my teeth; a complex music of bass drums and cymbals, falling masonry, sustained mortar fire and the high whine of an electric drill skidding across sheet metal. The sea had gone rigid beneath us. We banged and pounded over waves as hard and sharp as rocks. Behind us, the water stretched out in a mile-long train of billowing white lace. Swart, standing behind the wheel, his meaty forearms shuddering, was wearing a grin as wide as his face. This, I gathered from his expression, was the life.

It took five minutes to get out to the reef—a journey to which I had tentatively assigned a full half day's sail on *Sea Mist.* Swart was shouting something about my needing ear drops.

I took the plugs out. "What?"

He throttled down. "Air drops. This is a favorite spot for air drops." One time, after a tip-off, he had been waiting here at night in the Blue Thunder. The runners' boat failed to show, but a light aircraft turned up, flying low. When Swart shone his flashlight at the fuselage to read its markings, he was unexpectedly rewarded. A door opened on the plane, and the customs boat was showered from stem to stern with bales of marijuana.

We circled round the holiday crowd of charter fishing boats and scuba divers, then turned east and headed up the line of keys. They whipped past on the port beam: Boca Chica, Geiger, Pelican, Saddlehill, Sugarloaf. At the entrance to Cudjoe Bay, Swart slowed and turned out of the channel into shallow water. Our props ground into the soft sand and kicked up a mess behind us of what looked like boiling potato soup. But the boat kept going, wading rather than floating, toward the wall of mangroves ahead. The bow was very nearly in the bushes when a secret door opened to admit us to a long dark corridor of slimy water, ten feet deep. We slid through, scaring the pelicans and the ducks.

"This is a useful little back alley," Swart said. For more than a quarter of a mile, the slough wound through the overhanging mangroves, then it emerged into open swamp country. The Blue Thunder came to a stop beside a burned-out wooden bridge whose brick pilings were crumbling away on both banks. "We had a stake-out here. Couple of years back. I put a guy in those bushes, right there. Sent him out with a scrambler radio, a pile of sandwiches, a bottle of sunblock and a canister of mosquito repellent, and told him to sit tight until something happened. He was here three days before the bad guys showed up. We recovered sixty kilos out of that boat."

"Street price?"

"Not far shy of a million bucks. But you should have seen his mosquito bites. He was bit bad."

We wormed our way out to sea again, tore west for a minute or two and put into a crooked side-channel off Sugarloaf Key.

"This is another place they used to use before we found out what was happening. There was this guy, older man, grandad-type, bought a house on the water to retire in. Liked to fish. A lonely feller. Widower. One day he gets a phone call from a stranger, saying has he ever wanted to go on a visit to Disneyworld? Turns out it's been the old guy's dream. He's always wanted to go to Disneyworld. He's never been. He wants Mickey Mouse's autograph, or whatever the hell it is you get at Disneyworld. 'Okay,' the voice says, 'you're booked in for a week from next Thursday, and it's on us. Look in your mailbox now, and you'll find some spending money.' There's a thousand bucks in there. It's what the old guy dreamed of when he moved down to Florida—money on trees. So he goes away, has his week at Disneyworld, gets to shake Mickey Mouse's hand—and when he comes back there's a brand new Pontiac in his driveway, with twenty thousand bucks in the glove compartment. Well, says the old guy, this is the Keys, and he takes the car and the money and says nothing to nobody. When we arrest him, he's all injured innocence. *He*'s done nothing wrong—he can't understand it. Uh, huh, looks like he's home . . ."

Sitting under a parasol, wearing a straw hat and a boiler-suit, the man was fishing from the edge of his back yard. His grizzled black lab, Gypsy's double, barked at the Blue Thunder. Swart drove the boat in close. The old man, who had looked up at first, now had eyes only for his float.

"Hi," called Swart. "How ya doin'?"

No answer.

"Hey, I'm talking to you! How ya doin'?"

The man raised a skinny wrist and flapped his hand. It might have been a limp wave or an attempt to ward off a no-see-um.

"Real good," he said grayly.

"See ya," Swart said, gunning the engines.

"He got sentenced?" I asked.

"No. Insufficient evidence."

We bounced over the sea.

"How's your back?" I yelled.

"Holding up," Swart shouted over the mad music of the twin Chevies.

In Safe Harbor, just short of Key West, we rumbled up and down the lines of moored shrimpers. Swart said: "The bad guys keep close tabs on every fisherman in town. If a guy falls behind with payments on his boat, if his kid gets sick and needs hospitalization, the bad guys make it their business to be in the know. They'll call around at his house. Tea and sympathy. The bad guys have got an easy solution to everybody's problem. So we like to keep an eye out for any fisherman who's in trouble."

A shrimping trip lasted around five days. A drug run, to Jamaica or Colombia, in a big shrimper, would take ten days to two weeks. So Swart would hang out in his car in the parking lot of the supermarket near Safe Harbor.

"Guy comes out pushing a shopping cart with two weeks of supplies on board, you can bet your life that it's not shrimp he's after. I'll put a marker out on his boat, with the Coast Guard and Marine Patrol, and as soon as he's back in territorial waters, he gets boarded."

Back at the marina on Stock Island, after six hours of thundering around the lower keys, Swart said: "Friday, there's a meeting of the Poets' Club. That's something that might interest you."

This was a side of Swart's character that I'd missed.

"You're a poet?"

"Kind of. Stands for Piss on Everything, Tomorrow's Saturday."

"I thought every day was Saturday on the Keys."

"Some more than others. Friday, five-thirty, bar of the Santa Maria motel. Be there."

I had been buying supplies for the boat at Fausto's Grocery, and was waiting for a cab. It was eleven in the morning and the city was grilling under the sun. Squatting on the sidewalk, my paper sacks ranged round me like a bag lady's, I nursed a headache and dreamed of air conditioning.

"So who put shit in your corn flakes this morning?"

Dully, I took in my interrogator: a scrawny boy-man, thirtyish, in torn jeans and T-shirt. Hay hair. Recessed eyes. A missing tooth. He was using a litter-bin as his breakfast table and was washing down his portion of carry-out fried chicken with what was left of a six-pack of Coors.

"I look *that* bad?"

He studied me seriously. "Yeah." He looked over his stock of liquor. "You want a beer?"

"Thanks, but no. It'd make things worse."

"Know what you mean . . ." He took a mouthful of wing. "You here on vacation?"

"No. Not exactly. I'm on a boat."

"I been on boats."

I could imagine. He was natural deckhand material for the Bahamas run, though his presence on any boat would court the attention of Customs and Coast Guard. You'd have to keep him belowdecks.

"What do you do?" I said.

"Do? Like *work?* I don't work—this is Key West, man. I do jobs . . . sometimes. Lot of jobs in Key West. Why? You looking for a job?"

"No. I was just wondering."

"You want an apartment? I could get you an apartment. You got three fifty a month? I could find you an apartment for that."

"I've got the boat."

"Right." He munched. I could see, uncomfortably clearly, how the two of us would strike any passer-by. Being a boat bum was one thing; being a street bum was something else.

When the cab drew up, the driver gave me a wary once-over before he opened the trunk. My new friend helped me with the sacks of groceries. As I got into the car, he shook my hand.

"Bri," he said.

I missed a beat before coming back with "John."

In Pepe's Bar, I ran into the man I nailed at once as Blanco Robinson. His beard was going white at the edges, like the once-gold braid on his captain's cap. He had two faces. One was beaky and bespectacled, a northern face, shaped by short rations and cloudy skies. The other was the face of southern Florida—heedless, brown, abundantly fed, like the face of a fifth-century Roman emperor. He first caught my attention because his voice had once been English, though it had been long overlaid with American speech rhythms.

"Where does that accent come from originally?" I asked. "Derby?"

"Not far off. Nottingham." *Knotty-gum.* The whiffling, adenoidal twang of the English midlands struck an exotic note in Pepe's Bar. It conjured a whole world, of head colds that went on for months, of warm beer, pork pies, Odeons and umbrellas.

He was a charter skipper. His thirty-six-foot Westerly was moored on the same pier as *Sea Mist,* and we walked down to the boats together. I said that, with the season coming to an end, he must be looking forward to a lazy summer.

"No," he said. "I'm onto a good wheeze here. You see, I've got the gay trade all sewn up. Come on board, I'll show you."

From a cabin locker, he produced a sheaf of flyers. BEEF ON THE REEF, they announced: *Exclusively All Gay Snorkeling Trips.* "You can't go wrong," said Blanco Robinson, "if you get the gays on your side in Key West. I'm busy all year round."

He performed gay weddings at sea. Also burials. He'd just buried the ashes of a Cuban woman that morning, off the Marquesas. "That's why I'm wearing my whites," he said, taking off his captain's cap and replacing it with a disreputable object that even Red would have envied.

If Blanco could make himself so comfortable here . . . I asked him what the chances were of setting up as a charter captain. "It's a cinch," he said, "if you use your imagination. Trouble with most of the guys round here is they think along tramlines. You've just got to diversify. With me, it's the gays. You'd have to think up a line for yourself. And get yourself some good advertising. Be creative. Think up a good slogan. Like my 'Beef on the Reef.' Everyone remembers that."

He'd been on the Keys for six years, and he'd come here by a classic route. Back in England, he'd run into some trouble with the Inland Revenue. There had been a spot of confusion about certain receipts for "equipment"—Blanco was vague on details—and a summons to appear at a court hearing that Blanco thought it wise not to attend. He was on the Scilly Islands at the time, reason unspecified. In the nick of time, a job came up—the delivery of a yacht to the West Indies. Blanco had jumped at it and scarpered, leaving St. Mary's the night before the police arrived to interview him.

It had been a wild crossing. Blanco's crew for the voyage was a Scilly Islander who revealed himself, twelve hours out from port, as a religious maniac. "A real nutter. The minute the wind got up, the bugger was up in the fo'c's'le saying his prayers. I couldn't get him out. I was trying to reef the main in a force seven, and all this clown would do was lie on the Vee-berth and talk to Jesus."

He had dumped the crew in the Canaries and sailed on alone. After delivering the boat in Antigua, he'd bummed his way north through the Caribbean. In Fort Lauderdale, he'd taken odd jobs aboard other people's boats. He'd met a woman who . . . Like Newton's apple, obeying the law of gravitational force, Blanco had fallen gently into Key West.

His story took some following. "That was when I was in computers . . .," he said. "That was when I was going under the name of Barry Roper." "That was when I was working for MI5—when I was in the Committee of 100, digging up stuff to get Ralph Schoenmann out of the country." "Oh—that was when I was Bill Richards . . ." "That was when I was being paid by Mossad. When I was in the National Front. D'you remember Colin ———? You know how he suddenly dropped out of the news pretty smartish? Well, that was me," Blanco said modestly.

I had to admit that I was losing track. I got out my notebook.

"Hey, you won't use my real name in this, will you?"

"Promise."

I have the page in front of me where I listed as many of Blanco Robinson's occupations as he could remember. He worked as a surveyor. He joined the RAF as a flight engineer. He owned a nightclub ("not by myself, with a partner"). He was with MI5. He was employed ("on a freelance basis") by Mossad. He became an expert in card storage and retrieval with a computer firm. He was a contractor. He sold dictating machines ("but that was only for six weeks"). He had a business consultancy ("Well, *everybody*'s been a 'consultant,' haven't they?"). His "soon-to-be-ex" wife was assistant headmistress of a comprehensive school in Nottingham.

It was only the most quotidian parts of Blanco's story that I felt inclined to doubt. The wife, the jobs in dictating machines and card storage, sounded like transparent covers. He was a man who stood at an oblique angle to ascertainable reality, and in Key West he'd found the one place on the English-speaking earth whose attitude to reality exactly matched his own.

"Do you think you'll ever leave?" I asked.

"They'd have to serve a deportation order on me now." His double-face looked serious. I guessed that Blanco must have seen the print on a deportation order in his time.

The bar in the Santa Maria was the coldest place in the city, fanned by a welcoming refrigerated breeze. It was also one of the darkest. The members of the Poets' Club were seated in dim silhouette around a long table. Searching in the gloom, I found the expansive shadow of Swart, who was with his girlfriend, Violet. I was introduced to an area of darkness said to be the president of the hotel and motel owners' association, and to the black outlines of an attorney, a plumber, a journalist from the *Key West Citizen,* something or somebody who was in computers, a realtor and a pharmacist. As my sun-blinded eyes recovered their night vision, I was surprised to see that the burly, crepuscular shape across the table from me consisted of a business suit, a white shirt and, improbably, a striped tie. It had no face yet, but its voice announced that it belonged to the superintendent of the Monroe County school system.

An outsider, hearing the poets in session, would have mistaken them for a gang of good old boys, all beer and banter. Sitting in on the group, I caught the undercurrent of a serious agenda beneath the backslapping and laughter. The poets were settling the affairs of Key West for the next week. Deals were being struck, legal advice taken. Here, in the dark, the unacknowledged legislators of the world were busy at their legislation.

I had seen no schools at all during my selective encounter with the Keys, and I asked the superintendent how many Keys children made it into universities.

"You just asked him his favorite question," said the attorney. "I'm on the school board, and we're proud of the answer. Go on, tell him, Dickie."

The superintendent said that, well, he didn't like to boast, but in fact Monroe County was top of the league in the whole state for college admissions. Kids from Monroe County were going to some of the best universities in the United States. He rattled off the Harvards, Yales, Cornells, Columbias.

I was incredulous. In this landscape made for loafing in, with its torpid climate and its insistent buzz of criminality, I found it hard to credit that there were local children with their noses deep in books, mugging up for college entrance. I had been inclined to take as gospel the word of a sozzled Hollywood screenwriter, met in a bar in Key Largo, who'd said "This is brain-death country."

"How do you do it?" I said.

"I tell you," said the attorney, *sotto voce,* in my ear: "this guy's a marvel. We like to give him all the grief we can on the school board, but he's *made* our schools. I do hate to admit it, but just about everything that's right about the school system is down to that man there."

"And it'd be a whole lot better if it wasn't for that son-of-a-bitch attorney," said the superintendent. "He thinks education is a fine thing, so long as it doesn't cost a cent in taxes. This is the man who's trying to starve the schools to death."

"There you go again . . . Will you *listen* to that? That's what we have to put up with every school board meeting—the sound of a whining superintendent who can't meet his budget."

Patiently, I said, again: "How do you do it?"

"Teachers," the superintendent said. *"If* I could ever get any."

"I swear, I won't listen to this," said the attorney. "Do you want to drive me to an early grave?"

The superintendent told me how he traveled, in and out of state, to recruit his teachers from the colleges. "The secret is to get 'em young. And *pay* 'em. Pay 'em when they need it, right at the start of their careers. Get 'em housing. Then you've got 'em hooked. If I can get teachers down to the Keys when they're fresh out of college, I can keep them here. Once they're into the boating and the fishing and the sunshine, they won't go. It doesn't matter so much what you pay them once they're in their thirties. It's up front where it counts, when they're in their twenties, and if I could only get that damn attorney to see sense, I could have the best teachers in the whole United States working down here."

Sitting at table with the poets, I was in a place that I found myself surprised to recognize. That evening, Key West turned suddenly into a small, intimate, hard-working Southern town. I thought how, in another life, I might have come here in my own twenties, to live in a wooden cabin with a gingerbread porch, to teach Wordsworth to the shrimpers' children, to live blamelessly in this blameful city of guises and disguises.

Every excursion that I made from the boat took me through the graveyard. The more I saw of it, the more I liked the place, its quiet streets of little whitewashed houses, its birds and lizards, its odd epitaphs. It would be a good spot to be buried in, and I could think of no better site for an American ending. After the continuous motion of life in the United States, the striving and becoming, you'd land up here to rot in sunny indolence in a whitewashed building within the sound of the sea.

I wasn't ambitious. I didn't want a grand place. I would settle for a modest, Alice-sized apartment, a one-bed affair in a multi-story block.

From a pay phone on the dock, I called the public works department at city hall, and asked for Cemeteries. I had been thinking, I said, of ordering a tomb.

"For a relative?"

"No."

"Is this for a deceased party?"

"No, not yet. Actually, it's for me."

"I get you. What exactly do you have in mind?"

"You know those kind of condo blocks at the south end?"

"The multiple occupancy units. And this would be just one unit, right?"

"Yes. What's the cost on those?"

"Well, the price has just been raised. Like everything else, cost's going up all the time. Two years back, you could have had one for six hundred dollars. Right now, it'll cost you eight twenty-five clear."

"Is that leasehold or freehold?"

"I don't follow you."

"Is it for eternity?"

After an uneasy pause, the man laughed.

"Yeah, it's yours for keeps."

"It sounds like a good buy."

"It's the only property not taxed in the city."

"Could I buy one this afternoon?"

"Well—no. There's been a lot of demand for those units lately. We're doing what we can to stay ahead of the game; we used to build sixteen of 'em at a time, but last time we were up to sixty-four . . . Next time, we may be going up as high as ninety-six."

"How long would I have to wait?"

"That's difficult. You think you can hold out for two years?"

High clouds were moving in the sky. The wind was from the southwest, the water was flecked with small waves. There were many things I wanted to do. For a start, I wanted to sail up the Atlantic side of the Keys, go under the Seven Mile Bridge and strike north for the Everglades. After that . . .

"Well, I can try," I said.

ALSO BY JONATHAN RABAN

BAD LAND

An American Romance

In 1909 maps still identified eastern Montana as the Great American Desert. But in that year Congress offered 320-acre tracts of land to anyone bold or foolish enough to stake a claim to them. Drawn by inventive brochures, countless homesteaders went west to make their fortunes. Most failed. In *Bad Land*, Jonathan Raban travels through the unforgiving country that was the scene of their dreams and undoing, and makes their story come miraculously alive.

Winner of the National Book Critics Circle Award for Nonfiction
A New York Times Editors' Choice for Book of the Year

History/Current Affairs/0-679-75906-9

OLD GLORY

A Voyage Down the Mississippi

As a child in England, Jonathan Raban read *Huckleberry Finn* and dreamed of floating down the Mississippi. Thirty years later he realized his dream in a spartan sixteen-foot motorboat, navigating the river from Minneapolis to Morgan City, Louisiana. In the course of his voyage, Raban records the mercurial caprices of the Mississippi and the astonishingly varied lives of the people who live along its banks.

Travel/Literature/0-375-70100-1